# Lexical Access in Speech Production

# Cognition Special Issues

The titles in this series are paperbacked and readily accessible, in some cases expanded and updated editions of the special issues of *COGNITION: An International Journal of Cognitive Science*, edited by Jacques Mehler and produced by special agreement with Elsevier Science Publishers B.V. The first six issues are available from M.I.T. Press.

*VISUAL COGNITION*, Steven Pinker, guest editor

*THE ONSET OF LITERACY: Cognitive Processes in Reading Acquisition*, Paul Bertelson, guest editor

*SPOKEN WORD RECOGNITION*, Uli H. Frauenfelder and Lorraine Komisarjevsky Tyler, guest editors

*CONNECTIONS AND SYMBOLS*, Steven Pinker and Jacques Mehler, guest editors

*NEUROBIOLOGY OF COGNITION*, Peter D. Eimas and Albert M. Galaburda guest editors

*ANIMAL COGNITION*, C. R. Gallistel, guest editor

*LEXICAL AND CONCEPTUAL SEMANTICS*, Beth Levin and Steven Pinker guest editors

*LEXICAL ACCESS IN SPEECH PRODUCTION*, Willem J. M. Levelt, guest editor

*NUMERICAL COGNITION*, Stanislas Dehaene, guest editor

# Lexical Access in Speech Production

## Edited by

## Willem J. M. Levelt

## BLACKWELL
Cambridge MA & Oxford UK

Copyright © 1991 Elsevier Science Publishers, B.V., Amsterdam, The Netherlands.

This edition published by Blackwell Publishers, 1993

238 Main Street
Cambridge, MA 02142, USA

108 Cowley Road
Oxford, OX4 1JF, UK

Reprinted from *Cognition: International Journal of Cognitive Science*, Volume 42, Numbers 1–3, 1992. Blackwell Publishers have exclusive licence to sell this English-language book edition throughout the world.

*Library of Congress Cataloging-in-Publication Data*

Lexical access in speech production / edited by Willem J. M. Levelt.
    p.   cm.
    Originally published in Cognition: international journal of
cognitive science, v. 42, nos. 1–3, 1992.
        Includes indexes.
        ISBN 1-55786-355-5
        1. Lexicology. 2. Psycholinguistics. I. Levelt, W. J. M.
(Willem J. M.), 1938–
P326.L378   1993
413'.028 — dc20                                          92-42764
                                                              CIP

*British Library Cataloging in Publication Data*

A CIP catalog record for this book is available from the British Library.

Printed and bound in the United States of America.

This book is printed on acid-free paper.

# Contents

**1    ACCESSING WORDS IN SPEECH PRODUCTION:**
**Stages, processes and representations**                          1
Willem J. M. Levelt

**2    FROM CONCEPTS TO LEXICAL ITEMS**                          23
Manfred Bierwisch and Robert Schreuder

**3    PICTURE NAMING**                                          61
Wilhelm R. Glaser

**4    A SPREADING-ACTIVATION THEORY OF**
**LEMMA RETRIEVAL IN SPEAKING**                                107
Ardi Roelofs

**5    DISORDERS OF LEXICAL SELECTION**                         143
Merrill Garrett

**6    INVESTIGATION OF PHONOLOGICAL ENCODING**
**THROUGH SPEECH ERROR ANALYSES:**
**Achievements, limitations, and alternatives**                 181
Antje S. Meyer

**7    THE ROLE OF WORD STRUCTURE IN**
**SEGMENTAL SERIAL ORDERING**                                  213
Stefanie Shattuck-Hufnagel

**8    DISORDERS OF PHONOLOGICAL ENCODING**                     261
Brian Butterworth

**9    STAGES OF LEXICAL ACCESS IN LANGUAGE**
**PRODUCTION**                                                 287
Gary S. Dell and Padraig G. O'Seaghdha

**LANGUAGE INDEX**                                             315

**NAME INDEX**                                                316

**SUBJECT INDEX**                                             323

# 1

# Accessing words in speech production: Stages, processes and representations*

Willem J.M. Levelt

*Max-Planck-Institut für Psycholinguistik, Wundtlaan 1, NL 6525 XD Nijmegen, Netherlands*

> Ich glaube, daß mancher großer Redner, in dem Augenblick, da er den Mund aufmachte, noch nicht wußte, was er sagen würde (Heinrich von Kleist, 1809).

Levelt, W.J.M., 1992. Accessing words in speech production: Stages, processes and representations. Cognition, 42: 1–22.

*This paper introduces a special issue of* Cognition *on lexical access in speech production. Over the last quarter century, the psycholinguistic study of speaking, and in particular of accessing words in speech, received a major new impetus from the analysis of speech errors, dysfluencies and hesitations, from aphasiology, and from new paradigms in reaction time research. The emerging theoretical picture partitions the accessing process into two subprocesses, the selection of an appropriate lexical item (a "lemma") from the mental lexicon, and the phonological encoding of that item, that is, the computation of a phonetic program for the item in the context of utterance. These two theoretical domains are successively introduced by outlining some core issues that have been or still have to be addressed. The final section discusses the controversial question whether phonological encoding can affect lexical selection. This partitioning is also followed in this special issue as a whole. There are, first, four papers on lexical selection, then three papers on phonological encoding, and finally one on the interaction between selection and phonological encoding.*

## Issues of lexical access

How do we access words when we speak? This question has not received serious scrutiny until relatively recently. But as soon as it was asked, a whole range of issues emerged.

*I am grateful to Aditi Lahiri for her important remarks on syllable representation and the association process, and to Antje Meyer for her helpful comments on an earlier version of this paper.

What is the rate of lexical access in normal conversation? Some 120–150 words per minute on the average (Maclay & Osgood, 1959), but there are spurts of up to double this rate (Deese, 1984).

How many words do we have to select from? We don't know. There are reliable ways of estimating the size of our word recognition lexicon (Oldfield, 1963, estimated the vocabulary size of Oxford undergraduates at about 75 000 words), but no such tests exist for measuring the active production lexicon. Levelt (1989) estimated the production lexicon of normal educated adults at about 30 000 words, but this can easily be out by a factor two. Still, there is no doubt that we can access a huge lexical database at high rates, over long stretches of time, and without signs of fatigue worth mentioning. This alone characterizes lexical access as a cognitive skill par excellence. The skill is further marked by an astonishingly low error rate. Garnham, Shillcock, Brown, Mill, and Cutler (1982) found 86 errors of lexical selection in a spoken text corpus of 200 000 words, and 105 other slips of the tongue. That is an error rate of about one per thousand. Butterworth (this issue) gives similar data. It is important to stress this low error rate, because much of what we know about lexical access is based on careful analyses of naturally occurring speech errors. Reading this literature may create the misleading impression that felicitous lexical access is a matter of good luck rather than of exquisite design.

Are we aware of how we do it? As for most other high-speed skilled behaviour, the answer is "no". We can muse about the meanings of lexical items. We can even reject a word that jumps to mind and go for a more appropriate one. But we cannot trace the process by which we retrieve a word to start with. Introspection is largely useless in the study of lexical access.

This being so, another important issue became how to study the process. Since the 1960s and 1970s (and in fact since Meringer & Mayer, 1895), the dominant answer has been to study failures of access, slips of the tongue, speech errors (Cohen, 1965; Fromkin, 1971, 1973; Garrett, 1975; MacKay, 1970; Nooteboom, 1967; Shattuck-Hufnagel, 1979; see Cutler, 1982, for a bibliography of the early work). And indeed, this work has provided us with the main outlines of the processing architecture subserving speech in general, and lexical access in particular. Another approach has been the analysis of pre-lexical hesitations in spontaneous speech (Beattie and Butterworth, 1979; Goldman-Eisler, 1968).

It took longer until issues of lexical access were put to experimental test at any scale, or at least so its seems. The initial steps were to *elicit* speech errors in the laboratory, with Baars, Motley, and MacKay (1975) as the pioneers, or to elicit tip-of-the-tongue effects (Brown & McNeill, 1966). But in addition, reaction time paradigms intruded the study of lexical access, with Oldfield and Wingfield (1965) as pioneers and discoverers of the word frequency effect (see also for early reaction time studies Glaser & Düngelhoff, 1984; Klapp, 1974; Levelt & Maassen, 1981; Lupker, 1979). In fact, the reaction time study of lexical access was much older, going under headings such as picture naming, colour naming, or even more disguised under the name of "Stroop effect" (cf. La Heij, 1988).[1] Glaser (this issue) reviews this history.

No less important, finally, is the study of the neuropathology of lexical access. Over the last decade or two there has been an increasing integration of the study of normal lexical access and its pathology. Garrett (this issue) and Butterworth (this issue) review the state of the art, but see also Caramazza and Hillis (1990) and Bub and Caplan (in press, chapter 4).

At present, research in lexical access has a pluralistic methodology, ranging from the analysis of naturally observed slips of the tongue, via error elicitation, to picture naming and picture–word interference studies. In addition, the pathology of lexical access in aphasic patients is increasingly contributing to our understanding of the underlying mechanisms.

This brings us to the main issue that emerged. What kind of processing mechanism governs the skill of accessing words? If we cannot introspect the mechanism, we are at the mercy of our theoretical inventiveness. The first serious proposal was Morton's (1969) logogen theory, which is still a significant competitor on the theoretical battleground. The mental lexicon was conceived of as a pandemonium, a collection of so-called *logogens*, each sensitive to its own specific information. For speech production (exclusive of reading) a logogen's relevant information stems from the "cognitive system", which is semantically active. The logogen becomes activated by semantic information relevant to "its" word. When the activation exceeds some threshold value, the logogen fires, and sends the phonological code of its word to a so-called "response buffer", from which an overt articulatory response can be initiated.

The logogen theory has (at least) two attractive features. One is that all logogens are simultaneously active in "watching" the cognitive system. There is parallel processing, which makes the speed of access largely independent of the size of the lexicon. The other is that lexical access is a two-step process. The first step, the logogen's activation to threshold, is semantic in nature. The second step, the logogen's firing and the preparation of response execution, is phonological in nature.

This two-step approach to lexical access is, in one guise or another, common to all modern views of lexical access (cf. Butterworth, 1989). There are two component processes to lexical access. The first one is *lexical selection*, retrieving the one appropriate word from among thousands of alternatives. The second one is *phonological encoding*, computing the phonetic shape from the selected item's phonological code or form specification as it is stored in the mental lexicon (Kempen & Huijbers, 1983, called this stored phonological code the *lexeme* as

---

[1]The Stroop effect: it is relatively hard to name the colour of a printed word (for instance red) if that word is itself the name of a different colour (for instance green), a case of lexical interference or competition. See Glaser (this issue) for details.

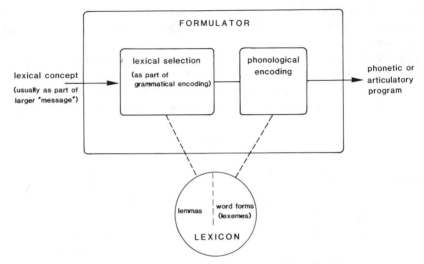

Figure 1.   *An outline of lexical access in speech production.*

opposed to the *lemma*). This scheme is presented in Figure 1; it will be used as a guideline for the present introductory chapter of this special issue. In the following section I will first present some thoughts on lexical selection. This will be followed by a section on phonological encoding. The final section will consider some aspects of interaction between these two component processes.

This ordering corresponds to the layout of the present special issue. There are, first, four contributions on lexical selection. This is followed by three contributions on phonological encoding. And, finally, there is one paper on the staging and potential interaction between lexical selection and phonological encoding.

## Lexical selection

A speaker's mustering of words usually serves the performance of some speech act. And a speech act is a way of revealing some communicative (and hence interactive) intention by means of spoken language. It is important not to ignore this larger perspective when discussing matters of lexical selection.

Recent years have seen substantial convergence on the following general picture of the initiation of a speech act. In order to reveal some communicative intention (e.g., to commit oneself or the interlocutor to some action, to share certain experiences with the interlocutor), the speaker will encode a so-called "message" whose expression can be effective in revealing that intention. So, for instance, if the speaker intends the addressee to recognize that his intention is to let her know that her sister has arrived, an effective message might be the declaration that her sister has arrived. But it need not be, dependent on the context. It may, for instance, be more effective to declare that an angel or a witch (as the matter may be) has arrived. Or the context may make it even more effective for the speaker to express the question whether he might just have seen a woman entering the door.

The choice of message is a subtle function of the relation between the interlocutors, their common ground, the existence of secondary intentions, such as to understate or to express irony, and other factors (cf. Clark & Wilkes-Gibbs, 1986; Levelt, 1989). And these choices have an immediate impact on lexical selection (*sister*, *angel*, *witch*, *woman* in the above example, all intended to make reference to the same person).

It is widely held that a message is a conceptual structure, cast in a propositional language of thought. It forms the input to the so-called *formulator*, whose task it is to map the message onto linguistic form. Its final output is a phonetic plan that can be executed by the articulatory motor system. The formulator involves two component processes: *grammatical* and *phonological encoding* (see Figure 1).

Grammatical encoding takes a message as input, retrieves lexical items from the mental lexicon, and delivers a surface structure as output. A surface structure is a hierarchical organization of syntactic phrases. Its terminal elements are *lemmas*. These are lexical items unspecified for phonological form. They are, however, semantically and syntactically specified. Their semantic specification is a set of conceptual conditions whose fulfilment in the message is a necessary requirement for their retrieval. Their syntactic specification involves category and subcategorization information, as well as the way in which grammatical subcategory functions of the lemma are mapped onto the conceptual arguments in its semantic description (the thematic role assignments, see especially Jackendoff, 1990). So, for instance, the lemma *swallow* has as part of its semantics that some theme Y is ingested by some agent X. That is, these conceptual conditions must be fulfilled for the appropriate use of that lemma. Syntactically *swallow* is a transitive verb, subcategorizing for two grammatical functions: subject and direct object. The canonical thematic mapping for this verb is agent (X) to subject and theme (Y) to direct object.

Lexical selection drives grammatical encoding. Lemmas are retrieved (activated, selected) when their semantic conditions are met in the message. In their turn, they call (activate, trigger) syntactic procedures that correspond to their syntactic specifications. A verb will instigate the construction of a verb phrase, a noun the construction of a noun phrase, etc. Grammatical encoding is somewhat like solving a set of simultaneous equations, simultaneously realizing the appropriate thematic role assignments for all lemmas retrieved. Not quite simultaneous, however, because lemmas can become available at different moments in time, dependent on the speaker's unfolding of the message. Different orders of lemma selection can lead to vastly different syntactic constructions (see Levelt, 1989, for an extensive review of grammatical encoding).

But there is a special set of lemmas whose retrieval is not conceptually driven. They all belong to the closed class vocabulary. In *the woman that arrived* the relative pronoun *that* is itself called by the syntactic procedure that constructs relative clauses. The retrieval of *that* is not semantically driven, such as the retrieval of *woman*. Here, in other words, grammatical encoding drives lexical selection. Notice, however, that many other closed class items do have some semantic specification, such as sex or definiteness; these specifications must be met at the message level for the item to be selected (except when they are syntactically derived by agreement).

I will now formulate some major problems for a theory of lexical selection. They are my own selection; others in this special issue will add several more of their own.

### The hyperonym problem

It was noticed by Levelt (1989) that no existing theory of lexical selection, including Morton's logogen theory and Miller and Johnson-Laird's (1976) decision table theory, can account for unique convergence of the conceptual information onto the one appropriate lexical item. This is due to the hyperonym[2] problem, which was formulated as follows:

> When lemma A's meaning entails lemma B's meaning, B is a hyperonym of A. If A's conceptual conditions are met, then B's are necessarily also satisfied. Hence, if A is the correct lemma, B will (also) be retrieved.

So, when a speaker intends to express the concept CAT, then all conceptual conditions for the retrieval of the lemma *animal* are also satisfied, because the meaning of *cat* entails the meaning of *animal*. Why then does the speaker not say *animal* instead of *cat*?

There are two types of approach to this problem. The first one is to maintain some degree of compositionality in semantic representations. Bierwisch and Schreuder (this issue) argue this to be imperative anyhow. But then one should implement what I called a *principle of specificity* (Levelt, 1989). It should be clear that the hyperonym problem derives from an assumption of compositionality: if A is a lemma, and B one of its hyperonyms, then the meaning of B is assumed to be a constituent part of the meaning of A. As long as one maintains this much compositional semantics in the mental lexicon, then any theory of lexical selection

---

[2] In Levelt (1989) I introduced the term *hypernym* (as opposed to *hyponym*). The correct Latin–Greek compound should, however, be *hyperonym*, as Michael Studdert-Kennedy explained to me.

must involve a principle of specificity, which says that of all lemmas whose conditions are satisfied by the concept-to-be-expressed the most specific one (the most entailing one) should be selected. So, if the intention is to express the concept CAT, which satisfies the semantic conditions of the lemmas *cat*, *animal*, *thing*, etc., the most specific lemma (*cat*) should be retrieved. Notice that distributed connectionist representations of word meaning are also subject to the hyperonym problem (cf. Roelofs, this issue). I am not aware of any explicit effort to implement a specificity principle in such network representations.

The second approach is to give up compositionality altogether, as has been proposed by Fodor, Garrett, Walker, and Parkes (1980) and Dik (1987). The classical non-compositional implementation of lexical knowledge is by Collins and Quillian (1969) and Collins and Loftus (1975). Here concept nodes (such as for CAT) are directly linked to word form nodes (such as for /kat/). Intending to express the concept CAT means activating the corresponding node, which then spreads its activation to the appropriate word form node. Here, the hyperonym problem doesn't arise. The node for CAT may spread some of its activation via the *is-a* link to the node for ANIMAL, but the latter node's activation will normally be less than the former node's, so that the connected word form node for *animal* will receive relatively minor activation. Roelofs (this issue) has extended a non-compositional Collins/Quillian/Loftus-type network to incorporate lemma-level nodes. Then it becomes not only possible to correctly predict many of the naming results reviewed by Glaser (this issue), but also some new and unexpected ones in the realm of picture–word interference. Garrett (this issue) also argues for a lemma level as interface between conceptual and form representations, but his arguments stem from the pathology of lexical selection in aphasic patients.

It is hard to anticipate which of these two approaches will ultimately be more successful. Bierwisch and Schreuder (this issue) at least make us cautious not to give up compositionality altogether, and so does Jackendoff (1990). But to the extent that compositionality is maintained, the hyperonym problem will keep haunting us. Garrett (this issue) analyses hyperonym substitutions in Alzheimer patients and featurally defined semantic field effects in aphasics. These deficits underline the importance of the compositionality issue.

*The dissection problem*

How do we dissect an idea to be expressed into *lexical concepts*, that is, into conceptual "chunks" that map neatly onto lemmas? What makes a speaker say *John is Mary's father* rather than *John is Mary's male parent*? There are certainly thinkable contexts in which the latter is the more appropriate expression. Is it the same idea here that is dissected into one or into two lexical concepts? Or is there

no full synonymy here between *father* and *male parent*, following Eve Clark's (1987, 1990) "principle of contrast"? Clearly, the dissection problem is related to the issue of compositionality as Bierwisch and Schreuder (this issue) explicate. If each lemma has a unique relation to a single concept, the dissection problem will not arise (cf. Roelofs, this issue). The speaker will either have an active FATHER node, or two active nodes MALE and PARENT. This "solution", however, shifts the weight of the problem to the speaker's conceptual intentions. Is this the right level of analysis? Our preference for using so-called "basic level" terms (Glaser, this issue; Rosch, Mervis, Gray, Johnson, & Boyes-Braem, 1976; Seymour, 1979) indicates that we have a preference for chopping up our message in such a way that it can be mapped onto this basic level vocabulary. But it may be intractable what is the chicken and the egg here. We may, after all, prefer to think in "basic level concepts", whether or not we intend to express them in language.

## The imitation problem

There is both conversational (Schenkein, 1980; Harley, 1984) and experimental (Levelt & Kelter, 1982) evidence that speakers tend to have some preference for words that have recently been used by the interlocutor or by themselves. This tendency cannot be fully explained by the interlocutors sharing the same topic of discourse (if the topic is for instance the American president, it is likely – anno 1991 – that the partners in speech will tend to use the word *Bush* a lot). The experimental evidence shows that the preference for re-using words even extends to words that are semantically non-discriminative. There is, in addition, a strong recency effect (Levelt & Kelter, 1982), which makes it likely that the effect is caused by a temporary extra activation of the relevant lemma, due to the speaker's hearing or using the word. Bock and Loebell (1990) found that, similarly, syntactic constructions can be induced without there being any conceptual-level grounds for it. This syntactic induction may, in turn, induce the selection of particular closed class items (such as *by* when a passive is induced). This might explain some of the Levelt and Kelter results, which concerned closed-class items. More generally, the fluency of formulating seems to be served by re-using recently activated words. In short, as long as a theory of lexical selection only acknowledges semantic or syntactic reasons for selecting words, these imitation phenomena cannot be explained.

## The problem of collocations

This problem was recently formulated by Ward (1988, 1991). The selection of one word can depend on the selection of another word, without there being conceptual reasons for this. Ward gives the example of *strong air currents* versus *high winds*. Conceptually, the modification is identical in the two cases, but different words (*strong, high*) have to be selected in dependence on the head that is modified. Another example is *to fall into disuse* versus *to sink into oblivion*. In this context *fall* and *sink* are virtually synonymous, but cannot be exchanged. Probably, the lemmas for *disuse* and *oblivion* carry phrasal information involving *fall* and *sink* respectively.

The collocation problem is not well separable from what one might call the *idiom problem*. Certain concepts are well expressed by idiomatic phrases, such as *red tape*. That this is a phrase, not a compound, appears from its iambic stress pattern. It differs from the trochaic stress pattern of a compound like *hot dog*. But an idiomatic phrase is peculiar as a phrase for two reasons. First, its meaning is opaque, not compositional (*red tape* has very little to do with either *tape* or *red*), and second it allows for only restricted syntactic variations (**my tape is even redder than yours*, **two red tapes*, etc.). It is not entirely clear how the speaker's production of idioms should be modelled. Probably, an idiom is a special kind of lexical entry, specified for the (opaque) meaning. If that semantic condition is met by the message, the idiom is retrieved, just as for any other content word. It calls the constituent lemmas (like *red* and *tape*) and imposes its degraded or limited syntax on the further process of grammatical encoding, in ways that are still to be explored.

These are some problems of lexical selection to be solved, and more will be added in the final section of this chapter and in the paper by Dell and O'Seaghdha (this issue), where the potential influence of phonological encoding on lexical selection is discussed. The main problem, however, is to develop theoretical frameworks in which these problems can be addressed. Such frameworks will be at issue in the following papers by Bierwisch and Schreuder, Glaser, Roelofs, Garrett, and Dell and O'Seaghdha.

**Phonological encoding**

The second phase of lexical access in speech production is phonological encoding. Eventually, the selected lexical item must be given phonetic shape. A word's phonetic form is not a ready-made template that can be retrieved as a whole. Speech error research has made it abundantly clear that a word's ultimate shape is to be *constructed* time and again. An error such as *peel like flaying* (instead of the intended *feel like playing*) reveals that a word's "skeleton" can (at least to some extent) be specified independently from the segments that have to fill it. In the process of constructing *feel* the speaker apparently missed the segmental information /f/. But the fact that the speaker didn't say *eel* then, but *peel* makes it likely that there was already an active word skeleton requiring an onset consonant. The onset slot was then erroneously filled by the already available segment /p/. Though the segment /p/ had been used now, the speaker did not proceed to say *laying* instead of *playing*. Rather, the word *flaying* was constructed. Presumably also here the word's skeleton was already available; its first consonantal slot was then filled by the now available /f/, thus creating a second error. Probably the most fundamental insight from modern speech error research is that a word's skeleton or frame and its segmental content are independently generated. Shattuck-Hufnagel's (1979) slot-and-filler theory was the first formal rendering of this insight (see Meyer, this issue, for a review).

Far less attention has been paid in the literature to the question why this should be so. In fact, the frame-filling notion seems quite paradoxical. Why would a speaker go to the trouble of first generating an empty skeleton for the word, and then filling it with segments? In some way or another both must proceed from a stored phonological representation, the word's phonological code in the lexicon. Isn't it wasteful of processing resources to pull these apart first, and then to combine them again (on the risk of creating a slip)? As Meyer (this issue) shows, this question has been essentially ignored in the standard accounts of phonological encoding.

The answer must probably be sought in the generation of connected speech (cf. Levelt, 1989). Talking is mapping discrete linguistic representations onto pronounceable and continuous phonetic programs. The construction of frames serves the purpose of creating a pronounceable metrical pattern for the utterance as a whole. And that metrical pattern is *not* just a concatenation of individual word frames. It is rather more the exception than the rule that a word's stored skeleton will eventually turn up as a frame to be filled. The speaker produces frames for *phonological words* ($\omega$). These are metrical units, not lexical units. A phonological word is the domain of syllabification (see below) and of word stress assignment. It is never smaller than a morpheme, but it can be larger. In English (but not in all other languages) a phonological word is composed of a head word with its affixes and clitics; there may even be two or more head words involved (as in certain compounds).[3] In *Black Bear gave it him*, there are two phonological words: *Black Bear* and *gavitim*. The former one is a compound with its characteristic trochaic word stress, and corresponds to a single (compound) item in the mental lexicon. The latter one derives from a head word (*gave*) and two dependent words (*it* and *him*) that are cliticized to the head word.

The domain of syllabification in speech production is precisely the phonological

---

[3]Nespor and Vogel (1986) distinguish between a phonological word and a clitic group. The phonological word is the domain of syllabification. The clitic group allows for more limited syllabic interactions only. However, Lahiri, Jongman, and Sereno (1990) argue that the clitic group notion might be superfluous, at least for the phonology of Dutch. I will follow the latter authors in assuming that cliticization results in the creation of a phonological word.

word. So, for instance, *gavitim* is syllabified as *ga-vi-tim* (here the /v/ may be ambisyllabic), which violates all lexical boundaries. This shows that at the level of frames-to-be-filled lexical boundaries have lost their significance. It is therefore not generally the case that phonological encoding consists of filling pre-existing *lexical* skeletons. Rather, new phonological word frames are constructed, dependent on the context of utterance. It is these newly constructed frames that have to be filled with segmental materials. Hence, there is no paradox.

There are four major questions to be answered by a theory of phonological encoding. They are:

Question 1: how are a word's segments made available and to what detail are they specified in the lexicon?
Question 2: how are phonological frames constructed?
Question 3: how are segments associated with slots in the frame?
Question 4: how is a filled frame translated into a phonetic or articulatory program?

Of these, Questions 1 and 3 have received abundant attention. Questions 2 and 4, however, have been largely disregarded.

Let us first consider Question 1, the spelling out of a word's phonological segments. Here, the most important addition on last decade's theoretical scene has been the connectionist modelling of segmental activation and selection (Dell, 1985, 1986; MacKay, 1987; Stemberger, 1985; and others). What these accounts have in common is the notion of the lexicon as a multilayer network of nodes, connected by arcs. The nodes can be in different states of activation, and they can spread their activation over (weighted) arcs to connected nodes. As far as phonological encoding is concerned, the relevant part of the network consists of a layer of lexical nodes at the "top" level, a layer of phonological feature nodes at the bottom level, and a number of layers mediating between these two. In these models, the phonological segments, or rather their features, are made available through activation spreading from the lexical nodes. More details can be found in Dell and O'Seaghdha (this issue).

But the theories differ substantially in detail. They differ in the kinds and numbers of mediating layers (morpheme, syllable, cluster, segment and other layers), in the directionality of activation spreading (one-way or two-way), in the presence or absence of inhibitory connections between same-level nodes, in the amount of extraneous (structurally determined) activation impinging on the network, in the amount of over- or underspecification of segmental information in the network, and in their degree of explicit computer modelling and quantification. In short, theorizing is very much in flux here, and it seems to me that an exclusive reliance on speech error data will not suffice to sort out the theoretical differences (see Meyer, this issue, for more details).

More in particular, there is an increasing need for reaction time studies of phonological encoding. Connectionist models, if sufficiently explicit, may lend themselves well to experimental test by reaction time paradigms, as the work by Dell (1986, 1988), Meyer (1990, 1991), Schriefers, Meyer, and Levelt (1990), and Levelt et al. (1991a) has shown (see also below). In addition, as Butterworth (this issue) argues, the pathology of phonological encoding may tell us something about the underlying, stored representations and their spell-out mechanisms in lexical access. Segments may well be underspecified in our word form lexicon, as Stemberger (1983) already suggested. And this is in accordance with recent phonological theory (cf. Archangeli, 1988). How a complete phonetic specification arises from such underspecified segments is part of our Question 4, to which we will return below.

Turning now to Question 2, the connected speech perspective introduced above requires one to ask: how does a speaker generate the frame of a phonological word? Levelt (1989) assumes the existence of a prosody generator that takes as input the phrasal syntactic information and the metrical spell-out of words, and produces as output an organization of metrical units (in particular phonological words and phonological phrases).

For each incoming metrical pattern, the prosody generator will decide whether the pattern is to stay alone as a phonological word, or whether it is to be attached to the previous, or maybe a following head element. Here the syntactic information accessible to the prosody generator is crucial. For instance, pronouns can be attached to the main verb of the same clause, but nouns cannot. In *leave me alone*, *leave* and *me* can compose a phonological word, but in *leave Maureen alone*, *leave* and *Maureen* cannot (cf. Nespor & Vogel, 1986). It is also impossible to form phonological words across phonological phrase boundaries. For instance, *I wanna go* is possible, but the sentence *What I want, to be honest, is to go* cannot be uttered as *\*What I wanna be honest, is to go*. There is a phonological phrase boundary between *want* and *to* here.

For the construction of phonological words, the prosody generator must further have access to the metrical information that is stored with the words in the mental lexicon. A lexeme's metrical information is "spelled out" at an early stage in phonological encoding, according to Levelt (1989). So, for instance, a speaker in the "tip-of-the-tongue" state often knows a word's number of syllables and stress pattern without having access to most or all of the segmental information. Apart from being non-segmental (or "non-melodic" as the unhappy phonological term goes), the precise character of the metrical spell-out is as yet undecided.

Following Hayes (1989), the word's metrical spell-out could, among other things, contain its $\sigma, \mu$ pattern, that is, its syllable/mora structure. This amounts to saying that the metrical spell-out contains at least the following two pieces of information:

(1) the word's *number* of syllables (not the syllables themselves);

(2) the weight of the subsequent syllables (strong/weak – a two-morae syllable is strong, a one-mora syllable is weak).

In addition, the metrical spell-out may contain:

(3) the word's foot structure or stress pattern (this is only necessary in languages where a word's stress pattern is not fully determined by the weights of its syllables).

The latter is in phenomenological agreement with the just mentioned tip-of-the-tongue state of metrical information.

To represent the above three pieces of information, one minimally needs a string of $\sigma$'s (syllable nodes) each specified for weight (i.e., number of morae), and one for the word's main stress.

Hence, something like

$$[\sigma \quad \sigma']$$
$$| \quad /\backslash$$
$$\mu \; \mu \; \mu$$

for the word *neglect*. The word has two syllables, the last of which is heavy and stressed. It is notationally convenient to have word boundary symbols ("[" and "]"). This makes it easier to discuss the formation of phonological words, to which we turn now.

If the word *neglect* in the utterance is part of the verb phrase *neglect it* (as in *I neglect it*), the prosody generator can construct the phonological word *neglectit*. The first step here is to concatenate the metrical frames of the two constituting lexical items, which can be diagrammed as follows:

$$
\begin{array}{ccccc}
neglect & & it & & neglectit \\
[\sigma \quad \sigma'] & & [\sigma] & & [\sigma \quad \sigma' \; \sigma]_\omega \\
| \quad /\backslash & + & | & \rightarrow & | \quad /\backslash \quad | \\
\mu \; \mu \; \mu & & \mu & & \mu \; \mu \; \mu \; \mu
\end{array}
$$

Here the subscript $\omega$ indicates that *neglectit* is a phonological word frame.

The next step is to fill this frame with the spelled-out segmental information stemming from the two matrix lexical items (*neglect* and *it*) and to syllabify the resulting phonological word.

This brings us to Question 3: how are the segments (or "planning units") associated with positions in the phonological word frames? The reader is again referred to Meyer's review in the present issue. There is, in addition, Shattuck-Hufnagel's paper, which argues for the special status of the word-initial slot in this process of association. That slot is the most vulnerable position in the process of filler-to-slot association, testifying to the reality of word frames in phonological

encoding. Nothing in the latter paper is in disagreement with the notion introduced here that these word frames are in fact *phonological word* frames. As we
will shortly see, the vulnerability of the word-initial segment may in part be due to
the restrictions these phonological word frames impose on their filler segments. In
his paper for the present issue, Butterworth discusses various disorders of
assembling and syllabifying words in phonemic paraphasias.

Here I will only exemplify the filling process and the concurrent syllabification
by returning to the phonological word *neglectit*, whose frame was presented
above:

$$neglectit$$
$$[\sigma \quad \sigma' \quad \sigma]_\omega$$
$$\mid \quad /\backslash \quad \mid$$
$$\mu \quad \mu \quad \mu \quad \mu$$

Experimental reaction time evidence (Meyer & Schriefers, 1991) shows that the
process of filler-to-slot association is a rather strictly "left-to-right" one. What I
propose now is that syllabification takes place "on the fly" as this left-to-right
association of segments to metrical positions is taking place. For this to occur, the
spelled-out segments from the matrix items are assumed to be ordered – or more
precisely, to become available in the right order (speech errors show that this
ordering can be occasionally disrupted). So, for the present phonological word,
the planning units /n/, /i/, /g/, /l/, /ε/, /k/, /t/, /I/, /t/ (or their less specified
equivalents) are spelled out in this order. They are then one by one associated to
the frame, from "left to right" and following a set of association rules that are – in
part – language specific. A general convention here is that attachment to $\sigma$, the
syllable node, can only occur *on the left-hand side of a syllable*, that is, to the left
of any unfilled morae of that syllable.[4]

Among the rules for English are:

(1) A vowel only associates to $\mu$.
(2) The default association of a consonant is to $\sigma$. A consonant associates to $\mu$ if
    and only if any of the following conditions holds:
    (a) the next element is lower in sonority;
    (b) there is no $\sigma$ to associate to;
    (c) associating to $\sigma$ would leave a $\mu$ without associated element.

Rule (1) says that a vowel is always involved in a syllable's weight. Or in

---

[4]On a traditional account, this means that a consonant attaches by default to the onset of a
syllable. In Hayes' (1989) theory, which I follow here at least notationally, there are no onsets and
rhymes. Still, essentially the same process of association can be notated in an onset/rhyme representation of the syllable. In that case syllable weight is not represented by the number of morae, but by the
branchingness of the rhyme.

traditional rhyme terminology: a vowel is always part of a syllable's rhyme. The default association of rule (2) is what is traditionally known as "maximization of onset" (cf., for instance, Selkirk, 1984). Consonants between two vowels in a word (i.e., between two syllabic nuclei) are as much as possible associated with the second syllable (i.e., maximizing the second syllable's onset). Condition (a) of rule (2) is traditionally known as the sonority gradient. In a syllable's onset the sonority of segments increases (or at least does not decrease) towards the nucleus. After the nucleus, sonority decreases again (or at least doesn't increase). This makes, for example, /slorp/ a possible syllable but /lsopr/ an impossible one. Checking for condition (a) requires a one-element look-ahead in the association process. Condition (b) takes care of "left-over" consonants at the end of a word; they have no new syllable to go to, and are added to the last $\mu$ (traditionally: to the rhyme of the final syllable). Condition (c) takes care that, where necessary, a consonant will carry the weight of a syllable. A mora should not stay unfilled because that would change a syllable's weight.

These rules suffice to exemplify the association process and syllabification of the phonological word *neglectit*. The first spelled-out element is /n/. Since neither of the conditions (a) through (c) of (2) hold, /n/ is associated to the first $\sigma$ on the left in the frame. The next element is /i/. It is a vowel, and must be associated to $\mu$ according to rule (1). The next element /g/ is a consonant. It will, by default, be attached to $\sigma$ (condition (2a), for instance, doesn't apply, because /l/ is higher in sonority than /g/). Since right attachment to the first $\sigma$ is excluded by general convention, /g/ attaches to the next $\sigma$. The next consonant, /l/, also attaches to (the same) $\sigma$, following the default of rule (2). The vowel /ε/ then attaches to $\mu$ according to rule (1). The next element, /k/, must associate to $\mu$ for two reasons. First, attaching it to the next $\sigma$ would leave the second $\mu$ of the current syllable without associate (condition (2c)). Second, the following element (/t/) is lower in sonority (condition (2a)). The /t/, however, will by default be attached to the following $\sigma$, thus creating a syllable boundary between /k/ and /t/. (The fact that /t/ is syllable initial and preceding a vowel has as an important phonetic consequence that it will be aspirated.) The vowel /I/ attaches to the final $\mu$, and the last element /t/ attaches to the same $\mu$, following condition (b) of rule (2). The end result (with syllables indicated) is:

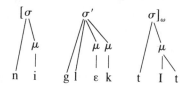

Using the same set of rules, the syllabification of the phonological word *regret it* will be re-gret-it. The first /t/ is not syllable initial here, because that would leave one $\mu$ of the second syllable without dependent, violating condition (2c). As a consequence, this /t/, not being syllable initial, will not be aspirated.

This picture of the association process differs from the standard accounts (reviewed in Meyer's paper) in that the one-slot-one-segment idea is given up. The frame doesn't completely specify the number of slots to be filled. For instance, the number of segments to be associated with $\sigma$ is not specified beforehand. It depends on the ordered string of spelled-out segments and on the fulfilment of conditions in rule (2) whether a syllable's onset will be a single segment or a cluster.

Another difference is that we are dealing now with *phonological* words, not *lexical* words. On the traditional account, the error *peel like flaying* (for *feel like playing*) involves exchanging consonants across an intermediate word. But the speaker who produced this error was probably planning just two phonological words here, [*feelike*]$_\omega$ and [*playing*]$_\omega$. On the phonological word account, Shattuck-Hufnagel's finding (this issue) that word onsets are more vulnerable to error than other syllable onsets now predicts that the mentioned error is a more likely one than, for instance, *leel fike playing*. The /l/ in *like* is internal to the phonological word; it is *not* word initial and hence less vulnerable.

The sketched account, moreover, provides us with one possible reason for Shattuck-Hufnagel's finding (1987, this issue) that word-final consonants are less vulnerable to error in phrases than in lists. For instance, the word-final consonants in a tongue-twister like *parade fad foot parole* are relatively more vulnerable than in a tongue-twister like *the parade is a fad and the foot has parole*. This may be due to the formation of phonological words in the phrasal context. In the example, [*paradis*]$_\omega$ and [*footas*]$_\omega$ are potential phonological words. When they are, the critical consonants are no longer word final, as they are in the list. However, under the phrasal condition nothing changes for the word-internal consonants, such as /r/ in *parade*. They keep being word internal. And indeed, as Shattuck-Hufnagel (this issue) shows, the relative vulnerability of these word-internal consonants is not affected by phrasal context.

The present account of the association process in connected speech is a highly preliminary one. It needs further elaboration, but is presented here to highlight the notion that syllabification is a late process in phonological encoding, that it is a consequence of the left-to-right association of segments to a metrical frame, and that the domain of syllabification is the phonological word.

Let us now turn to the fourth issue formulated above: how is a filled frame translated into a phonetic or articulatory program? The slot-and-filler theory has nothing to say about this problem. It is a theory about how phonemic segments find their ultimate positions in a metrical frame. It does not specify the allophonic phonetic shapes of segments within the word or syllable. Similarly, none of the connectionist theories address this issue. On first view, they do seem to take a step in the right direction by adding a level of feature nodes at the bottom of the network. But these feature nodes represent discrete *phonological* features, not scaled phonetic ones. In particular, there is no mechanism for making feature values dependent on a segment's context in the syllable or word.

Here, I only want to signal this hiatus in theory construction. In Levelt (1989) I adopted an important suggestion by Crompton (1982), which in my view indicates one way in which this hiatus can be filled. Crompton proposed that the syllables composed in phonological encoding function as addresses for stored phonetic syllable templates. One can conceive of these syllable templates as motor instructions for complex articulatory gestures. Following Browman and Goldstein (1990) one would call these "gestural scores", that is, specifications of articulatory tasks to be performed in pronouncing the syllables. I added that these syllable scores still have a few free parameters to be fixed, such as stress, rate and pitch parameters. Still, they are genuine phonetic, not phonological representations. The idea that we have a "phonetic syllabary" is certainly not obvious. It is quite an attractive idea for a language such as Chinese, which has no more than about 400 different syllables. But what about English or Dutch, which have somewhere between 6500 and 7000 different syllables? Would they all be stored in the speaker's head as phonetic templates or scores? One straightforward prediction from the theory is a frequency effect. It should take more time to retrieve a low-frequency syllable template than a high-frequency template. In our laboratory, Linda Wheeldon and I (in preparation) could confirm that prediction for Dutch. Naming latencies (not reading latencies) were slower for words consisting of low-frequent syllables than for words consisting of high-frequent syllables. This effect was completely independent of the word frequency effect, but is (as could be expected) related to the phonetic complexity of the syllables.

But even if the notion of an independent phonetic syllabary receives further experimental support, it cannot be the whole story. The syllable is not the only context of phonetic variation; there are cross-syllable and cross-word phonetic effects that are still to be explained.

## The interaction between lexical selection and phonological encoding

Lexical selection and phonological encoding are wildly different processes. Lexical selection is semantically (or syntactically) driven search for an appropriate item in a huge lexical store. Phonological encoding is the creation of an executable phonetic program for a single item in context. On first view, it would not seem like a great feat of psychological engineering if these two kinds of process were to interact with one another. It would add unnecessary error proneness to both aspects of the accessing system. Still, in an important paper, Dell and Reich (1981) presented statistical evidence from speech errors showing that errors of selection and errors of phonological encoding were not entirely independent. Moreover, there is a lexical bias effect (already reported by Baars, Motley, & MacKay, 1975), which means that trouble in phonological encoding tends to create real words more often than should be expected by chance. These findings have been replicated by Stemberger (1983), Harley (1984), Dell (1986), Martin, Weisberg and Saffran (1989) and form a challenge to the above modular view of the accessing process.

The observed interactions between lexical selection and phonological encoding found a natural theoretical explanation in connectionist models of lexical access. In particular, models that allowed for both forward and backward spreading of activation between levels of representation (Stemberger, 1985; Dell, 1986) could account for the statistical speech error evidence.

But Levelt et al. (1991a) argued that models of that kind also have specific implications for the time course of lexical access – implications that can be tested by appropriate reaction time experiments. Specifically, all connectionist models would predict that coactivated semantic alternatives to the target item (e.g., *goat* when the target item is *sheep*) would, at some moment during lexical access, undergo some degree of phonological activation. In addition, the models that allow for backward spreading of activation should predict that there is a late rebound of semantic activation following phonological activation. However, neither of these predictions could be experimentally substantiated.

The authors then argued for two directions in further research. The first one would be a careful exercise in the parametrization of connectionist models. Or, would it be possible to have *just* enough interactiveness between levels in the network to account for the above-mentioned statistical effects, but still so little that no measurable phonological coactivation of semantic alternatives and no measurable semantic rebound would occur? In his contribution to the present issue, Dell argues that appropriate parameters can indeed be found. For a full appreciation of this claim, the reader is referred to an ongoing discussion: Dell and O'Seaghdha (1991) and Levelt et al. (1991b). One issue raised there is what functional sense feedback could have in a lexical production network (it surely cannot be merely to cause a specific type of speech error). Dell (1988) suggested that a deep reason for feedback could be that the same lexical network is also used for lexical access in comprehension, which obviously would involve activation spreading in the reverse direction. For this double use of the same network we pay by occasionally making specific kinds of speech errors. This is a challenging suggestion: are the accessing mechanisms of production and comprehension making use of the same unified lexical network, or are there independent input and output networks? The latter view would find support if a double dissociation could be found in the pathology of lexical access. Allport (1984) explicitly raised this issue, but could not find convincing evidence of this kind. On the other hand, Howard and Franklin's (1988) patient MK seems to provide one half of this double dissociation.

A second direction, proposed by Garrett (personal communication), is to look more carefully into the situations in which mixed errors arise. They may be "environmentals", that is, intrusions of words that happen to be in the speaker's span of attention. In the Martin et al. (1989) study, for instance, the response set in the experiments contained a highly apparent subset of items that were not only semantically related to one another, but also phonologically. No surprise that the subjects tended to make confusions among these items. This probably has nothing to do with the fact that these items were *phonologically* related; any other marked relation among the items would have produced the same result. If Garrett is right, the occurrence of mixed errors may, after all, not exceed chance level if "environmentals" are excluded.

The third direction would be to give renewed attention to the possibility that the observed interactions are due to *post-lexical* processes. The speaker monitors his lexical productions to some extent (see also Butterworth, this issue), and can intercept imminent errors before they are overtly produced. This might account for some of the above statistical findings on speech errors. So, for instance, if a phonological error creates a non-word, it is more likely to be intercepted than when it creates a word; a word is well formed, a non-word is not. This "editor" theory was originally proposed by Baars et al. (1975), and elaborated in several subsequent publications. See Levelt (1989, chapter 12) for a review, and for a comparison between editor theories and connectionist accounts of the phenomena under discussion. My conclusion there was that it will not be easy to distinguish these two approaches experimentally. And indeed, the game is still as open as it was at the time. Only new, sophisticated research on the speaker's self-monitoring can end this deadlock.

Let me, finally, add one more issue to the already disquieting list of problems reviewed in this introductory paper. What we have just discussed with respect to phonological encoding and lexical selection, namely whether there is a real feedback there, can also be considered at the next higher level. Is our selection of concepts-to-be-expressed to any extent dependent on lexical selection? There is not only the general Whorfian problem looming on the horizon here (cf. Schlesinger, 1990, for an excellent review); but there is also a more specific processing issue involved. The aphorism from Kleist (1809) heading this paper suggests that there can be spontaneous activity in a speaker's formulator, generating words or phrases that present themselves to the speaker as potential issues to talk about.[5] One important question then is, What is the "routing" of that feedback? Is an active lemma directly feeding back to the conceptual level? The present evidence for such a direct link is minimal (cf., Levelt, 1989, pp. 275 ff.). Or is it feeding back via internal speech, i.e., does it involve (internal)

[5]Daniel Dennett (personal communication) alerted me to the idea of spontaneous activity in the formulator feeding back to the conceptual level (see also Dennett, 1991).

phonological encoding of the activated word? The latter view has some phenomenological face value. But as I said earlier, phenomenology is not of much help in dissecting the process of lexical access.

## References

Allport, D.A. (1984). Speech production and comprehension: One lexicon or two? In W. Prinz & A.F. Sanders (Eds.), *Cognition and motor processes* (pp. 209–228). Berlin: Springer.

Archangeli, D. (1988). Aspects of underspecification theory. *Phonology, 5*, 183–207.

Baars, B.J., Motley, M.T., & MacKay, D. (1975). Output editing for lexical status from artificially elicited slips of the tongue. *Journal of Verbal Learning and Verbal Behavior, 14*, 382–391.

Beattie, G., & Butterworth, B. (1979). Contextual probability and word frequency as determinants of pauses in spontaneous speech. *Language and Speech, 22*, 201–211.

Bock, J.K., & Loebell, H. (1990). Framing sentences. *Cognition, 35*, 1–40.

Browman, C.P., & Goldstein, L. (1990). Gestural specification using dynamically-defined articulatory structures. Haskins Laboratories Status Report on Speech Research. SR-103/104, 95–110.

Brown, R., & McNeill, D. (1966). The "tip of the tongue" phenomenon. *Journal of Verbal Learning and Verbal Behavior, 5*, 325–337.

Bub, D., & Caplan, D. (in press). *Aphasiology for speech–language pathologists.*

Butterworth, B. (1989). Lexical access in speech production. In W. Marslen-Wilson (Ed.), *Lexical representation and process* (pp. 108–135). Cambridge, MA: MIT Press.

Caramazza, A., & Hillis (1990). Where do semantic errors come from? *Cortex, 26*, 95–122.

Clark, E.V. (1987). The principle of contrast: A constraint on language acquisition. In B. MacWhinney (Ed.), *Mechanisms of language acquisition* (pp. 1–33). Hillsdale, NJ: Erlbaum.

Clark, E. (1990). On the pragmatics of contrast. *Journal of Child Language, 17*, 417–431.

Clark, H., & Wilkes-Gibbs, D.L. (1986). Referring as a collaborative process. *Cognition, 22*, 1–39.

Cohen, A. (1965). Versprekingen als verklappers bij het proces van spreken en verstaan. *Forum der Letteren, 6*, 175–186.

Collins, A.M., & Loftus, E.F. (1975). A spreading-activation theory of semantic processing. *Psychological Review, 82*, 407–428.

Collins, A.M., & Quillian, M.R. (1969). Retrieval time from semantic memory. *Journal of Verbal Learning and Verbal Behavior, 8*, 240–247.

Crompton, A. (1982). Syllables and segments in speech production. In A. Cutler (Ed.), *Slips of the tongue and language production.* Berlin: Mouton.

Cutler, A. (1982). *Speech errors: A classified bibliography.* Bloomington: Indiana Linguistics Club.

Deese, J. (1984). *Thought into speech: The psychology of a language.* Englewood Cliffs, NJ: Prentice-Hall.

Dell, G.S. (1985). Positive feedback in hierarchical connectionist models: Applications to language production. *Cognitive Science, 9*, 3–23.

Dell, G.S. (1986). A spreading activation theory of retrieval in sentence production. *Psychological Review, 93*, 283–321.

Dell, G.S. (1988). The retrieval of phonological forms in production: Tests of predictions from a connectionist model. *Journal of memory and language, 27*, 124–142.

Dell, G., & O'Seaghdha (1991). Mediated and convergent lexical priming in language production: A comment on Levelt et al. (1991). *Psychological Review, 98*, 604–614.

Dell, G.S., & Reich, P.A. (1981). Stages in sentence production: An analysis of speech error data. *Journal of Verbal Learning and Verbal Behavior, 20*, 611–629.

Dennett, D.C. (1991). *Consciousness explained.* Boston: Little, Brown & Co.

Dik, S.C. (1987). Linguistically motivated knowledge representation. In M. Nagao (Ed.), *Language and artificial intelligence* (pp. 145–170). Amsterdam: Elsevier Science Press.

Fodor, J.A., Garrett, M.F., Walker, E.C.T., & Parkes, C.H. (1980). Against definitions. *Cognition, 8*, 263–367.

Fromkin, V.A. (1971). The non-anomalous nature of anomalous utterances. *Language, 47*, 27–52. (Reprinted in: Fromkin, V.A. (Ed.) (1973). *Speech errors as linguistic evidence.* The Hague: Mouton.)

Fromkin, V.A. (Ed.) (1973). *Speech errors as linguistic evidence.* The Hague: Mouton.

Garnham, A., Shillcock, R.S., Brown, G.D.A., Mill, A.I.D., & Cutler, A. (1982). Slips of the tongue in the London–Lund corpus of spontaneous conversations. In A. Cutler (Ed.), *Slips of the tongue and language production* (pp. 251–263). Berlin: Mouton.

Garrett, M.F. (1975). The analysis of sentence production. In G. Bower (Ed.), *Psychology of learning and motivation* (Vol. 9, pp. 133–175). New York: Academic Press.

Glaser, W.R., & Düngelhoff, F.J. (1984). The time course of picture–word interference. *Journal of Experimental Psychology: Human Perception and Performance, 10*, 640–654.

Goldman-Eisler, F. (1968). *Psycholinguistics: Experiments in spontaneous speech.* New York: Academic Press.

Harley, T.A. (1984). A critique of top-down independent levels of speech production: Evidence from non-plan-internal speech errors. *Cognitive Science, 8*, 191–219.

Hayes, B. (1989). Compensatory lengthening in moraic phonology. *Linguistic Inquiry, 20*, 253–306.

Howard, D., & Franklin, S. (1988). *Missing the meaning? A cognitive neuropsychological study of the processing of words by an aphasic patient.* Cambridge, MA: MIT Press.

Jackendoff, R. (1990). *Semantic structures.* Cambridge, MA: MIT Press.

Kempen, G., & Huijbers, P. (1983). The lexicalization process in sentence production and naming: Indirect election of words. *Cognition, 14*, 185–209.

Klapp, S.T. (1974). Syllable-dependent pronunciation latencies in number naming, a replication. *Journal of Experimental Psychology, 102*, 1138–1140.

Kleist, H. von (1809). Über die allmähliche Verfertigung der Gedanken beim Reden. In H. von Kleist, *Sämtliche Werke und Briefe* (pp. 320–327). München: Carl Hanser Verlag.

Lahiri, A., Jongman, A., & Sereno, J. (1990). The pronominal clitic [dər] in Dutch: A theoretical and experimental approach. *Yearbook of Phonology, 3*, 1–13.

La Heij, W. (1988). Components of Stroop-like interference in picture naming. *Memory and Cognition, 16*, 400–410.

Levelt, W.J.M. (1989). *Speaking: From intention to articulation.* Cambridge, MA: MIT Press.

Levelt, W.J.M., & Kelter, S. (1982). Surface form and memory in question answering. *Cognitive Psychology, 14*, 78–106.

Levelt, W.J.M., & Maassen, B. (1981). Lexical search and order of mention in sentence production. In W. Klein & W.J.M. Levelt (Eds.), *Crossing the boundaries in linguistics: Studies presented to Manfred Bierwisch* (pp. 221–252). Dordrecht: Reidel.

Levelt, W.J.M., Schriefers, H., Vorberg, D., Meyer, A.S., Pechmann, T., & Havinga, J. (1991a). The time course of lexical access in speech production: A study of naming. *Psychological Review, 98*, 122–142.

Levelt, W.J.M., Schriefers, H., Vorberg, D., Meyer, A.S., Pechmann, T., & Havinga, J. (1991b). Normal and deviant lexical processing: A reply to Dell and O'Seaghdha. *Psychological Review, 98*, 615–618.

Lupker, S.J. (1979). The semantic nature of competition in the picture–word interference task. *Canadian Journal of Psychology, 36*, 485–495.

MacKay, D. (1970). Spoonerisms: The structure of errors in the serial order of speech. *Neuropsychologia, 8*, 323–350. (Reprinted in Fromkin, V.A. (Ed.) (1973). *Speech errors as linguistic evidence.* The Hague: Mouton.)

MacKay, D. (1987). *The organization of perception and action: A theory for language and other cognitive skills.* New York: Springer.

Maclay, H., & Osgood, C.E. (1959). Hesitation phenomena in spontaneous English speech. *Word, 15*, 19–44.

Martin, N., Weisberg, R.W., & Saffran, E.M. (1989). Variables influencing the occurrence of naming errors: Implications for a model of lexical retrieval. *Journal of Memory and Language, 28*, 462–485.

Meringer, R., & Mayer, K. (1895). *Versprechen und Verlesen*. Stuttgart: Goschensche Verlag. (Re-issued, with introductory essay by A. Cutler and D.A. Fay (1978). Amsterdam: John Benjamins.)

Meyer, A.S. (1990). The time course of phonological encoding in language production: The encoding of successive syllables of a word. *Journal of Memory and Language, 29*, 524–545.

Meyer, A.S. (1991). The time course of phonological encoding in language production: Phonological encoding inside a syllable. *Journal of Memory and Language, 30*, 69–89.

Meyer, A.S., & Schriefers, H. (1991). Phonological facilitation in picture–word interference experiments: Effects of stimulus onset asynchrony and types of interfering stimuli. *Journal of Experimental Psychology: Learning, Memory, and Cognition, 17*.

Miller, G.A., & Johnson-Laird, P.N. (1976). *Language and perception*. Cambridge, MA: Harvard University Press.

Morton, J. (1969). The interaction of information in word recognition. *Psychological Review, 76*, 165–178.

Nespor, M., & Vogel, I. (1986). *Prosodic phonology*. Dordrecht: Foris.

Nooteboom, S. (1967). Some regularities in phonemic speech errors. *Annual Progress Report. Institute for Perception Research IPO, 2*, 65–70.

Oldfield, R.C. (1963). Individual vocabulary and semantic currency: A preliminary study. *British Journal of Social and Clinical Psychology, 2*, 122–130.

Oldfield, R.C., & Wingfield, A. (1965). Response latencies in naming objects. *Quarterly Journal of Experimental Psychology, 17*, 273–281.

Rosch, E., Mervis, C.B., Gray, W., Johnson, D., & Boyes-Braem, P. (1976). Basic objects in natural categories. *Cognitive Psychology, 8*, 382–439.

Schenkein, J. (1980). A taxonomy for repeating action sequences in natural conversation. In B. Butterworth (Ed.), *Language production: Vol. 1. Speech and talk* (pp. 21–47). London: Academic Press.

Schlesinger, I.M. (1990). *The wax and wane of Whorfian views*. Working paper #32. The Goldie Rotman Center for Cognitive Science in Education. Jerusalem: Hebrew University.

Schriefers, H., Meyer, A.S., & Levelt, W.J.M. (1990). Exploring the time course of lexical access in production: Picture–word interference studies. *Journal of Memory and Language, 29*, 86–102.

Selkirk, E. (1984). *Phonology and syntax: The relation between sound and structure*. Cambridge, MA: MIT Press.

Seymour, P.H.K. (1979). *Human visual cognition*. New York: St Martin's Press.

Shattuck-Hufnagel, S. (1979). Speech errors as evidence for a serial order mechanism in sentence production. In W.E. Cooper & E.C.T. Walker (Eds.), *Sentence processing: Psycholinguistic studies presented to Merrill Garrett* (pp. 295–342). Hillsdale, NJ: Erlbaum.

Shattuck-Hufnagel, S. (1987). The role of word onset consonants in speech production planning: New evidence from speech error patterns. In E. Keller & M. Gopnik (Eds.), *Motor and sensory processing in language* (pp. 17–51). Hillsdale, NJ: Erlbaum.

Stemberger, J.P. (1983). *Speech errors and theoretical phonology: A review*. Bloomington: Indiana Linguistics Club.

Stemberger, J.P. (1985). An interactive action model of language production. In A.W. Ellis (Ed.), *Progress in the psychology of language* (Vol. 1, pp. 143–186). Hillsdale, NJ: Erlbaum.

Ward, N. (1988). *Issues in word choice*. Budapest: COLING-88.

Ward, N. (1991). *A flexible, parallel model of natural language generation*. Report No. UCB/CSD 91/629. Computer Science Division (EECS), UC Berkeley.

2

# From concepts to lexical items*

Manfred Bierwisch

*Academy of Sciences, Tiergartenstraße 21A–23/Hildebrandstraße 1–3, 1000 Berlin 30, Germany; and Max-Planck-Institut für Psycholinguistik, Wundtlaan 1, NL 6525 XD Nijmegen, Netherlands*

Robert Schreuder

*Interfaculty Research Unit for Language and Speech, University of Nijmegen, Netherlands*

Bierwisch, M., and Schreuder, R., 1992. From concepts to lexical items. Cognition, 42: 23–60.

*In this paper we address the question how in language production conceptual structures are mapped onto lexical items. First we describe the lexical system in a fairly abstract way. Such a system consists of, among other things, a fixed set of basic lexical entries characterized by four groups of information: phonetic form, grammatical features, argument structure, and semantic form. A crucial assumption of the paper is that the meaning in a lexical entry has a complex internal structure composed of more primitive elements (decomposition). Some aspects of argument structure and semantic form and their interaction are discussed with respect to the issue of synonymy. We propose two different mappings involved in lexical access. One maps conceptual structures to semantic forms, and the other maps semantic forms to conceptual structures. Both mappings are context dependent and are many-to-many mappings. We present an elaboration of Levelt's (1989) model in which these processes interact with the grammatical encoder and the mental lexicon. Then we address the consequences of decomposition for processing models, especially the nature of the input of lexical access and the time course. Processing models that use the activation metaphor may have difficulties accounting for certain phenomena where a certain lemma triggers not one, but two or more word forms that have to be produced with other word forms in between.*

## 1. Introduction

In normal discourse, speakers utter two to three words per second. Each word is chosen from a set of some tens of thousands of entries – depending on what

*Requests for reprints should be sent to Robert Schreuder, Max-Planck-Institut für Psycholinguistik, Wundtlaan 1, NL 6525 XD Nijmegen, Netherlands.

counts as one entry of a normal speaker's lexical knowledge. Even though these figures are impressive, they do not tell much about the complexity of the process by which lexical items are selected in the production of meaningful, coherent utterances.

First of all, the choice of lexical items is based on the speaker's mental model of his or her external and internal environment, which incorporates all sorts of information – visual, auditory, motoric, inferential, background knowledge, etc. – leading to the actual message to be verbalized. Whatever the modular nature of the pertinent mental system and the eventual interaction of information they provide might be, the choice of lexical items ultimately reflects a wide range of different, but somehow integrated conditions determining the truth, appropriateness, and communicative effect of linguistic utterances.

Secondly, the ingredients or constitutive parts of a pre-verbal message do not in general correspond to ready-made lexical items. The different ways in which the same thought or intended message is to be expressed in different languages (or even within one and the same language) indicate this problem. Thus the message expressed by the two word utterance *Stand here!* would come out, for example, as *Stell dich hierhin!* or *Stellen Sie sich hierher!* in German. More drastic examples could easily be adduced. Hence the question arises: how are the parts of an intended message that are appropriate candidates for lexicalization identified in the first place? This question has various ramifications, some of which will be discussed later on, and it is anything but trivial, once we realize that the way in which experience is conceptualized is no simple isomorphism of the way in which it is verbally expressed.

Thirdly, the set of lexical items from which words are selected is by no means a mere list of simple, isolated entries. Not only does it comprise syntactically complex entries of various sorts, like phrasal verbs such as *look up* or idioms such as *make headway*. Lexical knowledge also provides procedures to set up new words not listed in the stored set of lexical items, such as *unexpectedness*, *paperclip production system*, etc. The system of lexical knowledge is furthermore structured by various relations and dependencies by means of which the access of lexical items is constrained.

Further aspects contributing to the complexity of lexical access could be adduced, and we will discuss some of them later. In general, then, the choice of lexical items as a constitutive process of language production cannot be construed as a straight mapping that triggers simple entries of a fixed list by means of clear-cut matching concepts.

Practically all empirical studies of this process as well as attempts to set up explicit models that account for it are forced either to radically simplify the complexity of the knowledge involved, or to restrict the conditions under which selection takes place, or both. So, studies of lexical access are usually bound to highly specific and more or less unnatural conditions, such as selecting individual words to name, or to limited domains of concepts and corresponding lexical items, like nouns of classificatory taxonomies, leaving out most of the complications, mentioned earlier, that are characteristic for normal, spontaneous use of language.

The present paper cannot, of course, overcome these difficulties and solve the problems they raise. We neither want to propose an even remotely adequate model for the process of lexical access, or of the mechanisms that lead from concepts to words, nor to offer new experimental evidence bearing on the mechanisms. The aim of this paper is rather to discuss various problems any account of lexical access must eventually deal with. More specifically, we will explore principles by which the structure of lexical knowledge is organized (section 2), indicate the consequences of this knowledge for its use in production (section 3), and then discuss questions these considerations raise for the processes of lexical access (sections 4 and 5).

For the sake of orientation, we presuppose the overall schema of language production proposed in Levelt (1989), which distinguishes an (essentially pre-linguistic) *conceptualizer*, a crucially linguistic *formulator* and an also language-dependent *articulator*. Schematically:

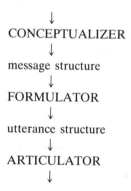

CONCEPTUALIZER

message structure

FORMULATOR

utterance structure

ARTICULATOR

The conceptualizer, which draws on all sorts of perceptual, motoric, emotional, conceptual and possibly other information, delivers message structures, which must then be verbalized and grammatically organized by the formulator. We will call the representational system of message structure "conceptual structure" (or CS for short), assuming that CS is to a large extent language independent and based on general principles of conceptual organization, including common-sense ontology, conceptualization of space and time, general conditions underlying encyclopedic knowledge or systems of belief.

The formulator operates in terms of linguistic elements, that is, lexical items and the properties and relations by means of which they are characterized and related. A crucial aspect of these structures is the lexical meaning determining the range of conceptual configurations to which lexical items and their combinations might correspond. We will call the representational system of lexical meanings and their combination "semantic form" (or SF for short), where the properties related to SF are part of the knowledge of a given language and crucially involved in the operation of the formulator.

The distinction between largely pre-linguistic conceptual structures and the structure of semantic form, which is determined by linguistic knowledge, plays a crucial role for the processes of lexical access and will be discussed and motivated in more detail in section 2.2.

An essential part of linguistic knowledge concerns the association of lexical meanings with the invariant conditions on their phonetic realization. These conditions comprise the abstract "phonetic form" (or PF for short) for lexical items. It is the information of PF by means of which the articulator develops the articulatory output of an utterance.

The correspondence between the semantic and phonetic form of complex combinations of lexical items is determined by the morpho-syntactic structure of those combinations. Hence the formulator must both select appropriate lexical items and integrate them into a syntactic structure or grammatical form.

The focus of the present paper is the contribution the mental lexicon makes to the utterance structure originating from a message the conceptualizer creates, and more specifically the conditions according to which the formulator selects the lexical items to be integrated into the utterance structure.

## 2. Aspects of lexical knowledge

Lexical knowledge is an essential aspect of knowledge of a given language, which is to be construed as a highly complex, more or less stable state of the mind/brain. Those parts of this state, the structure of which is determined by the lexical system of the language, will be called the mental lexicon. We will first outline linguistically motivated assumptions about the lexical system of language, and then discuss how it might be realized in the mental lexicon.

### 2.1. The structure of the lexical system

As there is a great deal of discussion of various issues about the lexical system, we will concentrate on largely uncontroversial issues, ignoring notational variants as far as possible but indicating crucial alternatives, where necessary.

The lexical system LS of a language *L* consists of all of the fixed set BLE of basic lexical entries of *L*. A canonical entry E of this set is a data structure comprising various sorts of information, which can be grouped into four components. Consider an approximate entry of the verb *enter*:

(1) $\underbrace{/\text{enter}/}_{\text{PF}} \; \underbrace{[+V, -N]}_{\text{GF}} \; \underbrace{\lambda x \, \lambda y}_{\text{AS}} \; \underbrace{[y \, DO \, [MOVE \, y] : FIN \, [y \, LOC \, IN \, x]]}_{\text{SF}}$

PF(E), the phonetic form PF of an entry E, is a redundancy-free, multi-dimensional array of phonetic features specifying the segmental and suprasegmental conditions E imposes on the phonetic realization of an expression in which it occurs. Hence /enter/ abbreviates the segmental information that distinguishes *enter* from other entries of BLE.[1]

GF(E) is a structured set of grammatical features determining the syntactic and morphological properties of E and of higher-order constituents of which E is the head. Thus [+V, −N] classifies *enter* as a verb that can be the head of a verb phrase. Besides category features as in (1), GF(E) might contain features indicating person, number, or tense, and also case and other grammatical properties to which rules and principles of grammatical organization are sensitive.[2]

AS(E), the argument structure of E, is a sequence of (one or more) argument positions specifying the number and type of complements required by E. We will return to this sort of information shortly.

SF(E), the semantic form of E, represents the specific contribution E makes to the meaning of complex expressions containing E. The nature of this contribution is a matter of dispute among various approaches to semantics, and we will discuss some of the issues involved. A general assumption of all approaches is that SF constrains the propositional content of an utterance containing E. We will in fact assume the SF(E) is a propositional condition to be integrated into the semantic representation of complex expressions according to systematic principles of grammar.

As the SF of *enter* in (1) shows, we take the lexical meaning of an entry to have a complex internal structure composed of more primitive elements, just as PF is composed of more primitive elements, even though the elements and their combination are rather different. It must be noted that this contention, pursued in different ways, for example in Katz (1972), Jackendoff (1983, 1990), Miller and Johnson-Laird (1976), Dowty (1979), Bierwisch (1982) and many others, is at

---

[1] For systematic discussion of the principles of lexical phonology underlying PF(E) see, for example, Kiparsky (1985). Although this aspect will not be considered in the present paper, the way in which PF relates to input and output information reveals interesting analogies to corresponding problems at the semantic side. See footnote 6.

[2] We cannot here go into the details concerning the more specific organization of GF(E) and the principles according to which it determines the syntactic behaviour of a given entry E. Although grammatical features clearly participate in the constraints by which lexical access is governed, we will not include these problems in our further discussion.

variance with the holistic position most rigorously advocated by Fodor (1975, 1983, and related work). According to this view, the meaning of lexical items is an unanalysable whole that cannot be decomposed into smaller components in any systematic way. The SF of *enter* would consist of a single element ENTER representing the relational concept expressed by this verb. Semantic relations among different entries in the lexicon, which we assume are inferred from their compositional structure, are accounted for by means of so-called meaning postulates within the holistic approach to lexical meaning. We will endorse the decompositional over the holistic view for three reasons:

(a) There is growing evidence, ranging from linguistic analyses to speech errors resulting in lexical mis-selection, and to language acquisition, that strongly supports decomposition. We will discuss experimental work directly testing the decomposition hypothesis in section 4.1.

(b) There are clear cases of systematic lexical relations that are captured in a straightforward way by decomposition, but cannot plausibly be expressed with meaning postulates. (We turn to this point in more detail in section 3.3.)

(c) The problem of lexical access cannot reasonably be formulated under the view of meaning holism, because that would require a pre-established congruity between concepts and the semantic form of lexical items. Under this (clearly counterfactual) assumption, the conceptualizer would have to operate essentially in terms of lexical items, so that the real problem of lexical access is trivialized.

Returning to the SF illustrated in (1), we notice that there are two sorts of elements: semantic constants like DO, MOVE, FIN, LOC, etc., and variables like x, y, z. While constants have a fixed, albeit context-dependent interpretation in terms of conceptual, perceptual, motoric, and possibly other mental structures, variables are open slots that are to be filled in one of two ways: they are either specified by other linguistic expressions, or they are to be fixed by appropriate conceptual values.

Both constants and variables are assigned to specific semantic categories determining on the one hand the type of conceptual interpretation that can be associated with them, and on the other hand the combinatorial structure of SF based on these components.

We now turn to the argument structure AS(E), which is instrumental in providing syntactically specified values for the variables in SF(E).

According to various conceptions that emerged from Chomsky's (1981) theta theory, argument positions in AS(E) are based on thematic roles (or $\theta$-roles, for short), such as agent, theme, experience, source, or goal.[3] Within this framework,

---

[3]The intuitive notion of thematic roles has been developed in a number of ways. For recent discussion see, for example, Grimshaw (1990), Di Sciullo and Williams (1987), Jackendoff (1990). The exposition sketched below follows proposals developed in Bierwisch (1982, 1989).

*enter* should have an agent and a goal position in AS. Obviously, these argument positions determine an important aspect of the syntactic behaviour of E not covered by the features in GF(E). As a matter of fact, AS(E) provides the information encoded in subcategorization frames in earlier versions of syntactic theory, such as Chomsky (1965). Thus, the goal of *enter* must be realized by its direct object, and the agent by the grammatical subject. On the other hand, argument positions are clearly based on the conceptual content to be associated with a lexical entry. In sum, AS(E) functions in a sense as the interface between the syntactic and semantic information provided by its lexical entry.

Formally, it consists of operators binding variables in SF(E), which provide the semantic aspect of AS(E). Each of these operators is associated with (in part predictable) grammatical features, specifying the case (and possibly other categories) of the appropriate syntactic arguments. This information constitutes the grammatical aspect of AS(E).

The information in AS(E) directly reflects the fact that lexical items are $n$-place predicates assigning properties or relations to $n$-tuples of entities (or sets of entities). As SF(E) is a propositional condition to which the sequence of lambda-operators of AS(E) is prefixed, AS(E) and SF(E) taken together define a predicate that has just the number and type of places, that is, the valency, identified by the abstractors in AS(E). Thus *enter* is a two-place predicate that assigns a relation to the entities identified by its grammatical subject and object.

Besides canonical entries like *enter*, the lexical system contains functional elements of various sorts, in particular derivational and inflectional affixes, such as *-ed* for past tense, or *-s* for plural. Even though these non-canonical entries consist of the same types of information as major lexical categories, they differ in characteristic respects that we cannot discuss here. The main point is this: affixes combine with major lexical entries to create combinations like *entered*, *entering*, *entrance*, or *entrances*, that are again lexical items. In other words, the lexical system LS is not just a fixed set BLE of basic entries organized according to principles of LS, but also contains elements and principles extending BLE to the more inclusive set LE of lexical entries that comprises both basic and complex entries. Complex entries that are regular, that is, predictable on the basis of their constituent parts, need not be included in the set of actual entries, but constitute what might be called the set of virtual lexical entries. Schematically, this yields the following structure of the set of lexical items (see Figure 1).

Obviously, VLE contains only complex entries, the properties of which are predictable from their constituent parts.

The classification in (6) has important consequences for the status of the different types of lexical items in the mental lexicon, although it does not reflect their actual arrangement within the mental lexicon.

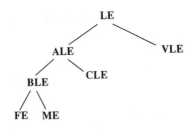

Figure 1.    The structure of the set of lexical items.

ALE is the set of actual lexical entries
VLE is the set of virtual lexical entries
BLE is the set of basic lexical entries
CLE is the set of complex lexical entries
FE is the set of functional elements
ME is the set of major category entries

## 2.2. Semantic form and conceptual structure

The lexical information discussed so far has two major aspects: on the one hand it determines the combinatorial properties of lexical items. The argument structure AS(E) specifies the syntactic arguments required or licensed by E; GF(E) provides the grammatical categorization of the constituents resulting from the combination of E with its complements. Furthermore, AS(E) and SF(E) together determine the way in which the meaning of E combines with that of its complements, where the latter provide the value for the variables in SF(E) related to the $\theta$-roles in AS(E). On the other hand, lexical information defines the contribution of an item E to the articulatory realization and the conceptual interpretation of an utterance containing E: SF(E) constrains the interpretation in the conceptual domain, very much like PF(E) constrains the range of articulatory gestures and defines the targets of auditory patterns. For obvious reasons, the relation between SF and its conceptual interpretation CS is of particular concern in the present context. We will therefore discuss it in somewhat more detail.

The first point to be noted is the fact that a systematic distinction between linguistic and extralinguistic determinants of meaning must be made. Even though many of the facts that are relevant in this respect have been noted repeatedly, the distinction between SF and CS we are proposing is still controversial. This seems at least in part due to the fact that assumptions about non-linguistic aspects of meaning depend to a large extent on evidence coming from the linguistic utterance used to express the conceptual structures in question. Thus SF tends to be conflated with CS, very much like phonology tended to be conflated with articulatory phonetics.[4] There are, however, strong reasons to distinguish SF and CS (just as PF is to be distinguished from articulatory patterns). We will briefly discuss three of them.

First, CS is based on principles and information that account for all sorts of factual knowledge or belief that are clearly not part of linguistic knowledge. Our mental representations of situations, objects, and of spatial, temporal, causal, and many other relations within and between them contain a great deal of distinctions not represented in the semantic form of utterances used to talk about them. They must be organized and constrained by conditions that are independent of linguistic knowledge. To illustrate this point by just one example: linguistically, we know that *John* is a proper name by means of which we may refer to male persons identified by this name. This is the information represented in the corresponding lexical entry in the format discussed above. Conceptually, we have a varying amount of more specific knowledge about each John we happen to know. This knowledge is mentally organized in systematic ways, although it has nothing to do with the knowledge of English. If you learn more about the John living next door that might have important consequences for part of your conceptual knowledge. But it does not at all affect your lexical knowledge related to *John*.

Second, as a consequence of this, a linguistic expression may have different interpretations, although it is not ambiguous on either syntactic or semantic grounds. Consider the following examples:

(2) Who do you want to leave?
(3) Who do you want to leave the bank?
(4) Who do you want to leave the institute?

Example (2) is a well-known case of syntactic ambiguity, turning on a transitive and an intransitive reading of *leave*. Lexically, the θ-role that *leaves* assigns to its object must be marked as optional, leaving behind a free variable in its SF for contextual specification in the intransitive use. In (3), this ambiguity is dissolved by the overt realization of the object position, but a semantic ambiguity comes in, as *bank* is lexically associated with (at least) two different SFs. In (4), there is neither a syntactic nor a semantic ambiguity, as *institute* is not ambiguous in the way *bank* is, but still it has clearly different conceptual interpretations. This can be highlighted in various ways, for instance by temporal adverbials as in (5):

(5) (a) He left the institute an hour ago.
    (b) He left the institute a year ago.

---

[4]Positions are often not quite clear in this respect. Thus Miller and Johnson-Laird (1976) distinguish a level of perceptual representation from conceptual structure, which they seem to identify with what we have called semantic form. Jackendoff (1983, 1990) quite explicitly identifies semantic representation with conceptual structure. In a similar vein, Fodor (1975) identifies semantic structure with what he calls language of thought or message structure, that is, conceptual representation.

In (5a), *the institute* most likely refers to a building, and *leave* is interpreted as a change of place, while in (5b) *the institute* refers to an institution and *leave* is interpreted by a change in affiliation. The different time intervals in (5a) and (5b) do not resolve a semantic ambiguity, but rather bring in different background knowledge. This sort of background knowledge has been dealt with in recent literature on artificial intelligence by means of "frames" or "scripts".[5]

Cases of this type can be multiplied at will; the phenomenon is in fact ubiquitous. Here are two more examples:

(6) The office is closed.
(7) You will get coffee on the third floor.

It is not contradiction, if (6) is uttered by a servant standing in the open door of the office, even though in a different situation the utterance might say that the door of the office is locked. Similarly (7) has conceptually quite distinct interpretations, if it is an announcement at a conference break or an information given at the entrance of a food store.

The third reason relates to situational knowledge that is involved in the specification of CS, but cannot be derived from linguistic knowledge. This does not only hold for variables of SF that can only be fixed by contextual or situational information, such as the initial and the final location in *John left* and *John came in*, respectively; it also applies to various semantic constants. Thus, how the possessor relation in *my chair*, or the distal region in *over there* is to be determined, depends crucially on the situational setting of utterances containing those expressions. Other notorious cases are anaphoric and demonstrative pronouns and adverbials.

To sum up, the conceptual structure CS, in terms of which the actual interpretation of linguistic expressions is specified, merges the conditions specified by SF with information coming from different domains of encyclopedic background knowledge, contextual information and situational conditions.

The assumption that there are two levels or aspects of meaning to be distinguished immediately raises two questions. First, how is CS explicitly to be characterized in a way that is comparable to the linguistically motivated assumptions about SF? Secondly, how are SF and CS related to each other with respect to actual linguistic expressions?

Let us assume for the sake of further discussion that there is a unified representational system of the mind/brain that provides the conceptual structures under discussion. It should be obvious that any substantive discussion of specific assumptions about this system goes far beyond the scope of the present paper. It

[5]The notion of scripts has been developed in various ways we need not go into here (see Schank, 1986, for illustrations). The crucial point is that, for example, "institutional affiliation" provides an organized body of conceptual knowledge that has no direct relation to the structure of lexical knowledge.

would have to deal with and to evaluate work that comes from a wide range of disciplines, from linguistic and formal semantics to artificial intelligence and philosophy of the mind. Relevant topics include scripts and frames, mental models, conceptual dependencies, common-sense ontology, to mention just a few. (For surveys from different perspectives see, for example, Jackendoff, 1990; Johnson-Laird, 1983.) With respect to the present purpose, we will make the following minimal assumptions about the nature of CS and its relation to SF.

First, the most parsimonious conception would ascribe to SF and CS essentially the same representational format with the primes and relations of SF being a proper or improper subset of those of CS. Under this perspective, the conceptual interpretation CS of a given SF would have to contain SF as a proper substructure. A somewhat more flexible relation between SF and CS, which we will assume here, requires SF to be embeddable into representations of CS, where embedding is to be conceived as the relation of a partial model to a more complete model the partial model is compatible with. This notion, which has been developed in Kamp (1981), Kamp and Reyle (forthcoming), does not require the primes and relations of SF to be identical with those of CS, but merely requires CS to preserve certain properties holding in SF. (Obviously, the stronger relation mentioned before is just a special case of embedding.) Under both conceptions, SF can be subject to principles that do not hold for CS, and vice versa. Thus the tree-like organization, which seems to be crucial for SF, does not necessarily carry over to CS. CS on the other hand is likely to exhibit constraints on ontological types, spatio-temporal organization and other aspects of knowledge structure that are not explicitly reflected in SF. This seems to be a natural consequence of the modular organization of the mind/brain, according to which the computational structure of language might be partially autonomous with respect to the organization of general world knowledge.

So much for the overall relation between SF and CS. Consider now the interpretation of actual utterances in CS. To this effect, we will introduce an interpretation mapping *Int* which effectively determines the representation in CS on the basis of the SF of a given utterance. As the above illustrations clearly show, *Int* must be crucially dependent on the contextual setting and the background knowledge with respect to which SF is interpreted. We will indicate the overall conceptual context of a given instance $E_i$ of an expression E by $Ct_i$, where $Ct_i$ is a representation in CS that might be determined by encyclopedic knowledge, previous utterances, and situational conditions. The value of the mapping *Int* applied to semantic form $SF(E_i)$ of $E_i$ and the context $Ct_i$ will be a conceptual structure that modifies $Ct_i$ by the particular contribution that $E_i$ makes under the condition of $Ct_i$. If we indicate the resulting conceptual structure, that is, the value of *Int* for $SF(E_i)$ and $Ct_i$ by $Ct_j$, the general format of *Int* can be given as:

(8)  $Int(SF(E_i), Ct_i) = Ct_j$

One might want to sort out in $Ct_j$ the original context $Ct_i$ and the particular conceptual structure $CS(E_i)$ assigned to E relative to $Ct_i$, such that $Ct_j$ is the extension of $CT_i$ by $CS(E_i)$. With this proviso, (8) comes out as:

(9)  $Int(SF(E_i), Ct_i) = (CS(E_i), Ct_i)$

Even though in the pair $(CS(E_i), Ct_i)$ the particular conceptual interpretation of $E_i$ is separated from its contextual setting $Ct_i$, it should be noted that this does not in general mean that $CS(E_i)$ is an independent conceptual unit or configuration. To see this point, one might think of the interpretation of (5a) and (5b), where the scripts of physical motion on the one hand and change of social affiliation on the other integrate the conditions specified by the SF of *leave* and *institute*, so that no conceptual unit that corresponds to all and only the conditions specified by the SF of *leave* needs to show up in the conceptual structures in question. Similar comments apply to the different interpretations of *office* and *closed* in (6). To put it differently, the ingredients of $CS(E_i)$ that are due to $SF(E_i)$ need not be conceptually autonomous against those that are due to $Ct_i$. This close integration will have important consequences for what we call the chunking problem and the selection problem of lexical access in language production.

It should be clear that the eventually required precise and explicit formulation of the mapping effected by *Int* can only be given on the basis of a formal characterization of the structure of CS. In the present state of discussion we can only add two remarks of clarification.

First, *Int* must be characterizable by a constructive procedure, such that the interpretation of more inclusive configurations of SF can effectively be computed on the basis of the interpretation of its parts. Hence the operation of *Int* must ultimately be based in the primitives of SF, that is, the conceptual purport of constants like DO, CAUSE, MOVE FIN, etc.

Second, the operation of *Int* cannot in general be compositional in the specific Fregean sense, according to which the value of a complex expression must not change the independently determined values of the parts from which it is made up. According to the above considerations, precisely this sort of change might happen in the conceptual interpretation: the interpretation of *closed* may differ, depending on the spatial or institutional interpretation required for its argument *the office*.

It might be noted that both the groundedness of the interpretation of SF in its primes and the not strictly compositional nature of the interpretation are similar to the articulatory interpretation of PF and its primes.

So far, we have discussed the mapping from SF to PF. The essential point for lexical access in production is, of course, the existence of an equally effective mapping from CS to SF. We will call this mapping verbalization *Vbl*. Although *Vbl* is the inverse mapping of *Int*, it cannot simply be defined as its mirror image, because it must assign values in SF, rather than pairs of SF and conceptual context. We may account for this condition by the following definition of *Vbl*:

(10)  $Vbl(CS_i, Ct_i) = SF_i$, if there is some $E_i$ such that
   (a)  $SF_i = SF(E_i)$, and
   (b)  $Int(SF_i, Ct_i) = (CS(E_i), Ct_i)$

Three comments on this definition are indicated. First, a conceptual configuration of $CS_i$ extending a background $Ct_i$ can only be mapped into some $SF_i$, if $SF_i$ is the semantic form of an expression $E_i$. Second, (10b) requires this $CS_i$ to be the value of *Int* for $SF_i$ relative to the setting $Ct_i$, that is, the expression $E_i$ that is to verbalize $CS_i$ must be related to the context in question. Third, *Vbl* must therefore be based on or controlled by the interpretation mapping *Int*.

The last point can be viewed in two ways. From a structural perspective, the dependence of *Vbl* on *Int* corresponds to the fact that language, and hence lexical meaning (and semantic form in general) is imposed on conceptual structure, rather than the other way round. In other words, lexical knowledge and linguistic structure must be made up from interpretable elements, rather than conceptual representations from verbalizable configurations. From a processing perspective, we may construe (10) as accounting for the fact that verbalization is at least implicitly monitored and controlled by the condition that the utterance created by the formulator has the given conceptual structure as a (contextually appropriate) interpretation.

To conclude this discussions about the relation between SF and CS, we notice that both *Int* and *Vbl* are many-to-many-mappings, that is, one SF might have various CS interpretations (as shown by the above examples), and one CS might be the interpretation of different SFs. This case can be illustrated by examples like *John is shorter than Bill* and *John is not as tall as Bill*, to which we will return below.[6]

Presupposing an intuitive understanding of identity or differences in conceptual structure, we will now turn to some of the lexical structures their verbalization is confronted with.

---

[6] It might be useful to point out that the invariance of relative to the variability of CS has a close parallel on the phonetic side of language. Just as one and the same SF can have various conceptual interpretations, a given PF interpretation might allow for different articulatory and hence acoustic realizations. Conversely, the same auditory input might be assigned to different invariants at the level of PF. Thus the same acoustic signal might be identified as /impossible cases/ or as /in possible cases/, depending on context, style of speech, etc. In other words, the fact that both *Int* and *Vbl* are many-to-many mappings directly corresponds to the fact that the articulatory and perceptual mapping between PF and the input/output representation is flexible and non-unique. Hence flexibility and invariance are characteristics of the relation between linguistic and extralinguistic structures at the semantic level as well as at the phonetic level.

## 2.3. *Semantic relations between lexical items*

Lexical knowledge represented by lexical items as discussed in section 2.1 defines a wide range of more general properties and relations of particular lexical items, such that the lexical system LS turns out to be a highly organized structure, rather than a mere list of entries. Definable properties and relations include, for example, phonological neighbourhood, identity of argument structure, identity of derivational suffixes, synonymy, antonymy, identity or incompatibility of lexical presuppositions, and many others. The properties and relations that are relevant in the present context are, of course, meaning relations. Before we are going to discuss them in some detail, three general remarks are indicated.

First, the properties and relations in question apply to actual as well as virtual entries. They may furthermore apply to phrases outside the lexicon. Synonymy or antonymy, for example, can hold between two lexical items, two phrases, or even a phrase and a lexical item.

Second, for this reason, the relations in question cannot explicitly be represented in LE, even though they account for relevant structural properties of the lexical system. They rather follow from the information specified in the entries of LE and from the properties of complex expressions.[7]

Third, the semantic relations comprise essentially the relations which meaning postulates are supposed to account for under the non-compositional view of SF(E) mentioned above.

The semantic relations to which lexical access is sensitive include the following:

(11) For any two expressions A and B, lexical or phrasal:
    (a) A is synonymous with B, if A and B have the same meaning.
    (b) A is a hyponym of B, if the meaning of A is more specific than the meaning of B.
    (c) A is a hypernym of B, if B is a hyponym of A.
    (d) A is an antonym of B, if the core meaning of A contrasts with the core meaning of B.
    (e) A is semantically ambiguous, if A has more than one meaning.

These notions can be made explicit by means of the structure of SF and its interpretation in CS. For reasons of space, we will restrict our discussion to synonymy, illustrating some of the intricacies it involves for lexical access. One important point that applies to all the notions in (11) has to be noted in advance, however.

Given the two-level approach to meaning with the distinction between SF and CS outlined above, the intuitive notion "meaning of A" must be split up into SF(A) on the one hand and CS(A) in context Ct on the other. This is not only

---

[7]For an extensive discussion of the definition of semantic relations and their place in a theory of linguistic knowledge see Katz (1972).

helpful in clarifying traditional puzzles, but also of primary importance for formulating the issues in lexical access.

The issues of synonymy can now be made more precise by distinguishing the following four possibilities for any two (lexical or phrasal) expressions A and B:

(12) (a) SF(A) is identical to SF(B).
    (b) SF(A) is equivalent to SF(B).
    (c) CS(A) is identical to CS(B) relative to Ct.
    (d) A and B are identical in reference (or denotation).

According to the previous considerations, two expressions with identical SF should have the same conceptual interpretation in all contexts. This is the strictest view of synonymy. With respect to lexical access, this creates a typical problem for the selection task, as a choice has to be made between two equally appropriate options. There is an ongoing debate whether this situation does occur at all in natural languages. There seems to be a tendency for strictly synonymous entries to develop differences in meaning, as argued, for example, in Di Sciullo and Williams (1987). If this is true, then certain items nevertheless resist this tendency. *Someone* and *somebody* or *anyway* and *anyhow* are cases in point, which are rarely considered in this connection.

More intricate issues arise when A or B is a complex expression. Let us assume for the sake of discussion that the phrases in (13) are a case in point:[8]

(13) (a) enter the garden
    (b) go into the garden

Given the lexical entry of *enter* (repeated here as (14)), the SF of (13a) comes out as (15), where the SF of *the garden* – abbreviated as DEF GARDEN – replaces the variable of the object position:

(14) /enter/   [+V,−N]   $\lambda x\, \lambda y$ [y DO [MOVE y]:[FIN [y LOC IN x]]]
(15) /enter the garden/ VP
    $\lambda y$ [y DO [MOVE y]:[FIN [y LOC IN [DEF GARDEN]]]]

To see how the same SF results for (13b), consider the following entries for *go* and *into*:

(16) /go/   [+V,−N]   $\lambda P\, \lambda y$ [y DO [MOVE y]:[P y]]
(17) /into/   [−V,−N, +Dir]   $\lambda x\, \lambda z$ [FIN [z LOC IN x]]

---

[8]This assumption is not quite correct: *enter* and *go into* cannot be exchanged in all contexts: *He was allowed to enter the country*, but not *?He was not allowed to go into the country*, and *He didn't go into more detail*, but not *?He didn't enter into more detail*. Whether those differences must be captured by further components to be included in the SF of the lexical items can be left open here. What we want to show is how the SF of expressions like (13a) and (13b) has the same compositional structure, although it is put together in different ways. This aspect would not be changed, even if *enter* or *go into* would bring in additional specifications.

The directional preposition *into* relates a theme z to a goal x, such that the directional PP *into the garden* defines a property of the theme z, namely, the location of the final part of some dimension associated with z in the interior of the garden..

(18)  (a)  $[_{PP} [_P$ into$] [_{NP}$ the garden$]]$
      (b)  $[\lambda z [FIN [z LOC IN [DEF GARDEN]]]]$

This PP can now be combined with the verb *go*, where its SF substitutes the variable P ranging over path-properties assigned to the subject of the verb:

(19)  /go into the garden/ VP
      $\lambda y [y DO [MOVE y]: [FIN [y LOC IN [DEF GARDEN]]]]$

The SF of (19) is in fact identical to that of (15). In spite of various oversimplifications, this example highlights certain points that are important for lexical access. First, (15) and (16), because of their identical SF, are options for verbalizing the same range of conceptual structures, hence a choice must be made in formulating the utterance. Second, although *enter* in a sense incorporates the SF of *into*, there is still no single constituent *go into* in (19), since *into* is the head of a PP containing an NP that corresponds to the object of *enter*. In other words, the choice between (15) and (19) implies a difference in breaking up the message to be encoded into constituent parts that can be lexicalized and integrated according to grammatical principles. This is one instance of the general phenomenon of conceptual chunking, which plays a crucial role in speech production and lexical access.

Turning next to (12b) – expressions with different, but equivalent SFs – we might consider pairs like

(20)  (a)  John is not tall enough (to be in the team).
      (b)  John is too short (to be in the team).

Even though these sentences express the same thought, they cannot have the same SF because they are based on antonymous adjectives that obviously must differ in their SF. The entries for *tall* and *short* are roughly as in (21) and (22):

(21)  /tall/   [+V,+N]   $(\lambda z) \lambda x [QUANT MAX x = v PLUS z]$
(22)  /short/  [+V,+N]   $(\lambda z) \lambda x [QUANT MAX x = v MINUS z]$

The SF of *tall* represents the condition that the quantity of the maximal dimension of x equals some value v of comparison plus a difference of degree z. Both x and z are bound by abstractors specifying argument positions, so that *tall* is a two-place predicate specifying a relation between an object and the degree of its height. The parentheses around $\lambda z$ indicate the optionality of this argument, as *tall* can in fact appear as a one-place predicate with the degree of height being computed from contextual information as in *John is tall* as opposed to *John is six feet tall*. The variable v is not bound to an argument position. It is a free parameter to be fixed as 0 if possible, and a context-dependent norm N otherwise. The entry for *short* differs only by the negative difference represented by the functor MINUS, which makes it the marked antonym of the unmarked *tall*, with characteristic consequences for the possible choice of values for both z and v. For further discussions of gradable adjectives see, for example, Cresswell (1976), Hellan (1981), Stechow (1985), Seuren (1985), and Bierwisch (1989).

Ignoring technical detail, we now get (23a) and (23b) as the SF of (20a) and (20b) by means of the functional elements *too*, *enough* and *not* in ways we need not spell out here:

(23)  (a)  NEG [QUANT MAX [JOHN] = 0 PLUS C]
     (b)      [QUANT MAX [JOHN] = C MINUS z]

Both *too* and *enough* introduce a criterial extent C (which might in fact be specified by a complement clause such as *to be in the team*). While *too* turns this criterion into the value of the free variable v, *enough* substitutes it for the degree z, which in turn causes v to take the default value 0. Finally *not* contributes the negation NEG in (23a). Obviously, (23a) and (23b) are not identical, but they are equivalent, as they express the same condition, namely that the maximal dimension of John be below some criterion C. Three remarks are to be added to this illustration.

First, the equivalence in question must be established by certain rules or axioms. Their status is similar to that of the meaning postulates mentioned earlier. They are crucially different, however, as they are not restricted to idiosyncratic lexical items, but rather apply to general configurations in SF. Second, even though (20a) and (20b) are equivalent, they still differ in their combinatorial properties: only (20b), but not (20a), does allow for measure phrases. Thus we might have, for example, *two feet too short*, while *\*not two feet tall enough* is out. This follows from the fact that the optional degree position is saturated in *tall enough*, while it is still available in *too short*. In other words, the SF of *not tall enough* and *too short* is equivalent, while their AS is different.

Third, the problem of conceptual chunking shows up here in an even more intricate fashion. The relevant differences do not come as separable parts of SF associated with different lexical entries, as in *go into* versus *enter*, but are due to identical values assigned to different variables in contrasting lexical entries. In other words, the choice of lexical items depends on the interaction with specific combinatorial conditions triggered by the items selected.

Whereas sameness of meaning as discussed so far concerns relations between expressions based on their SF only, conceptual identity envisaged in (12c) involves interpretation relative to situational and background knowledge. In other words, while identity and equivalence of SF define conditions on interpretation and verbalization, identity of CS involves these processes directly. The effects can be of basically two types: either the same SF receives different conceptual interpretations, due to the abstractness of SF – we have illustrated this phenomenon in section 2.2 – or two expressions with different SFs might receive identical conceptual interpretation under different conceptual conditions. Thus even though *square* and *box* are likely to have different SFs, the sentences in (24) can represent the same instruction:[9]

(24) (a) Draw a square around the box!
     (b) Draw a box around the square!

As a matter of fact, the shift from (24a) to (24b) involves both a differentiation and an identification in the interpretation of the SF of *square* and *box*.

As shown above, such interpretive processes may have combinatorial consequences. Thus in *He left the institute some time ago* one might plausibly replace *the institute* by *the building* only if *some time* ranges over hours, but not if it ranges over years.

Finally, identity of reference or denotation listed as (12d) should be distinguished from identity of conceptual interpretation. This is obvious in cases like (25), which refer to the same person, if John's brother happens to be the president:

(25) (a) We just talked about the president.
     (b) We just talked about John's brother.

Even if the speaker and the addressee do know this identity, the person is conceptualized in quite different ways. Thus while in cases like (24) we only have a different verbalization, in (25) we also have a different conceptualization.

We will not go through the other relations mentioned in (11), but only notice that on the level of SF hyponymy, hyperonymy, and antonymy all turn on partial identity. Again, intriguing problems arise with respect to selection and chunking (as was seen, for example, with respect to the antonymous adjectives *tall* and *short*) and conceptual interpretation.

We will conclude this discussion by mentioning the fact that differences in style and register are obviously involved in verbalization, even though they are not to be included in either SF or CS directly. For the sake of illustration, consider *buck*, which has several SFs, one of which is identical to that of *dollar*. It is this – and only this – SF which is stylistically marked as colloquial. Notice that it is neither the lexeme *buck* nor the meaning "dollar" which is so marked, but rather the meaning expressed by that lexeme. This is precisely what Hjelmslev (1953) called connotation. The purport of connotation is not the conceptual interpretation of an expression, but rather the social, situational, and regional conditions of its use. Connotations might also combine to more complex conditions according to

---

[9]The type of contextual specification has been pointed out to us by Herbert Clark (personal communication).

certain principles (see Bierwisch, 1989, for some discussion). With respect to lexical access, they are related to the choice of both the lemma and the lexeme. In this paper we will ignore this aspect throughout, which amounts to considering lexical access under strictly homogeneous connotational conditions.

## 3. Conditions on the use of lexical knowledge in language production

### 3.1. Lexical knowledge in language production

The implementation of lexical knowledge as discussed so far in the mind/brain of the individual speaker/hearer constitutes what is usually called the mental lexicon (ML). Besides variation corresponding to the differences in individual knowledge, ML must be assumed to contain additional information, reflecting, for example, frequency of use or familiarity. Information in the mental lexicon must furthermore be organized according to the conditions of use in comprehension and production.

While assumptions about the structural knowledge of the lexical system (LS) are essentially motivated by linguistic analysis of natural languages, models of the mental lexicon are based on evidence from two fields of research: memory and language processing. The most ambitious attempts to model the mental lexicon are developed within the framework of neo-connectionism (see Rumelhart, McClelland & the PDP Research Group, 1986). The basic elements of neo-connectionist models are nodes of memory structure organized on various levels or layers and connected to each other by activating or inhibitory connections of different strength. A lexical entry under this conception is a collection of nodes related by a specific net of activating connections. Lexical access can then be construed as creating specific patterns of activated nodes within the overall network representing the speaker's lexical knowledge. Even though this overall view provides a unified framework integrating the structure of knowledge with the processes of using it, there are at least two serious problems with this approach in its present state.

First, there are no actual models that even remotely approach the complexity of structure defined by lexical systems of natural language, so that neo-connectionist proposals of ML simply cannot be assessed. In spite of interesting insights derived with respect to certain restricted phenomena, such as Dell's (1986) account of phonological speech errors, it is unclear how these insights can be generalized to less circumscribed problems.

Second, it is obvious that language use cannot merely consist of the generation of different activation patterns in the network representing the knowledge of lexical items. First, regular use of lexical knowledge must account for the conceptually determined and syntactically realized connections between activated words. Thus to produce *The dog came in*, it does not suffice to activate the collections of nodes that make up *the*, *dog*, *come*, and *in*, they must also be integrated in the way discussed above. But as *dog* can occur in innumerable different combinations, the pertinent relations cannot all be stored as connections in the network representing lexical knowledge. One might, of course, try to enrich the technical machinery allowed for connectionist networks, so that they can implement the combinatorial processes determined by syntactic and semantic rules. But even if a connectionist syntax of this type could be designed, it would just be an arbitrary way of implementing combinatorial processes. And in any case, it violates the basic notion of sets of connected nodes representing the knowledge of lemmas and lexemes. It might be noted that this problem arises not only for syntactically organized phrases, but also for productive processes of inflection and word formation, that is, within the lexical system. Second, even if syntactically determined relations could be accommodated in a connectionist network, a mere activation pattern could in no way account for cases like *Then the second car crashed into the first car*, as the lemma for *car* would have to have two different types of connections simultaneously. This is a fundamental problem that shows up even in simple sentences like *Children like children*, which is systematically different from *Children like themselves*. In other words, the formulator, which integrates accessed lexical items, cannot merely establish additional connections in the network representing lexical knowledge, but must dispose of some sort of buffer or intermediate storage where activated lexical items can be integrated into more complex utterance structures. We will return to another aspect of this problem, namely the time course of activation, in section 5.2.

Instead of speculating about more appropriate models of the mental lexicon, we will merely indicate by means of the following schema (see Figure 2) the

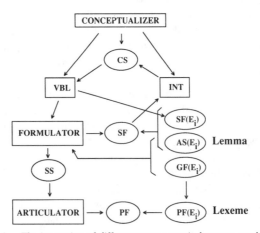

Figure 2.   *The interaction of different components in language production.*

interaction of different components, which any model must account for in one way or the other. This schema, which elaborates on Levelt's general model of language production, must not be considered as an actual flow chart, as it only represents the way in which different types of information and mapping processes depend on each other.

This schema is simplified in several respects, in order to keep it perspicuous for the present discussion. Thus, we left out the way in which morphological aspects of actual words relate to the lexicon and enter the formulator. Some of the relevant categories, such as tense and number, have a clear and extensively studied conceptual interpretation and must therefore originate from CS. Other morphological categories, such as agreement or structural case, are a matter of purely grammatical, language internal structure and bear no direct relation to CS. We also did not try to indicate the fact that both verbalization and interpretation are sensitive to the distinction between the context Ct of (a part of) an utterance, and its conceptual purport in the narrower sense.

We have nothing to say about the various sorts of input to the conceptualizer and the way in which it generates a conceptual structure CS. In the light of what has been said earlier, we have to assume, however, that there is a mechanism that takes CS as input and realizes the mapping *Vbl*. This mechanism has to effect two things: first, it must split up CS into chunks that can be lexicalized, thereby registering the relation between them and making them available for the formulator; second, it must feed chunks into the system of lemmas where they must be matched with the semantic form $SF(E_i)$ of appropriate lexical entries $E_i$. The selection of some $SF(E_i)$ is directly connected with the determination of the argument structure $AS(E_i)$ and the grammatical features $GF(E_i)$, both of which must be available to the formulator, which constructs the syntactic structure SS in accordance with the relational information provided by *Vbl*. The integrated semantic form SF, compiled from the $SF(E_i)$ of the accessed lexical items of an utterance, is best understood as a criterion against which monitoring of the result of lexical access and integration into a connected utterance structure is possible. This monitoring must be effected by the interpretation mechanism *Int*, which also maps SF into CS in language comprehension.

While we assume that $SF(E_i)$, $AS(E_i)$, and $GF(E_i)$ are different, but directly related types of information constituting the lemma of $E_i$, the phonetic form $PF(E_i)$ – and the graphemic form, for that matter – belongs to the system of lexemes, which is a different component of the mental lexicon delivering its information to the articulator. We will not make any further comments on the access of lexemes and their integration.

Two final points should be noted with respect to the schema given above. First, while the formulator and the articulator must be central processing units operating sequentially on the input provided by *Vbl* to produce SF and SS (and ultimately the articulatory output), this does not hold for the mechanism realizing

*Vbl.* This becomes quite obvious, if we recognize that the lemma component containing $SF(E_i)$, $AS(E_i)$, and $GF(E_i)$ abbreviates the whole system of lemmas, that is, the proper memory basis of the mental lexicon. Second, while assembling an integrated SF and constructing the corresponding SS by the formulator is largely a matter of sequential processing, the matching of conceptual chunks against the lemmas to be accessed is a distributed process that allows for extensive parallel processing. If this assumption is correct, then *Vbl* does not only sort out conceptual chunks, thereby registering their relationship, but also feeds on the one hand into the sequentially operating formulator, and triggers on the other hand parallel processes on the system of lemmas. We will return to this aspect of temporal organization of lexical access in section 5.2.

## 3.2. Input representations and their lexicalization

In section 2.2 we have distinguished between SF and CS, assuming that CS is the level of pre-verbal message structures. We will now look somewhat more closely at the input the mechanism realizing *Vbl* is actually confronted with. A plausible assumption in this respect can be stated as follows:

(26) Only conceptualized information can be input to the formulator and to lexical access.

Although this is a rather general claim, it has fairly specific consequences. It excludes, for instance, direct lexical access by means of perceptual information, let alone physical stimuli, even if special conditions like object naming or word–picture matching suggests the contrary. Hence experiments exploiting the apparent direct mapping from sensory input to lexical items might be revealing in various respects, but they do not demonstrate lexical access without conceptualization.

More important for (26), conceptualized information must be assumed to come in integrated representations drawing on conceptual structure, encyclopedic and situational knowledge. Such representations are not only richer than their eventual verbalization (as, for instance, *The shop is closed*), they also do not in general exhibit the partitioning or chunking required for matching of individual lexical items.

A further question related to (26) is whether thoughts or messages, that is, structures to be verbalized, are necessarily pre-linguistic, free of any lexical or grammatical ingredients. We need not go here into the controversy about language and thought, inner speech, etc. We adopt the view that, in general, pre-verbal message structures precede the process of utterance formation as attested by introspections that we normally know what we want to say, before we have worked out how to say it.

There are two alternatives to be considered:

(27) (a) Message structures are related to (or even structured in terms of) linguistic structures right from the beginning.

  (b) Message structures are strictly pre-linguistic and only later mapped onto linguistic expressions.

We have already rejected (27a), the strict and complete correspondence of language and thought. Notice that under this view lexical access would either disappear altogether or become part of conceptualization, rather than language production.

Example (27b) cannot be true either, however, as attested by simple cases like (28):

(28) A: Did you go to the movie last night?

  B: No, I could not go to the movie last night, because I had to prepare my lecture notes.

Comprehending the question of A involves the construction and interpretation of much of what reappears in the answer. Obviously, it does not disappear from short-term memory before the answer is generated. It would be pointless to claim that the message underlying B's answer is conceptualized in a strictly non-linguistic way. Phenomena like these are quite pervasive even if they do not take the form of a somewhat redundant repetition as in (28). What these considerations suggest is the assumption that the conceptualizer, even though it operates essentially in pre-linguistic terms, can rely on and integrate linguistic material already formulated if it is directly accessible. So, neither (28a) nor (28b) is correct. The input to the formulator, although essentially conceptual in nature, might be mixed under special conditions. The assumption just adumbrated is by no means at variance with the requirement in (26) that the input to the formulator be conceptualized information: obviously, elements of the message structure that are already verbalized for whatever reason do have a conceptual interpretation. Otherwise they were not (parts of) a message to be integrated with other conceptual information. In (28), verbalized parts of the message structure have both a conceptual *and* a linguistic representation, in much the same way in which non-verbal parts of the conceptual input acquire a conceptual and a linguistic aspect through lexical access.

Mixed – that is, partially verbalized – input nevertheless requires standard processes of the formulator, including lexical access, as even simple examples like (28) show: the question *did you go* is replaced by *I could not go* in the answer, which not only brings in new material (*could not*), but also reorganizes preserved components in grammatically and lexically determined fashion. Retelling a joke, where crucial parts are stored in verbalized form, is another example.

So the relation between CS and SF, that is, the pre-linguistic and the linguistic aspect of an utterance, is essentially the same whether or not parts of the generated utterance come already verbalized. The main difference is that lexical access might be vacuous in certain cases, whatever that means.

With this proviso, we will abstract in what follows from particular problems related to mixed, partially verbalized input representations, treating the generation of utterances from a non-verbal conceptual structure as the standard case, with utterances based on previously verbalized input as short-cut results with the same output processes.

## 4. Decomposition and its consequence for processing systems

### 4.1. Decomposition

Our basic assumption (see section 2.1) is that the lexical meaning of a lemma has a complex internal structure composed of more primitive elements. It is exactly this assumption that leads to a large number of problems for a theory about the mapping of conceptual structures onto lemmas. Most, if not all, of these problems are solved if one adopts Roelof's (this volume) approach, where the conceptual system presents the formulator with a conceptual structure with a one-to-one mapping between conceptual properties and lemmas. This guarantees that activation of the right lemma is possible in principle. This is an attractive possibility. But, if there were relevant empirical evidence in favour of the decomposition hypothesis, then this would indicate that lemma activation by the conceptual system might indeed be as complex and problematic as the previous paragraphs try to show. It is therefore important what empirical evidence might tell us about decomposition.

Unfortunately, there is not much evidence. Most evidence has been obtained in so called "complexity" studies. In these studies the processing of two words is compared where the semantic representation of one ("simple") word is assumed to be a subset or substructure of the other ("complex") word, for example, *man* versus *bachelor*, *go* versus *walk*. In most cases it is predicted that, in some way, the semantically more complex word will take more time to process, be more difficult to remember, or be more difficult to verify against a picture. This line of research has generally shown negative results, finding no differences between simple and complex words (cf. Fodor, Fodor, & Garrett, 1975; Kintsch, 1974; Thorndyke, 1975). One exception to these negative results, however, was obtained by Carpenter and Just (1975) and Clark (1974), who found in picture–sentence matching tasks a systematic pattern of results, where pairs such as *present/not present* behave in a similar way to pairs such as *present/absent*. Some other positive evidence was obtained by Schreuder (1978). In these experiments subjects had to verify descriptions containing either "simple" or "complex" verbs of motion against simple objects moving on a computer screen (e.g., comparing *move* vs. *rise*, *reach* vs. *crash*). Surprisingly, these experiments showed a reversed complexity effect. The descriptions using a complex verb were verified faster than the descriptions using a simple verb. The fact that semantic complexity played a clear role in these experiments argues against the assumption that all lemmas have a representation of just one, unanalysable, concept (Fodor et al., 1975; Roelofs, this volume). The negative results obtained by others are more difficult to evaluate. Complexity effects can be explained by the decomposition hypothesis, but they are by no means a necessary consequence of decomposition. Meaning components could be processed in parallel, without any additional processing load for words with more components than others.

Another way to look at this issue, however, is by comparing not the number of components, but the way these primitives are connected (as, for example, in the structures proposed by Jackendoff, 1976, 1983). Surprisingly little testing has been done on proposals like this. There are two exceptions. Gentner (1981) tested the "connectivity" hypothesis. This hypothesis views verb semantic structures as frames for sentence representations and predicts that memory strength between nouns in a sentence increases with the number of underlying verb subpredicates that connect the nouns. In Gentner's experiments, subjects were given subject nouns as cues to recall SVO sentences. General verbs with relatively few subpredicates (*damage*, *clean*, *give*) were compared with more specific verbs (*smash*, *scrub*, *sell*) whose additional subpredicates provided additional connections between the nouns in the sentences. For instance, *sell* conveys more connective information than *give*, because there are connections between the subject and structures dealing with change of possession and connections between the subject and change of possession of money. ("Ida gave her tenants a clock" vs. "Ida sold her tenants a clock".) Gentner found that the subject nouns as a recall cue produced better recall for the sentence with specific verbs.

In Schreuder's (1978) approach the assumption was that in the semantic structure of verbs describing human locomotions one part deals with a change of place and another part deals with the motion of the body (our example (4b) is similar to this). Schreuder paired up verbs with adverbial phrases that gave information either about the part dealing with change of place or about the part dealing with motion of the body. For instance, in *She swam leisurely on her back*, the two adverbial phrases both pertain to a meaning representation dealing with body movement. And in *She swam through the river to the island*, both phrases pertain to a meaning representation dealing with path and location. The pattern of results indicated that the "link" between the two aspects of verb meaning could be severed, suggesting that the two meaning structures have an independent structure. In an incidental learning task subjects saw sentences with a motion verb combined with two adverbial phrases. Either the phrases both modified one of the two substructures or one of them modified one substructure and the other phrase the other substructure. Level of recall of one of the adverbial phrases was measured given the other one as a retrieval cue. Performance was better in the condition where both adverbial phrases modified the same substructure. These memory tasks are rather "off-line" tasks and provide indirect evidence for decomposition during processing. But this is also the case for the careful study of Fodor, Garrett, Walker, and Parkes (1980), which showed no evidence for decomposition using different scaling measures. Since there is some positive empirical evidence, and given our earlier remarks on decomposition, we feel strongly that it is necessary to have semantic decomposition as our main assumption and explore problems associated with it. In what follows we explore the consequences of this assumption for a theory of lemma retrieval from a psycholinguistic point of view. We look at the way the first step, from CS to lemma, might be implemented in a psycholinguistic model of lemma retrieval and discuss the various problems that arise, assuming that there is no one-to-one mapping of primitives in the CS and lemma representations in contrast to the proposal of Roelofs (1992). In doing so, we will retrace some of the issues mentioned in previous sections.

## 4.2. *From the conceptual system to the verbalization system*

In section 3.1, Figure 2 shows that the conceptualizer sends a conceptual structure to *Vbl*, a processing system that transforms a non-linguistic conceptual structure into a representation containing an SF, as described so far. Let us assume, with Levelt (1989), that the conceptualizer produces "fragments", that is, not the full representation of a message, but certain parts of it. At several places in the previous sections we have noted that arbitrary chunking of a CS might lead to problems (cf. section 2.2 comparing *enter* vs. *go into*). Is there any guarantee that, whichever way the conceptualizer breaks up the CS, the *Vbl* can handle the resulting chunk? Can the *Vbl* mechanism always create an SF that is guaranteed to trigger a lemma? This problem does not disappear when the *Vbl* function is left out. It merely shifts to lemma access. Without a *Vbl* the question becomes whether it is guaranteed that any way of breaking up a CS will allow the resulting structures to be lemmatized at all. This is the first problem for a theory of lemma access, the chunking problem. It is caused by two important assumptions of Levelt's (1989) model and our version of it. The first is that the conceptualizer has *no* access to the lexicon proper and does not have any information about the SFs that are available in the lexicon. The second is that no interaction is possible between conceptualizer and the formulator in Levelt's proposal, and between conceptualizer and *Vbl* in our proposal. If the conceptualizer could be signalled that a certain fragment could not be lemmatized or translated into an SF then the problem would be solved, though at the high price that now two different, formerly fully independent subsystems can influence each other, which goes against the modular spirit of Levelt's model. Since the exact nature of CS representations remains a riddle, and since there is also no empirical, psycholinguistic evidence about how messages are chunked, we can only point to this as a serious problem for any processing model assuming fragmented messages and no interaction between conceptualizer and formulator.

Another problem of assuming semantic decomposition is word-to-phrase synonymies. How can the system make a choice between producing "Peter is a bachelor" versus "Peter is an unmarried human adult male"? Lexicalizations of the supposedly primitive elements can be a choice of a speaker (Roelofs, 1992). We think that this problem can be solved in the following way. By default *Vbl* will try to map a certain fragment onto as few lemmas as possible. But when the conceptualizer prefers decomposed lemmatization, it could achieve this by supplying the *Vbl* with additional information "marking" certain parts of a CS with a request for separate lemmatization.

## 4.3. The verbalization function

In section 2.2 we argue why the *Vbl* mapping might be necessary. To summarize, it maps a certain conceptual structure (given a certain representation of the conceptual context) onto an SF representation. In example (16) the SF of "The office is closed" might be the result of many different combinations of conceptual structures and contexts. Examples (13a) and (13b) show how one CS may be mapped onto two different SFs. The *Vbl* mapping therefore is many-to-many.

Simplifying, what the *Vbl* process does is to translate a certain CS into a set of SFs. These SFs in their turn have to be mapped onto the lemma lexicon, probably partly in parallel. That is, given a certain fragment CS(i) *Vbl* delivers a set of SFs, $\langle SF(E_j), SF(E_k), \ldots, SF(E_k) \rangle$. Such a process *must* have knowledge about which SF representations can be lemmatized, and it must choose between different but equivalent ways of chunking a CS representation into a series of fragments to be lemmatized. In section 2.3 it was argued that a particular CS could be expressed either as "The man went into the garden" or as "The man entered the garden". It is clear that the series of chunks accepted by *Vbl* in order to trigger lemmas differ for the two series. The choice for the SF of the lemma *go* entails that *Vbl* now also has to deliver the SF of *into*.

It is not clear on what basis the system would chose between alternative verbalizations like these. In creating these series of SFs, furthermore, the process needs to know in which way information from CS can be combined within a certain SF to be lemmatized within this particular language. Let us illustrate this point with an example from Talmy (1985):

(29) The bottle floated into the cave.
(30) La botella entró a la cuave flotando.

Let us assume that the CS of these two sentences is the same and looks like

(31) [DO [MOVE BOTTLE]: FIN[BOTTLE LOC IN CAVE]]:
     FLOAT BOTTLE

The lexicalization patterns differ across these two languages. English can "con-flate" MOVE with the manner condition FLOAT in a single lemma, that is, *Vbl* can create an SF as a request for a lemma in which both the motion and the manner are expressed. In Spanish, this is not possible. So, depending on the language, the *Vbl* mapping may combine different elements of the CS into SF representations. Talmy (1985), in an overview of these different lexicalization patterns across languages, shows that they can vary extensively. The *Vbl* mapping, therefore, should have this knowledge. There are other language-specific considerations that the *Vbl* mapping needs to know. For instance, languages differ in spatial deixis. Some have a three-step contrast on distance to ego, others have a two-step system. The processing within the *Vbl* mapping, therefore, is language specific and has access to knowledge of language-specific requirements. It can be considered the interface between the conceptualizer and language-specific infor-mation-processing systems. This proposal is in contrast with Levelt's (1989) model. In his discussion of language-specific requirements (pp. 103–105) he concludes that the conceptualizer has this knowledge. In our proposal the conceptual system need have no linguistic knowledge at all; it is not constrained by any linguistic considerations (cf. section 2.2). If we consider *Vbl* to be a part of the formulator, conceptualizer and formulator are now two completely in-dependent modules. Within the formulator the *Vbl* module may have access to lexical knowledge. How *Vbl* does its work is unclear, but it has to be a fast and efficient process, since speakers usually produce around 150 words per minute. And producing a series of SFs to lemmatize is just the beginning. The next step in the process is to trigger the *right* lemma.

### 4.4. *From semantic form to lemma*

The problem of lemma access is to explain what kind of system can find the right lemma fast. Finding the right word is what Levelt (1989) called the convergence problem: the system must converge on a *single* item, the correct one. Levelt (pp. 199–212) discusses different ways in which the convergence problem might be solved. We will not review these proposals here but concentrate on one specific problem, the "hypernym" problem (Levelt 1989, p. 201): "When lemma A's meaning entails lemma B's meaning, B is a hypernym of A. If A's conceptual conditions are met, then B's are necessarily also satisfied. Hence if A is the correct lemma, B will also be retrieved." Why don't we say *dog* when we want to say *poodle*? So, in our terminology, how will the right lemma be retrieved given an SF produced by the *Vbl* process? No available theories can solve this problem. Levelt solves the problem by three principles:

1. Uniqueness principle: no two lexical items have the same core meaning.
2. Core principle: a lexical item is retrieved only if its core condition is satisfied by the concept to be expressed.
3. Principle of specificity: of all items whose core conditions are satisfied, the most specific one is retrieved.

Together these three principles solve the hypernym problem in theory, but it is not clear what type of processing system could *implement* these principles. The principles form a constraint on processing theories but are themselves no solution to the processing problem. There is, however, a simpler formulation of the three principles that also leads to a solution of the processing problem:

(32) An SF(i) triggers Lemma(m) if and only if there exists complete match of *all* structures in SF(i) with all structures in the semantic representation of the lemma.

That is, all elements in the SF should also be present in the lemma's representation and all elements in the lemma's representation should also be present in the SF that the *Vbl* has produced.

This one-to-one mapping will usually solve the problem of retrieving a lemma (given a certain SF). One exception may complicate matters. For idiomatic expressions, one SF has to trigger not one but many lemmas at the same time, but the principle remains the same assuming that a combination of lemmas also can have its own SF.

How could such a principle be implemented? There are many different possibilities but we will discuss one way in terms of an activation model. Figure 3 shows two lemma nodes and a number of nodes that represent SF information.

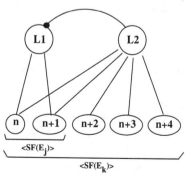

Figure 3. *Solution of the hypernym problem in an activation model.*

The lemma L1 is a hypernym of lemma L2. What happens when the *Vbl* function produces SF(Ek)?

Nodes *n* up to *n* + 4 are activated and they will start to activate both L1 and L2. L2 has a bias (threshold) that it needs more than 4 units of activation. Since it is activated by 5 units L2 will become activated. Assuming inhibitory links between words and their hypernyms, L2 will deactivate L1, the hypernym of L2. That is, after activation of SF(Ek) the system will stabilize into a situation where only L2 will be activated. SF(Ej) will not activate L2 because L2 needs more than 4 units of activation. This is one, simplified way of modelling lemma access by semantic representations. One of its simplifications is that an SF is treated as an unordered set of primitive elements. If the SF is highly structured, as we have argued, the principle of one-to-one mapping can still be the same, and guarantees that no hypernyms will be produced. In discussing the hypernym problem we have appealed to activation models, as introduced by Dell (1986). In the next section we will discuss one specific problem for all activation models.

## 5. Activation models and discontinuities in time

### 5.1. Activation and deactivation of lemmas

In Dell's (1986) activation model semantic features activate lemma representations. Lemma representations, in combination with activation of diacritical features like tense or number, activate word form representations. These, in their turn, activate representations at the syllabic and phonological level. It is crucial in these models that activation develops over time, where representations become activated and then deactivated. At each level and each discrete moment, there is always one and only one "current" node. To produce the different elements in the right order, one lemma must become the most highly activated and will then decrease in activation, so that now the next lemma in the utterance can become activated. All nodes at all levels show an exponential decay of activation. Similar considerations apply, of course, to units representing word forms, syllables, and so on.

There is empirical evidence showing that lemma deactivation occurs rather rapidly. These experiments investigated the two-stage theory of lexical access of Garrett (1976, 1988). The first stage, lexical selection, gives information about lexical items that are used to construct the functional level representation. In the second stage, word forms are retrieved. At the first stage, there is no information about phonology available. When word forms are accessed, semantic and syntactic information is no longer available. Schriefers, Meyer, and Levelt (1990) tested this seriality hypothesis experimentally using a task where the naming of picture is interfered by an accompanied word. The interfering words were presented auditorily. They obtained interference effects for semantically related words on picture-naming latencies at an early stimulus-onset asynchrony, or SOA, (−150 ms). Phonologically related words produced interference effects at later SOAs (0 ms, +150 ms). Since at later SOAs semantic interference effects disappeared the authors concluded that this gives evidence for the notion of a two-step model where once form information is computed the semantic information disappears. Deactivation of lemmas, however, is problematic for certain types of lemmas and certain kinds of idioms. To see why this is a problem we have to discuss some aspects of temporal order of access.

## 5.2. Discontinuity in time

Where in the time course of language production does lexical access take place? The structural aspect of linguistic (and conceptual) knowledge does not say. Structural representations of both lexical items and complex expressions are abstract schemata specifying the units in question in an essentially atemporal manner. There is, however, a basic correspondence between the linear order of constituents in syntax and of segments in phonetic form on the one hand and the temporal organization of the speech signal and the articulatory program on the other: the ordering of segments and constituents determines the potential time course in which these elements are processed in comprehension and production.

We may distinguish three time-dependent aspects interlocked in lexical access in language production.

First, there is the time course controlling the articulatory realization of the phonetic form of an utterance.

Second, there is the order in which the formulator accesses lemmas on the basis of the conceptual input.

Third, there is the time course that for each lexical item leads from the initial steps accessing the lemma to spelling out the pertinent lexeme.

Schematically, these three aspects can be indicated as follows (see Figure 4). The two "horizontal" aspects (B) and (A) represent the temporal structure determined by the formulator and the articulator, respectively, while the "vertical" aspect (C) symbolizes the time course of the individual lexical items from access to their articulatory pattern. This schema is, of course, simplified. The time course (A) is obviously not realized by a uniform, continuous sequence of articulatory processes, but is subject to interruptions, hesitations, etc., depending

Figure 4.   *Three time-dependent aspects interlocked in lexical access.*

on higher-order operations of the formulator and the time course (C) of accessing individual lexical entries. Its parts are therefore delayed relative to their counterparts in the temporal sequence (B). However, the order of segments in phonetic form and of syntactic surface constituents must conform to the sequential ordering of time units in (A) realizing these segments and constituents. A strict correspondence of this sort does not hold for the ordering in (B). Indeed, the articulatory realization of a word may follow that of others whose access starts at a later time point. A simple case in point is (33), where *up* must be accessed together with *put*:

(33) They could not put their friends up.

This means not only that the time lines (C) do not in general project in a straightforward manner from (B) to (A), but they may cross each other with intermediate storage of lemmas or lexemes that have to wait for their output realization. This happens especially for verbs with separable particles in languages like German, Dutch or Afrikaans:

(34) *vallen*: "to fall"      *aan*: "on"      *af*: "down"
    *aanvallen*: "to attack"      *afvallen*: "to lose weight"

Example (34) gives two of these verbs. These often have idiosyncratic meanings. This poses interesting problems not only for recognition processes handling these verbs (See Schreuder, 1990), but also for processes in producing them. This is because they can occur separated in time:

(35) Zij *vielen* de hele dag, in grote aantallen *aan*.
    (They attacked all day, in large numbers.)
    Dat *aan* te willen *vallen*, is gevaarlijk.
    (It is dangerous to want to attack that.)

Given the idiosyncratic meaning aspects of these verbs they *must* have their own lemma representation. But this lemma representation must then be connected to two different form representations. Simple spread of activation cannot do the job of selecting the right word form. Having activated the lemma together with the diacritical features does not help in deciding *which* of the two forms is to be chosen, the particle or the verb. This is a selection problem and cannot be handled by the lexicon but should be taken care of within the grammatical encoder.

It is now clear why the decay of lemma representation discussed in the previous paragraph leads to problems. How can an activation model keep a certain node activated for an essentially, unlimited amount of time? There is no theoretical limit to the amount of linguistic information insertable between a verb and its later occurring particle. After production of the verb part the conceptualizer might introduce a new message fragment that has to be inserted between verb and particle. So, at the moment that the verb part is produced the system does not know how long it will take before the other half of the compound verb has to be produced. In certain idioms, many different word forms may have to be kept active:

(36) De leugenaars *vielen*, ook al deden zij nog zo hun best, *door de mand.*
     Literal meaning: The liars fell, despite all their efforts, through the basket.
     Idiomatic meaning: The liars were caught out, despite all their efforts.

In cases like, this *one* SF triggers *one* lemma, which in its turn will have to trigger several forms. Either one form is triggered or all of them are triggered. When one form is triggered, then, according to the two-step theory, the semantic information represented at the lemma level will decay fast. It is not clear how the other form(s) could be produced later, since "their" lemma is no longer activated. Keeping the lemma activated during this time, or keeping all the forms activated during an unknown amount of time, runs counter to Dell's principle of one "current" node. In activation models the different patterns of activation and deactivation are tuned such that at a given moment only one node can be selected, because it is more activated, given certain criteria, than others are. Getting the right word form out at the right time depends on this mechanism. Having more than one word form activated for some time poses serious problems for activation models like those of Dell (1986).

Accessing verbs with separable particles and idiomatic verbs is, however, no problem for algorithmic models of language production like the incremental production grammar of Kempen and Hoenkamp (1987). In these models, word forms that are part of a verb with a separable particle may be put "on hold" in a buffer. The syntactic processor or grammatical encoder can decide when to send this word form to the phonological encoder, based on syntactic considerations.

## 6. Conclusion

### 6.1. *Conditions on lexical access in language production*

Taking the step from concepts to lexical items as a crucial ingredient of language production, one faces three major problems:

(37) (a) The nature of conceptual structures.
     (b) The structure of lexical knowledge.
     (c) The mapping between conceptual and lexical structures.

Although the processes underlying (37c) are the focus of the present paper, very little can be said about them without an appropriate understanding of (37a) and (37b). We have therefore dealt at some length with the rich structure that must be assumed for lexical knowledge, especially its meaning-oriented, semantic aspect, according to presently available linguistic insights. In contrast, problems of conceptual structure must be approached in a largely indirect, less conclusive way. Summarizing the main observations we made with respect to (37a)–(37c) from a bird's-eye perspective, the following assumptions seem to us essential.

1. Concepts and lemmas belong to different mental domains determined by largely independent systems of knowledge. The interface between representations of these two systems is provided by what we have called the verbalization mapping *Vbl* and its converse, the interpretation mapping *Int*. Both *Vbl* and *Int* are many-to-many mappings, and the processes determined by *Vbl* are assumed to constitute the main part of the step from concepts to lexical items. As the verbalization is clearly dependent on language-specific information, *Vbl* must be considered a part of the language-dependent formulator, if the system of conceptual knowledge operates in basically pre-linguistic terms.

2. Both concepts and lexical items – or, more specifically, the semantic form SF and lexical items – must be assumed to be structured in terms of more basic components that enter the general combinatorial structure of their respective domains. Even though this assumption has been the object of controversies and extensive discussion, we have argued that some sort of decomposition must be assumed for a variety of reasons, including semantic interpretation in cases like *This little dog is made of ivory*, or the anomaly of phrases like *five feet short* as opposed to the well-formedness of *five feet tall*.

3. Conceptual structures and the semantic form of lexical items are determined by different mental systems, so they are not in general congruent. *Int* and *Vbl* are many-to-many-mappings and allow for a fair range of flexibility – very much like the perceptual and articulatory functions that relate phonetic form representations to variable input and output representations. Conceptual structures might also differ from semantic form in the way in which basic components and complex configurations of them are integrated into larger structures. These incongruities lead to crucial requirements that the mechanism realizing the verbalization function has to deal with.

4. The first requirement is characterized by what we have called the chunking problem: the necessity to identify those conceptual configurations that are available for lexicalization. As we have tried to show, a given conceptual structure might be split up in different chunks corresponding to lexical items, depending on language-specific conditions of the lexical system. How the decisions required by the chunking problem are actually made is one of the most intricate issues in lexical access, as the lexical items to be accessed must be anticipated in order to break up a formulated message structure into appropriate parts. The relations among these parts must correspond, moreover, to the relations established among the accessed lexical items according to the rules and principles of the lexical and grammatical system of the language.

5. Assuming that the chunking problem is solved somehow, the verbalization must decide the specificity lexical items are to preserve relative to a given message structure and its contextual setting. Once again, conditions embodied in the lexical system, the structure of the available lemmas and the relations among them play a crucial role for these decisions.

6. As both the chunking problem and the specificity of the selected lemmas cannot be treated independently for the lexical items in an utterance, the time course of the decisions in question and the lemmas eventually accessed play a crucial role. We have argued that the decisions involved in the verbalization cannot proceed in a simple left-to-right sequential ordering, corresponding to the linear order in which selected items occur in the surface of a formulated utterance. A plausible assumption emerging from these considerations acknowledges a certain amount of parallel processing with a strictly sequential timing imposed only by the resulting surface structure, according to certain relevant syntactic domains.

7. An important conclusion about lexical access is the fact that the activation metaphor, in which access to a lexical item is tantamount to an activation pattern within the network of nodes representing the lexical system, is untenable. Lexical items can be syntactically complex, so that the pertinent lexemes appear at distant places of the resulting surface structure, and hence intermediate storage will be necessary. But this is at variance with the very notion of activation pattern and their decay.

As mentioned before, these considerations by no means lead in any direct way to a model describing, let alone explaining, the processes that lead from conceptual structures to utterances. They merely specify a number of conditions any such model must account for.

## 6.2. Additional problems?

The previous discussion is incomplete in many respects. There are many facts and problems bearing on lexical access we have not even mentioned.

One of the phenomena we did not deal with is the influence of discourse conditions or communicative settings on lexical access. Thus, for instance, the referential specificity related to a given situation, as studied by Olson (1970), might lead directly to effects on lexical access. For one particular situation and conversational background, a certain object might uniquely be identified by the phrase *the big square*, while under different conditions the same effect would be achieved by means of *the black painting* or *the famous Malevich*. Thus, objects will be classified in different ways depending on situational and discourse requirements.

A related aspect concerns the whole range of direct and indirect illocutionary forces and conversational implicatures controlled by conversational maxims of the Gricean type. As Sperber and Wilson (1986) have argued, phenomena like these can all be reduced to some sort of cognitive economy, which controls the conceptualization messages and the formulation of utterances.

Problems of the sort just indicated clearly have to do with the operations of the conceptualizer that determine how the message is to be delivered to the formulator. Thus, to the extent to which the phenomena in question are covered by the operation of the conceptualizer – that we have simply taken for granted – they do not go beyond the scope of the discussion summarized in the previous section.

Second, to the extent to which the phenomena in question directly concern the choice of lexical items over and above the construction of messages performed by the conceptualizer, they might be relevant for lexical access directly. This will indeed be the case if, for example, the principle of cognitive economy proposed by Sperber and Wilson turns not only on conceptual representations, but depends also on their verbalization. Here it becomes relevant that both *Int* and *Vbl* have been assumed to be context dependent. Although we have explicitly stated this fact, we made no specific assumptions about the nature and range of the context on which these function depend. If we assume that *Vbl* (and *Int*, for that matter) can access both conceptual and linguistic representations, which is a plausible assumption, given the interface character of these mappings, then linguistic factors determining cognitive economy are within the range of *Vbl*, and hence within lexical access in the sense assumed here. Whether these speculations are correct depends crucially on the pertinent assumptions about the nature of available context information. For obvious reasons, we have been deliberately unspecific in this respect – as practically all approaches that respect the relevance of context. Things do not only become extremely complicated, if one tries to be explicit about this additional aspect. It is also practically impossible at present to go beyond the obvious claim that contextual information plays a crucial role for the verbalization of formulated messages. Hence, in a trivial sense, additional phenomena are already covered by the constraints we have discussed. Whether they turn out to go beyond these constraints in a non-trivial way must be left open until a more explicit characterization of the nature of conceptual structures and contextual information is available.

## References

Bierwisch, M. (1982). Formal and lexical semantics. *Linguistische Berichte, 80,* 3–17.

Bierwisch, M. (1989). The semantics of gradation. In M. Bierwisch & E. Lang (Eds.), *Dimensional adjectives: Grammatical structure and conceptual interpretation* (pp. 71–271). Berlin: Springer.

Bierwisch, M., & Lang, E. (1989). Somewhat longer, much deeper, further and further. In M.

Bierwisch & E. Lang (Eds.), *Dimensional adjectives: Grammatical structure and conceptual interpretation*. Berlin: Springer.

Carpenter, P.A., & Just, M.A. (1975). Sentence comprehension: A psycholinguistic processing model. *Psychological Review, 82*, 45–73.

Chomsky, N. (1965). *Aspects of the theory of syntax*. Cambridge, MA: MIT Press.

Chomsky, N. (1980). *Rules and representations*. Oxford: Blackwell.

Chomsky, N. (1981). *Lectures on government and binding*. Dordrecht: Foris.

Clark, H.H. (1974). Semantics and comprehension. In T.A. Sebeok (Ed.), *Current trends in linguistics, Vol. 12: Linguistics and Adjacent Arts and Sciences*. The Hague: Mouton.

Cresswell, M. (1976). The semantics of degree. In B. Partee (Ed.), *Montague grammar* (pp. 261–292). New York: Academic Press.

Dell, G.S. (1986). A spreading activation theory of retrieval in sentence production. *Psychological Review, 93*, 283–321.

Di Sciullo, A.M., & Williams, E. (1987). *On the definition of word*. Cambridge, MA: MIT Press.

Dowty, D.R. (1979). *Word meaning and Montague grammar*. Dordrecht: Reidel.

Fodor, J.A. (1975). *The language of thought*. Hassocks: Harvester Press.

Fodor, J.A. (1983). *The modularity of mind*. Cambridge, MA: MIT Press.

Fodor, J.D., Fodor, J.A., & Garrett, M.F. (1975). The psychological unreality of semantic representations. *Linguistic Inquiry, 6*, 515–531.

Fodor, J.A., Garrett, M.F., Walker, E.C.T., & Parkes, C.H. (1980). Against definitions. *Cognition, 8*, 263–367.

Garrett, M.F. (1976). Syntactic processes in sentence production. In R.J. Wales & E. Walker (Eds.), *New approaches to language mechanisms* (pp. 231–256). Amsterdam: North-Holland.

Garrett, M.F. (1988). Processes in language production. In F.J. Newmeyer (Ed.), *Linguistics: The Cambridge survey, Vol. III. Biological and psychological aspects of language* (pp. 69–96). Cambridge, MA: Harvard University Press.

Gentner, D. (1981). Verb semantic structures in memory for sentences: Evidence for componential representation. *Cognitive Psychology, 13*, 56–83.

Grimshaw, J. (1990). *Argument structure*. Cambridge, MA: MIT Press.

Hellan, L. (1981). *Towards an integrated analysis of comparatives*. Tübingen: Narr.

Hjelmslev, L. (1953). *Prolegomena to a theory of language*. Bloomington: Indiana University Publications.

Jackendoff, R. (1976). Toward an explanatory semantic representation. *Linguistic Inquiry, 7*, 89–150.

Jackendoff, R. (1983). *Semantics and cognition*. Cambridge, MA: MIT Press.

Jackendoff, R. (1990). *Semantic structures*. Cambridge, MA: MIT Press.

Johnson-Laird, P.N. (1983). *Mental models*. Cambridge, UK: Cambridge University Press.

Kamp, H. (1981). A theory of truth and semantic representation. In J. Groenendijk, T. Janssen, & M. Stokhof (Eds.), *Formal methods in the study of language* (pp. 277–322). Amsterdam: Mathematisch Centrum.

Kamp, H., & Reyle, U. (forthcoming). *From discourse to logic*. Dordrecht: Kluwer.

Katz, J.J. (1972). *Semantic theory*. New York: Harper & Row.

Kempen, G., & Hoenkamp, E. (1987). An incremental procedural grammar for sentence formulation. *Cognitive Science, 11*, 201–258.

Kintsch, W. (1974). *The representation of meaning in memory*. Hillsdale, NJ: Erlbaum.

Kiparsky, P. (1985). Some consequences of lexial phonology. In C.J. Ewens & J.M. Anderson (Eds.), *Phonology yearbook 2* (pp. 85–138). Cambridge, MA: MIT Press.

Levelt, W.J.M. (1989). *Speaking: From intention to articulation*. Cambridge, MA: MIT Press.

Miller, G.A., & Johnson-Laird, P.L. (1976). *Language and perception*. Cambridge, MA: Belknap Press.

Olson, D. (1970). Language and thought: Aspects of a cognitive theory of semantics. *Psychological Review, 77*, 257–273.

Roelofs, A. (1992). A spreading-activation theory of lemma retrieval in speaking. *Cognition, 42*, 107–142.

Rumelhart, D.E., McClelland J.L., & the PDP Research Group (1986). *Parallel distributed processing* (2 Vols.). Cambridge, MA: MIT Press.

Schank, R.C. (1986). *Explanation pattern: Understanding mechanically and creatively.* Hillsdale, NJ: Erlbaum.

Schriefers, H., Meyer, A.S., & Levelt, W. (1990). Exploring the time course of lexical access in language production: Picture–word interference studies. *Journal of Memory and Language, 29,* 86–102.

Schreuder, R. (1978). *Studies in psycholexicology with special reference to verbs of motion.* PhD thesis, University of Nijmegen.

Schreuder, R. (1990). Lexical processing of verbs with separable particles. In J. van Marle & G. Booy (Eds.), *Yearbook of morphology 3,* pp. 65–79. Dordrecht: Foris.

Seuren, P.A.M. (1985). *Discourse semantics.* Oxford: Blackwell.

Sperber, D., & Wilson, D. (1986). *Relevance.* Oxford: Blackwell.

Stechow, A. von (1985). Comparing semantic theories of comparison. *Journal of Semantics, 3,* 1–77.

Talmy, L. (1985). Lexicalization patterns: Semantic structure in lexical forms. In T. Shopen (Ed.), *Language typology and syntactic description* (Vol. III, pp. 57–138). Cambridge, UK: Cambridge University Press.

Thorndyke, P.W. (1975). Conceptual complexity and imagery in comprehension and memory. *Journal of Verbal Learning and Verbal Behaviour, 14,* 359–369.

# 3

# Picture naming*

Wilhelm R. Glaser

*Psychological Institute, University of Tübingen, Friedrichstrasse 21, D-7400 Tübingen, Germany*

Glaser, W.R., 1992. Picture naming. Cognition, 42: 61–105.

*Picture naming has become an important experimental paradigm in cognitive psychology. To name a picture can be considered an elementary process in the use of language. Thus, its chronometric analysis elucidates cognitive structures and processes that underlie speaking. Essentially, these analyses compare picture naming with reading, picture categorizing, and word categorizing. Furthermore, techniques of double stimulation such as the paradigms of priming and of Stroop-like interference are used. In this article, recent results obtained with these methods are reviewed and discussed with regard to five hypotheses about the cognitive structures that are involved in picture naming. Beside the older hypotheses of internal coding systems with only verbal or only pictorial format, the hypotheses of an internal dual code with a pictorial and a verbal component, of a common abstract code with logogen and pictogen subsystems, and the so-called lexical hypothesis are discussed. The latter postulates two main components: an abstract semantic memory which, nevertheless, also subserves picture processing, and a lexicon that carries out the huge amount of word processing without semantic interpretation that is necessary in hearing, reading, speaking and writing.*

## 1. Basic data and early hypotheses

Concrete objects, natural or man-made, constitute the inventory of our everyday world. Only a small part of our actions consist of direct physical operations with these objects; most of them are symbolically mediated. There are two comprehen-

*I am grateful to Margrit O. Glaser for many helpful discussions and her assistance in formulating this text. The help of Hanne Bonnelycke in all questions concerning English usage is gratefully acknowledged. Furthermore, I thank Wido La Heij and an anonymous reviewer for many substantial suggestions to improve this article.

sive classes of symbols for concrete objects: pictures, that is, photographs, line drawings or pictograms, and words, in particular nouns. Pictures become symbols of their objects or object classes by physical similarity. Therefore, it is a very plausible hypothesis that recognizing pictures comprises essentially the same cognitive processes as perceiving the objects themselves (Potter, 1979). Recognizing pictures does not require particular steps of learning or development beyond learning to know the represented objects. On the other hand, the relation between a noun and the corresponding class of objects is determined, in a certain sense arbitrarily, during the centuries of evolution of a language. Nouns are, furthermore, often polysemous because an individual word can represent very different objects. Likewise, any given object can be named with different words depending on its context and the intentions of the speaker. Everybody has to learn spoken words, their meaning, and their written form. Both kinds of symbolism, picture and word, play a fundamental role in human culture.

The psychological analysis of symbol use postulates basic mapping processes between objects and symbols as well as between different symbol systems and modalities. Therefore, the early experimental psychologists had already begun to investigate these processes. The most promising method was until now chronometric analysis.

Cattell (1885) found that reading aloud a printed list of 100 nouns in the speaker's native tongue took about 25–35 s, whereas 50–60 s were required for naming a comparable list of 1-cm wide line drawings or small colour dots. Because tachistoscopic experiments had shown that his pictures were recognized slightly faster than his words, Cattell concluded that the naming time is prolonged due to particular difficulties to retrieve the name of a recognized object. The high speed of the reading response, on the other hand, is explained by a strong association between a written word and its pronounciation caused by extensive practice (Cattell, 1885, p. 650, 1886, p. 65). Eventually, Cattell conjectures that loud reading responses became *automatic* because they are repeated very often in everyday life, whereas naming requires *a voluntary effort*. Thus, Cattell anticipated the modern distinction of automatic and controlled cognitive processes. However, we will neither discuss what exactly Cattell means by the word *automatic*, nor to what degree overt reading is really practised by the average adult.

This line of investigating picture (or colour) naming by comparing it with reading was continued by Brown (1915). He predicted from the differential practice hypothesis that sufficient additional training should bring naming times down to the reading times, whereas reading times should not show considerable improvement. The two predictions failed: although the naming responses were accelerated by 25.8% during 12 days of extensive training, the time for naming remained 41% longer than that for reading. The latter was still reduced by 16.8% due to the same amount of training (Brown, 1915, Table I). With these results, it appeared impossible to explain the difference in reading and naming times by a different amount of practice. Later on, Lund (1927) and Ligon (1932) found a constant reading–naming difference over age for all subjects who had learned to read, although reading as well as naming times strongly decreased from the first to the ninth grade among students.

Fraisse (1969) reported experiments which confirmed that the reading–naming difference cannot be reduced by practice. Therefore he rejects the differential-practice hypothesis. Furthermore, like Cattell (1885), he obtained almost the same tachistoscopic recognition threshold for line drawings and for words. Eventually, Fraisse (1969) outlined a tentative explanation in terms of higher compatibility between written and spoken word, compared to the picture and its name. For each word, there is only one reading response, which is uniquely determined by the print. On the other hand, there are several ways to name a common object. They cause a response uncertainty in the naming task which increases the reaction time because the correct answer is to be determined by additional restrictions given in the instruction. Beyond these theoretical considerations, Fraisse (1967, 1969) presented a particular experimental highlight: the identical symbol O was named as *circle* in 619 ms, as *zero* in 514 ms, and read as *oh* in 453 ms.

Since then, this reading–naming difference was often replicated by several authors: 260 ms (Potter & Faulconer, 1975); 348 ms (Smith & Magee, 1980, Experiment 3); 173 ms (Irwin & Lupker, 1983, Experiment 3); 222 ms (Glaser & Düngelhoff, 1984, Experiment 1, neutral condition at stimulus onset asynchrony (SOA) = 0 ms); 257 ms (Potter, So, Von Eckardt, & Feldman, 1984); 133 ms (Glaser & Glaser, 1989, Experiment 6, control condition, mean over SOAs); 145 ms (Theios & Amrhein, 1989); 178 ms (Bajo, 1988).

In these experiments, the number of response alternatives was not less than four, and was often far greater. Gholson and Hohle (1968) compared reading and naming times for different numbers of alternatives. The usual difference as found for six alternatives decreased for four and disappeared for two alternatives. In a picture-naming task, La Heij and Vermeij (1987) found response times in the magnitude of the reading times for two alternatives. Similarly, Virzi and Egeth (1985, Experiment 2, "vocal" condition) did not obtain a reading–naming difference in a spatial variant of a Stroop-like experiment with two alternatives. On the other hand, this difference was fully preserved in the Stroop experiment with two colour and colour–word alternatives by Simon and Sudalaimuthu (1979). However, I will not discuss why naming can become so efficient in the special case of two alternatives.

It is noteworthy that Potter et al. (1984) and Biederman and Tsao (1979) obtained reading–naming differences of 305 ms and 266 ms, respectively, in the Chinese language. This contradicts an explanation of the reading–naming difference due to a close grapheme–phoneme correspondence in Western languages.

Oldfield and Wingfield (1965) obtained further fundamental data on picture naming. They investigated the influence of word frequency (as counted by Thorndike & Lorge, 1944) on picture naming and found a negative linear relation between naming latency and the logarithm of word frequency. The slope was −254 ms per ten-log frequency unit. Oldfield and Wingfield (1965) attributed this frequency effect to the process of name retrieval. It seemed plausible that frequent words are retrieved faster than rare ones, but an explanation for the log-linear shape of this relation is lacking. It is reasonable to compare this result with reading. Here, the log-linear relation between word frequency and reading latency holds as well, but with a much lesser slope of about −30 ms per ten-log frequency unit (Frederiksen & Kroll, 1976; Huttenlocher & Kubicek, 1983). That argues again for a more automatic or more compatible access of the internal word code by printed words rather than by pictures.

Concerning the theoretical explanations, it was the cognitive revolution that provided the preconditions for greater progress, because now structures of internal processing stages together with their codes and procedures could be modelled.

## 2. Important models for picture naming

In the late 1960s, several models that are relevant for picture naming emerged from different starting points. The logogen model (Morton, 1970) was centred around internal word codes (logogens) that are necessary to recognize, produce and understand words. Seymour (1973) and Warren and Morton (1982) further elaborated the logogen model in order to cover naming and semantic comparisons of pictures and physical objects. Starting from an early computerized language comprehension system, Collins and Quillian (1969) developed a first network model of semantic memory which was essentially improved by Collins and Loftus (1975). Smith, Shoben, and Rips (1974) presented a featural model of semantic decisions, but it proved impossible to decide empirically between network and feature models (cf. Hollan, 1975).

Starting from phenomena of mental imagery, Paivio (1971) proposed his dual code hypothesis of semantic memory. It states that semantic knowledge is represented internally by a verbal as well as a pictorial code. Which one of them is retrieved depends on the demands of the task; generally, picture stimuli tend to activate pictorial codes, and word stimuli are first encoded as word codes. Of course, there are internal translations between both coding systems. This hypothesis was soon disputed with profound methodological and, to some extent, philosophical arguments by Pylyshyn (1973). The core of this critique is that the attributes *verbal* and *pictorial* characterize modes of experience in perception or imagery, but not explanatory theoretical constructs. Therefore, "the need to postulate a more abstract representation – one which resembles neither pictures nor words and is not accessible to subjective experience – is unavoidable" (Pylyshyn, 1973, p. 5).

Thus, with the cognitive revolution, the central questions began to address the modality or the "format" of the internal codes and their transformations in naming, reading and different novel types of tasks. I hypothesize that five different, fundamental classes of hypotheses can be discerned, although not all of their demarcations are already clear:

(1) There is only one word-like internal code system. Its units represent clusters of associations among perceived objects, their properties and functions, experiences from actions with them, and the spoken and written modalities of their verbal labels (e.g., Deese, 1962). This hypothesis is a heritage from behaviourism and difficult to reconcile with a great deal of present-day empirical data.

(2) There is only one internal semantic code of concepts but not of words. The concepts are represented pictorially; the traces in long-term memory represent past perceptions and experiences. Essentially, this hypothesis is also a historical reminiscence. Nevertheless, it can explain some phenomena of mental imagery as well as the superior memory performance for pictures rather than for words (cf. Paivio, 1969). However, it remains unresolved how processes of abstraction and generalization could operate on an internal picture code and how they are functionally connected with verbal symbols.

(3) The dual-code hypothesis tries to escape these problems by combining hypotheses 1 and 2. Thus, the concrete, perceptual properties of concepts should be coded as internal pictures, the abstract and functional features as well as all linguistic attributes in an internal word system (Paivio, 1971, 1978). This hypothesis was the starting point of many experimental tests which are reported below. It implies some form of a simple architecture of human cognition. Thus, its fundamental structure is given in Figure 1(a). However, the dual-code hypothesis, too, does not fully explain higher cognitive processes like comparison, classification, abstraction and inference, and it is seriously disputed by many experimental data.

(4) At present, the most accepted hypotheses postulate a central, abstract, amodal and propositional internal code for long-term storage. This code is generally unconscious and not accessible to introspection. It provides the informational basis for the more complex cognitive operations. The percepts of external objects and events are translated into this code if they are to be stored or used in cognitive tasks. The contents of this storage can be read out for conscious operations in working memory, among them mental imagery, and they can be used for perception and action. The connection of this abstract code system with perception and action on the one hand, and with language understanding and

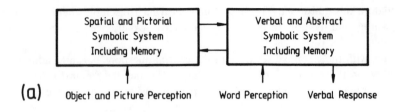

**(a)**

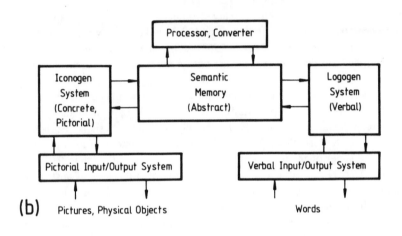

**(b)**

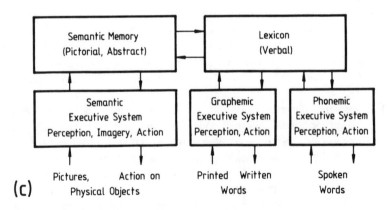

**(c)**

Figure. 1.    *Pictorial, verbal, and abstract components of the cognitive system according to different hypotheses: (a) dual-code hypothesis (after Pellegrino, Rosinski, Chiesi, & Siegel, 1977, Figure 1, p. 384); (b) hypothesis of a central, abstract code (after Seymour, 1973, Figure 2, p. 39); (c) lexical hypothesis (after Glaser & Glaser, 1989, Figure 5, p. 31).*

production on the other, requires large recoding systems with extended processing capacity and inherent long-term storage (Potter, 1979; Seymour, 1976; Snodgrass, 1980, 1984; Theios & Amrhein, 1989). Their long-term components contain canonical or prototypical pictures of everyday objects, productions for skilled actions, and the morphemes of all words that an individual knows together with their syntax as well as their phonemic and orthographic properties (e.g., Seymour, 1976; Snodgrass, 1984). Figure 1(b) shows a configuration of systems according to this hypothesis that is close to Seymour's (1973) modification of Morton's logogen model. It is essentially based on Seymour's (1973, 1976) ideas.

(5) Recently, psycholinguists have shown that the production of speech embodies large and complicated operations with morphemes or words outside the central propositional system (for a comprehensive review see Levelt, 1989). On the other hand, Glaser and Glaser (1989) tried to integrate the known data of studies on Stroop and picture–word interference into a unique cognitive model. In particular, they found that the Stroop-like word–word interference does not exhibit semantic components. This provides further evidence for an extensive internal word processing without semantic components. Thus, they suggested a modification of Seymour's model, which is presented in Figure 1(c). It rests on two ideas. First, the amount of autonomous, semantically uninterpreted word processing that is necessary in language use is underestimated in Seymour's model. Thus, the logogen component of Seymour's model is upgraded to the linguistic one of two central parts of the long-term memory. It contains the complete thesaurus of morphemes that an individual knows, perhaps in several different languages. Second, whereas a word as a perceptual object has its graphemic and phonemic features which are internally connected with representations of morphemes and lexemes, the features of physical objects are essential components of the meaning of their concepts. Thus, an iconogen system in addition to the semantic memory seems to be unnecessary. Although the concepts of the semantic memory are abstract nodes in a network, they essentially comprise physical features. Thus, we suggest eliminating the iconogen system from Seymour's model and implementing its functions, the semantic analysis of perceived pictures and objects, into the semantic system. This leads again to a relatively simple architecture with only one fundamental distinction between a large concrete and abstract, semantic and non-verbal system on the one side and an equally large verbal and linguistic system on the other. For lack of an established name, we will call this the *lexical hypothesis*. At first glance, it seems to be similar to the dual-code hypothesis (3). However, there are at least two clear demarcations. First, in the lexical hypothesis, picture stimuli are functionally tied with the abstract module. Second, the word module provides no semantic processing, not even of abstract meanings or relations. Of course, it is still to be demonstrated that the essentials of the lexical hypothesis, the extension of the logogen system and the deletion of a separate iconogen system besides the semantic memory are empirically justified.

## 3. Experimental methods

These hypotheses were developed in close connection with a growing repertory of experimental methods. At the beginning, there were only naming and reading latencies and their comparison. Later on, a great methodological progress arose from the techniques of double stimulation (Kantowitz, 1974). Thereby, two pictures, two words, or a picture and a word are presented simultaneously or in close temporal succession. There are three main types of double-stimulation experiments:

(1) In the matching paradigm, both stimuli are to be compared according to a given rule. This technique descends from the same–different matching task as initiated by Posner and Mitchell (1967). It became a very productive tool for tackling hypothetical internal stages and processes.

(2) In the priming paradigm (Beller, 1971), the facilitating influence of the voluntary or involuntary processing of one stimulus (prime) on the latency of the response to the other stimulus (target) is investigated.

(3) In the Stroop paradigm any reaction to the irrelevant stimulus (distractor) is to be suppressed. Nevertheless, the distractor often interferes strongly with responding to the target. The amount and time course of this interference provide information on internal structures and processes (e.g., Glaser & Glaser, 1989). Although the logic of priming and Stroop experiments are very similar, both techniques were developed independently and were only recently systematically compared with each other (see La Heij, Dirkx, & Kramer, 1990; La Heij, Van der Heijden, & Schreuder, 1985).

However, the study of picture processing was not only extended by these recent experimental techniques but also by an extension of picture naming itself. If presented with a picture of a chair and asked "what is that?", a subject can well respond *furniture*, *chair*, or *kitchen chair*. All three responses are labels for categories of objects which form a taxonomy. Apparently, these three labels represent different levels of categorization. In particular Rosch (1975) and Rosch, Mervis, Gray, Johnson and Boyes-Braem (1976) elaborated the different psychological functions of these levels. The response *chair* belongs to the *basic level*. This level contains the fundamental classifications of everyday life. The labels of this level represent classes of objects that share a great number of perceptual and functional features. Basic level objects are easiest to be drawn. In contrast, superordinate categories as, for example, *furniture*, comprise many visually and functionally different objects that share only a few properties. They are defined by rather abstract rules, and they can be visualized only by prototypes at basic level. Finally, the *subordinate* level results from additional distinctions within basic level categories. They are less relevant for everyday life but become far more important in professional work. To picture at subordinate level requires again drawing a basic object but with emphasis on special features that underlie a subordinate delineation.

This *level of designation* was introduced as an independent variable into the naming task towards the end of the 1960s. Thereby, the term *picture naming* was usually restricted to the verbal responses at basic level, whereas naming responses at superordinate level were called *categorizing*. We will adopt this terminology in the following, but it must be emphasized that for a given picture both tasks consist of retrieving a verbal label in the mental lexicon.

Now, we will present the most important recent results concerning picture processing that are based on the aforementioned experimental methods. We will begin with the categorizing studies, then proceed to the priming investigations, and end with the Stroop-like experiments.

## 4. Pictures and their superordinate labels

If pictures of everyday objects like chair, hat, or saw are presented and subjects are asked "what is that?", then they respond almost solely at basic level, that is, they answer "chair", "hat", and "saw" (Potter & Faulconer, 1975; Rosch et al., 1976, Experiment 10; Segui & Fraisse, 1968). Nevertheless, instructed to do so, they can also easily respond with the superordinate labels, for example "furniture", "clothes", or "tool", but now the reaction times are usually longer than in the naming task at basic level. This *categorizing–naming* difference was often reported in the literature. Its amount was 162 ms (Segui & Fraisse, 1968), 71 ms (Smith, Balzano, & Walker, 1978), 152 ms (Irwin & Lupker, 1983, Experiment 3), 266 ms (Smith & Magee, 1980, Experiment 4) and 102 ms (Glaser & Düngelhoff, 1984, Experiments 1 and 2, neutral condition at SOA = 0 ms). However, small amounts of this difference (47 ms; Glaser & Glaser, 1989, Experiment 6, control condition, mean over SOAs) were also obtained.

There is another important variant of the categorizing task. Now, the concept at basic level is not presented as a picture but as a word. Therefore, the subject has to name the superordinate category of a concept that is activated by reading silently the stimulus word. Of course, the reaction time in this *word-categorizing* task is longer than that in reading, but it is also prolonged compared to picture categorizing. This *word–picture* difference for categorizing was already reported by Segui and Fraisse (1968). For the categories *furniture*, *clothes*, *musical instrument*, *vegetable*, and *weapon*, these authors obtained a word–picture difference of 75 ms. Other researchers found 66 ms (Irwin & Lupker, 1983, Experiment 3), 126 ms (Glaser & Düngelhoff, 1984, Experiment 2, neutral condition at SOA = 0 ms), 95 ms (Glaser & Glaser, 1989, Experiment 6, control condition, mean over SOAs).

The word–picture difference for categorizing is theoretically at least as important as the naming–reading difference. Assuming that sensory encoding of the stimulus takes about the same time for pictures and for words (Fraisse, 1969; Potter & Faulconer, 1975; Potter et al. 1984; Theios & Amrhein, 1989), then the following predictions can be derived. If there is only one internal code with verbal format, then picture categorizing should take longer than word categorizing, because picture stimuli must be translated into the word code which is directly accessed by word stimuli. This assumption is at odds with the data. If the single internal code has pictorial format, then picture categorizing should be faster than word categorizing, as is indeed the case, because pictures should have more direct access to the internal code. However, as mentioned above, this hypothesis has other problems: it cannot explain abstract cognitive operations as, for example, the build-up of type-token relations of mentally stored to perceived objects (cf. Pylyshyn, 1973, p. 7). Also the categorizing–naming difference of pictures is difficult to reconcile with this hypothesis. If the internal code had a visual format, recognizing, for example, a chair as an instance of furniture should need less feature detection than its identification at basic level.

The dual-code hypothesis, too, cannot predict the word–picture difference in categorizing. Because the demarcations at the superordinate level are rather abstract, they should be stored in the verbal system that is accessed faster by word than by picture stimuli. Thus, contrary to the data, word categorizing should require less time than picture categorizing.

According to the hypothesis of a single abstract code, picture as well as word stimuli are translated into an abstract format that allows their superordinate category membership to be determined. Thus, equal reaction times for categorizing pictures and words are predicted as long as two auxiliary hypotheses hold. Firstly, not only perceptual encoding, but also access to the abstract semantic code take the same time for picture and word stimuli, and secondly, the times for selection and articulation of the response are equal in both cases. Therefore, the abstract-code hypothesis remains only in line with the observed word–picture difference in categorizing, if at least one of the auxiliary hypotheses is rejected. Because the verbal responses are the same in picture and word categorizing, there is no reason to doubt that the times to select and articulate them are equal in both tasks. On the other hand, the abstract-code hypothesis can only be reconciled with the word–picture difference in categorizing, if the first auxiliary hypothesis is rejected, that is, if faster access of the abstract system for pictures than for words is assumed. This leads over to the lexical hypothesis.

The lexical hypothesis states close functional connections of object and picture perception to the abstract semantic system, whereas word processing contains extended linguistic functions that are carried out in the lexical system without semantic evaluation (Glaser & Glaser, 1989; Levelt, 1989). Considered as a speech act, the categorizing task requires only little linguistic processing. Nevertheless, the processing of word stimuli should pass a linguistic stage before the abstract code is reached. Thus, pictures have privileged access to the semantic system. The lexical hypothesis predicts the observed word–picture difference in categorizing.

As these theoretical considerations have shown, the picture–word difference in categorizing latency is one of the most important data. Thus, many experiments addressed its reliability. We will give a short survey. In addition to vocalizing the category name (Glaser & Düngelhoff, 1984; Glaser & Glaser, 1989; Segui & Fraisse, 1968; Smith et al., 1978; Smith & Magee, 1980, Experiment 4), often a semantic decision was demanded from the subjects whether two objects belong to the same superordinate category or whether one object belongs to a certain category. For example, Potter and Faulconer's (1975) subjects had to say *yes* if a stimulus object belonged to a pre-specified superordinate category. Otherwise, they had to say *no*. The objects were represented by line drawings or their printed basic-level names, respectively. Altogether, 96 concepts from 18 different categories were used. The "yes" responses were on the average 57 ms faster for pictures than for words, the "no" responses by 44 ms. The mean of both measures was 51 ms. This is a clear picture–word difference that argues for a privileged access of the picture to the semantic code (see also Hogaboam & Pellegrino, 1978). Potter et al. (1984) replicated these results with Chinese native speakers who later lived in English-speaking countries. They were still more fluent in Chinese than in English, and on average they categorized pictures 34 ms faster than Chinese word symbols.

Rosch (1975) investigated the categorization task with the same–different matching technique. In each trial, two line drawings or two words that represented basic-level objects were given. The subjects had to indicate by pressing a "yes" or "no" key whether or not both objects belonged to the same superordinate category. Altogether, ten different categories were used. The author obtained a general picture advantage of about 260 ms (my calculation from Rosch, 1975, Figure 1, "yes" responses). Friedman and Bourne (1976) used a technique they called *speeded-inference* task. It is closely related to same–different matching: in each trial, a pair of words or pictures was presented in close succession. Both signified objects at basic level that could match either in a physical property such as size, or in a conceptual property, like membership in a common superordinate category. The subjects had to utter aloud the value of that property that was equal for both stimuli. As an illustration, suppose the item pool would contain only the four concepts *hippo*, *mouse*, *bus*, and *car*. Hippo and mouse are both animals, bus and car are both vehicles; besides that, hippo and bus are large, mouse and car are small, compared to the other animal or vehicle, respectively. Now the subject had to respond, for example, "large" to the stimulus pair *bus–hippo* or "vehicle" to the pair *bus–car*. In Experiment 1, these responses were given to picture pairs on an average of 96 ms and 128 ms faster than to word pairs.

Pellegrino, Rosinski, Chiesi, and Siegel (1977) extended the same–different categorical judgment task. They presented not only word–word and picture–picture pairs, but also mixed pairs of one word and one picture. The mixed pairs were called *picture–word* if the left element was the picture and the right element was the word. *Word–picture* designated the opposite case. Thus, the four modality conditions picture–picture, picture–word, word–picture, and word–word resulted. Both stimuli were simultaneously exposed and the subjects had to press either a "yes" key if both stimuli belonged to the same superordinate category or a "no" key if they did not. The two categories *animals* and *articles of clothing* were used.

The authors formulated models of additive stages for three theoretical alternatives: (1) dual code with category information in the pictorial and in the verbal system; (2) dual code with category information only in the verbal system; and (3) common abstract code for semantic information including category membership. Hypothesis 1 was extended by the auxiliary hypothesis that the subjects process the stimulus pair from left to right, according to reading habits. Thus, the category codes of picture–word stimuli should be matched in the word system, and those of word–picture pairs in the pictorial system. A set of four linear equations made it possible to estimate the internal transfer times between both systems under hypothesis 1 from the mean reaction times of the four stimulus conditions. conditions.

The results showed mean latencies of 715 ms for picture–picture pairs, 810 ms for picture–word pairs, 851 ms for word–picture pairs, and 900 ms for word–word pairs. The estimators for the internal transfer times were not significantly different from zero, so that the hypothesis of dual code with dual category information (1) was rejected. The difference of 185 ms between word–word and picture–picture pairs argues furthermore against a dual code with category information in the word system (2). Thus, the authors accept the hypothesis of a common semantic code (3). However, this hypothesis is only tenable if it is assumed that pictures have faster access to the semantic code than words. The mathematical model yields $185/2$ ms $= 92.5$ ms as the advantage of the pictures in retrieving semantic information.

There have been some similar experiments with essentially the same results (e.g., Klimesch, 1982; Rosinski, Pellegrino, & Siegel, 1977). Harris, Morris, and Bassett's (1977) Experiment 1 was almost identical to Experiment 1 by Pellegrino et al. (1977), but showed one fundamentally different result: the shortest latencies for "same category" responses were observed in the word–word condition. This is contrary to almost all other experimental evidence, and could be a serious challenge for the common-code hypothesis with privileged access for pictures. To my knowledge, the reason for this divergence is not yet known. However, I suppose there is an artifact in the work by Harris et al. (1977). As stimulus materials, they used only the two categories *animals* and *vehicles* with four instances each. The four animals had very similar and in part rhyming three-letter names: *pig*, *dog*, *cat*, and *rat*. The four vehicles had names with a different number of letters: *car*, *bicycle*, *train*, and *boat*. That means that – with the exception of *car* – the subjects had to respond "yes" for every word pair in which no word or both words had three letters, and "no" if one word had three and the other word had more than three letters. It is likely that the subjects utilized these redundancies and matched length and similarity of the words. That could well have accelerated the desired semantic decision. Thus, the first-glance evidence against the common-code hypothesis is questionable. Nevertheless, it demonstrates the possibility that the subjects take advantage of linguistic surface similarity among the verbal labels of the instances of the categories.

The latter argument became very important with regard to picture stimuli. Snodgrass and McCullough (1986) try to explain the picture superiority in categorizing tasks with the *visual similarity hypothesis*. It states that the pictures are classified or matched at superordinate level not through the internal semantic code but by use of the visual surface similarity that is higher among pictures of the same category than among pictures of different categories. If this hypothesis is true, then "picture categorization is a poor task to use in evaluating hypotheses about the form of representation of semantic knowledge" (Snodgrass & McCullough, 1986, p. 153).

The authors provided a first experimental test of this hypothesis. In their Experiment 1, word–word or picture–picture stimuli were to be classified into two categories by key-pressing responses (cf. Hogaboam & Pellegrino, 1978). In the *visually dissimilar* condition the categories *fruits* and *animals*, and in the *visually similar* condition *fruits* and *vegetables*, were used. The instances of the latter categories were selected for high visual similarity between categories, for example *apple*, *orange* as fruits and *tomato*, *potato* as vegetables. Indeed, the picture superiority was replicated only in the visually dissimilar condition: pictures were classified as fruits or animals 40 ms faster than words. In the visually similar condition, the results were reversed: to discriminate between fruits and vegetables required 96 ms more for pictures than for words.

There is no doubt that the authors could reverse the word–picture difference in the categorizing task. But is their conclusion justified that the usual categorizing task does not tap semantic access by pictures and by words because picture categorizing is "artifactually" accelerated by the higher intra-category than inter-category similarity of the pictures? To answer this question by "yes" implies the assumption that Snodgrass and McCullough's (1986) *visually similar* condition is the standard, the ecologically most valid case, the control condition, to which the usual results are to be compared. However, that is unlikely. Everyday objects that are different at *basic* level as defined by Rosch (1975) are visually different among (e.g., *guitar*, *chair*) as well as within (e.g., *guitar*, *trumpet*) superordinate categories, even if there are more visually similar object pairs within (e.g., *guitar*, *violin*) than among (e.g., *racket, violin*; cf. Flores d'Arcais & Schreuder, 1987, Fig. 1c) superordinate categories. Thus, the adequate control experiment should contain basic objects with a low or medium visual similarity that is kept constant among and within categories. Many experimenters carefully controlled this variable (e.g., Flores d'Arcais & Schreuder, 1987; La Heij, 1988; La Heij et al., 1990).

However, the argument can be extended. According to Rosch's definition, the basic level is "the most inclusive (abstract) level at which the categories can mirror the structure of attributes perceived in the world" (Rosch, 1978, p. 30; cf. Rosch et al., 1976). Basic and superordinate levels of classification are essentially delineated.with respect to visual features: "A working assumption . . . is that (1) in the perceived world, information-rich bundles of perceptual and functional attributes occur that form natural discontinuities, and that (2) basic cuts in categorization are made at these discontinuities." Thus, concepts at basic level are defined by "attributes in common, motor movements in common, objective similarity in shape, and identifiability of averaged shapes" (Rosch, 1978, p. 31). In contrast, superordinate categories are characterized by a very reduced set of common features, different motor movements, and the impossibility of drawing or imaging an average instance. Thus, it is questionable whether *fruits* and *vegetables* are really different superordinate categories at all, although they were explicitly considered as such by Rosch (1975). On the contrary, according to Rosch's definitions, at least the instances that were used by Snodgrass and McCullough (1986) share too many visual features for belonging to different superordinate categories, and thus they are delineated by rather abstract properties (cf. the subsequent discussion of the experiments by Hoffmann and by Flores d'Arcais).

Consequently, the results of Snodgrass and McCullough (1986) demonstrate that an extreme visual similarity among all basic objects that are to be discriminated according to an abstract criterion reverses the word–picture difference in categorizing. However, the usual picture superiority in categorization tasks is not disputed by these data.

In the German language, the problem of visual similarity in categorization tasks was tackled by Hoffmann and Klimesch (1984). In preliminary studies (e.g., Hoffmann & Ziessler, 1982), the subjects had to name characteristic features for the elements of an item pool which consisted of common nouns that belonged to subordinate, basic, or superordinate level in Rosch's (1975) terms. Two main results were obtained: (1) about 30% of the responses were concrete properties (e.g., *tree: green, large,* or *has leaves*), the rest were abstract (e.g., *tree: solid, of wood,* or *shelter from rain*); and (2) the proportion of concrete to abstract features decreased with an increasing level of a concept. Furthermore, the authors introduced a terminology which is different from that of Rosch (1975) to characterize three-level hierarchies: the lowest level is called *sublevel*, the highest *superlevel*; the *medium* level lies between them. Thus the superlevel of categorizing experiments usually contains categories like *musical instrument, vehicle,* or *weapon*. These examples include *string* and *wind instrument, street, rail, air,* and *water vehicle,* or *stabbing* and *firearm* as medium-level categories. *Violin, trumpet, car,* and *dagger* are examples of corresponding sublevel nouns.

In their experiments, Hoffmann and Klimesch (1984) used three-step hierarchies with sublevel, medium-level and superlevel concepts. The preliminary data (Hoffmann & Ziessler, 1982) gave strong evidence that three types of hierarchies were to be distinguished:

(1) In the *sensory superlevel* hierarchies, concrete features dominated from sublevel up to superlevel concepts. For example, the superlevel concept *tree* shares with the medium-level concepts *deciduous tree* and *coniferous tree* and with sublevel concepts like *oak, birch, pine,* and *fir* the characteristic visual features of trees.

(2) In the *sensory medium-level* hierarchies, salient visual features comprise sublevel and medium level as, for example, *dagger* and *sword* as *stabbing arms,* and *colt* and *gun* as *firearms,* whereas the superlevel concept *weapon* is characterized by abstract properties.

(3) In the *sensory sublevel* hierarchies, eventually, concrete, visual features only discriminate among sublevel objects, whereas the medium level as well as the superlevel are characterized by abstract features. It is noteworthy that Hoffmann and Ziessler (1982) found *food* to be a sensory sublevel hierarchy with the abstract medium-level categories *vegetables, fruits,* and *baked goods.*

Based on this preliminary work, Hoffmann and Klimesch (1984) replicated the category-matching experiment of Pellegrino et al. (1977) with picture–picture, picture–word, and word–word stimulus pairs that were administered to three different groups of subjects. The stimuli were selected at sublevel and were to be categorized, as usual, at superlevel. However, the type of hierarchy was strongly controlled as an independent variable. On the average, picture–picture pairs had a latency of 886 ms; picture–word pairs exhibited longer responses by 285 ms, and word–word pairs by 624 ms. That replicates the usual order of the differences. The relatively long latencies are due to seven different categories (instead of two in other experiments; e.g., Harris et al., 1977; Pellegrino et al., 1977; Snodgrass & McCullough, 1986), and the fact that the subjects did not know the stimuli in advance and that each concept was exposed only once. The "yes" responses for the picture–picture pairs exhibited clear effects of type of hierarchy. The pairs of pictures that belonged to the *sensory superlevel* hierarchies were classified with a mean latency of 729 ms. The instances of the *sensory sublevel* hierarchies, on the other hand, required an average of 1048 ms. Most interesting was the *sensory medium-level* hierarchy. If both stimuli were instances of the same medium-level category, then the mean latency was 728 ms; if they belonged to different medium-level categories, they required 999 ms. Essentially the same results were obtained with picture–word stimuli, whereas the word–word stimuli did not show any significant effect of hierarchy type.

The authors interpret this result within the framework of the common code hypothesis with privileged access for pictures: the internal concept code contains concrete and abstract properties. If the access goes through pictures, then the concrete properties are activated first. Thus, if the concrete properties of a pair of pictures are sufficient for categorizing, then a fast response occurs. On the other hand, if the later activated abstract properties are necessary for categorizing, then the response is delayed. Picture–word stimuli exhibit the same pattern of results for the same reason, that is, because one picture stimulus is sufficient to start the internal categorizing with the concrete properties. In contrast, word–word stimuli activate concrete and abstract properties about simultaneously so that categorizing responses due to concrete properties are not faster than those due to abstract ones. However, there are counterexamples in the literature to the latter conclusion, although it is clearly justified by Hoffmann and Klimesch's data. In a priming study with reading and lexical-decision tasks, Flores d'Arcais, Schreuder, and Glazenborg (1985) obtained data which suggest that also verbal stimuli activate the perceptual properties of a concept faster than the abstract and functional ones.

However, from the work of Hoffmann (e.g., Hoffmann & Klimesch, 1984) and of Flores d'Arcais (e.g., Flores d'Arcais & Schreuder, 1987) it is obvious that perceptual and functional properties of objects play different roles in categorization. Further research is required to clear the discrepancies. It is noteworthy that the results and conclusions of Hoffmann and Klimesch (1984) do not contradict those of Rosch (1975). In Rosch's terms, Hoffmann and Klimesch's types of hierarchies are characterized by the position of the basic-level concepts: they can be placed at superlevel (e.g., *tree* in the hierarchy of *oak*, *deciduous tree*, *tree*), medium level (e.g., *stabbing arm* in the hierarchy of *sword*, *stabbing arm*, *weapon*), or sublevel (e.g., *apple* in the hierarchy of *apple*, *fruit*, *food*).

So far, we are inclined to take for granted that the mean latencies increase monotonically from word reading over picture naming and picture categorizing up to word categorizing.[1] The first of these latency differences, that between reading and naming, is beyond dispute. The second one, the categorizing–naming difference for pictures, was clearly demonstrated, but by a lesser number of experi-

---

[1]An anonymous reviewer emphasized that these comparisons of response times for verbal and pictorial stimuli are valid only if the two sets of materials require about the same time for the early visual-recognition stage. Of course, this time depends essentially on the kind of drawing of the pictures and on the type font of the words. Thus, careful experimenters match their verbal and pictorial materials for tachistoscopic threshold (e.g., Potter & Faulconer, 1975) or for recognition time (e.g., Potter, Kroll, Yachzel, Carpenter, & Sherman, 1986). On the other hand, there are no hints that this condition could be seriously violated if clear outline drawings in the style of those by Snodgrass and Vanderwart (1980) and functional fonts (e.g., Courier, Helvetica) are used in sufficient contrast and size.

ments (e.g., Glaser & Düngelhoff, 1984; Glaser & Glaser, 1989; Irwin & Lupker, 1983; Segui & Fraisse, 1968; Smith et al., 1978). It decisively supports an important supplement of the common abstract code hypothesis: the basic level provides the entry points of the semantic system for pictures (Glaser & Glaser, 1989, pp. 30, 32), and categorization as well as other semantic tasks are mediated by internal concept nodes at basic level. In other words, there is no semantic processing of pictures that circumvents this level, although that could be an attractive theoretical alternative: in categorizing, it could well be that the pictures are only partially analysed up to the point at which the category, for example *furniture* with the picture of a chair, is recognized. If that were the case, then the categorizing–naming difference should show the reverse direction: pictures should be categorized faster than named.

The third difference, that between word and picture categorizing, was more often demonstrated – and disputed. It provides the most conclusive evidence that category membership is stored in an internal abstract code which is accessed faster by pictures than by words. Thus, we have to discuss the recent criticism by Theios and Amrhein (1989). These authors also adhere to the hypothesis of one abstract semantic code as a basis for semantic processing, but they deny a privileged access of pictures to that code. They argue that the often observed picture superiority is an artifact due to the greater viewing angle for pictures than for words in these experiments. Surely, Theios and Amrhein (1989) are right that stimuli with greater size or energy are processed faster. But does this really justify the conclusion that the word–picture difference in categorizing "disappears when the pictorial stimuli are controlled for size, area, and featural line width" (Theios & Amrhein, 1989, p. 22)?

In their Experiment 1, these authors obtained a mean reading–naming difference of 160 ms for word and picture stimuli that were equalled for averaged visual width on the three levels of 1.5, 3.0, and 6.0 degrees. The means for reading were 640 ms, 591 ms, and 596 ms, and those for naming were 819 ms, 750 ms, and 738 ms, respectively, for the three size conditions. As concepts, five geometrical figures such as *circle*, *square*, and so on were used. The authors conclude that their reading–naming difference of 160 ms is an estimator for this difference if words and pictures are equal in size. They argue that the usually observed reading–naming difference is reduced with regard to its true value because cognitive picture-processing times are confounded with an artifactual acceleration that results from picture stimuli being far greater than word stimuli. For example, if their reading time for the small words is compared with their naming time for the large pictures, the reading–naming difference is reduced to 98 ms. In other words, the artifactual component amounts to 62 ms.

After that, Theios and Amrhein (1989, p. 11) take a reading–naming difference from Fraisse (1969) that amounts to 90 ms and argue that this value would approach the "true" 160 ms if it were corrected for an artifactual loss of 62 ms. Of course, this is a fascinating result with these numbers; however, it cannot be generalized. Most reading–naming differences as reported in the literature are greater than 90 ms; moreover, they often exceed these authors' "true" value of 160 ms (cf. the values quoted in the first paragraph of this article). Fraisse (1960) himself reports 219 ms as reading–naming difference for a set of four geometric figures like those of the present authors. Furthermore, if the word width exceeds 3 degrees, then the artifact practically disappears in the data of Theios and Amrhein (1989). Thus, there remains the fact that the reading–naming difference may be artifactually reduced in empirical data if pictures and words are not equalled in size, but only if the word stimuli were less than 3 degrees wide.

It is our main question whether or not these results of Theios and Amrhein (1989) invalidate the naming–categorizing difference for pictures and the word–picture difference in categorizing. Obviously, the naming–categorizing difference is completely independent from these data because under both conditions pictures of the same size are used. The word–picture difference in categorizing, on the other hand, would be jeopardized. Because word categorizing is longer than picture categorizing, this difference would be artifactually increased, or, in the worst case, brought about, if picture processing were accelerated by an artifact. This is far more critical than the attenuated reading–naming difference.

However, according to present knowledge, we can argue as follows: Theios and Amrhein (1989) could not establish the artifact if the word stimuli were more than 3 degrees wide, disregarding picture size. Therefore, the observed word–picture differences in categorizing tasks can be taken for granted, if the word components of the stimuli fulfilled this condition. That is undoubtedly the case in the studies of Glaser and Düngelhoff (1984; width of the five-letter word 4 degrees), Glaser and Glaser (1989; 5 degrees), Pellegrino et al. (1977; 14 degrees; my calculation, W.G.), Rosch (1975; 7 degrees for word pairs).

The conclusion is that the hypothesis of the faster access to the abstract semantic system for pictures rather than for words is not affected by the criticism of Theios and Amrhein (1989). The conviction of these authors that the often observed faster semantic processing of pictures than words results only from the usually different size of picture and word stimuli in those experiments is not justified by the available data. Of course, their claim for a control of this variable in further experiments is worth following (e.g., Snodgrass & McCullough, 1986; Bajo, 1988).

So far, the essential results were discussed that follow from a comparison between naming pictures at basic and at superordinate level. Converging evidence for the theoretical conclusions was sought from the comparison with word naming at both these levels and with matching tasks. We will now turn to the priming studies.

## 5. Picture naming in priming studies

The term *priming* designates two matters: an experimental paradigm and an effect that is often observed in these experiments. In principle, the target stimulus or stimulus pair in a reading, naming, categorizing, or matching task is preceded by another stimulus, the prime. The main independent variables are the instruction concerning the prime and the semantic or associative relatedness between prime and target. The instructions go from ignoring the prime over using its information for a more efficient response to the target up to responding in a similar way as to the target. The usual results show that the response latencies to the target are gradually reduced depending on prime–targe similarity and on depth of processing of prime and target (Irwin & Lupker, 1983). This effect is called *priming*. Theoretically, it is explained as follows. The voluntary or involuntary processing of the prime activates internal nodes or links so that they are more readily available for the processing of a related target. Thus, the network along which internal codes activate one another should be mapped onto a pattern of observable priming effects.

Indeed, a large number of priming studies were undertaken to investigate the structures of long-term memory. We will give a short review of only the most important ones that concern picture naming. As in the last paragraph, we include studies of reading as well as of categorizing and matching pictures and words. On the other hand, we leave aside the numerous investigations that used the lexical decision task.

One of the first priming studies in picture naming was published by Sperber, McCauley, Ragain, and Weil (1979). In a picture–picture condition, the subjects had to name prime and target at basic level. The response to the prime triggered an interstimulus interval of 1000 ms followed by the target. If both pictures were instances of the same superordinate category, the response latency to the target was 51 ms shorter than otherwise. In one additional condition, the target pictures were blurred by defocusing the projection lens. Now, they were primed by 112 ms. That indicates that semantic priming has a perceptual component, at least if the targets are visually degraded (cf. Reinitz, Wright, & Loftus, 1989). In the word–word condition, when subjects had to read aloud prime and target, a priming by 19 ms was obtained if the targets were in focus, and by 56 ms if they were degraded. This is in accordance with the often quoted results by Meyer, Schvaneveldt, and Ruddy (1975). Following the Sternberg (1969) logic, that means that both the visual quality of the stimulus and the semantic relatedness of the prime influence at least one common stage in the reading or picture-naming pathway.

In Experiment 3 by Sperber et al. (1979), the four stimulus conditions word–word, word–picture, picture–word, and picture–picture were administered in mixed blocks. Compared to the blocked conditions of word–word and picture–picture pairs, the priming effects were considerably reduced. Reading was primed 10 ms by word and 8 ms by picture stimuli, picture naming 31 ms by picture and 13 ms by word stimuli. These data show that there was within-modality as well as, though to a lesser degree, between-modality priming. The picture was more effective as prime and more susceptible to priming as target.

McCauley, Parmelee, Sperber, and Carr (1980) and Carr, McCauley, Sperber, and Parmelee (1982) conducted similar experiments. As additional independent variables, (1) exposure duration of the prime with the three levels below threshold, at threshold, and suprathreshold, and (2) interstimulus interval from prime offset to target onset with two levels of 90 ms and 490 ms were introduced. The four modality conditions picture–picture, picture–word, word–picture, and word–word were blocked. For the target, a speeded response was required, whereas the prime was to be named after the target. Averaged over threshold conditions and interstimulus intervals, the pattern of results was very similar to that from Sperber et al. (1979), but the priming effects were about twice as large: 23 ms (word–word), 15 ms (picture–word), 36 ms (word–picture) and 54 ms (picture–picture). Apparently, the blocked variation of the modality condition and, perhaps, naming the prime after the target, raised the priming effect. Again, picture naming was particularly prone to be primed and pictures were more effective as primes than words. Thereby, the primes that were presented below threshold exhibited essentially the same effects. The authors conclude that the semantic priming does not depend on conscious identification of the primes by the subject. However, that was disputed by Merikle (1982) and by Purcell, Stewart, and Stanovich (1983). We will not pursue this discussion (see, for example, Hines, Czerwinski, Sawyer, & Dwyer, 1986). Generally, the authors favour the common-code hypothesis and assume a functional closeness of pictures to that code: "Stimuli that are more similar to semantic representations will prime more effectively because they are able to activate semantic representations more rapidly. Such stimuli will also be more primeable as targets because activated semantic representations will make greater or more efficient contact with target stimuli that are more similar to them" (Carr et al., 1982, p. 772).

A similar study, which used the repetition-priming technique and included categorizing responses, was conducted by Durso and Johnson (1979). Ninety concepts at basic level, together with additional filler items, were presented in random order. In every trial, one concept was given. In mixed blocks, one half of the stimuli were words, the other half were line drawings. The reading–naming group of subjects had to name the pictorial and to read the verbal stimuli. The categorizing group had to categorize the stimuli as natural or man-made by pressing keys. The priming conditions were created by repeating some of the stimulus concepts with a controlled distance to their first presentation. This repetition was factorially crossed with stimulus modality, so that picture–picture, picture–word, word–picture, and word–word presentations of the same concept emerged. In the picture–picture condition, two different pictures of the same object were used in order to avoid "physically same" matches.

In the reading–naming group, the same rank order of priming effects was found as in the studies by Sperber et al. (1979) and by Carr et al. (1982): 32 ms (word–word), 15 ms (picture–word), 109 ms (word–picture), and 175 ms (picture–picture). Thus, the high primeability of the picture-naming response was demonstrated again. On the other hand, the high efficiency of the picture prime is almost completely restricted to picture naming and does not work in reading. Thus, the authors conjecture "that a word trace contains information capable of aiding subsequent processing of both pictures and words, whereas picture traces are more specific in that they aid the processing of pictures to a large extent while aiding the processing of subsequent words to a small extent" (Durso & Johnson, 1979, p. 457). Unfortunately, that is scarcely more than a paraphrase of the data. Similar data which also showed that using a word as a response in a naming task does not prime later recognition of this word were also found by Scarborough, Gerard, & Cortese (1979).

The categorizing task yielded priming effects of 90 ms (word–word), 45 ms (picture–word), 27 ms (word–picture), and 51 ms (picture–picture). They were generally lower than in the reading–naming task, and now picture processing was markedly less primed. It is difficult to integrate these data theoretically. The authors sketch a "generic-specific" hypothesis. According to that hypothesis, a word stimulus should activate rather general features of its concept, whereas a picture should activate more specific aspects (see also Lupker, 1988). Furthermore, semantic excitation should spread rather from the general to the specific than in the opposite direction. That would explain that picture primes had practically no effect on word reading. The categorizing task, on the other hand, should force the activation of these specific properties that are important for the decision between natural and man-made objects. Because that, in particular, is difficult for word stimuli, priming should become effective. Durso and O'Sullivan (1983) tried to support this hypothesis by further experiments, but essentially it remains ad hoc. A superior hypothesis states that naming a picture can only prime a later reading of the picture's label if the subject's strategy connects reading of the word stimulus with semantic processing (Bajo, 1988).

Irwin and Lupker (1983) aimed at a systematic comparison of the effects of prime and target modality (word or picture), the task concerning the prime (categorizing, reading–naming, or naming the colour in which the prime is printed), and the task concerning the target (reading–naming, categorizing). As usual, prime and target modality were factorially crossed (picture–picture, picture–word, word–picture, and word–word). These four conditions were presented in mixed blocks, whereas the task concerning prime and target was blocked. As materials, 72 concepts at basic level from six superordinate categories were used.

The results were as follows. When the target had to be read or named, there was no significant facilitation by a picture or word prime regardless of whether the prime had to be categorized, named or its colour had to be named. When the target had to be categorized, words and pictures were primed to an equal degree and the amount of facilitation depended on the task concerning the prime. Related primes facilitated by 231 ms, if they were to be categorized; by 119 ms, if they were to be named; and by 57 ms, if their colour was to be named. Thus, the degree of semantic processing of the prime was the only independent variable that exhibited graded facilitatory effects on the latency in target categorizing. The authors interpret their results within the framework of the semantic network model by Collins and Loftus (1975) and the model of a common code with logogen and iconogen subsystems by Seymour (1973). Thus, the observed priming in the categorizing task results from deeper target processing in the common code system. The dependency of this effect from the priming task is explained in the same way by different levels of prime processing. However, it remains un-explained why the naming of target pictures was not primed, not even by picture primes. This result is contrary to almost all other data. One hypothetical reason may be that every stimulus concept was presented four times to each subject. However, if the fourfold krepeated use of the same stimulus concepts would "wash out" the priming effects, then at least the first presentation of each stimulus should exhibit priming, but this, too, was not the case in the data of Irwin and Lupker (1983).

Bajo (1988) conducted a comprehensive study in order to clarify the inconsistencies of the results of Sperber et al. (1979), Carr et al. (1982), Irwin and Lupker (1983), and Durso and Johnson (1979). Furthermore, Bajo (1988) sought priming data that contributed to the decision between the dual-code and the common abstract code hypotheses of semantic memory. As stimulus materials, a pool of 128 picturable concepts at basic level were chosen in such a way that always two of them were taxonomically related. Relatedness was widely defined as semantic association (e.g., *cat–dog*) or as membership in categories of a rather low superordinate level (e.g., *part of the face: nose–eye*; *part of the body: arm–leg*). Thus, 64 different category terms were available for the categorizing task, and each instance of a category was considered to be an effective prime if the other instance was the target. In the unrelated priming condition, instances of two different categories were combined.

In Experiment 1, a name-verification and a category-verification task were given. The modalities of primes and targets were factorially crossed so that picture–picture, picture–word, word–picture, and word–word pairs resulted. The subjects in the name-verification group were instructed to answer the question

"Does the stimulus name match the name of the concept . . . ?" for the target, disregarding the prime, by pressing a "yes" or "no" key. The subjects in the category-verification group heard the question "Does the stimulus belong to the category . . . ?" Pictures and words were equalled for visual angle at a width of 3 degrees. Thus, Theios and Amrhein's (1989) objection does not apply. The prime was visible for 1000 ms and then followed by a 50-ms visual noise mask and the target. The prime–target relation (related, unrelated), the prime–target modalities (picture–picture, picture–word, word–picture, word–word), and the responses (yes, no) were factorially crossed and varied within subjects at random from trial to trial.

The results exhibited the rank order of mean latencies from verifying words (538 ms) over verifying pictures (559 ms) and verifying categories of pictures (625 ms) up to verifying categories of words (644 ms). Thus, they mirrored the reading–naming difference, the naming–categorizing difference for pictures, and the word–picture difference for categorizing as discussed in the last paragraph. Of course, the reduced amount of the word–picture difference in verifying, compared to reading and naming, is due to this task. Most interesting are the priming results. Firstly, there was no effect of prime modality, that is, word and picture primes had always the same effects. Secondly, the priming effect was about equal in verifying names of pictures (101 ms) and in verifying categories of pictures (112 ms) as well as of words (100 ms). On the other hand, verifying names of words showed only a small, residual effect of 11 ms from picture and 13 ms from word primes.

The common code hypothesis accords with these data. Verifying the name of a picture as well as verifying the category of a picture or a word requires semantic processing of the target that takes place in the abstract system. Thus, it is plausible that the subjects translate not only the target, but also the prime in its abstract semantic code, regardless if it is a word or a picture. In this system, processing of targets that are related to the primes takes advantage of codes that are pre-activated by the primes. Verifying the word, on the other hand, requires a match between spoken and printed modality of the word symbol that is carried out in the verbal system without semantic processing. Of course, this interpretation of the results provides new, independent evidence for the lexical hypothesis which postulates an extended system for word processing without semantic components.

However, there are two possible criticisms. Firstly, if the picture has privileged access to the semantic system, why, then, did picture primes have no greater effect than word primes? A plausible answer is that the SOA of 1050 ms was sufficient even to complete the slower semantic interpretation of the word primes. Secondly, the lack of facilitation of the word targets in the name verification task could result from functional differences between this task and the reading task.

In order to test this objection, Bajo (1988) carried out Experiment 2. Now, the usual reading and picture-naming instructions were given and two additional independent variables were introduced:

(1) Type of instruction: half of the subjects were instructed to try using the prime information as far as possible to process the target more efficiently; half received a neutral instruction as in Experiment 1.

(2) For half the subjects, the modality conditions of picture–picture, picture–word, word–picture, and word–word were randomized between trials as in Experiment 1; for the other half of subjects they were blocked.

These two factors were crossed between subjects; all other factors were varied within subjects. The results exhibited the following pattern of facilitations. Again, naming picture targets was on the average 100 ms facilitated by related primes, disregarding modality of the prime, instruction, and mixed or blocked trial sequence. On the other hand, word targets now also showed a priming by 50 ms under "semantic" instruction and mixed presentation and by 48 ms under neutral instruction and blocked presentation. "Semantic" instruction together with blocked presentation yielded 65 ms facilitation. No priming effect (7 ms) occurred only if the neutral instruction was combined with mixed presentation.

The interpretation is clear: the task to read words aloud is usually carried out without activation of the word's meaning and thus there is no effect of a word or picture prime. On the other hand, the subjects can voluntarily use semantic information also in word reading if they are instructed to do so or if there is no uncertainty about the modality of prime and target because modality is kept constant throughout blocks of trials. Now, semantic processing takes place as is indicated by the observed priming. Taken together, this result indicates an asymmetry of access to the common abstract code for pictures and words. Whereas pictures always contact the semantic code, words do only if the task requires semantic processing or if the subjects choose a strategy to use semantic information. This leads unambiguously from the common code hypothesis to the lexical hypothesis as presented in our second paragraph.

Two important further variables were introduced in the priming task with picture–picture and word–word pairs by Huttenlocher and Kubicek (1983). Firstly, these authors asked whether the priming effects arise automatically from the repeated activation of semantic features that were common to prime and target, or from the controlled expectation of a target that is semantically similar to the prime. Since Posner and Snyder (1975), this question has been investigated by varying the predictive validity of the prime. Thus, a low-expectancy group of subjects was given 12.5% semantically related prime–target pairs in the trial sequence, whereas the high-expectancy group received 87.5% related pairs. Secondly, the influence of word frequency on the naming and reading latencies as well as on the priming effect was evaluated. The modality of the stimulus pairs, picture–picture or word–word, was blocked, and there were no picture–word or word–picture pairs.

In picture naming, related targets exhibited a mean latency of 765 ms in the low-expectancy and of 781 ms in the high-expectancy group. The responses to the respective unrelated targets were 59 ms longer under low and 175 ms longer under high expectancy. The authors conclude that the first of these numbers represents an automatic facilitation by similarity between prime and target that is also contained in the second number as a component. The far greater amount of the second number is explained as an effect of "surprise" in those rare trials in which the target was not similar to the prime in the high-expectancy group. Although the authors do not explicitly mention this source, that result fits perfectly the inhibition that Posner and Snyder (1975) found if controlled expectation was directed to a stimulus other than the presented one. The responses to high-frequency pictures were 116 ms faster than to low-frequency ones, but the interaction of frequency and relatedness was not significant. In word reading, high-frequency words were read by 24 ms faster than low-frequency words, but there were only marginal priming effects in all conditions.

Huttenlocher and Kubicek (1983) divide the processing chain of picture naming into four parts: visual processing, activation of the concept, retrieving of its name, and articulation. Given this, the results were interpreted as follows:

(1) In picture naming, there is an automatic priming by similarity between prime and target of about 59 ms. If a controlled expectation is induced, then processing of unexpected targets is inhibited by about 116 ms, a result which is in line with theory and data by Posner and Snyder (1975). Because these effects are not obtained in reading, they can be attributed only to the first three stages.

(2) Because object decision tasks concerning pictures (cf. Kroll & Potter, 1984) showed priming effects in the same magnitude without naming responses, the name-retrieving stage is also eliminated as a source of this effect, and there remains only visual processing or activation of the concept.

(3) The large effect of name frequency should arise in other stages than visual processing or concept activation, because there was no interaction between this factor and relatedness. Because frequency effects are far less in reading, the articulation stage is also eliminated and only the name-retrieval stage remains. In short, priming effects originate in concept identification, frequency effects in name retrieval. However, there remains the question why some authors found priming effects in reading. Huttenlocher and Kubicek (1983) hypothesize that in the reading task access to the articulatory plan and to the meaning are independent from one another. If easily readable words are to be spoken aloud, then their meaning plays no role. On the other hand, different experimental conditions can activate the access to meaning and thus render reading primeable. Visual degradation of word stimuli (Meyer et al., 1975; Sperber et al., 1979) seems to be such a condition.

Taken together, the priming study by Huttenlocher and Kubicek (1983) also provides evidence for the hypothesis of a common semantic code together with a word system that can operate uninfluenced by word meanings. This is the lexical hypothesis of our section 2.

## 6. Stroop-like interference

The reading–naming difference as introduced in our first section was often investigated with colour words and colour patches as stimuli. Stroop (1935) looked for an explanation in terms of associative interference: every object, including colours, can be named in several ways, and these different naming tendencies could inhibit one another, whereas a reading response is uniquely determined by the print. This gave him the idea to add intentionally an irrelevant response tendency to the colour-naming task by writing a different colour word using the colour that is to be named, for example the word *red* in GREEN ink.[2] The idea led to a discovery: the latency to name the colour of such a stimulus is seriously increased compared to naming a colour patch, and the subjects show strong signs of stress and effort. The rise of naming latency due to the irrelevant word is called Stroop interference. Often, it amounts to more than 80–100 ms and sometimes it reaches the reading–naming difference. Thus, it is one of the most marked effects in cognitive psychology. It is very reliable and, because of its magnitude, easy to replicate.

To read the word component of a Stroop stimulus, on the other hand, is practically not longer than to read a word that is printed in black. This difference, the serious impact of the irrelevant word on colour naming and the immunity of the reading response against the irrelevant colour, is called the *asymmetry* of the Stroop effect.

From the beginning, Stroop research had two aims which were tightly interwoven: to look for an explanation of this strong effect, and to use this effect as a tool to investigate reading, naming, and selective attention. (For comprehensive reviews see Dyer, 1973; Glaser & Glaser, 1989; MacLeod, 1991.) In this article, we confine ourselves to applications of the Stroop technique to picture naming and picture categorizing. Our main interest concerns the question how far Stroop interferences can provide evidence in favour of the particular hypotheses given in the second section.

Glaser and Glaser (1989) present a general characterization of the Stroop experiment. They started from two premises:

(1) The colour of the Stroop stimulus is the limiting case of a picture. Therefore, colour–word/colour and word–picture interference are both instances of a general reading–naming interference.

---

[2]In the following text, concepts as represented by colours, pictures, or internal concept codes are given in capitals; words that are meant as physical symbols, stimuli, or internal word codes are given in italics.

(2) The word and the colour or picture, respectively, of the Stroop-like stimulus can be considered as two stimuli. That is, the Stroop stimulus is the limiting case of double stimulation (Kantowitz, 1974) in which both stimuli are spatially integrated and temporally synchronized.

A further characteristic of the Stroop experiment is the instruction. The subject has to respond to one stimulus component, the *target*, according to a certain rule. The usual instructions demand reading, naming, categorizing, or some kind of matching or semantic decision. The other stimulus component, the *distractor*, must be ignored. Therefore, the Stroop experiment is similar to the priming experiment, although the instruction to ignore the prime is given only rarely.

In the Stroop experiment, the following independent variables play a role:

(1) Stimulus modality: the conventional Stroop stimulus is modally mixed, that is, it contains a pictorial and a verbal component. Modally pure word–word stimuli were used by Dallas and Merikle (1976a, 1976b), Warren (1977), Shaffer and LaBerge (1979), and La Heij et al. (1985). The systematic investigation of Stroop effects with word–word and colour–colour stimuli, compared to conventional colour–word stimuli, began with the studies by Van der Heijden (1981) and Glaser and Glaser (1982). Stroop effects of picture–picture stimuli were investigated by Glaser and Glaser (1989). The main results of these studies are that the interference fails to appear only if the word of a modally mixed stimulus is to be read. Modally pure, that is colour–colour, picture–picture, and word–word stimuli, always exhibit Stroop interference as well as modally mixed stimuli in the naming task. The categorizing task, on the other hand, reverses this result in a dramatic way. Word–word and picture–picture stimuli show again the interference (Glaser & Glaser, 1989), with modally mixed stimuli now word processing is disturbed by adequate picture distractors, whereas picture categorizing becomes immune against distracting words (Smith & Magee, 1980; Glaser & Düngelhoff, 1984).

(2) A central independent variable in Stroop experiments is *distractor–target pairing*. It determines essentially the amount of interference. In the *congruent* condition of this variable, both stimulus components match at basic level (e.g., RED–*red*, HOUSE–*house*). Usually, the congruent distractor facilitates the processing of the target, whereby picture targets are more facilitated than word targets (e.g., Glaser & Glaser, 1989, Experiment 6). That is in accordance with the results from priming studies as discussed in the previous section. The *control* condition is created by using a neutral distractor, that is, a non-word, non-colour or non-picture. In Stroop research, this condition provides the usual baseline for the evaluation of the distractor effects, whereas only a part of the priming studies contain such a non-word control. *Incongruent* distractor–target pairings cause the usual Stroop inhibition (e.g., RED–*green*). In picture naming, they show a *semantic gradient*: naming a picture is more disturbed by a distractor from the

same superordinate category (e.g., HOUSE–*castle*, same category BUILDING) than by a distractor from another category (e.g., HOUSE–*fish*, different category ANIMAL; Glaser & Düngelhoff, 1984; Glaser & Glaser, 1989; Guttentag & Haith, 1978; Lupker, 1979). It is noteworthy that a mere associative relatedness between distractor and target (e.g., MOUSE–*cheese*) does not cause the rise of interference that results from common membership in a superordinate category (Guttentag & Haith, 1978; Lupker, 1979). In the categorizing task, interference is observed if the instruction concerning the target would lead to a different response if it would be applied to the distractor. That is, if the category name "building" is to be said as response to the target word *house*, then the distracting picture of a FISH (different category ANIMAL) strongly interferes, whereas that of a CASTLE (same category BUILDING) does not (Glaser & Düngelhoff, 1984).

(3) Despite its semantic components, the Stroop interference is very sensitive to variations of the *spatial configuration* of distractor and target. Maximum interference is obtained if both components are spatially integrated, for example if the colour is used to print a different colour word, or if the picture surrounds the word, as is the case in the usual picture–word stimulus pairs. On the other hand, the facilitation in the congruent condition is less dependent on stimulus geometry. We will not pursue this complicated matter further here (see Glaser & Glaser, 1989, p. 14).

(4) In the priming studies, the prime usually precedes the target by about 400–1000 ms. In the Stroop studies, the distractor is most often presented synchronously with the target. However, there are some investigations that systematically varied the SOA between distractor and target within a range from about −500 ms (distractor pre-exposed) to about +400 ms (distractor post-exposed) in order to trace the time course of the interference (Dyer, 1971; Flowers, 1975; Flowers, Nelson, Carson, & Larsen, 1984; Glaser & Düngelhoff, 1984; Glaser & Glaser, 1982, 1989; Goolkasian, 1981; Neumann, 1980; Posner & Snyder, 1975; Warren, 1977).

In the resulting SOA functions, three characteristic components are observed:

(1) The facilitation due to congruent distractors is often weak at SOA = 0 ms and shows a flat maximum at distractor pre-exposure by 200–400 ms. Thus, facilitation is a slow effect. It can contain automatic and controlled components (Taylor, 1977). This facilitation in the Stroop experiment seems to be the same effect that is observed in priming studies.

(2) There is an inhibition that has a similar time course as the facilitation, that is, it also shows a flat maximum at distractor pre-exposure of 200–400 ms and more. It seems to be the inhibitory counterpart of the facilitation, and it occurs when an unexpected target is presented after the voluntary build-up of a certain expectation by the subject (cf. Glaser & Glaser, 1982; Posner & Snyder, 1975; Taylor, 1977). Thus, it is essentially a controlled effect.

(3) The Stroop inhibition shows a strong maximum within a small SOA window around synchrony of distractor and target; usually, it is observed from distractor pre-exposure of 100 ms over simultaneous exposure of distractor and target up to distractor post-exposure of 100 ms. Thus, it is a fast effect. It is essentially automatic because it occurs without conscious strategies, but it is intensified by voluntarily directed expectations.

Almost all theoretical explanations share the assumption that the distractor in the Stroop task is involuntarily processed up to a certain stage. The response to the target is delayed because the internal distractor signal absorbs mental capacity or hampers the accumulation of evidence in favour of the target or its response. The main question for any Stroop theory arose from the asymmetry, the immunity of the reading task against an interfering picture, and the immunity of the picture-categorizing task against an interfering word. For a long time, the horse-race or relative-speed hypothesis was most widely accepted (Dyer, 1973; Morton & Chambers, 1973; Palef & Olson, 1975; Posner & Snyder, 1975; Warren, 1972, 1974): the internal signals from distractor and target are processed in temporal proximity and in parallel; interference occurs only if the distracting signal "wins the race", that is, reaches a certain stage before the target's signal. Thereby, the critical stage is captured by the irrelevant signal and released for target processing only after a refractory period.

However, the relative-speed hypothesis of the Stroop interference was un-ambiguously rejected by the studies with SOA variation (Glaser & Düngelhoff, 1984; Glaser & Glaser, 1982, 1989; Neumann, 1980): they showed that it is impossible to disturb the reading response by giving the colour or picture distractor a head start. According to a similar logic, Dunbar and MacLeod (1984) demonstrated that the Stroop asymmetry is preserved even if the words of the Stroop stimuli are transformed so that reading becomes longer than naming. Thus, Glaser and Glaser (1989) concluded that occurrence or absence of the Stroop inhibition does not depend on the speed with which target and distractor are processed. Rather, the Stroop interference should exhibit the degree to which one pathway from perception to action (e.g., from printed word to reading it aloud) is functionally privileged compared to another one (e.g., from picture to pronouncing its name). Thus, the pattern of Stroop interference in adequate series of experiments should provide information on cognitive structures that go beyond that from basic reaction times and from priming data.

Now, let us have a look at Stroop-like results with picture naming. The first investigations were carried out by Rosinski, Golinkoff, and Kukish (1975), Ehri (1976), and Rosinski (1977) using stimulus matrices. These studies aimed at the development of reading skills in children. The main idea was that the degree to which the word stimuli interfere with picture naming should indicate the level of reading ability. The results showed that the interference was very high after the children read fairly well as second graders. Later on, the interference decreased steadily up to adulthood. Underwood (1976) used the picture–word interference to explore attentional effects in reading of adults.

Lupker (1979) carefully investigated the influence of several independent variables:

(1) A non-word distractor (e.g., MOUSE–*wydem*) prolonged the naming latency by 65 ms, compared to the lack of any distractor.

(2) A neutral word without any relation to the target (e.g., MOUSE–*hand*) inhibited 21 ms more.

(3) The same effect was produced by a distractor with an associative relation to the target (e.g., MOUSE–*cheese*). This means that associative relatedness has no particular influence on the Stroop interference.

(4) If the distracting word belonged to the target picture's superordinate category (e.g., MOUSE–*dog*), then the interference increased by an additional 31 ms.

(5) Whether the distractor had a high or low typicality as an instance of the target's superordinate category (cf. Rosch, 1975) did not influence the amount of interference.

(6) A distracting word without semantic or associative relatedness to the target inhibited target naming by 24 ms more if it had a high imageability (e.g., BUTTERFLY–*newspaper*) than if its imageability was low (e.g., BUTTERFLY–*law*).

In a very accurate study, La Heij et al. (1990) conducted a time-course analysis of the effects on picture naming of a common category membership of distractor and target on the one hand and of associative relatedness between them on the other hand. The results demonstrate that common category membership produces the fast Stroop-like inhibition at SOAs from 0 ms (synchrony) to +150 ms (slight post-exposure of the distractor; cf. Glaser & Düngelhoff, 1984), whereas associative strength facilitates markedly with pre-exposed distractors from SOA = −800 ms up to −400 ms. Because the two variables are confounded in most priming and Stroop studies, these results contribute importantly to a solution of the fundamental question why "semantic relatedness" facilitates in priming and inhibits in Stroop experiments.

Taken together, these results show that the Stroop interference is a sensitive indicator of cognitive processes which responds differentially to different independent variables: associative relatedness between distractor and target as well as typicality of the distractor show no inhibition, whereas membership in the target's superordinate category and imageability are very effective. Lupker (1979) supposes that this interference originates in a semantic common code system. Its partially hierarchical structure (see Collins & Loftus, 1975) should cause the effect of common category membership of distractor and target. The stronger effect of highly imageable distractor words should result from their easier access to the semantic system.

Lupker and Katz (1981) investigated Stroop-like effects in a semantic decision task. The targets were a set of (1) different pictures of a dog, (2) pictures of four-legged animals that were not dogs, and (3) pictures of inanimate objects. The subjects had to decide whether the target represented a dog or not. In the control condition, there was no distractor word. The "yes" responses were facilitated 7 ms by the distractor word *dog*. A non-word distractor inhibited the "yes" response by 11 ms, the name of an inanimate object by 15 ms, and an animal name other than *dog* by 39 ms. The "no" responses were only inhibited 25 ms by the distractor word *dog*. It is noteworthy that these effects are very low compared with the Stroop inhibition as obtained in naming tasks that often exceed 100 ms. The authors conclude "that the automatically available semantic information from the word only causes problems in making decisions (a) when the word can supply information similar to but obviously not identical with that available from the picture and (b) when the two stimulus components are not compatible with the same decision" (Lupker & Katz, 1981, p. 277).

In a second experiment, the subjects had to name the superordinate category label of the target picture. Distracting words inhibited under several conditions by 22–33 ms without any significant difference. Only a category label that was an element of the set of the responses, but was different from the actual response, inhibited by 53 ms. Now, the authors conclude: "words do not cause problems for the response selection process by suggesting responses other than their names" (Lupker & Katz, 1981, p. 279). Later on, this conclusion was corroborated by the lack of any semantic component of the word–word interference in the reading task as given in the experiments by Glaser and Glaser (1989). Generally, these results by Lupker and Katz (1981) are to be interpreted in the context of the results by Smith and Magee (1980) and by Glaser and Düngelhoff (1984): the semantic processing of pictures is relatively immune against distracting words, except if the distracting words are possible responses as is the case in the usual picture-naming task.

Of course, the experiments of Lupker and Katz (1981) require complementary studies in which the targets are words and the distractors are pictures. Such a study was reported by Lupker and Katz (1982). Generally, greater inhibitions were now obtained. That means that in semantic decision tasks word processing is more inhibited by picture distractors than picture processing by word distractors. This is in accordance with the priming results discussed above. However, the experiments by Lupker and Katz of 1981 deviated in detail from those of 1982, so that subtle comparisons are not possible.

Smith and Magee (1980) presented a very important study with four experiments. The reading–naming and categorizing tasks were factorially crossed with word or picture as modality of the target. In three of the four experiments, the stimuli were presented as tables; in the categorizing task, the subject had to give a "yes–no" decision whether or not the target was an instance of a pre-specified superordinate category. The time to work through the table was divided by the number of its elements. In Experiment 1, picture naming was inhibited 191 ms by an incongruent word, and word categorizing 194 ms by an incongruent picture. On the other hand, reading was prolonged 19 ms if a distracting picture was given, and categorizing a picture was prolonged 50 ms by an incongruent word.

The authors interpreted this result in terms of the relative-speed hypothesis of the Stroop inhibition: reading is faster than naming, and thus only the naming response should be disturbed by an irrelevant word. On the other hand, picture categorizing is faster than word categorizing, and thus now word categorizing should be disturbed by an irrelevant picture but not vice versa. These data agree with the relative-speed hypothesis of the Stroop interference as well as with the hypothesis of a faster access of the picture to the internal semantic code:

> Experiment 1 examined the hypothesis that a reversal in the pattern of interference would occur when the task was changed from naming to categorization, a task that requires semantic analysis. In accordance with the hypothesis of more rapid semantic access by pictures, the pattern of interference did indeed reverse: Word categorization was delayed in the presence of distracting pictures, whereas picture categorization was left relatively immune to interference by the simultaneous presentation of incongruent words (Smith & Magee, 1980, p. 389).

It is noteworthy that the authors base this argument on the usual word–picture difference in categorizing, although they failed to replicate this difference in three experiments: words were categorized 16 ms or 11 ms faster than pictures (Experiments 1 and 3), and pictures were categorized only 2 ms faster than words in Experiment 2. Thus, the argument must be reversed: word categorizing is disturbed by an incongruent picture distractor even in experiments that do not show a faster picture than word categorizing. That is the same result for categorizing as was found for naming by Dunbar and MacLeod (1984): the word retains its power to inhibit the naming response even if word processing is experimentally delayed.

This line of argument was further pursued by Glaser and Düngelhoff (1984). They used a set of 36 basic objects that belonged to nine superordinate categories. All stimuli consisted of a word and a picture; four Stroop conditions were used. In the *congruent* condition, word and picture matched at basic level (e.g., *chair*–CHAIR). In the *control* condition, a non-picture or non-word provided neutral stimulation at the time and place of the distractor. In the *category–congruent* condition, words were different from pictures, but had their superordinate category in common (e.g., *chair*–TABLE). Finally, in the *incongruent* condition, words and pictures were different and were instances of different superordinate categories (e.g., *chair*–RABBIT). Beside that, SOA was the essential independent variable. Thus, the time courses of the Stroop-like effects were obtained.

Three essential results were found:

(1) Congruent and category-congruent stimuli showed the same amounts and time courses of facilitation and inhibition, respectively, as the conventional Stroop

stimuli that consist of colour words and colours. Thus, the identification of Stroop and picture–word interference with one another is further justified. Again, also a head start of the picture could not inhibit reading, whereas the word disturbed picture naming maximally within a SOA range from −100 ms to +100 ms.

(2) The incongruent distractor words exhibited less interference than the category-congruent ones. This replicated the results of Guttentag and Haith (1978) and of Lupker (1979) that picture naming is maximally disturbed by distractor words of the same superordinate category. In particular, the fast, steep maximum of Stroop interference at −100 ms ⩽ SOA ⩽ +100 ms was slurred with incongruent distractors.

(3) Word categorizing showed essentially the same time course of a strong inhibition as picture naming, whereas picture categorizing was only scarcely influenced by distracting words. Again, a head start of the word could not improve the word's impact on picture categorizing. That fits well with the data, but not with the theory of Smith and Magee (1980) insofar as the latter rests on the relative-speed hypothesis.

Glaser and Düngelhoff (1984) rejected the relative-speed hypothesis and concluded that the Stroop asymmetry, which is so dramatically reversed if the reading–naming task is changed to categorizing, indicates different priorities of internal pathways. Glaser and Glaser (1989) went a further step in this direction: if the Stroop asymmetry as found with modally mixed stimuli results from different internal priorities of the stimulus modalities in different tasks, then both components of modally pure stimuli should be processed along pathways with equal priorities. Thus, modally pure word–word or picture–picture stimuli should exhibit interference that again should provide information about these pathways. This was corroborated empirically: the authors found strong Stroop-like inhibitions with the usual time courses for modally pure stimuli. Strikingly, the word–word interference lacked semantic components in the reading task, whereas the picture–picture interference showed them. Thus, new evidence was obtained that the pathway of reading aloud does not contain a mandatory stage for semantic evaluation. That is also in accordance with the results of some priming studies (e.g., Bajo, 1988; Irwin & Lupker, 1983).

Further research was devoted to the variables that determine the amount of Stroop inhibition. La Heij et al. (1985) accentuated the similarity between priming and Stroop-like experiments and asked why semantic similarity between prime or distractor, respectively, and target facilitates in the priming and inhibits in the interference experiments. They identified two important variables that contribute to these different results: (1) number of "semantic domains" and (2) the relation between the sets of distractors and targets.

(1) In the usual Stroop experiment, only one semantic domain, that of colour concepts, is used. Picture–word interference is usually investigated using a small

number of two to ten superordinate categories, whereas in priming studies often more categories are used (e.g., 64 by Bajo, 1988). Furthermore, in Stroop-like experiments, a small number of stimuli are repeated several times, whereas in most priming studies a large number of stimuli is presented only one or two times. In a word–word variant of the Stroop experiment, La Heij et al. (1985) could demonstrate a facilitation by associative relatedness between distractor and target that increased with increasing number of associated stimulus pairs that were active within a block of trials.

(2) In the usual Stroop experiments, the set of the distractor words is identical to the set of the spoken responses. However, these two sets can also be intersecting or disjoint. Generally, other conditions being constant, target processing is far more inhibited by distractors that are elements of the response set than by those that are not (Glaser & Glaser, 1989; Klein, 1964; Proctor, 1978). We called that variable *set relation* (Glaser & Glaser, 1989, p. 25). La Heij et al. (1985) found that the degree of inhibition due to set relation decreases with increasing number of categories.

La Heij and Vermeij (1987) varied the stimulus set size in the steps of 2, 4, or 8 stimulus alternatives in a picture-naming experiment and found that the interference due to incongruent words decreased and the facilitation due to congruent words increased with ascending number of target alternatives.

A very careful investigation of the variables that influence the Stroop-like interference of word distractors on picture naming was carried out by La Heij (1988). In Experiment 1, six pictures from the two categories *musical instruments* and *tools* were used as targets. The visual similarity of the pictures was kept constant within and between categories. Thus, the increased interference due to semantically related distractors compared to unrelated ones (Glaser & Düngelhoff, 1984; Guttentag & Haith, 1978; Lupker, 1979) should disappear if it resulted only from different visual similarity within and between categories as supposed by Neumann and Kautz (1982) and, for a face–name interference task, by Young, Ellis, Flude, McWeeny, and Hay (1986). It should also be remembered that Snodgrass and McCullough (1986) suggested this as the cause for the word–picture difference in categorizing.

Semantic *relatedness* was varied by combining a picture with a distracting word from the same (e.g., PIANO–*guitar*) or from a different (e.g., PIANO–*chisel*) category. Furthermore, one half of these distractors were labels of the pictures used in the experiment, the other half were not. Thus, *set relation* was combined factorially with relatedness. As *control* distractors, series of Xs were used, and names of objects that were neither musical instruments nor tools provided an additional semantically *irrelevant* condition. The results exhibited four independent effects: (1) the mere presence of a distracting word prolonged the latency by 45 ms compared with the non-word distractor; (2) the task relevance of the distractor, that is, its usefulness as a potential response in the task to name musical instruments and tools, prolonged the latency by a further 23 ms; (3) semantic relatedness contributed an additional inhibition of 13 ms; and (4) set relation added 25 ms. There was no interaction between semantic relatedness and set relation so that the effects of these two factors are orthogonal to one another. In his Experiment 2, La Heij (1988) essentially replicated these results with other pictures that were controlled for visual similarity by an additional reaction-time experiment.

In line with Lupker and Katz (1981) and Huttenlocher and Kubicek (1983), La Heij (1988) supposes four stages in the picture-naming pathway: visual processing, semantic activation of the concept, retrieving of its name, and articulation. Because some studies have shown a very reduced Stroop interference if the response to the non-verbal stimulus component is given by pressing keys or with other non-naming responses like sorting cards or humming tones (McClain, 1983; Palef, 1978; Virzi & Egeth, 1985), La Heij (1988) concludes that the reading–naming interference does not arise whilst the picture is semantically identified, but during name retrieval. Glaser and Glaser (1989, p. 32) also tried to incorporate these empirical results in a model and arrived at the same theoretical conclusions. The Stroop interference is generated in the lexicon, because the code of the distracting word is activated from three sources: semantic spread of excitation from the target in the semantic system that is transferred to the lexicon, an increased basic activation as a potential response in the block of trials, and an activation through automatic reading. The Stroop inhibition is explained by the extra effort to select the target's label against this strong evidence in favour of the distracting word.

An additional property of the picture–word interference was found by Lupker (1982) and by Rayner and Springer (1986). In Lupker's (1982) Experiment 1, an un-related word inhibited picture naming by 78 ms compared to a picture-alone condition. This interference was reduced by 72% to 22 ms if the word was orthographically similar to the picture's name. In his Experiment 2, an inhibition of 69 ms was reduced by 23 ms (33%) if the distractor word rhymed with the response word, and by a further 32 ms (46%) if in addition it was orthographically similar.

In Rayner and Springer's (1986) picture-naming task, there were *congruent* (e.g., BALL–*ball*, category TOY), *category–congruent* (e.g., BALL–*drum*), and *incongruent* (e.g., BALL–*pear*) distracting words as in the study by Glaser and Düngelhoff (1984). Additionally, there were distractors that shared initial letter and word contour with the label of the picture (e.g., category-congruent: BALL–*bell*; incongruent: BALL–*bill*). With the usual distractors, the usual results also were replicated: a congruent distractor facilitated the response, and a category-congruent distractor inhibited far more than an incongruent one. However, if the distracting word was not identical to the picture's label, but had the initial letter and the shape in common with it, then the interference was reduced on average by

61% in the category-congruent and by 37% in the incongruent condition. This means that the distractor produces two involuntary effects: its property of being a readable word and its semantic relatedness to the target inhibit, whereas its graphemic similarity to the response word facilitates target processing.

At first glance, it does not seem to be impossible to reconcile these data with some kind of logogen model (Rayner & Springer, 1986). However, there remains a fundamental theoretical problem. The interference due to semantic relatedness is explained by assuming that the decision between target and distractor signal becomes more difficult with increasing similarity. This is a known fact about discrimination in psychology. On the other hand, increasing graphemic similarity of the distracting word facilitates target processing, although it should activate a different word that is also very similar to the correct response word and that should also compete with it for the control of the spoken response. In other words, the data of Rayner and Springer (1986) claim two different discrimination processes: one that becomes more difficult with increasing similarity among the alternatives and that operates on the semantic components of the naming task, and another that becomes easier with increasing similarity and works on the graphemic components.

However, perhaps a solution can be found within the framework of Levelt's (1989, p. 231) hypothesis that the word entries of the lexicon have two separate components: (1) the *lemma* which contains syntax and meaning (the latter refers to the semantic information that is necessary for the selection of the word by activated concepts in the semantic system); and (2) the *morpho-phonological form* which governs the articulatory programming. That means that lemma retrieval and articulatory programming are distinct processes which occur in strong temporal seriality. Thus, the semantic features of the distractor could become effective by activating their lemma that would compete with the correct response at the level of the lemmas, but the resulting inhibition terminates at this stage and does not reach articulatory programming (Levelt et al., 1991). On the other hand, linguistic features of the distractor work by activating phonemes on the basis of grapheme–phoneme correspondence at the morpho-phonological level of the lexicon. Thus, rhyme, orthography, and shape of the distractor could prime the particular phonemes that are used in an incremental articulatory programming of the correct response.

Levelt's hypothesis was essentially derived from analyses of speech errors (e.g., Dell & Reich, 1981; Fay & Cutler, 1977; Garrett, 1988). Later on, Levelt and his co-authors looked for additional evidence in Stroop-like experiments. Thus, Schriefers, Meyer, and Levelt (1990) gave their subjects a picture-naming task in which verbal distractors were presented acoustically. Beside *neutral* and *unrelated* words, *semantically* and *phonetically* related distractors were presented at the three SOA levels of −150 ms (distractor first), 0 ms, and +150 ms (distractor second). The main results were an increased inhibition due to semantically related pre-exposed distractors and a facilitation due to phonologically related post-exposed distractors.

These data clearly demonstrate two temporal windows for semantic inhibition and phonological facilitation of the naming response. Semantic interference is maximal, if the distractor is exposed early, whereas phonological facilitation profits most from a post-exposed distractor. This is well in accordance with the assumption of two separate steps of lexical access that follow one another, even if it does not uniquely reject the alternative hypothesis of an overlapping or continuously flowing transition between these two stages.

By the way, there is an undiscussed discrepancy between these authors' results and those of the other Stroop-like experiments that varied SOA (Glaser & Düngelhoff, 1984; Glaser & Glaser, 1982, 1989; La Heij et al., 1990). Whereas the semantic interference usually reaches its maximum at SOAs from 0 ms (synchrony) up to a post-exposure by +50 ms to +150 ms of the distractor, Schriefers et al. (1990) found it only at a pre-exposure by −150 ms. Perhaps this is caused by the auditory modality of the distractors. An experimental clarification of this issue is still lacking.

Of course, there remains the problem that semantic similarity inhibits, whereas phonological similarity of the distractor facilitates target processing. The authors hypothesize that the articulation of the target's label does not use the distractor word in its entirety – that should lead to the activation of a different, competing response – but have accelerated access to the single phonemes that are primed by the distractor. As discussed above, this hypothesis can also explain the data from other investigations (e.g., Lupker, 1982; Rayner & Springer, 1986). Nevertheless, further converging evidence would be useful.

In a series of six experiments, Levelt et al. (1991) looked for further evidence for the two-step hypothesis of lexical access. Their subjects received a speeded picture-naming task. In the relevant trials, an additional word or non-word stimulus, respectively, was presented acoustically. Contrary to the usual picture–word interference task, now the subjects had to make a lexical decision concerning the acoustical stimulus as a secondary task that was also timed. The main dependent variable was now the latency of the lexical decision. Besides SOA, the relatedness of picture and word was the essential independent variable. It was varied in seven steps:

(1) In the *identical* condition, the name of the picture matched the word (e.g., SHEEP–*sheep*).

(2) In the *semantically related* condition, the word was a close associate of the picture (e.g., SHEEP–*wool*).

(3) In the condition of *semantic alternatives*, the word denoted a concept of the same superordinate category as the picture (e.g., SHEEP–*goat*).

(4) The *phonologically related* condition was made up by words that shared the initial phonemes of the target's name (e.g., RADIO–*radar*).

(5) There were also *unrelated* words that were associatively as well as semantically and phonemically distant to the picture's label.

(6) A further condition contained words that were *phonemically similar to a close associate of the target* (e.g., SHEEP–*wood* because *wool* is an associate of *sheep*).

(7) A final condition contained words that were *phonemically similar to a semantic alternative* of the target (e.g., SHEEP–*goal* because *goat* belongs to the same superordinate category as *sheep*).

SOA was varied in the three steps *short* (word on average 73 ms after picture), *medium* (word on average 373 ms after picture, and *long* (word on average 673 ms after picture).

The main results were as follows. The *unrelated* condition was used as a baseline with respect to which inhibitions and facilitations were evaluated.

(1) The lexical decision of words that were *identical* to the response was inhibited at short and facilitated at long SOAs. This is reasonable if one assumes that at short SOAs phonological access of picture and word overlap and hamper one another. At long SOAs, on the contrary, word processing is facilitated because the identical word is already phonologically activated as a response to the picture.

(2) *Semantically related* words were inhibited at short SOAs but showed no effects at medium and long SOAs. Apparently, this semantic interference occurs only if the word stimulus taps into the semantic processing of the picture. If this stage of picture processing is terminated, there are no more semantic effects on word processing.

(3) At short SOAs, *semantic alternatives* were inhibited far more than *semantically related* words (Experiment 6). That is in accordance with the data from the usual picture–word experiments (cf. Lupker, 1979).

(4) The *phonologically related* words were strongly inhibited at all three SOA levels. This result contrasts to the data from picture–word interference studies in which phonological similarity between the distracting word and the target's label always facilitated the response (Lupker, 1982; Rayner & Springer, 1986; Schriefers et al., 1990). This discrepancy, of course, needs further discussion which, however, is beyond the scope of the present article.

(5) Finally, words that were phonologically related to an associate or a semantic alternative of the target's label did not show any effect different from unrelated words. This is strong evidence for the two-step hypothesis of lexical access: if a spoken word is required as a response in picture naming, then other semantically related concept codes are coactivated through a spreading semantic excitation. This activation terminates at their lemmas. That means that only the one word that has to control the overt response is also programmed phonologically, whereas the coactivated codes do not reach the phonological and articulatory stages.

# 7. Conclusions

The three domains of experimental investigations on picture naming arrived at an impressive corpus of data:

(1) The comparison of naming with reading as well as with picture and word categorizing showed three reliable effects: reading is markedly faster than picture naming, naming pictures is faster than categorizing pictures, and picture categorizing is faster than word categorizing. Furthermore, picture categorizing is accelerated for superordinate categories that share characteristic visual features with objects at basic level (Hoffmann & Klimesch, 1984), and it is inhibited if the pictures are especially similar to one another between the categories (Snodgrass & McCullough, 1986). The word-frequency effect is far greater in naming than in reading responses.

(2) The priming results are partially different from one another, so that it is difficult at present to integrate them all into a completely consistent theoretical framework (cf. Snodgrass, 1984, p. 14). Nevertheless, one characteristic result is that in the reading and naming tasks pictures are more effective as primes and are more primeable as targets. Within-modality priming is more effective than between-modality priming. Often, the reading response is only marginally or not at all primed. In some cases, even picture naming was not primed (e.g., Irwin & Lupker, 1983), whereas in other cases the reading response was markedly primed depending on voluntary strategies of the subjects (cf. Bajo, 1988). Thus, the contribution of the priming studies to the evaluation of the hypotheses given in the second section seems so far to be limited. Nevertheless, further productive contributions of priming studies could be possible (e.g., De Groot, 1990).

(3) Although the Stroop-like interferences have been used only recently as a tool to investigate picture processing, they have provided some strong, reliable, and consistent effects. Thus, the Stroop asymmetry is reversed if the reading and naming task is replaced by the categorizing task: word processing is inhibited by an incongruent picture distractor. Modally pure stimuli, that is, word–word and picture–picture pairs, always exhibit interference, but lack semantic components in the reading task. In a way that is not yet fully understood, the Stroop-like interference is very sensitive to a common category membership of target and distractor, but unaffected by typicality (e.g., Lupker, 1979). Associative relatedness among distractor and target label facilitates to a small degree at synchronous exposure and to a marked degree if the distractor precedes the target by about $-400$ ms and more (La Heij et al., 1990). Task relevance of the distractor, set relation between target and distractor and number of semantic domains are also theoretically informative independent variables (cf. La Heij, 1988). Finally, there is a nearly complete paradox insofar as a distractor that is semantically similar to the target inhibits its processing, whereas a phonemically similar distractor facilitates. Perhaps this effect is related to the facilitation by associative strength.

As was demonstrated in detail throughout this article, these data can be integrated within a theoretical framework that contains two large components as shown in Figure 1(c): (1) an abstract semantic memory that nevertheless is functionally connected with picture processing and, in a broader sense, with perception and action; and (2) a lexicon that provides storage and processing facilities for all linguistic knowledge and abilities beyond semantics.

## References

Bajo, M.-T. (1988). Semantic facilitation with pictures and words. *Journal of Experimental Psychology: Learning, Memory, and Cognition, 14*, 579–589.

Beller, H.K. (1971). Priming: Effects of advance information on matching. *Journal of Experimental Psychology, 87*, 176–182.

Biederman, I., & Tsao, Y.-C. (1979). On processing Chinese ideographs and English words: Some implications from Stroop-test results. *Cognitive Psychology, 11*, 125–132.

Brown, W. (1915). Practice in associating color-names with colors. *Psychological Review, 22*, 45–55.

Carr, T.H., McCauley, C., Sperber, R.D., & Parmelee, C.M. (1982). Words, pictures, and priming: On semantic activation, conscious identification, and the automaticity of information processing. *Journal of Experimental Psychology: Human Perception and Performance, 8*, 757–777.

Cattell, J.M. (1885). Über die Zeit der Erkennung und Benennung von Schriftzeichen, Bildern und Farben [The time to recognize and name letters, pictures, and colors]. *Philosophische Studien, 2*, 635–650.

Cattell, J.M. (1886). The time to see and name objects. *Mind, 11*, 63–65.

Collins, A.M., & Loftus, E. (1975). A spreading-activation theory of semantic processing. *Psychological Review, 82*, 407–428.

Collins, A.M., & Quillian, M.R. (1969). Retrieval time from semantic memory. *Journal of Verbal Learning and Verbal Behavior, 8*, 240–247.

Dallas, M., & Merikle, P.M. (1976a). Response processes and semantic-context effects. *Bulletin of the Psychonomic Society, 8*, 441–444.

Dallas, M., & Merikle, P.M. (1976b). Semantic processing of non-attended visual information. *Canadian Journal of Psychology, 30*, 15–21.

De Groot, A.M.B. (1990). The locus of the associative-priming effect in the mental lexicon. In D.A. Balota, G.B. Flores d'Arcais, & K. Rayner (Eds.), *Comprehension processes in reading* (pp. 101–123). Hillsdale, NJ: Erlbaum.

Deese, J. (1962). On the structure of associative meaning. *Psychological Review, 69*, 161–175.

Dell, G.S., & Reich, P.A. (1981). Stages in sentence production: An analysis of speech error data. *Journal of Verbal Learning and Verbal Behavior, 20*, 611–629.

Dunbar, K., & MacLeod, C.M. (1984). A horse race of a different color: Stroop interference patterns with transformed words. *Journal of Experimental Psychology: Human Perception and Performance, 10*, 622–639.

Durso, F.T., & Johnson, M.K. (1979). Facilitation in naming and categorizing repeated pictures and words. *Journal of Experimental Psychology: Human Learning and Memory, 5*, 449–459.

Durso, F.T., & O'Sullivan, C.S. (1983). Naming and remembering proper and common nouns and pictures. *Journal of Experimental Psychology: Learning, Memory, and Cognition, 9*, 497–510.

Dyer, F.N. (1971). The duration of word meaning responses: Stroop interference for different preexposures of the word. *Psychonomic Science, 25*, 229–231.

Dyer, F.N. (1973). The Stroop phenomenon and its use in the study of perceptual, cognitive, and response processes. *Memory and Cognition, 1*, 106–120.

Ehri, L.C. (1976). Do words really interfere in naming pictures? *Child Development, 47*, 502–505.

Fay, D., & Cutler, A. (1977). Malapropisms and the structure of the mental lexicon. *Linguistic Inquiry, 8*, 505–520.

Flores d'Arcais, G.B., & Schreuder, R. (1987). Semantic activation during object naming. *Psychological Research, 49*, 153–159.

Flores d'Arcais, G.B., Schreuder, R., & Glazenborg, G. (1985). Semantic activation during recognition of referential words. *Psychological Research, 47*, 39–49.

Flowers, J.H. (1975). "Sensory" interference in a word–color matching task. *Perception and Psychophysics, 18*, 37–43.

Flowers, J.H., Nelson, S.M., Carson, D., & Larsen, L. (1984). Automatic and expectancy-based priming effects in a digit naming task. *Journal of Experimental Psychology: Human Perception and Performance, 10*, 65–74.

Fraisse, P. (1960). Recognition time measured by verbal reaction to figures and words. *Perceptual and Motor Skills, 11*, 204.

Fraisse, P. (1967). Latency of different verbal responses to the same stimulus. *Quarterly Journal of Experimental Psychology, 19*, 353–355.

Fraisse, P. (1969). Why is naming longer than reading? *Acta Psychologica, 30*, 96–103.

Frederiksen, J.R., & Kroll, J.F. (1976). Spelling and sound: Approaches to the internal lexicon. *Journal of Experimental Psychology: Human Perception and Performance, 2*, 361–379.

Friedman, A., & Bourne, L.E. (1976). Encoding the levels of information in pictures and words. *Journal of Experimental Psychology: General, 105*, 169–190.

Garrett, M.F. (1988). Processes in language production. In F.J. Newmeyer (Ed.), *Linguistics: The Cambridge Survey, Vol. III: Psychological and biological aspects* (pp. 69–96). Cambridge, UK: Cambridge University Press.

Gholson, B., & Hohle, R.H. (1968). Verbal reaction times to hues vs hue names and forms vs form names. *Perception and Psychophysics, 3*, 191–196.

Glaser, M.O., & Glaser, W.R. (1982). Time course analysis of the Stroop phenomenon. *Journal of Experimental Psychology: Human Perception and Performance, 8*, 875–894.

Glaser, W.R., & Düngelhoff, F.-J. (1984). The time course of picture–word interference. *Journal of Experimental Psychology: Human Perception and Performance, 10*, 640–654.

Glaser, W.R., & Glaser, M.O. (1989). Context effects in Stroop-like word and picture processing. *Journal of Experimental Psychology: General, 118*, 13–42.

Goolkasian, P. (1981). Retinal location and its effect on the processing of target and distractor information. *Journal of Experimental Psychology: Human Perception and Performance, 7*, 1247–1257.

Guttentag, R.E., & Haith, M.M. (1978). Automatic processing as a function of age and reading ability. *Child development, 49*, 707–716.

Harris, P.L., Morris, P.E., & Bassett, E. (1977). Classifying pictures and words: Implications for the dual-coding hypothesis. *Memory and Cognition, 5*, 242–246.

Hines, D., Czerwinski, M., Sawyer, P.K., & Dwyer, M. (1986). Automatic semantic priming: Effect of category exemplar level and word association level. *Journal of Experimental Psychology: Human Perception and Performance, 12*, 370–379.

Hoffmann, J., & Klimesch, W. (1984). Die semantische Codierung von Wörtern und Bildern [Semantic coding of words and pictures]. *Sprache & Kognition, 1*, 1–25.

Hoffmann, J., & Ziessler, M. (1982). Begriffe und ihre Merkmale [Concepts and their features]. *Zeitschrift für Psychologie, 190*, 46–77.

Hogaboam, T.W., & Pellegrino, J.W. (1978). Hunting for individual differences in cognitive processes: Verbal ability and semantic processing of pictures and words. *Memory and Cognition, 6*, 189–193.

Hollan, J.D. (1975). Features and semantic memory: Set-theoretic or network model? *Psychological Review, 82*, 154–155.

Huttenlocher, J., & Kubicek, L.F. (1983). The source of relatedness effects on naming latency. *Journal of Experimental Psychology: Learning, Memory, and Cognition, 9*, 486–496.

Irwin, D.I., & Lupker, S.J. (1983). Semantic priming of pictures and words: A levels of processing approach. *Journal of Verbal Learning and Verbal Behavior, 22*, 45–60.

Kantowitz, B.H. (1974). Double stimulation. In B.H. Kantowitz (Ed.), *Human information processing: Tutorials in performance and cognition* (pp. 83–131). Hillsdale, NJ: Erlbaum.

Klein, G.S. (1964). Semantic power measured through the interference of words with color-naming. *American Journal of Psychology, 77*, 576–588.

Klimesch, W. (1982). Die semantische Encodierung von Bildern [Semantic encoding of pictures]. *Zeitschrift für experimentelle und angewandte Psychologie, 29*, 472–504.

Kroll, J.F., & Potter, M.C. (1984). Recognizing words, pictures, and concepts: A comparison of lexical, object, and reality decisions. *Journal of Verbal Learning and Verbal Behavior, 23*, 39–66.

La Heij, W. (1988). Components of Stroop-like interference in picture naming. *Memory and Cognition, 16*, 400–410.

La Heij, W., Dirkx, J., & Kramer, P. (1990). Categorical interference and associative priming in picture naming. *British Journal of Psychology, 81*, 511–525.

La Heij, W., Van der Heijden, A.H.C., & Schreuder, R. (1985). Semantic priming and Stroop-like interference in word-naming tasks. *Journal of Experimental Psychology: Human Perception and Performance, 11*, 62–80.

La Heij, W., & Vermeij, M. (1987). Reading versus naming: The effect of target set size on contextual interference and facilitation. *Perception and Psychophysics, 41*, 355–366.

Levelt, W.J.M. (1989). *Speaking: From intention to articulation*. Cambridge, MA: MIT Press.

Levelt, W.J.M., Schriefers, H., Vorberg, D., Meyer, A.S., Pechmann, T., & Havinga, J. (1991). The time course of lexical access in speech production: A study of picture naming. *Psychological Review, 98*, 122–142.

Ligon, E.M. (1932). A genetic study of color naming and word reading. *American Journal of Psychology, 44*, 103–122.

Lund, F.H. (1927). The role of practice in speed of association. *Journal of Experimental Psychology, 10*, 424–433.

Lupker, S.J. (1979). The semantic nature of response competition in the picture–word interference task. *Memory and Cognition, 7*, 485–495.

Lupker, S.J. (1982). The role of phonetic and orthographic similarity in picture–word interference. *Canadian Journal of Psychology, 36*, 349–367.

Lupker, S.J. (1988). Picture naming: An investigation of the nature of categorical priming. *Journal of Experimental Psychology: Learning, Memory, and Cognition, 14*, 444–455.

Lupker, S.J., & Katz, A.N. (1981). Input, decision, and response factors in picture–word interference. *Journal of Experimental Psychology: Human Learning and Memory, 7*, 269–282.

Lupker, S.J., & Katz, A.N. (1982). Can automatic picture processing influence word judgments? *Journal of Experimental Psychology: Learning, Memory, and Cognition, 8*, 418–434.

MacLeod, C.M. (1991). Half a century of research on the Stroop effect: An integrative review. *Psychological Bulletin, 109*, 163–203.

McCauley, C., Parmelee, C.M., Sperber, R.D., & Carr, T.H. (1980). Early extraction of meaning from pictures and its relation to conscious identification. *Journal of Experimental Psychology: Human Perception and Performance, 6*, 265–276.

McClain, L. (1983). Stimulus–response compatibility affects auditory Stroop interference. *Perception and Psychophysics, 33*, 266–270.

Merikle, P.M. (1982). Unconscious perception revisited. *Perception and Psychophysics, 31*, 298–301.

Meyer, D.E., Schvaneveldt, R.W., & Ruddy, M.G. (1975). Loci of contextual effects on visual word-recognition. In P.M.A. Rabbitt & S. Dornic (Eds.), *Attention and performance V* (pp. 98–118). New York: Academic Press.

Morton, J. (1970). A functional model for memory. In D.A. Norman (Ed.), *Models of human memory* (pp. 203–254). New York: Academic Press.

Morton, J., & Chambers, S.M. (1973). Selective attention to words and colours. *Quarterly Journal of Experimental Psychology, 25*, 387–397.

Neumann, O. (1980). *Informationsselektion und Handlungssteuerung* [Selection of information and control of action]. Unpublished doctoral dissertation, University of Bochum, Germany.

Neumann, O., & Kautz, L. (1982). *Semantische Förderung und semantische Interferenz im Be-*

*nennungsexperiment* [Semantic facilitation and semantic interference in a naming experiment] (Bericht Nr. 23/1982). Bochum, Germany: University of Bochum.

Oldfield, R.C., & Wingfield, A. (1965). Response latencies in naming objects. *Quarterly Journal of Experimental Psychology, 17,* 273–281.

Paivio, A. (1969). Mental imagery in associative learning and memory. *Psychological Review, 76,* 241–263.

Paivio, A. (1971). *Imagery and verbal processes.* Hillsdale, NJ: Erlbaum.

Paivio, A. (1978). A dual coding approach to perception and cognition. In H.L. Pick, Jr., & E. Saltzman (Eds.), *Modes of perceiving and processing information* (pp. 39–51). Hillsdale, NJ: Erlbaum.

Palef, S.R. (1978). Judging pictorial and linguistic aspects of space. *Memory and Cognition, 6,* 70–75.

Palef, S.R., & Olson, D.R. (1975). Spatial and verbal rivalry in a Stroop-like task. *Canadian Journal of Psychology, 29,* 201–209.

Pellegrino, J.W., Rosinski, R.R., Chiesi, H.L., & Siegel, A. (1977). Picture–word differences in decision latency: An analysis of single and dual memory models. *Memory and Cognition, 5,* 383–396.

Posner, M.I., & Mitchell, R.F. (1967). Chronometric analysis of classification. *Psychological Review, 74,* 392–409.

Posner, M.I., & Snyder, C.R.R. (1975). Facilitation and inhibition in the processing of signals. In P.M.A. Rabbitt & S. Dornic (Eds.), *Attention and performance V* (pp. 669–682). London: Academic Press.

Potter, M.C. (1979). Mundane symbolism: The relations among objects, names, and ideas. In N.R. Smith & M.B. Franklin (Eds.), *Symbolic functioning in childhood* (pp. 41–65). Hillsdale, NJ: Erlbaum.

Potter, M.C., & Faulconer, B.A. (1975). Time to understand pictures and words. *Nature, 253,* 437–438.

Potter, M.C., Kroll, J.F., Yachzel, B., Carpenter, E., & Sherman, J. (1986). Pictures in sentences: Understanding without words. *Journal of Experimental Psychology: General, 115,* 281–294.

Potter, M.C., So, K.-F., Von Eckardt, B., & Feldman, L.B. (1984). Lexical and conceptual representation in beginning and proficient bilinguals. *Journal of Verbal Learning and Verbal Behavior, 23,* 23–38.

Proctor, R.W. (1978). Sources of color–word interference in the Stroop color-naming task. *Perception and Psychophysics, 23,* 413–419.

Purcell, D.G., Stewart, A.L., & Stanovich, K.E. (1983). Another look at semantic priming without awareness. *Perception and Psychophysics, 34,* 65–71.

Pylyshyn, Z.W. (1973). What the mind's eye tells the mind's brain: A critique of mental imagery. *Psychological Bulletin, 80,* 1–24.

Rayner, K., & Springer, C.J. (1986). Graphemic and semantic similarity effects in the picture–word interference task. *British Journal of Psychology, 77,* 207–222.

Reinitz, M.T., Wright, E., & Loftus, G.R. (1989). Effects of semantic priming on visual encoding of pictures. *Journal of Experimental Psychology: General, 118,* 280–297.

Rosch, E. (1975). Cognitive representations of semantic categories. *Journal of Experimental Psychology: General, 104,* 192–233.

Rosch, E. (1978). Principles of categorization. In E. Rosch & B.B. Lloyd (Eds.), *Cognition and categorization* (pp. 27–48). Hillsdale, NJ: Erlbaum.

Rosch, E., Mervis, C.B., Gray, W.D., Johnson, D.M., & Boyes-Braem, P. (1976). Basic objects in natural categories. *Cognitive Psychology, 8,* 382–439.

Rosinski, R.R. (1977). Picture–word interference is semantically based. *Child Development, 48,* 643–647.

Rosinski, R.R., Golinkoff, R.M., & Kukish, K.S. (1975). Automatic semantic processing in a picture–word interference task. *Child Development, 46,* 247–253.

Rosinski, R.R., Pellegrino, J.W., & Siegel, A.W. (1977). Developmental changes in the semantic processing of pictures and words. *Journal of Experimental Child Psychology, 23,* 282–291.

Scarborough, D.L., Gerard, L., & Cortese, C. (1979). Accessing lexical memory: The transfer of word repetition effects across task and modality. *Memory and Cognition*, 7, 3–12.

Schriefers, H., Meyer, A.S., & Levelt, W.J.M. (1990). Exploring the time course of lexical access in language production: Picture–word interference studies. *Journal of Memory and Language*, 29, 86–102.

Segui, J., & Fraisse, P. (1968). Le temps de réaction verbale. III. Réponses spécifiques et réponses catégorielles à des stimulus objets [Verbal reaction time. III. Specific and categorical responses to stimulus objects]. *L'année psychologique*, 68, 69–82.

Seymour, P.H.K. (1973). A model for reading, naming and comparison. *British Journal of Psychology*, 64, 35–49.

Seymour, P.H.K. (1976). Contemporary models of the cognitive processes: II. Retrieval and comparison operations in permanent memory. In V. Hamilton & M.D. Vernon (Eds.), *The development of cognitive processes* (pp. 43–108). New York: Academic Press.

Shaffer, W.O., & LaBerge, D. (1979). Automatic semantic processing of unattended words. *Journal of Verbal Learning and Verbal Behavior*, 18, 413–426.

Simon, J.R., & Sudalaimuthu, P. (1979). Effects of S–R mapping and response modality on performance in a Stroop task. *Journal of Experimental Psychology: Human Perception and Performance*, 5, 176–187.

Smith, E.E., Balzano, G.J., & Walker, J. (1978). Nominal, perceptual, and semantic codes in picture categorization. In J.W. Cotton & R.L. Klatzky (Eds.), *Semantic factors in cognition* (pp. 137–168). Hillsdale, NJ: Erlbaum.

Smith, E.E., Shoben, E.J., & Rips, L.J. (1974). Structure and process in semantic memory: A featural model for semantic decisions. *Psychological Review*, 81, 214–241.

Smith, M.C., & Magee, L.E. (1980). Tracing the time course of picture–word processing. *Journal of Experimental Psychology: General*, 109, 373–392.

Snodgrass, J.G. (1980). Towards a model for picture–word processing. In P.A. Kolers, M.E. Wrolstad, & H. Bouma (Eds.), *Processing of visible language* (Vol. 2, pp. 565–584). New York: Plenum Press.

Snodgrass, J.G. (1984). Concepts and their surface representations. *Journal of Verbal Learning and Verbal Behavior*, 23, 3–22.

Snodgrass, J.G., & McCullough, B. (1986). The role of visual similarity in picture categorization. *Journal of Experimental Psychology: Learning, Memory and Cognition*, 12, 147–154.

Snodgrass, J.G., & Vanderwart, M. (1980). A standardized set of 260 pictures: Norms for name agreement, image agreement, familiarity, and visual complexity. *Journal of Experimental Psychology: Human Learning and Memory*, 6, 174–215.

Sperber, R.D., McCauley, C., Ragain, R.D., & Weil, C.M. (1979). Semantic priming effects on picture and word processing. *Memory and Cognition*, 7, 339–345.

Sternberg, S. (1969). The discovery of processing stages: Extension of Donder's method. *Acta Psychologica*, 30, 276–315.

Stroop, J.R. (1935). Studies of interference in serial verbal reactions. *Journal of Experimental Psychology*, 18, 643–662.

Taylor, D.A. (1977). Time course of context effects. *Journal of Experimental Psychology: General*, 106, 404–426.

Theios, J., & Amrhein, P.C. (1989). Theoretical analysis of the cognitive processing of lexical and pictorial stimuli: Reading, naming, and visual and conceptual comparisons. *Psychological Review*, 96, 5–24.

Thorndike, E.L., & Lorge, I. (1944). *The teacher's word book of 30 000 words*. New York: Teacher's College, Columbia University.

Underwood, G. (1976). Semantic interference from unattended printed words. *British Journal of Psychology*, 67, 327–338.

Van der Heijden, A.H.C. (1981). *Short-term visual information forgetting*. London: Routledge & Kegan Paul.

Virzi, R.A., & Egeth, H.E. (1985). Toward a translational model of Stroop interference. *Memory and Cognition*, 13, 304–319.

Warren, C., & Morton, J. (1982). The effects of priming on picture recognition. *British Journal of Psychology*, *73*, 117–129.

Warren, R.E. (1972). Simulus encoding and memory. *Journal of Experimental Psychology*, *94*, 90–100.

Warren, R.E. (1974). Association, directionality, and stimulus encoding. *Journal of Experimental Psychology*, *102*, 151–158.

Warren, R.E. (1977). Time and the spread of activation in memory. *Journal of Experimental Psychology: Human Learning and Memory*, *3*, 458–466.

Young, A.W., Ellis, A.W., Flude, B.M., McWeeny, K.H., & Hay, D.C. (1986). Face–name interference. *Journal of Experimental Psychology: Human Perception and Performance*, *12*, 466–475.

4

# A spreading-activation theory of lemma retrieval in speaking*

Ardi Roelofs

*Nijmegen Institute for Cognition Research and Information Technology, University of Nijmegen, P.O. Box 9104, 6500 HE Nijmegen, Netherlands*

Roelofs, A., 1992. A spreading-activation theory of lemma retrieval in speaking. Cognition, 42: 107–142.

*This paper presents a spreading-activation theory of conceptually driven lemma retrieval – the first stage of lexical access in speaking, where lexical items specified with respect to meaning and syntactic properties are activated and selected. The mental lexicon is conceived of as a network consisting of concept, lemma, and word-form nodes and labelled links, with each lexical concept represented as an independent node. A lemma is retrieved by enhancing the activation level of the node representing the to-be-verbalized concept. This activation then spreads towards the lemma level, and the highest activated lemma node is selected. The theory resolves questions such as the hypernym problem (Levelt, 1989). Furthermore, a computer model that implements the theory is shown to be able to account for many basic findings on the time course of object naming, object categorization, and word categorization in the picture–word interference paradigm. In addition, non-trivial predictions regarding the time course of semantic facilitation for hypernyms, hyponyms, and cohyponyms are experimentally tested, and shown to be valid.*

## 1. Introduction

A central problem in speech production concerns the process of lexical access.

*The work reported in this paper is part of a PhD project supported by the Nijmegen Institute for Cognition Research and Information Technology and the Max-Planck-Institut für Psycholinguistik, Nijmegen. I am indebted to my promoters Pim Levelt and Gerard Kempen, and to Pieter Bison, Edwin Bos, Koen De Smedt, Ton Dijkstra, Henk Haarmann, Jörg Jescheniak, Jan Peter de Ruiter, Linda Wheeldon, and two anonymous reviewers for helpful comments on the manuscript. I also want to thank W.R. Glaser for letting me use his raw data, so that I could compute a statistical measure of it.

During normal conversation, a speaker retrieves just the right word for a concept to be verbally expressed, both *fast* – up to five words per second – and *accurately* – with less than one whole-word error per 2000 words (Levelt, 1989). This is an enormous achievement given the vastness of the mental lexicon; it is conjectured that a speaker has an active vocabulary of some 30 000 words (the number varies greatly from speaker to speaker). How is such efficient word retrieval accomplished by a speaker?

This paper presents a theory of the first stage of lexical access in speaking, called *lemma retrieval*, where lexical items specified with respect to meaning and syntactic properties are activated and selected (the second stage is word-form encoding and will not be addressed). To set the stage for the exposition of the theory, I will first discuss the role of lemma retrieval in speech production. Next, I will distinguish between computational decomposition and non-decomposition approaches to lemma retrieval, and point to an important class of retrieval (i.e., convergence) problems for the existing decomposition theories, supporting the non-decompositional approach taken in this paper. Finally, I will briefly describe the experimental paradigm that has been used in initial tests of the theory: the picture–word interference paradigm. In the remainder of the paper, the theory will be outlined, and tested by computer simulation and empirical experiment. My aim is to show that the proposed theory resolves the retrieval problems in a simple fashion, and that it can account – both qualitatively and quantitatively – for many basic empirical phenomena associated with conceptually driven naming.

## 1.1. Lemma retrieval in speech production

Psycholinguists usually hold that speech production involves three types of mental processes. First, speaking starts with *conceptualization* processes, specifying which concepts are to be expressed verbally. Second, *formulation* processes select appropriate words for these concepts, and build a representation of (a) the syntactic structure (in case of sentence production) and (b) the sound structure of the utterance. Third, *articulation* processes realize the latter as overt speech (cf. Bock, 1982, 1986; Dell, 1986; Garrett, 1975, 1988; Kempen, 1977; Kempen & Hoenkamp, 1987; Levelt, 1983; for a review of the processes underlying speaking see especially Levelt, 1989).

Lexical access is assumed to comprise two major steps: *lemma retrieval* and *word-form encoding* (cf. Bock, 1986; Butterworth, 1980, 1989; Dell, 1986; Fromkin, 1971; Garrett, 1975, 1976, 1980, 1988; Kempen, 1977; Kempen & Hoenkamp, 1987; Kempen & Huijbers, 1983; Levelt, 1983, 1989; Levelt & Maassen 1981; Levelt & Schriefers, 1987; Schriefers, 1990; Van Wijk & Kempen, 1987). Lemma retrieval is the activation and selection of a *lemma* (a term coined by Kempen & Huijbers, 1983) on the basis of conceptual information to be verbally expressed. The latter is called the *message* (Garrett, 1975; Levelt, 1989) or the interfacing representation – the representation that interfaces between thought and language (Bock, 1982). Lemmas represent the meaning and the syntactic properties of a word (see Levelt, 1989, for a detailed description). For instance, the lemma of the word *dog* specifies the conceptual conditions for the appropriate use of the word, and indicates, inter alia, that the word is a noun. Lemma retrieval is a crucial component of the syntactic encoding process. The building of a phrasal, clausal, or sentential structure (e.g., making the noun *dog* head of a noun phrase) requires the syntactic part of lemmas. Word-form encoding is the process by which an articulatory program for the word is constructed. This involves retrieving its morpheme(s) and speech segments, and linking them to categorically labelled slots in word-form frames (Dell, 1986; Garrett, 1975; Levelt, 1989; Shattuck-Hufnagel, 1979). For example, the syllable frame for *dog* is filled with the retrieved segments /d/, /ɔ/ and /g/. A final step in word-form encoding involves addressing stored syllable programs, which will control the articulatory movements (Levelt, 1989). Following Kempen and Huijbers (1983), the mental representation of word-form information will be referred to as the *lexeme*.

The assumption of two accessing steps, instead of one for the whole word, is supported by experimental findings on speech latencies and word-order preferences (e.g., Bock, 1986; Kempen & Huijbers, 1983; Levelt & Maassen, 1981; Levelt et al., 1991a; Schriefers, Meyer, & Levelt, 1990), tip-of-the-tongue studies (e.g., Brown & McNeill, 1966; Jones & Langford, 1987), speech-error data (e.g., Dell, 1986; Fromkin, 1971; Garrett, 1975, 1976, 1980, 1988), and data from aphasia (e.g., Butterworth, 1989; Saffran, Schwartz, & Marin, 1980). For an extensive discussion of whether lemma retrieval and word-form encoding are not only distinct, but also discrete (i.e., temporally nonoverlapping) processes, I refer to Dell and O'Seaghdha (1991) and Levelt et al. (1991b).

## 1.2. Decomposed retrieval, yes or no?

The process of lexical access has not received as much attention in the study of language production as it has in the study of language comprehension. Theories of lexical access in speaking primarily address the process of word-form encoding (e.g., Dell, 1986, 1988; Meyer, 1990; Shattuck-Hufnagel, 1979; Stemberger, 1985). Although typically some assumptions are made about lemma retrieval (e.g., Bock, 1982; Brown & McNeill, 1966; Butterworth, 1989; Fay & Cutler, 1977; Fodor, 1976; Garrett, 1982; Morton, 1969; Oldfield, 1966; Stemberger, 1985), only a few theories address this process in depth (Dell & O'Seaghdha, 1991; Goldman, 1975; Miller & Johnson-Laird, 1976; for an extensive review, see Levelt, 1989).

Theories of lemma retrieval can be divided into two broad classes: decompositional and non-decompositional. Decompositional theories claim that semantically complex words (i.e., words whose meaning can be further analysed into more elementary concepts) are retrieved on the basis of a *combination of primitive concepts* (e.g., Bock, 1982; Dell, 1986; Dell & Reich, 1981; Dell & O'Seaghdha, 1991; Goldman, 1975; Miller & Johnson-Laird, 1976; Morton, 1969; Stemberger, 1985). They argue, for example, that the lemma of *father* is retrieved on the basis of representations like MALE(X) and PARENT(X, Y). In contrast, non-decompositional theories (cf. Collins & Loftus, 1975; Fodor, 1976; Fodor, Fodor, & Garrett, 1975; Fodor, Garrett, Walker, & Parkes, 1980; Garrett, 1982; Kintsch, 1974) assume that an abstract representation FATHER(X, Y) is used to retrieve *father*, and that properties such as MALE(X) and PARENT(X, Y) are specified *outside* the message, in semantic memory.[1]

Whereas both decomposition and non-decomposition theories seem to be able to account for several major empirical facts on word meaning quite well (e.g., Collins & Loftus, 1975; Smith, Shoben, & Rips, 1974), at least one class of problems relevant to lemma retrieval seems to require a non-decompositional approach. When a concept has to be expressed, and the mental lexicon contains the appropriate word, precisely that word's lemma should be retrieved and no other (Levelt, 1989). But the retrieval procedures proposed by the existing decompositional theories fail to do so. *Hypernymy* and *word-to-phrase synonymy* are especially troublesome (Levelt & Schriefers, 1987; Levelt, 1989; Roelofs, in preparation). If the meaning of word *a* implies the meaning of word *b*, *b* is a *hypernym* of *a*, and *a* is a *hyponym* of *b* (Cruse, 1986; Lyons, 1977). When the conceptual conditions of a hyponym (e.g., *father*) are met, then those of its hypernyms (e.g., *parent*) are automatically satisfied as well. Therefore, in accessing a particular word, all its hypernyms should also be retrieved (Levelt, 1989). The existing decompositional theories cannot explain how the retrieval process converges on the appropriate lemma. Word-to-phrase synonymy poses similar problems. According to decompositional theories, utterances such as . . . *is a father* and . . . *is a male parent* will have one and the same underlying conceptual structure (Fodor, 1976). But how, then, does the retrieval mechanism know to select one lemma (in the former case) or several lemmas (in the latter case)?

For a theory without decomposition of lexical-concept representations, hypernymy and word-to-phrase synonymy pose no difficulties. MALE(X), PARENT(X, Y), and FATHER(X, Y) are computational primitives, and are made part of the message to retrieve, respectively, *male*, *parent*, and *father* (for

---

[1]The decomposition at issue here concerns the computational primitives of the speech production system at the message level. Computational primitives, such as FATHER(X, Y) in a non-decompositional approach, are not necessarily also developmentally primitive (i.e., a starting point for concept acquisition) or definitionally primitive (i.e., without a definition) (for a discussion, see Carey, 1982; Fodor, 1976, p. 152; Fodor et al., 1980, p. 313; Roelofs, in preparation).

the feasibility of syntactic encoding without lexical decomposition see, for example, De Smedt, 1990; Kempen & Hoenkamp, 1987).

### 1.3. Theory and experimental paradigm

Below, a spreading-activation theory will be proposed that is designed to handle conceptually driven lemma retrieval. Following Dell (1986), Dell and Reich (1981), Harley (1984), Stemberger (1985), and others, the mental lexicon is conceived of as a network. It is assumed to consist of (a) a conceptual stratum with concept nodes and links, (b) a syntactic stratum with lemma nodes and links, and (c) a word-form stratum with input-lexeme and output-lexeme nodes and links. To solve the convergence problems mentioned (and variants of them, see Roelofs, in preparation), I assume that conceptual component nodes are only *indirectly* linked to lemma nodes, via non-decomposed concept representations. Within the message, there is no lexical decomposition. This is in contrast to Dell, Stemberger, and others, and in line with the proposals by Collins and Loftus, and Fodor, Garrett, and colleagues. A lemma is retrieved by enhancing the activation level of the node of the to-be-verbalized concept (similar to giving it *signalling activation* in the theory of Dell, 1986). This activation then spreads towards the syntactic stratum, and the highest activated lemma node is selected.

The theory will be applied to empirical findings on object naming, object categorization, and word categorization (among the simplest forms of conceptually driven word retrieval), both informally and by computer simulation. The simulations concern the time course of lemma retrieval in the so-called *picture-word interference paradigm* (cf. Glaser & Düngelhoff, 1984; Glaser & Glaser, 1989; La Heij, 1988; Lupker, 1979; Rosinski, 1977; Schriefers et al., 1990; Smith & Magee, 1980). Subjects have to name pictured objects (e.g., they have to say *dog* to a pictured dog) and ignore so-called *distractor* words. A distractor word is a written word superimposed on the picture or a spoken word presented via headphones. The naming response is affected depending on, inter alia, the *temporal* relationship (the stimulus onset asynchrony or SOA) and the *content* relationship between picture and word. Usually, the distractor is presented just before (e.g., −400, −300, −200 or −100 ms), simultaneously with, or right after (e.g., +100, +200, +300, or +400 ms) picture onset, and is either semantically related to the pictured object (e.g., distractor *fish*, henceforth the REL condition) or semantically unrelated (e.g., distractor *tree*, henceforth the UNR condition). Alternatively, the subjects are asked to refer to the picture or to the word printed in the picture by producing a hypernym – called, respectively, picture categorization and word categorization. For example, they have to say *animal* to a depicted dog, while trying to ignore the word printed in the picture. Or they have to say *animal* to the word *dog* and ignore the picture. Typically, one observes semantic inhibition (i.e., naming latencies are slower for REL than for UNR) at SOA ∈ [−100, +100] for picture naming, semantic facilitation (i.e., naming latencies are faster for REL than for UNR) at SOA ∈ [−400, −100] for picture categorization, and even more semantic facilitation at SOA ∈ [−400, +200] for word categorization (Glaser & Düngelhoff, 1984; Glaser, this issue).

Testing the theory on the basis of object naming, object categorization, and word categorization may seem rather restrictive. However, to date, these tasks have provided the most detailed information on the time course of conceptually driven naming (alone or in combination with an auxiliary task; see Levelt et al., 1991a). For a discussion of the importance of time-course analyses in studying lexical access in speaking, I refer to Levelt (1989), Levelt et al. (1991a, 1991b), and Schriefers et al. (1990); for a discussion of the importance of SOA functions in testing a process model, see especially Vorberg (1985).

One might be inclined to argue that naming and categorization are not suitable testing grounds for a theory of lemma retrieval, because the syntactic properties of a word do not play a role in naming isolated objects. Could not a concept be directly mapped onto a word form, as is advocated by Collins and Loftus (1975) and many theorists in the field of picture-word processing (cf. Glaser & Glaser, 1989; Nelson, Reed, & McEvoy, 1977; Potter, 1979; Seymour, 1979; Smith & Magee, 1980; Snodgrass, 1984; Theios & Amrhein, 1989)? A central assumption in this paper is that, in naming and categorization, speakers cannot bypass lemma retrieval, just as they cannot simply retrieve but have to construct articulatory programs (cf. Dell, 1986; Levelt, 1989). Both lemma retrieval and word-form encoding are of primary use in the production of connected speech. Lemma retrieval makes available the syntactic properties of words for the syntactic encoding process. Word-form encoding enables a speaker to resyllabify words: to enhance the fluency of articulation, a speaker often combines neighbour words in the utterance, which leads to a syllabification of words that differs from the syllabification specified in the mental lexicon. If articulatory programs were ready-made wholes, then such resyllabification of words would not be possible (Levelt, 1989).

Thus, it is assumed that there is only a *single* route from word meaning to word form, instead of one via a lemma, taken during sentence production, and another one bypassing lemmas, taken in the production of single words (for empirical support see, for example, Kempen & Huijbers, 1983). Moreover, lemma retrieval is claimed to be responsible for the semantic effects in the picture–word interference paradigm (cf. Schriefers et al., 1990), and not word-form retrieval, as is claimed by Glaser and Glaser (1989), La Heij (1988), and La Heij, Happel, and Mulder (1990). In a picture–word interference experiment with spoken distractor words, Schriefers et al. (1990) obtained a lexical semantic effect at a negative SOA (−150 ms), and a word-form effect at later SOAs (viz., 0 and +150 ms). For example, the naming of a pictured dog was inhibited at the early SOA by the semantically related distractor *fish* compared to the semantically unrelated distractors *tree* and *doll*. By contrast, the naming response was facilitated at the later SOAs by the phonologically related distractor *doll* compared to the phonologically unrelated distractors *fish* and *tree*. If one assumes, for object naming, a direct mapping from concepts onto word forms, one should not get an early lexical semantic effect and a late word-form effect. Schriefers et al. provided evidence that the semantic effect was indeed *lexical*: in a recognition task without naming the effect disappeared, as is typical for Stroop(-like) effects (for a review see, for example, La Heij, 1988). If we assume that a concept is mapped onto a word form via a lemma then, initially, semantic competitors could be active at lemma level and cause the early *lexical* semantic effect whereas, later on, the word form of the target becomes encoded, causing the word-form effect. (For further evidence, see Levelt et al., 1991a.)

### 1.4. A brief overview of the remainder

The remainder of this paper is organized as follows. In section 2, I will explain the theoretical assumptions. In section 3, the theory is applied (a) to object naming, object categorization, and word categorization by computer simulation, and (b) informally, and very briefly, to speech errors (i.e., word blends, substitutions, and exchanges). In addressing naming and categorization, I will mainly concentrate on findings obtained by Glaser and Düngelhoff (1984) and Glaser and Glaser (1989), because their time-course studies are among the most comprehensive available in the literature: they include the speech latencies for picture naming, picture categorization, and word categorization with both picture distractors as well as word distractors over an extended range of SOAs (i.e., −400 up to +400 in steps of 100 ms). Slips of the tongue will be addressed, because they have been central in developing theories of speech production, and, therefore, may not be ignored by the new theory proposed. In section 4, some novel, and non-trivial, empirical predictions of the theory are tested in a new experiment, and shown to be valid. And finally, section 5 comprises a summary and conclusions.

## 2. Theoretical assumptions

### 2.1. General architecture

I will assume that in the naming of a perceptually given object (at least) four processing stages are involved (see Figure 1). First, there is the stage of object identification based on perceptual input (conceptual identification of the stimulus). The target representations of this processing level are concepts. Second, there is

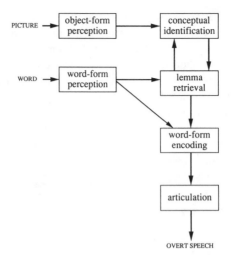

Figure 1.    *Stages of mental processing engaged in the picture–word interference paradigm. Boxes denote processing stages, and arrows indicate the relevant flow of information through the system.*

the stage of lemma retrieval (response selection). Third, there is the stage of word-form encoding (response programming). The fourth stage involves articulating the name of the object (response execution), resulting in overt speech. My theoretical claims will be restricted to the second stage. They will concern how a lemma is retrieved, *given* a concept to be verbalized.[2]

Figure 1 also indicates the mental stages assumed to be engaged in the picture–word interference paradigm; the perceptual stages that process pictures and words are shown on the left. The conceptual identification of an object involves mapping a representation of the object's form onto a concept, preferably a basic-level one (Jolicoeur, Gluck, & Kosslyn, 1984; Rosch, Mervis, Gray, Johnson, & Boyes-Braem, 1976). Categorization of the object (i.e., a dog as animal), then, requires the retrieval in memory of its superordinate (Jolicoeur et al., 1984). The information flow from conceptual identification to lemma retrieval and vice versa is continuous (for empirical support, see Humphreys, Riddoch, & Quinlan, 1988; Schriefers, 1990). No specific claims will be made about the other

---

[2]A theory of lemma retrieval presupposes that speakers have decided what to say, that is, have encoded a message, at the level of lexical concepts either in terms of conceptual components (in a decomposition view) or not (in a non-decomposition view). A theory of message encoding has to explain how speakers decide what to say, in particular, what kind of speech act to make and what conceptual content (i.e., conceptual component nodes or concept node) to include in the message to reach their communicative goals (for a review, see Levelt, 1989).

perceptual and production stages.[3] A written word will activate both its lemma and its articulatory program, as is shown by language comprehension research (cf. Rayner & Pollatsek, 1989) and the research on picture–word processing (cf. Nelson et al., 1977; Potter, 1979; Snodgrass, 1984). The existence of a direct route from written word to articulatory program is also indicated by interference effects obtained with the word pronunciation task. Glaser and Glaser (1989) and La Heij et al. (1990) observed an inhibitory effect of word distractors on reading a word aloud. For example, both *fish* and *tree* slowed down the reading aloud of *dog* (relative to pronouncing *dog* without a distractor word). However, there was no additional effect of semantic relatedness: *fish* (REL) did not cause *more* inhibition than *tree* (UNR). Furthermore, if instead of a distractor word a picture of a fish or tree was given, almost no effect on reading *dog* was observed (Glaser & Düngelhoff, 1984). These findings suggest that a word *can* be read aloud without explicitly selecting the word's lemma.

## 2.2. The memory structure of lexical entries

Figures 2 and 3 illustrate the main assumptions about the memory representation of a word. Figure 2 shows the structure of a single lemma. It illustrates the types of information linked to a lemma node: the sense of the word, its syntactic properties, and its input and output lexemes. Figure 3 shows a fragment of the lexical network representing the Dutch words *hond* (*dog*) and *dier* (*animal*).

First, at the conceptual stratum, there are *concept* nodes and conceptual links storing the meanings of the words. Each node represents a single concept, such as DOG, ANIMAL, and BARK (cf. Collins & Loftus, 1975; Fiksel & Bower, 1976; Norman & Rumelhart, 1975; Shastri, 1988). The links between the nodes are *labelled pointers*, which express a relationship between two concepts. For instance, the IS-A link indicates that DOG is a subtype of ANIMAL, and the CAN link specifies that a DOG can BARK. Links differ in their *accessibility* (cf. Collins & Loftus, 1975), which is determined by a weight (a positive real-valued number) on the link. Weights will be explained in the next section. Furthermore, outside the lexical network proper, there are nodes for the *visual form* of the objects

---

[3]In a network theory with labelled links (or pointers) such as proposed in this paper, a discreteness of stages may be obtained by limiting the availability of certain links for the spreading process. For example, if the link (pointer) between a lemma node and a word-form node only becomes available *upon* selection of the lemma node, then lemma retrieval and word-form encoding will be discrete (i.e., temporally non-overlapping) processes. In experimental studies of the time course of object naming, Levelt et al. (1991a) and Schriefers et al. (1990) obtained data fully compatible with a discreteness of lemma retrieval and word-form encoding. As already indicated, for an extensive discussion the reader might consult Dell and O'Seaghdha (1991) and Levelt et al. (1991b).

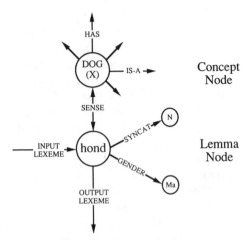

Figure 2.    *Structure of a lemma.*

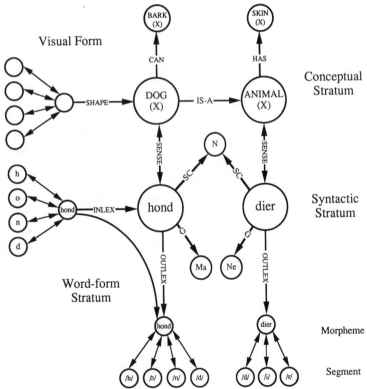

Figure 3.    *Fragment of the lexical network for the Dutch words* hond (dog) *and* dier (animal). *For an explanation, see text.*

denoted by the words. These form representations are involved in shape-based object identification.

Second, at the syntactic stratum, there are *lemma* nodes, and nodes and labelled links which correspond to the words' syntactic properties, such as gender (GENDER or G: Ne = neuter, Ma = masculine) and syntactic category (SYN-CAT or SC: N = noun). Third, at the word-form stratum, there are *input-lexeme* (INLEX) nodes and links for the orthography, and *output-lexeme* (OUTLEX) nodes and links for the morpho-phonological properties of the words in speaking. The output-lexeme part of the network is involved in word-form encoding (cf. Dell, 1986, 1988; Stemberger, 1985), and the input-lexeme part is involved in visual word-recognition (cf. McClelland & Rumelhart, 1981).

## 2.3. *The spreading of activation and the selection process*

Information is retrieved from the network by means of spreading activation (cf. Collins & Loftus, 1975; Dell, 1986). Activation is taken to be a positive real-valued quantity, spreading according to the equation

$$a(m, t + \Delta t) = a(m, t)(1 - d) + \sum_{n \in N} w(n, m)a(n, t) \qquad (1)$$

where $a(m, t)$ is the activation level of node $m$ at point in time $t$, $d$ is a decay rate $(0 < d < 1)$, and $\Delta t$ is the duration of a time step. The rightmost term denotes the amount of activation node $m$ receives between $t$ and $t + \Delta t$, where $a(n, t)$ is the output of neighbour node $n$ (the output of $n$ is equal to its level of activation), $N$ the set of direct neighbour nodes $n$ of $m$, and $w(n, m)$ the weight on the link between nodes $n$ and $m$. A weight determines the proportion of activation sent along the link.

In spontaneous speech, the retrieval of a lemma is a very simple process. The activation level of the node of the to-be-verbalized concept (*flagged* as being part of the message, as in the theory of Dell, 1986) is enhanced, followed by a spread of the activation from the conceptual stratum towards the syntactic stratum, and a selection of the highest activated lemma node.

In a picture–word interference experiment the selection is more complicated. The retrieval system must select the lemma activated by the picture, and prevent selection of the lemma activated by the distractor word. To solve this indexing problem I will assume, following Collins and Loftus (1975), that when activation spreads along the links of the network it leaves *activation tags* at each node reached, specifying the *source* of the activation (see also Charniak, 1983; Hendler, 1989; Quillian, 1967). So, in a picture–word interference experiment, there are picture tags and word tags. The lemma nodes that are permitted responses in the experiment receive a *flag* indicating that they are members of the response set. (In the experiments to be discussed, subjects studied a booklet showing the pictures and the names to be used, before the experiment began; I assume that during that period lemmas became flagged as permitted responses.) The determination of the response node is based on the *intersection* of the tag originating from the target source (e.g., the picture in picture naming) and a response-set flag on one of the lemma nodes. The node at which the intersection is established first will be the target lemma.[4]

I will assume that an intersection is by itself insufficient to trigger a response. The activation level of the target lemma node must also exceed that of the other nodes in the response set by some critical amount. Once this amount has been reached, the actual selection is a random event. Let $T$ denote time, let $s$ be the $s$th time step, $\Delta t$ the duration of a time step, and $t$ a particular moment in time, where $t = (s-1)\Delta t$, and $s = 1, 2, \ldots$ The probability that the target node $m$ will be selected at $t < T \leq t + \Delta t$ given that it has not been selected at $T \leq t$ (and provided that an intersection has been established and the critical amount has been reached) is given by the ratio (cf. Luce, 1959)

$$p(\text{selection } m \text{ at } t < T \leq t + \Delta t \,|\, \neg \text{ selection } m \text{ at } T \leq t)$$

$$= a(m, t) \bigg/ \sum_{e \in Exp} a(e, t) \tag{2}$$

The index $e$ ranges over the lemma nodes of all the targets and distractors occurring in an experiment, irrespective of response-set membership. Thus, the probability of actually selecting the target lemma node depends on the activation state of other salient lemma nodes in the mental lexicon. The selection ratio, hereafter referred to as the *Luce ratio*, equals the hazard rate $h(s)$ of the process of lemma retrieval at time step $s$ (cf. Luce, 1986; McGill, 1963; Townsend & Ashby, 1983). It is the probability that the retrieval of lemma $m$ is completed at $t < T \leq t + \Delta t$ given that it is not already completed. When no intersection has been established and/or the critical difference has not been exceeded, then $h(s) = 0$.

---

[4]If there are no a priori restrictions on the responses, the intersection mechanism might work as follows. Following Collins and Loftus (1975), assume that a person can diffusely activate (prepare) an entire stratum of the network, here the syntactic stratum. If the resulting activation tags do not spread but stay at their nodes (which makes sense, because they come from an unspecific source of activation), the target lemma node could be determined by the intersection of the target-source tag (picture or word) and one of these tags.

## 3. Application of the theory

### 3.1. *Picture naming, picture categorization, and word categorization*

In this section, I will show that the proposed theory can account for many empirical findings relevant to conceptually driven lemma retrieval. The findings are from studies of object naming, object categorization, and word categorization. First, I will briefly describe a computer model embodying the main theoretical assumptions. Next, I will present results from computer simulations of the time course (i.e., the SOA functions) of picture naming with a word distractor, picture categorization with a word distractor, and word categorization with a picture distractor.

In each simulation the procedure was as follows. For a particular experimental condition the expected lemma retrieval time $E(T)$ was computed on the basis of the activation equation (Equation 1), the selection ratio (Equation 2), and

$$E(T) = \sum_{s=1}^{\infty} h(s) \left\{ \prod_{j=0}^{s-1} [1 - h(j)] \right\} s \, \Delta t \tag{3}$$

where $h(s)$ is the hazard rate function of lemma retrieval in the model, $h(0) = 0$, and $1 - h(s)$ the probability that $m$ is not selected at time step $s$ given that it has not already been selected. The derivation of the formula for $E(T)$ is given in the Appendix.

Figure 4 illustrates the network configuration used in the simulations. The

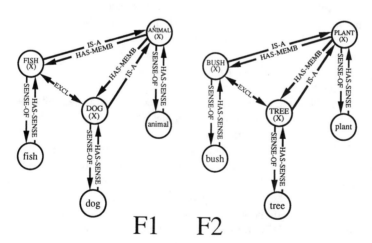

Figure 4. *Illustration of the network configuration used in the simulations. Two unrelated semantic fields (F1 and F2), each consisting of three concept nodes with their lemma nodes.*

network was kept as simple as possible. (Larger networks consisting of, for example, 50 or 100 nodes gave equivalent simulation results.) There were two different semantic fields, each consisting of a superordinate, two subordinates, and their lemma nodes. This configuration realized all the hypernymy (superordinate→ subordinate), hyponymy (subordinate→ superordinate), and cohyponymy (subordinate→ subordinate) relationships needed. There was an IS-A link (and vice versa a HAS-MEMBER link) between a subordinate and superordinate, and an EXCLUDES link between two mutually exclusive subordinates within a semantic field (cf. Collins & Loftus, 1975).

The presentation of a picture and a word was simulated by adding external input of size *exin*, representing the output of the perceptual stages, to the corresponding concept node and lemma node in the network. For example, in simulating picture naming with a word distractor, the picture input was assigned to DOG(X), and the distractor-word input was assigned to the lemma node of either *fish* (REL) or *tree* (UNR). Signalling activation of size *exin* (enhancing the activation level of the to-be-verbalized concept) was given as soon as the target-source tag arrived at the target concept (e.g., DOG(X) in picture naming, or ANIMAL(X) in picture categorization and word categorization). Signalling activation was given until the selection of a lemma node. An activation tag crossed a link in *tag_speed* ms. Distractor input was given to the network for *du* ms. The SOA was simulated by presenting the distractor input simultaneously with the target input, or at the appropriate number of time steps before or after the onset of the target input. The decay rate of each node in the lexical network was equal to *d*. The spreading rate within the semantic network was *sem_rate*, that is, all conceptual weights were identical. The spreading rate from concept to lemma node and vice versa was *lem_rate*. The critical difference for selection was of size *cd*. The simulations were run using time steps $\Delta t$ of 25 ms. (Steps of, for example, 5 or 1 ms gave equivalent simulation results.) For details of the computer simulations, I refer to Roelofs (in preparation).

The values of the seven model parameters described above (used in all simulations reported in this paper) were obtained by maximizing the fit between a restricted number of predictions of the model and corresponding findings in the literature. For the parameter estimations, the data obtained by Glaser and Düngelhoff (1984) were taken, because these data embody several of the most important findings on the time course of picture–word interference (cf. Cohen, Dunbar, & McClelland, 1990; MacLeod, 1991; Phaf, Van der Heijden, & Hudson, 1990; Rayner & Springer, 1986). In particular, the estimates were obtained by minimizing the deviation between the predicted and empirically obtained semantic effects (REL minus UNR) for each SOA (ranging from −400 to +400 in steps of 100 ms) for three tasks: picture naming with word distractor, picture categorization with word distractor, and word categorization with picture distractor. The fit was maximized for the tasks simultaneously, employing the well-known optimization technique proposed by Nelder and Mead (1965). The parameter values thus obtained were the following:

*tag_speed*  25 [ms per link]
*sem_rate*   0.0101 [proportion per ms]
*lem_rate*   0.0074 [proportion per ms]
*d*          0.0240 [proportion per ms]
*exin*       0.1965 [activation unit per ms]
$du_{pnam}$   75 [ms]              $du_{pcat}$ 200 [ms]              $du_{wcat}$ 125 [ms]
$cd_{pnam}$   3.6 [activation unit] $cd_{pcat}$ 3.2 [activation unit] $cd_{wcat}$ 3.0 [activation unit]

where $du_{pnam}$, $du_{pcat}$, and $du_{wcat}$ are the distractor durations, and $cd_{pnam}$, $cd_{pcat}$, and $cd_{wcat}$ the critical differences for picture naming, picture categorization, and word categorization, respectively. So, five parameters were kept constant across the tasks, while two parameters were allowed to vary. The $du$ and $cd$ were treated as free parameters for the purpose of fine-tuning only. Although the parameter values play a role in the quantitative fit between model data and real data, the explanations of the empirical findings do not depend on them. These findings will be accounted for in *structural* terms, such as the number of links to be traversed, the presence of response-set flags, and so forth.

To evaluate the fit between the simulated data and the real data (those of Glaser & Düngelhoff, 1984), a $\chi^2$ statistic was computed. (All statistics for fits reported in this paper are corrected for the number of estimated parameters.) Except for two data-points (to be discussed below), there was no statistical difference between model and data ($\chi^2$ with $df = 14$ was 23.4, $p > .05$). So, as far as the similarity in SOA functions is concerned, no real reason exists to reject the model.

### 3.1.1. Picture naming with word distractor

*Basic findings.* The effect on naming a pictured object (e.g., saying *dog* to a dog) of the presentation of distractor words (e.g., *fish* or *tree*) that are the name of other pictures in the experiment is to increase naming latencies. This increase is greater when the distractor word is semantically related to the picture name (*fish*) than when it is unrelated (*tree*): a semantic inhibition effect. Semantic inhibition is observed when the distractor is displayed between 100 ms before and 100 ms after picture onset. Figure 5 shows the amount of inhibition caused by a semantically related distractor compared to an unrelated one as a function of SOA. The empirical data are from Glaser and Düngelhoff (1984, Experiment 1; cf. Guttentag & Haith, 1978, for SOA = 0). Depicted (here and in all figures below) is the mean retrieval time with related distractors, REL, minus the mean retrieval time

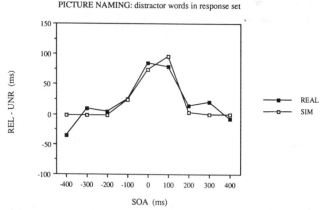

Figure 5.    *Mean latency difference (in ms) between REL and UNR per SOA: real and simulated data (real data are from Glaser & Düngelhoff, 1984, Experiment 1). A positive difference denotes semantic inhibition.*

with unrelated distractors, UNR. Thus, negative values indicate semantic facilitation, and positive values indicate semantic inhibition.

The theory explains the semantic inhibition as follows. The inhibition is the outcome of a *trade-off* between the priming of the distractor lemma node by the picture and the priming of the target lemma node by the distractor word. In the unrelated condition, the distractor word will activate its lemma node but not the target lemma node, and the picture will activate the target lemma node but not the distractor lemma node. In the related condition, however, the distractor word will activate its lemma node and also the target lemma node, and the picture will activate the target lemma node and also the distractor lemma node. Because the path from picture to distractor lemma node (DOG(X)→FISH(X)→fish) is shorter than from distractor word to target lemma node (fish→FISH(X)→ DOG(X)→dog), the picture will prime the distractor lemma node more than the distractor word will prime the target lemma node (see Figure 4). Furthermore, the target concept (i.e., DOG(X)) gets signalling activation, in addition to the picture input, making it a stronger source of activation than the distractor word. As a result, semantic inhibition will occur.

*Picture distractor.* According to the above explanation, similar SOA functions should occur if, instead of a distractor word, a picture distractor is given. However, now the signalling activation will be the only factor in the trade-off; the paths from distractor picture to target lemma node and from target picture to distractor lemma node will be of the same length (e.g., FISH(X)→ DOG(X)→dog and DOG(X)→FISH(X)→fish, respectively). Glaser and

Glaser (1989, Experiment 6) observed similar SOA functions for picture distractors.[5]

I will now show how the theory deals with findings that are considered to be problematic for network accounts of picture–word interference (Lupker, 1979, Experiments 1–3, utilizing SOA = 0).

*Same-category associations.* Lupker obtained a similar interference effect from *same-category* distractors that were bidirectional associates or non-associates of the name of the picture (e.g., from respectively *foot* and *ankle* printed in a pictured hand). The associative relatedness of category members is often seen in terms of the strength of the connection between their concept nodes (but see Levelt, 1989), where the connection between associated members is assumed to be stronger than between non-associated ones (cf. Collins & Loftus, 1975). In the simulation, increasing the bidirectional connection strength for associates from $1.0 \times sem\_rate$ to, for instance, $3.0 \times sem\_rate$ resulted in similar effects for associates (*foot*) and non-associates (*ankle*) at SOA = 0, complying with the results obtained by Lupker. Increasing the connection strength in both directions leaves the path from picture to distractor lemma node and from distractor word to target lemma node virtually intact.

*Different-category associations.* Lupker also obtained no difference in interference effect between *different-category* distractors that were associates or non-associates of the picture's name (e.g., respectively *cheese* and *hand* printed in a pictured mouse). An associative relationship between words from different semantic fields may correspond to a strong labelled (i.e., a conceptually mediated) or unlabelled link between their concept nodes. In Lupker's experiment, the connections were probably labelled, because they concerned links between two semantic fields connected by the fact that a concept in one field specified a property of a concept in the other field (e.g., a *mouse* likes *cheese*). Simulation of Lupker's experiment (with a connection strength of, for example, $3.0 \times sem\_rate$ for the associates) showed no difference between the associates (*cheese*) and non-associates (*hand*) at SOA = 0, just as Lupker observed.

*Typicality.* Finally, Lupker observed no difference in effect between distractors denoting typical category members and distractors denoting atypical ones (e.g., respectively distractor *arm* versus *lip* printed in a pictured foot). Typicality is often seen in terms of the connection strength between subordinates and superordi-

---

[5]In the experiment, subjects were instructed to name either the first or the second picture presented. Correspondingly, in the theory, the relevant intersection in determining the target lemma node involves either the first or the second picture tag.

nates, where typical subordinates have a stronger connection to the superordinate than atypical ones (cf. Collins & Loftus, 1975). In the simulation, reducing the connection strength between subordinate and superordinate from $1.0 \times sem\_rate$ to, for instance, $0.0001 \times sem\_rate$ for an atypical member, resulted in no difference between distractors denoting typical (*arm*) and distractors denoting atypical category members (*lip*) at SOA = 0, just as Lupker found. Decreasing the connection strength between a subordinate and its superordinate leaves the path from picture to distractor lemma node and from distractor word to target lemma node intact.

In summary, although varying the strength of connections in the network will affect the amount of activation that is sent along a link (and consequently, might explain effects of associative relatedness and typicality on the search of semantic memory, as proposed, for example, by Collins & Loftus, 1975), such a manipulation does not need to result in differences between *distractors* in a picture–word interference experiment.

### 3.1.2. Picture categorization with word distractor

*Basic findings.* When subjects have to name pictured objects using a hypernym (and the hypernyms of the distractors are part of the response set), for instance, they have to say *animal* instead of *dog* to a pictured dog, one obtains semantic facilitation at negative SOAs. A related distractor word (*dog* or *fish*) will reduce naming latencies compared to an unrelated distractor word (*tree*). Figure 6 shows the amount of facilitation caused by a semantically related distractor word relative to an unrelated one as a function of SOA. The empirical data are again from

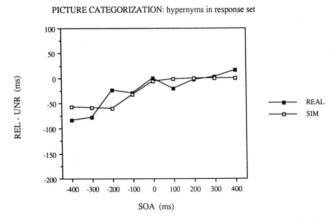

Figure 6.    *Mean latency difference (in ms) between REL and UNR per SOA: real and simulated data (real data are from Glaser & Düngelhoff, 1984, Experiment 2). A negative difference denotes semantic facilitation.*

Glaser and Düngelhoff (1984, Experiment 2; cf. Lupker & Katz, 1981, for SOA = 0).

As can be seen, the model overestimates the amount of facilitation at SOA = −200. (Decreasing, for example, the distractor duration *du* from 200 ms to 125 ms, reduces the amount of facilitation at SOA = −200 by half, but also diminishes the facilitation at the SOAs of −400 and −300.) Importantly, however, the model displays an increase in facilitation for the negative SOAs: a characteristic of the real data.

The theory explains the semantic facilitation as follows. In a categorization task, the lemma nodes of the hypernyms (e.g., *animal*, *plant*) will receive a response-set flag. If the distractor is a related hyponym (*fish* or *dog* in a pictured dog), the lemma node of the target hypernym (*animal*) will be primed by the distractor word via the conceptual network. However, when the distractor word is an unrelated hyponym (e.g., *tree*), the wrong hypernym node will be primed, in particular, the lemma node of the hypernym of the distractor word (*plant*), and not the lemma node of the hypernym of the name of the picture (*animal*). Therefore, one will observe facilitation for semantically related distractors compared to unrelated ones.

*Picture distractor.* Similar SOA functions are predicted if instead of a distractor word a picture distractor is given (e.g., a pictured fish or dog, REL; or tree, UNR). However, now distractors identical to the target (e.g., a picture of a dog repeated; once as distractor and once as target) should lead to more facilitation than distractors that depict other semantically related objects (e.g., a pictured fish as distractor for a pictured dog), due to priming at the object-form perception stage (see Figures 1 and 3). This is precisely what Glaser and Glaser (1989, Experiment 6) observed (cf. Flores D'Arcais & Schreuder, 1987).

*Comparison of picture naming and picture categorization.* According to the theory, picture categorization will take longer than picture naming, due to the difference in path length. In picture categorization, the target-source tag has to cross two links (e.g., DOG(X)→ ANIMAL(X)→ animal), whereas in picture naming it has to cross only a single link (DOG(X)→ dog). This corresponds to what is observed empirically (e.g., Glaser & Düngelhoff, 1984; Glaser & Glaser, 1989; Irwin & Lupker, 1983; Jolicoeur et al., 1984; Smith & Magee, 1980).

### 3.1.3. Word categorization with picture distractor

*Basic findings.* When subjects have to produce the hypernym of words printed in a picture (and hypernyms of the names of the distractor pictures are part of the response set), for instance, they have to say *animal* to the word *dog* printed in a picture of a dog or fish (related distractor, REL), or tree (unrelated distractor,

UNR), one obtains a great amount of semantic facilitation up to an SOA of +200 ms. A related distractor (picture of a dog or fish) will enormously decrease naming latencies compared to an unrelated distractor (picture of a tree). Figure 7 shows the amount of facilitation caused by a semantically related distractor picture relative to an unrelated one as a function of SOA. The empirical data are from Glaser and Düngelhoff (1984, Experiment 2).

As can be seen, the model underestimates the amount of facilitation at SOA = +200. Importantly, however, the model captures the main characteristics of the real data.

The semantic facilitation effect in word categorization can be explained in the same way as the same effect in picture categorization. However, we must also explain why the facilitation for word categorization is greater than for picture categorization. According to the theory, there are two reasons for this difference. First, picture distractors have more direct access (a shorter path) to the lemma nodes of the hypernyms (both the wrong one in the unrelated condition and the right one in the related condition) than distractor words. For example, in the unrelated condition, the path for a picture distractor will be

TREE(X)→PLANT(X)→plant (wrong hypernym via two links),

and the path for a word distractor will be

tree→TREE(X)→PLANT(X)→plant (wrong hypernym via three links).

Therefore, the wrong hypernym will be primed more by a picture distractor during word categorization than by a word distractor during picture categorization. In the related condition, the path for a picture distractor will be

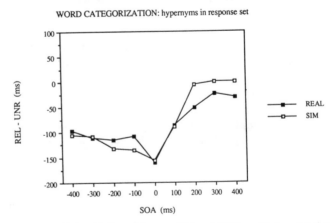

WORD CATEGORIZATION: hypernyms in response set

Figure 7.    *Mean latency difference (in ms) between REL and UNR per SOA: real and simulated data (real data are from Glaser & Düngelhoff, 1984, Experiment 2). A negative difference denotes semantic facilitation.*

FISH(X) → ANIMAL(X) → animal (right hypernym via two links),

and the path for a word distractor will be

fish → FISH(X) → ANIMAL(X) → animal (right hypernym via three links).

Therefore, the right hypernym will be primed more by a picture distractor during word categorization than by a word distractor during picture categorization. Consequently, the difference between REL and UNR will be larger for word categorization than for picture categorization. Second, the picture targets will activate the target lemma node in picture categorization more than the word targets will activate the target lemma node in word categorization. This is also due to the difference in path lengths. For example, the target path for picture categorization will be DOG(X) → ANIMAL(X) → animal (two links), and for word categorization dog → DOG(X) → ANIMAL(X) → animal (three links). Thus, word categorization will benefit more from a related hyponym than picture categorization.

*Word distractor.* Similar SOA functions are again predicted if instead of a picture distractor a word distractor is given. However, now distractors identical to the target (e.g., *dog* repeated; occurring once as distractor and once as target) should cause more facilitation than other semantically related ones (e.g., *fish* as distractor for *dog*), due to priming of input lexemes at the word-form perception stage (see Figures 1 and 3; cf. Rayner & Pollatsek, 1989). This is precisely what Glaser and Glaser (1989, Experiment 6) found.

*Comparison of picture categorization and word categorization.* The theory also predicts that word categorization will take longer than picture categorization, due to the difference in path length. In word categorization, the target-source tag has to cross three links (e.g., dog → DOG(X) → ANIMAL(X) → animal), whereas in picture categorization it has to cross only two links (DOG(X) → ANIMAL(X) → animal). When I ran the simulation without distractors, word categorization took, on average, 88 ms longer than picture categorization. In their neutral conditions (distractor xxxxxx) Glaser and Düngelhoff (1984) and Glaser and Glaser (1989) obtained differences (means across SOAs) of 100 and 95 ms, respectively (cf. Irwin & Lupker, 1983).

### 3.1.4. Summary of the major results

Above, I have shown that the theory can explain: (a) the semantic inhibition at SOA ∈ [−100, +100] by word and picture distractors in picture naming, and the absence of an effect of the distractor's typicality and bidirectional associative relatedness; (b) the semantic facilitation at SOA ∈ [−400, −100] by word and picture distractors in picture categorization, and the increase of the facilitation by picture repetition; (c) the huge amount of semantic facilitation at SOA $\in [-400,$ $+200]$ by word and picture distractors in word categorization, and the increase of the facilitation by word repetition. Furthermore, the theory explains the relative processing times for picture naming, picture categorization, and word categorization.

## 3.2. Speech errors: Blends, substitutions, and exchanges

In the simulation of a picture–word interference experiment, the right lemma will be selected due to the model's intersection mechanism. Nevertheless, the model allows for retrieval errors such as substitutions (e.g., in naming a pictured dog with the word *fish* superimposed, a subject might say *fish* instead of *dog*). These errors will occur if, for example, due to a lapse of attention, the selection is based on an irrelevant intersection (e.g., involving the word tag in picture naming).

The analysis of slips of the tongue occurring in spontaneous speech has been central in the development of theories of speech production (cf. Dell, 1986; Fromkin, 1971; Garrett, 1975, 1976). For instance, speech errors provide evidence for the distinction between lemma retrieval and word-form encoding. If one assumes that lemma retrieval takes place during syntactic encoding and that the retrieval of morphemes and speech segments takes place during the building of the utterance's sound structure, then one can explain the distributional properties of word and sound exchanges. Examples (taken from Dell, 1986) are *writing a mother to my letter* and *flow snurries* (for *snow flurries*). Word exchanges typically occur between items of the same syntactic category and across phrase boundaries (the lemmas of the nouns *letter* and *mother* are linked to each other's phrasal slots), while sound exchanges typically do not respect syntactic category and stay within a phrase (the consonant clusters /fl/ and /sn/ are linked to each other's form slots). The latter also holds for stem exchanges (morpheme errors). For example, in *slicely thinned* (for *thinly sliced*, taken from Dell, 1986), the stems of an adjective (*thin*) and a verb (*slice*) trade places.

Although a quantitative treatment of lemma retrieval failure in spontaneous speech (e.g., Dell's account of errors in word-form encoding) is not within the scope of the theory at its present level of development, a qualitative account is possible and will be given below. For an extensive treatment of errors in word selection, I refer to Dell (1986), Garrett (1980, 1988), Harley (1984), Levelt (1989), and Stemberger (1985), among others. (For reviews of speech errors see, for example, Cutler, 1982; Fromkin, 1973).

*Word blends* (e.g., a speaker says *it has a pretty nice flaste*, fusing *flavour* and *taste*, from Stemberger, 1985) typically involve semantically related words of the same syntactic category. Word blends might occur when two lemma nodes are activated to an equal level, and both get selected and encoded as one word form. That is, they may arise when the selection criterion in spontaneous speech (i.e., select the highest activated lemma node of the appropriate syntactic category) is satisfied simultaneously by two lemma nodes. Blends of semantically related words may reflect an indecision on the side of the speaker in encoding the message: two concept nodes that constitute alternative ways of conveying the same message are used to retrieve their lemma nodes, but there is only a single syntactic slot to fill. This would explain why these blends mostly involve near-synonyms, and why antonym blends are highly exceptional.

*Word substitutions* (e.g., a speaker says *don't burn your toes*, but meant to say *fingers*, from Fromkin, 1973) mostly involve words with a semantic and/or associative relationship to the intended word, to another word in the utterance under construction, or to a distractor in the environment (i.e., an object, word, or thought). The substituting word is virtually always of the same syntactic category as the intended one. A substitution might occur when, due to priming via a strong conceptual and/or associative link in the lexical network, a lemma node other than the target satisfies the selection criterion (i.e., has become the highest activated lemma node of the appropriate syntactic category), and is selected.

In *word exchanges* (e.g., a speaker says *a wife for his job*, interchanging *job* and *wife*, from Fromkin, 1973) two exchanged words typically lack a semantic and/or associative relationship, suggesting an aetiology different from substitutions. The words involved are mostly of the same syntactic category (though not as often as substitutions). Exchanges might occur when two to-be-verbalized concepts in the message simultaneously retrieve their lemma nodes, and the nodes get erroneously linked to each other's syntactic slot.

## 4. Experimental test of predictions

In this section, the theory is tested empirically on a new set of data. The experiment tests a prediction of the theory that already seems to be refuted by the empirical evidence in the literature. The prediction concerns the semantic effect in picture naming of hypernym, hyponym, and cohyponym distractors *that are not part of the response set*. For instance, a subject has to say *dog* to a pictured dog, where the distractor is the related hypernym *animal*, the related hyponym *dachshund*, or the related cohyponym *fish* (now not in the response set); or the distractor is the hypernym, hyponym, or cohyponym of the name of another picture, for instance, *plant*, *oak*, and *bush* (picture of a tree). The theory predicts semantic *facilitation* for these distractor words at negative SOAs. When a subject has to name a picture of a dog, and *animal*, *dachshund*, or *fish* is superimposed, the distractor will prime the target lemma node (of *dog*), but will not be a competitor itself, because it is not part of the response set. In contrast, when *plant, oak,* or *bush* is in the picture, there will be no priming of the lemma node of the target *dog*, but priming of a competitor lemma node in the response set: the node of *tree* (the name of another picture). Thus, semantic facilitation is to be expected for hypernyms, hyponyms, and cohyponyms alike. The prediction of semantic facilitation by the theory is *non-trivial*, because evidence against it already seems to exist: La Heij (1988), Lupker (1979), Schriefers et al. (1990), and others, obtained semantic *inhibition* for distractor words (i.e., cohyponyms) *not in the response set*. To anticipate the results of the current experiment: the prediction by the theory will be confirmed. Indeed, semantic facilitation will be found. Moreover, it will be shown – informally and by computer simulation – that the theory can resolve this paradoxical situation.

In the experiment, SOAs of −100, 0, and +100 ms will be used, because semantic *inhibition* by distractors on picture naming typically occurs at SOAs from −100 ms to +100 ms. Therefore, the prediction of *facilitation*, by the theory, receives its strongest test at these SOAs. The simulation predicts a semantic facilitation of about 25 ms for SOA = −100, and no effect for SOA = 0 and SOA = +100. To simulate related and unrelated hyponyms of hyponyms (e.g., *dachshund* and *oak*), the network used previously (see Figure 4) was expanded by attaching extra concept nodes, DACHSHUND(X) and OAK(X), to DOG(X) and TREE(X), and extra lemma nodes, for *dachshund* and *oak*, to DACH-SHUND(X) and OAK(X), respectively.

## 4.1. Method

*Subjects.* Eighteen native speakers of Dutch, from the subject pool of the Max-Planck-Institut für Psycholinguistik (Nijmegen), served as subjects in the experiment. They received Dfl. 8.50 for their participation.

*Materials.* Nine highly familiar objects were used as target items: dog, tree, car, knife, house, apple, chair, hammer, and coat. The pictures of the objects satisfied the following criteria: (1) subjects spontaneously named the pictures with the intended names, for example, *hond* (*dog*), *boom* (*tree*), *auto* (*car*), and so forth; (2) subjects considered the intended hypernym and hyponym of the target name to be appropriate labels for the pictures; for example, *voertuig* (*vehicle*) and *jeep* (*jeep*) were considered to be plausible names for the depicted car, but the intended cohyponym *tractor* (*tractor*) not; (3) the hypernym, hyponym, and cohyponym consisted of a single word; for example, *moker* (*sledge*) would be appropriate, but *Engelse sleutel* (*adjustable spanner*) not; (4) the hypernym, hyponym, and cohyponym did not contain the name of the target word as a proper part; for example, *keukenstoel* (*kitchen chair*) as a hyponym of *stoel* (*chair*) would not be suitable, whereas *troon* (*throne*) would; (5) the hypernym, hyponym, and cohyponym did not share initial letter(s) with the target word to prevent orthographic priming (cf. Rayner & Springer, 1986).

The nine pictures were selected from a set of 19 candidate pictures. These 19 pictures were presented to ten subjects (who did not participate in the actual experiment) with the instruction to name the depicted object. If subjects spontaneously gave the intended name, they were asked whether the hypernym, hyponym, and cohyponym were also suitable names for the pictured object. For nine selected pictures, all subjects spontaneously gave the correct name, and agreed on the appropriateness of the hypernym and hyponym, and on the inappropriateness of the cohyponym. Table 1 lists the experimental stimuli, for each of the nine target picture names, the distractor hypernym (SUPER/REL),

Table 1. *Materials. See text for explanation*

| Distractor | Picture name | | | | |
|---|---|---|---|---|---|
| | **auto** | **hond** | **boom** | **mes** | **huis** |
| SUPER/REL | voertuig | dier | plant | wapen | gebouw |
| COORD/REL | tractor | poes | struik | zwaard | flat |
| SUBOR/REL | jeep | tekkel | eik | dolk | bungalow |
| SUPER/UNR | plant | wapen | gebouw | fruit | meubel |
| COORD/UNR | flat | banaan | kast | trui | zaag |
| SUBOR/UNR | dolk | troon | goudreinet | bungalow | moker |
| CONTR | xxxxxx | xxxxxx | xxxxxx | xxxxxx | xxxxxx |
| | **appel** | **stoel** | **hamer** | **jas** | |
| SUPER/REL | fruit | meubel | gereedschap | kleding | |
| COORD/REL | banaan | kast | zaag | trui | |
| SUBOR/REL | goudreinet | troon | moker | colbert | |
| SUPER/UNR | gereedschap | kleding | voertuig | dier | |
| COORD/UNR | tractor | poes | struik | zwaard | |
| SUBOR/UNR | colbert | jeep | tekkel | eik | |
| CONTR | xxxxxx | xxxxxx | xxxxxx | xxxxxx | |

*English translation*

| Distractor | Picture name | | | | |
|---|---|---|---|---|---|
| | **car** | **dog** | **tree** | **knife** | **house** |
| SUPER/REL | vehicle | animal | plant | weapon | building |
| COORD/REL | tractor | puss | bush | sword | flat |
| SUBOR/REL | jeep | dachshund | oak | dagger | bungalow |
| SUPER/UNR | plant | weapon | building | fruit | furniture |
| COORD/UNR | flat | banana | cabinet | jumper | saw |
| SUBOR/UNR | dagger | throne | golden rennet | bungalow | sledge |
| CONTR | xxxxxx | xxxxxx | xxxxxx | xxxxxx | xxxxxx |
| | **apple** | **chair** | **hammer** | **coat** | |
| SUPER/REL | fruit | furniture | tool | clothes | |
| COORD/REL | banana | cabinet | saw | jumper | |
| SUBOR/REL | golden rennet | throne | sledge | jacket | |
| SUPER/UNR | tool | clothes | vehicle | animal | |
| COORD/UNR | tractor | puss | bush | sword | |
| SUBOR/UNR | jacket | jeep | dachshund | oak | |
| CONTR | xxxxxx | xxxxxx | xxxxxx | xxxxxx | |

hyponym (SUBOR/REL), and cohyponym (COORD/REL). The labels will be explained below.

*Design.* There were two crossed within-subjects factors. The first factor was SOA with three levels: the distractor was exposed *before* picture onset by 100 ms, *simultaneously with* the picture, or *after* picture onset by 100 ms. The second factor was distractor type with seven levels: SUPER/REL (name of a related superordinate or hypernym), SUBOR/REL (name of a related subordinate or hyponym), COORD/REL (name of a related coordinate or cohyponym), SUPER/UNR (name of an unrelated superordinate), SUBOR/UNR (name of an unrelated subordinate), COORD/UNR (name of an unrelated coordinate), and CONTROL. In the SUPER/REL, SUBOR/REL, and COORD/REL condition a picture was combined with, respectively, its hypernym, hyponym, or cohyponym. In the SUPER/UNR, SUBOR/UNR, and COORD/UNR condition the distractor was, respectively, the hypernym, hyponym, or cohyponym of the name of one of the other pictures. In the CONTROL condition the distractor consisted of a row of six x's (mean length of the distractor words). By taking the difference between the means of SUPER/REL and SUPER/UNR, SUBOR/REL and SUBOR/UNR, and COORD/REL and COORD/UNR one gets the semantic effect of, respectively, hypernymy, hyponymy, and cohyponymy. By taking difference scores, each distractor word serves as its own control. The CONTROL condition was included as a safeguard. If no difference between REL and UNR for all levels of abstraction and all SOAs would be found (in several SOA = 0 pilots conducted in preparation of this experiment, this was indeed the case), the CONTROL condition could be used as a check for whether or not this absence is due to an ability of the subjects to ignore the distractors. Normally, for the SOAs involved, presenting a word (either REL or UNR) as a distractor results in slower response latencies than presenting a string of x's (cf. Glaser & Düngelhoff, 1984).

Three different lists of picture–word stimuli were created (L1, L2, and L3). A list consisted of 63 picture–word combinations (7 distractors each of a different distractor type and 9 pictures) randomly ordered with the following restrictions: no particular picture or word occurred in two consecutive trials; target and distractor name never shared initial phonemes; the distractor in one trial and the target of the next trial were never semantically related, and vice versa, nor were the distractors in two consecutive trials of the same abstraction level (e.g., both subordinates). Within a list, every distractor word appeared once in the REL condition, and once in the UNR condition. Picture–word pairing was constant across lists; for the pairing, see Table 1. The lists (L1, L2, L3) were presented to each subject in constant-SOA blocks (SOA is −100, 0, or +100 ms), each list combined with a different SOA. The assignment of levels of SOA and lists to blocks (first, second, third) was counterbalanced across subjects.

*Apparatus.* The pictures were drawn by hand, then digitized using a Hewlett-Packard scan application, and tidied up with the editing facilities of MS-Paint. The pictured objects were approximately 15 cm high and 9 cm wide. In the centre of the pictured object a word field was kept free of lines of the drawing to avoid overlap with the distractor word. Distractor words were presented in lower-case letters, which were about 8 mm high and 6 mm wide. The stimuli were displayed on a high-resolution CRT screen (NEC-MULTISYNC). The picture outlines and the words were presented in white on a black background. Naming latencies were measured by means of a voice key. Presentation of the stimuli and registration of naming latencies were controlled by a HERMAC PC-AT computer.

*Procedure.* All subjects were tested individually in a darkened soundproof booth. They sat about 0.75 m away from the CRT screen. The subjects were told that they would see a series of pictures with words or a series of x's superimposed, and that their job was to name the pictures as rapidly as possible without making mistakes. Before the experiment, they were shown a booklet with the pictures and the names to be used. Each trial involved the following sequence. An asterisk appeared in the centre of the screen as the ready signal. After a button press by the subject, following an interval of 750 ms, the picture and word were presented at the appropriate SOA. The picture remained on the screen until the subject started speaking, with a maximum presentation duration of 1.5 s. The time between trials was 2.5 s. After each trial the experimenter coded the response for errors. Experimental sessions were recorded on audio tape. This recording was consulted after the experiment when the experimenter was in doubt about whether the response given was correct.

A session involved three constant-SOA blocks of 63 picture–word stimuli each. Between each block there was a short break. Before the experimental session, subjects received a practice session consisting of 28 picture–word stimuli (7 distractor types and 4 pictures) presented with SOA = 0. The structure of the practice block was the same as the experimental blocks. The practice pictures and distractors were not repeated in the experimental session, and were not semantically related to any of the experimental stimuli. A complete session lasted approximately half an hour.

## 4.2. Results and discussion

Excluded from the analysis were (1) responses where a subject gave an incorrect name, made a sound error, repaired, stuttered, or produced mouth clicks (in total 0.94% of all responses, see Table 2 for the error rate per condition), (2) responses where the apparatus malfunctioned, and (3) responses with a latency longer than 1500 ms and latencies deviating more than two standard deviations from a subject's and item's mean (5.7% of all responses). The excluded data points were replaced by estimates following Winer (1971). Table 2 lists the mean naming latencies per SOA and distractor type.

Table 2.    *Mean naming latencies (ms) per SOA and distractor type (n = 162).*
*Between brackets the error rate, and between parentheses the difference*
*between REL and UNR per level of abstraction*

| SOA = −100 | | | |
|---|---|---|---|
| CONTROL    588 [1.2] | | | |
| SUPER/REL    607 [1.9] | SUPER/UNR    615 [0.0] | (−8) | |
| COORD/REL    607 [1.2] | COORD/UNR    628 [1.2] | (−21) | |
| SUBOR/REL    613 [1.2] | SUBOR/UNR    642 [1.9] | (−29) | |
| | | (mean −19) | |
| | | | |
| SOA = 0 | | | |
| CONTROL    582 [0.0] | | | |
| SUPER/REL    626 [1.2] | SUPER/UNR    625 [1.9] | (+1) | |
| COORD/REL    645 [0.0] | COORD/UNR    636 [0.0] | (+9) | |
| SUBOR/REL    639 [0.0] | SUBOR/UNR    634 [0.0] | (+5) | |
| | | (mean +5) | |
| | | | |
| SOA = +100 | | | |
| CONTROL    590 [0.0] | | | |
| SUPER/REL    626 [0.6] | SUPER/UNR    629 [1.9] | (−3) | |
| COORD/REL    634 [1.2] | COORD/UNR    628 [0.6] | (+6) | |
| SUBOR/REL    630 [1.2] | SUBOR/UNR    640 [2.5] | (−10) | |
| | | (mean −2) | |

For each SOA the difference between the REL and UNR condition for each
level of abstraction (SUPER, SUBOR, COORD) was computed. The mean
differences are given in parentheses in Table 2. The *difference scores*, indicating
respectively the semantic effect of hypernymy, hyponymy, and cohyponymy, were
submitted to a by-subjects and by-items ANOVA, with SOA and level of
abstraction as fixed factors.

The ANOVA on the difference scores yielded a main effect of SOA
($F_1(2,34) = 6.01$, $MS_e = 1312$, $p < .006$; $F_2(2,16) = 8.16$, $MS_e = 481$, $p < .003$);
pairwise comparisons revealed that the difference between REL and UNR at
SOA = −100 was significantly greater than the difference at SOA = 0 and at
SOA = +100 (by-subjects, respectively $t(17) = 3.46$, $p < .005$, $t(17) = 1.89$, $p <$
.05; by-items, respectively $t(8) = 4.04$, $p < .005$, $t(8) = 2.84$, $p < .02$). The difference between REL and UNR at SOAs 0 and +100 did not differ significantly (by
subjects, $t(17) = 1.56$, $p > .1$; by items $t(8) = 1.20$, $p > .2$). The data therefore
show an SOA-dependent semantic effect.

There was no main effect of level of abstraction ($F_1(2,34) = 0.78$, $MS_e = 1520$,
$p > .4$; $F_2(2,16) = 0.68$, $MS_e = 1043$, $p > .5$). Furthermore, SOA and level of
abstraction did not interact ($F_1(4,68) = 1.09$, $MS_e = 1342$, $p > .3$; $F_2(4,32) = 0.69$,
$MS_e = 687$, $p > .6$), showing that the semantic effect did not differ for hypernyms,
hyponyms, and cohyponyms. I will therefore treat the levels of abstraction as
equivalent as far as their semantic effect is concerned. Figure 8 depicts for each

PICTURE NAMING: distractor words not in response set

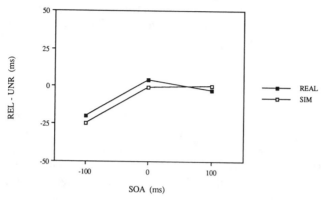

Figure 8. *Mean latency difference (in ms) between REL and UNR per SOA (collapsed over levels of abstraction): real and simulated data. A negative difference denotes semantic facilitation.*

SOA the mean difference between REL and UNR collapsed over levels of abstraction (SUPER, SUBOR, and COORD).

The data show a semantic facilitation at the negative SOA, as was predicted by the theory. Figure 8 shows that the quantitative predictions by the computer model are also met (means for the SOA of $-100$, 0, and $+100$, respectively, $-25$, $-1$, and 0 ms). (The size of the critical difference, $cd$, was estimated anew, keeping the rest of the parameters fixed. A critical difference of 1.1 appeared to minimize the deviation.) The $\chi^2$ measure of fit between simulated and real data was equal to 3.1 ($df = 2$, $p > .2$, n.s.). This means that the predictions of the simulation are statistically not different from the real data.

*An apparent contradiction.* La Heij (1988) and Lupker (1979), among others, observed semantic inhibition at SOA $= 0$ with cohyponym distractors that were not part of the response set (their studies did not include hypernyms and hyponyms). Although in the experiment reported above, the responses for the cohyponyms in the related condition differed from those in the unrelated condition by 9 ms, this difference was statistically not reliable (by subjects, $t(17) = 0.99$, $MS_e = 697$, $p > .1$; by items $t(8) = 1.44$, $MS_e = 165$, $p > .05$). These studies therefore seem to be in conflict.

How might this conflict be resolved? First, consider the experiments of La Heij. In contrast to the current study with only *one* response-set member per semantic field, his study had *three* response-set members from one semantic domain, for example, *piano, trumpet, guitar;* or *hammer, pincers, chisel* (cf. Cohen et al., 1990). So, although a number of distractor words (e.g., *violin* or *drill*) were not part of the response set, these words could nevertheless prime a competitor lemma node. For instance, in naming a pictured piano, the lemma nodes of *trumpet* and *guitar* would be primed by distractor *violin* in the REL condition; and the lemma nodes of *hammer*, *pincer*, and *chisel* would be primed by distractor *drill* in the UNR condition. Therefore, La Heij's results can be explained in the same way as the findings of Glaser and Düngelhoff (1984). In the related condition the picture and the distractor word activate the same response-set competitors of the picture name, whereas in the unrelated condition different competitors are activated by the picture and the distractor word. The only difference between the studies is that in the Glaser and Düngelhoff experiment the distractors were actually part of the response set, whereas in La Heij's experiments they were cohyponyms of response-set members. This also explains why La Heij did not find an interaction between semantic relatedness and response-set membership; that is, why the semantic effect was the same for distractors that were in the response set (e.g., *trumpet* vs. *hammer*) and distractors that were not in the response set (e.g., *violin* vs. *drill*). According to the theory, the distractors that were not part of the response set nevertheless behaved *indirectly* as response-set members, by activating response-set competitors of the picture name, in REL as well as in UNR.

Second, distractors that are not part of the response set may cause semantic inhibition if the retrieval mechanism is more sensitive to activation in the lexical environment of the target lemma (i.e., nodes that are close to a relevant intersection) than to activation outside that environment. According to the theory, the activation of the lemmas from the same semantic field as the target would receive a heavier weight in the Luce ratio than the activation of the lemmas from a different semantic field. The weighting *is the same* for the REL condition and the UNR condition. However, the *effect* on the lemma retrieval latency will be different for the semantically related and unrelated distractors. A semantically related distractor will activate the target but also the target's neighbours (including its own lemma node), thereby increasing the denominator of the Luce ratio, and decreasing the probability that the target node will be actually selected. For an unrelated distractor this will not be the case. Once again there is a trade-off between the priming of the target and the priming of competitors, now via the Luce ratio.

The computer simulation shows that increasing the sensitivity to activation in the lexical environment of the target lemma indeed results in semantic inhibition (as observed by Lupker, 1979, and Schriefers et al., 1990), instead of a null effect (as in the simulation and real data of the experiment reported above). Multiplying the activation values of neighbour lemma nodes by 2, 3, or 4 results in a semantic inhibition at SOA = 0 of about 15, 25, and 35 ms, respectively. At the earlier SOAs there may still be facilitation, as in the experiment reported above; at later SOAs, there may again be a null effect, similar to the experiment reported above and to what Schriefers et al. observed. Thus, variation on an attention parameter may underlie the differences between these studies.

## 5. Summary and conclusions

I have described a spreading-activation theory designed to explain certain aspects of lemma retrieval in speaking. In the theory the mental lexicon is conceived of as a network with concept, lemma, and lexeme nodes and labelled links, with each lexical concept represented as an independent node. A lemma is retrieved by enhancing the activation level of the node of the to-be-verbalized concept. The activation then spreads to the lemma level, where the highest activated lemma node is selected. For lemma retrieval in the picture–word interference paradigm, three extra assumptions were made. First, source tags are transmitted by the external sources of activation (picture and word). Second, response-set flags indicate which lemmas are permitted responses in an experiment. Third, the target lemma (the lemma searched for) is determined by the intersection of the tag from the target source (e.g., the picture in picture naming) and one of the response-set flags.

The theory has much in common with earlier proposals by Collins and Loftus (1975), Dell (1986), and others, but there are also some important differences. In contrast to Dell (1986), Dell and Reich (1981), and Stemberger (1985), a lexical concept is represented by an independent node in the network. This characteristic allows the retrieval mechanism to cope with hypernymy and word-to-phrase synonymy. In contrast to Collins and Loftus (1975) and many others (e.g., Glaser & Glaser, 1989; Nelson, Reed, & McEvoy, 1977; Potter, 1979; Seymour, 1979; Smith & Magee, 1980; Snodgrass, 1984; Theios & Amrhein, 1989), the theory postulates no direct connection between lexical-concept nodes and word-form nodes. These nodes are indirectly connected via a lemma node. Word retrieval therefore involves both a stage of lemma retrieval and a stage of word-form encoding. This characteristic of the theory is consistent with the findings of a variety of experimental paradigms, tip-of-the-tongue findings, speech-error data, and data on aphasia (see Introduction and section 3.2).

I have shown that the theory can account for many empirical findings on the time course of object naming, object categorization, and word categorization. Some novel and non-trivial predictions were also tested and confirmed in a new experiment. Future experiments could test the theory further by employing new paradigms, for example, paradigms requiring syntactic encoding (cf. Bock, 1986; Bock & Warren, 1985; Kelly, Bock, & Keil, 1986; Kempen & Huijbers, 1983; Levelt & Maassen, 1981; Levelt, 1989). It may also be possible to test whether the theory's predictions hold for words other than nouns, such as verbs and adjectives.

The theoretical assumptions I have made are very simple, and yet are sufficient to handle hypernymy and word-to-phrase synonymy, and to account for many empirical findings on conceptually driven lemma retrieval. The challenge is now for theorists to develop a decompositional theory that solves the retrieval problems and accounts for the data in a more parsimonious way.

**Appendix: Derivation of the expected retrieval latency $E(T)$**

Let $T$ denote time, let $s$ be the $s$th time step ($s = 1, 2, \ldots$), and $\Delta t$ the duration of a time step (in ms)

Definitions:

$$f(s) = p(\text{selection at } s)$$

$$h(s) = p(\text{selection at } s \mid \neg \exists u : (u < s \wedge \text{selection at } u))$$

respectively, the probability mass function and the hazard rate function.

Derivation of $f(s)$ from $h(s)$:

$$h(s) = p(\text{selection at } s \mid \neg \exists u : (u < s \wedge \text{selection at } u))$$

$$= \frac{p((\text{selection at } s) \wedge (\neg \exists u : (u < s \wedge \text{selection at } u)))}{p(\neg \exists u : (u < s \wedge \text{selection at } u))}$$

$$= \frac{p(\text{selection at } s)}{p(\neg \exists u : (u < s \wedge \text{selection at } u))}$$

$$= f(s) \bigg/ \prod_{j=0}^{s-1} [1 - h(j)]$$

$$\Rightarrow f(s) = h(s) \prod_{j=0}^{s-1} [1 - h(j)]$$

where $h(0) = 0$.

For the expectation of $T$ holds:

$$E(T) = \sum_{s=1}^{\infty} f(s) s \, \Delta t$$

$$= \sum_{s=1}^{\infty} h(s) \left\{ \prod_{j=0}^{s-1} [1 - h(j)] \right\} s \, \Delta t$$

## References

Bock, J.K. (1982). Toward a cognitive psychology of syntax: Information processing contributions to sentence formulation. *Psychological Review, 89*, 1–47.

Bock, J.K. (1986). Meaning, sound, and syntax: Lexical priming in sentence production. *Journal of Experimental Psychology: Learning, Memory, and Cognition, 12*, 575–586.

Bock, J.K., & Warren, R.K. (1985). Conceptual accessibility and syntactic structure in sentence formulation. *Cognition, 21*, 47–67.

Brown, R., & McNeill, D. (1966). The "tip of the tongue" phenomenon. *Journal of Verbal Learning and Verbal Behavior*, *5*, 325–337.

Butterworth, B. (1980). Some constraints on models of language production. In B. Butterworth (Ed.), *Language production* (Vol. 1, pp. 423–459). London: Academic Press.

Butterworth, B. (1989). Lexical access in speech production. In W. Marslen-Wilson (Ed.), *Lexical representation and process* (pp. 108–135). Cambridge, MA: MIT Press.

Carey, S. (1982). Semantic development: The state of the art. In E. Wanner & L.R. Gleitman (Eds.), *Language acquisition: The state of the art* (pp. 347–389). Cambridge, UK: Cambridge University Press.

Charniak, E. (1983). Passing markers: A theory of contextual influence in language comprehension. *Cognitive Science*, *7*, 171–190.

Cohen, J.D., Dunbar, K., & McClelland, J.L. (1990). On the control of automatic processes: A parallel distributed processing account of the Stroop effect. *Psychological Review*, *97*, 332–361.

Collins, A.M., & Loftus, E.F. (1975). A spreading-activation theory of semantic processing. *Psychological Review*, *82*, 407–428.

Cruse, D.A. (1986). *Lexical semantics*. Cambridge, UK: Cambridge University Press.

Cutler, A. (Ed.) (1982). *Slips of the tongue and language production*. Berlin: Mouton.

Dell, G.S. (1986). A spreading-activation theory of retrieval in sentence production. *Psychological Review*, *93*, 283–321.

Dell, G.S. (1988). The retrieval of phonological forms in production: Tests of predictions from a connectionist model. *Journal of Memory and Language*, *27*, 124–142.

Dell, G.S., & O'Seaghdha, P.G. (1991). Mediated and convergent lexical priming in language production: A comment on Levelt et al. (1991). *Psychological Review*, *98*, 604–614.

Dell, G.S., & Reich, P.A. (1981). Stages in sentence production: An analysis of speech error data. *Journal of Verbal Learning and Verbal Behavior*, *20*, 611–629.

De Smedt, K. (1990). *Incremental sentence generation: A computer model of grammatical encoding*. Doctoral dissertation, NICI Technical Report 90-01, University of Nijmegen.

Fay, D., & Cutler, A. (1977). Malapropisms and the structure of the mental lexicon. *Linguistic Inquiry*, *8*, 505–520.

Fiksel, J.R., & Bower, G.H. (1976). Question-answering by a semantic network of parallel automata. *Journal of Mathematical Psychology*, *13*, 1–45.

Flores D'Arcais, G.B., & Schreuder, R. (1987). Semantic activation during object naming. *Psychological Research*, *49*, 153–159.

Fodor, J.A. (1976). *The language of thought*. Hassocks: Harvester Press.

Fodor, J.D., Fodor, J.A., & Garrett, M.F. (1975). The psychological unreality of semantic representations. *Linguistic Inquiry*, *6*, 515–531.

Fodor, J.A., Garrett, M.F., Walker, E.C.T., & Parkes, C.H. (1980). Against definitions. *Cognition*, *8*, 263–367.

Fromkin, V.A. (1971). The non-anomalous nature of anomalous utterances. *Language*, *47*, 27–52.

Fromkin, V.A. (Ed.) (1973). *Speech errors as linguistic evidence*. The Hague: Mouton.

Garrett, M.F. (1975). The analysis of sentence production. In G.H. Bower (Ed.), *The psychology of learning and motivation* (Vol. 9, pp. 133–175). New York: Academic Press.

Garrett, M.F. (1976). Syntactic processes in sentence production. In R.J. Wales & E.C.T. Walker (Eds.), *New approaches to language mechanisms* (pp. 231–256). Amsterdam: North-Holland.

Garrett, M.F. (1980). Levels of processing in sentence production. In B. Butterworth (Ed.), *Language production* (Vol. 1, pp. 177–210). London: Academic Press.

Garrett, M.F. (1982). Production of speech: Observations from normal and pathological language use. In A.W. Ellis (Ed.), *Normality and pathology in cognitive functions* (pp. 19–76). London: Academic Press.

Garrett M.F. (1988). Processes in language production. In F.J. Newmeyer (Ed.), *Linguistics: The Cambridge survey* (Vol. 3, pp. 69–96). Cambridge, MA: Harvard University Press.

Glaser, W.R. (1992). Picture naming. *Cognition*, *42*, 61–105.

Glaser, W.R., & Düngelhoff, F-J. (1984). The time course of picture–word interference. *Journal of Experimental Psychology: Human Perception and Performance*, *10*, 640–654.

Glaser, W.R., & Glaser, M.O. (1989). Context effects in Stroop-like word and picture processing. *Journal of Experimental Psychology: General*, *118*, 13–42.

Goldman, N. (1975). Conceptual generation. In R. Schank (Ed.), *Conceptual information processing.* Amsterdam: North-Holland.

Guttentag, R.E., & Haith, M.M. (1978). Automatic processing as a function of age and reading ability. *Child Development, 49,* 707–716.

Harley, T.A. (1984). A critique of top-down independent levels models of speech production: Evidence from non-plan-internal speech errors. *Cognitive Science, 8,* 191–219.

Hendler, J.A. (1989). Marker-passing over microfeatures: Towards a hybrid symbolic/connectionist model. *Cognitive Science, 13,* 79–106.

Humphreys, G.W., Riddoch, M.J., & Quinlan, P.T. (1988). Cascade processing in picture identification. *Cognitive Neuropsychology, 5,* 67–103.

Irwin, D.I., & Lupker, S.J. (1983). Semantic priming of pictures and words: A levels of processing approach. *Journal of Verbal Learning and Verbal Behavior, 22,* 45–60.

Jolicoeur, P., Gluck, M.A., & Kosslyn, S.M. (1984). Pictures and names: Making the connection. *Cognitive Psychology, 16,* 243–275.

Jones, H.G.V., & Langford, S. (1987). Phonological blocking in the tip of the tongue state. *Cognition, 26,* 115–122.

Kelly, M.H., Bock, J.K., & Keil, F.C. (1986). Prototypicality in a linguistic context: Effects on sentence structure. *Journal of Memory and Language, 25,* 59–74.

Kempen, G. (1977). Conceptualizing and formulating in sentence production. In S. Rosenberg (Ed.), *Sentence production: Developments in research and theory.* Hillsdale, NJ: Erlbaum.

Kempen, G., & Hoenkamp, E. (1987). An incremental procedural grammar for sentence formulation. *Cognitive Science, 11,* 201–258.

Kempen, G., & Huijbers, P. (1983). The lexicalization process in sentence production and naming: Indirect election of words. *Cognition, 14,* 185–209.

Kintsch, W. (1974). *The representation of meaning in memory.* Hillsdale, NJ: Erlbaum.

La Heij, W. (1988). Components of Stroop-like interference in picture naming. *Memory and Cognition, 16,* 400–410.

La Heij, W., Happel, B., & Mulder, M. (1990). Components of Stroop-like interference in word reading. *Acta Psychologica, 73,* 115–129.

Levelt, W.J.M. (1983). Monitoring and self-repair in speech. *Cognition, 14,* 41–104.

Levelt, W.J.M. (1989). *Speaking: From intention to articulation.* Cambridge, MA: MIT Press.

Levelt, W.J.M., & Maassen, B. (1981). Lexical search and order of mention in sentence production. In W. Klein & W.J.M. Levelt (Eds.), *Crossing the boundaries in linguistics: Studies presented to Manfred Bierwisch* (pp. 221–252). Dordrecht: Reidel.

Levelt, W.J.M., & Schriefers, H. (1987). Stages of lexical access. In G. Kempen (Ed.), *Natural language generation: New results in artificial intelligence, psychology and linguistics* (pp. 395–404). Dordrecht: Martinus Nijhoff.

Levelt, W.J.M., Schriefers, H., Vorberg, D., Meyer, A.S., Pechmann, T., & Havinga, J. (1991a). The time course of lexical access in speech production: A study of picture naming. *Psychological Review, 98,* 122–142.

Levelt, W.J.M., Schriefers, H., Vorberg, D., Meyer, A.S., Pechmann, T., & Havinga, J. (1991b). Normal and deviant lexical processing: A reply to Dell and O'Seaghdha. *Psychological Review, 98,* 615–618.

Luce, R.D. (1959). *Individual choice behavior.* New York: Wiley.

Luce, R.D. (1986). *Response times: Their role in inferring elementary mental organization.* New York: Oxford University Press.

Lupker, S.J. (1979). The semantic nature of response competition in the picture–word interference task. *Memory and Cognition, 7,* 485–495.

Lupker, S.J., & Katz, A.N. (1981). Input, decision, and response factors in picture–word interference. *Journal of Experimental Psychology: Human Learning and Memory, 7,* 269–282.

Lyons, J. (1977). *Semantics* (Vol. 1, pp. 309–360). Cambridge, UK: Cambridge University Press.

MacLeod, C.M. (1991). Half a century of research of the Stroop effect: An integrative review. *Psychological Bulletin, 109,* 163–203.

McClelland, J.L., & Rumelhart, D.E. (1981). An interactive activation model of context effects in letter perception: Part 1. An account of basic findings. *Psychological Review, 88,* 375–407.

McGill, W.J. (1963). Stochastic latency mechanisms. In R.D. Luce, R.R. Bush, & E. Galanter (Eds.), *Handbook of mathematical psychology* (Vol. 1, pp. 309–360). New York: Wiley.

Meyer, A.S. (1990). The time course of phonological encoding in language production: The encoding of successive syllables of a word. *Journal of Memory and Language, 29*, 524–545.

Miller, G.A., & Johnson-Laird, P.N. (1976). *Language and perception.* Cambridge, MA: Harvard University Press.

Morton, J. (1969). The interaction of information in word recognition. *Psychological Review, 76*, 165–178.

Nelder, J.A., & Mead, R. (1965). A simplex method for function minimization. *Computer Journal, 7*, 308–313.

Nelson, D.L., Reed, V.S., & McEvoy, C.L. (1977). Learning to order pictures and words: A model of sensory and semantic encoding. *Journal of Experimental Psychology: Human Learning and Memory, 3*, 485–497.

Norman, D.A., & Rumelhart, D.E. (Eds.) (1975). *Explorations in cognition.* San Francisco: W.H. Freeman.

Phaf, R.H., Van der Heijden, A.H.C., & Hudson, P.T.W. (1990). SLAM: A connectionist model for attention in visual selection tasks. *Cognitive Psychology, 22*, 273–341.

Oldfield, R.C. (1966). Things, words and the brain. *Quarterly Journal of Experimental Psychology, 18*, 340–353.

Potter, M.C. (1979). Mundane symbolism: The relations among objects, names, and ideas. In N.R. Smith & M.B. Franklin (Eds.), *Symbolic functioning in childhood.* Hillsdale, NJ: Erlbaum.

Quillian, M.R. (1967). Word concepts: A theory and simulation of some basic semantic capabilities. *Behavioral Science, 12*, 410–430.

Rayner, K., & Pollatsek, A. (1989). *The psychology of reading.* Englewood Cliffs, NJ: Prentice-Hall.

Rayner, K., & Springer, C.J. (1986). Graphemic and semantic similarity effects in the picture–word interference task. *British Journal of Psychology, 77*, 207–222.

Roelofs, A. (in preparation). *Lemma retrieval in speaking.* Doctoral dissertation in preparation, University of Nijmegen.

Rosch, E., Mervis, C.B., Gray, W.D., Johnson, D.M., & Boyes-Braem, P. (1976). Basic objects in natural categories. *Cognitive Psychology, 8*, 382–439.

Rosinski, R.R. (1977). Picture–word interference is semantically based. *Child Development, 48*, 643–647.

Saffran, E.M., Schwartz, M.F., & Marin, O.S.M. (1980). Evidence from aphasia: Isolating the components of a production model. In B. Butterworth (Ed.), *Language production* (Vol. 1, pp. 221–242). London: Academic Press.

Schriefers, H. (1990). Lexical and conceptual factors in the naming of relations. *Cognitive Psychology, 22*, 111–142.

Schriefers, H., Meyer, A.S., & Levelt, W.J.M. (1990). Exploring the time course of lexical access in language production: Picture-word interference studies. *Journal of Memory and Language, 29*, 86–102.

Seymour, P.H.K. (1979). *Human visual cognition.* New York: St. Martin's Press.

Shastri, L. (1988). A connectionist approach to knowledge representation and limited inference. *Cognitive Science, 12*, 331–392.

Shattuck-Hufnagel, S. (1979). Speech errors as evidence for a serial-order mechanism in sentence production. In W.E. Cooper & E.C.T. Walker (Eds.), *Sentence processing: Psycholinguistic studies presented to Merrill Garrett* (pp. 295–342). Hillsdale, NJ: Erlbaum.

Smith, E.E., Shoben, E.J., & Rips, L.J. (1974). Structure and process in semantic memory: A featural model for semantic decisions. *Psychological Review, 81*, 214–241.

Smith, M.C., & Magee, L.E. (1980). Tracing the time course of picture–word processing. *Journal of Experimental Psychology: General, 109*, 373–392.

Snodgrass, J.G. (1984). Concepts and their surface representation. *Journal of Verbal Learning and Verbal Behavior, 23*, 3–22.

Stemberger, J.P. (1985). An interactive activation model of language production. In A.W. Ellis (Ed.), *Progress in the psychology of language* (Vol. 1, pp. 143–186). London: Erlbaum.

Theios, J., & Amrhein, P.C. (1989). Theoretical analysis of the cognitive processing of lexical and pictorial stimuli: Reading, naming, and visual and conceptual comparisons. *Psychologica Review*, *96*, 5–24.

Townsend, J.T., & Ashby, F.G. (1983). *Stochastic modeling of elementary psychological processes* Cambridge, UK: Cambridge University Press.

Van Wijk, C., & Kempen, G. (1987). A dual system for producing self-repairs in spontaneous speech Evidence from experimentally elicited corrections. *Cognitive Psychology*, *19*, 403–440.

Vorberg, D. (1985). Unerwartete Folgen von Zufälliger Variabilität: Wettlauf-Modelle für der Stroop-Versuch. *Zeitschrift für experimentelle und angewandte Psychologie*, *32*, 494–521.

Winer, B.J. (1971). *Statistical principles in experimental design*. New York: McGraw-Hill.

# 5

# Disorders of lexical selection*

Merrill Garrett

*Department of Psychology, Faculty of Social and Behavioral Science, College of Arts and Sciences, University of Arizona, Tucson, AZ 85721, USA*

Garrett, M., 1992. Disorders of lexical selection. Cognition, 42: 143–180.

*Errors in lexical processing are commonplace in language pathologies resulting from brain injury or disease. This discussion considers some of the major recent developments in the interpretation of such errors. The focus is on behavioral systems, rather than neuroanatomical or neurophysiological issues. The objective is to comment on some plausible mutual implications of generally attested pathologies and normal models of lexical retrieval for production, particularly with respect to the roles of semantic and syntactic categories.*

## 1. Introduction

### 1.1. Limits of the discussion

One or another kind of error in lexical processing is commonplace in language pathologies. Speaking and writing errors that seem to implicate failures to adequately control meaning, syntax, and form are rife in the aphasias, dyslexias, and dementias (see Marshall, 1986, for an incisive overview and area critique). The impulse to tame the polymorphous bestiary of anomias, alexias, paralexias, paraphasias, dysphasias, dyslexias, dysgraphias, and neologisms has occupied many. We will not survey the full scene, but sample only some of the major recent developments in the interpretation of lexical errors observed in some of the language disorders associated with brain injury or disease. Further, the focus here is on behavioral systems, setting aside interpretations of neuroanatomical or neurophysiological claims and aiming only to describe some of the major patterns

*I wish to thank W.J.M. Levelt, K.I. Forster and two anonymous reviewers for helpful suggestions concerning topics covered in this paper. Preparation of this paper was supported in part by a grant from the McDonnell-Pew Cognitive Neurosciences Program.

of lexical error and place them in the context of a working model that has proven viable for the description of normal language production processes.

The working distinctions to be drawn here include a background distinction between non-verbal and verbal thought (see section 2.4) and an assumption that lexical retrieval in production is, globally, a two-stage process in which the initial stage associates a conceptual structure with a lexical element whose entry provides its semantic and syntactic characteristics, and the second stage associates that conceptually nominated lexical element with a record that provides its phonological form. The terminological conventions followed here are those adopted in Levelt (1989). The pre-verbal conceptual representations that drive sentence formulation, including, of course, lexical selection, are referred to as *messages*; the conceptually driven first-stage lexical retrieval targets will be called *lemmas* and the second-stage retrieval targets *word forms*; each semantic/syntactic lemma representation is linked to a word-form representation that specifies the abstract phonological and morphological structure for that lexical item. The processes that interpret word-form information for the specific purposes of pronounciation are deemed to be subsequent to and consequent on the recovery of the word-form representations that are linked to lemmas. At this general level of description, these assumptions have much in common with a number of other proposals for normal and aphasic lexical processing (e.g., Butterworth, 1980, 1985; Caramazza, 1988; Fromkin, 1987; Marshall & Newcombe, 1973; Schwartz, 1987).

More detailed versions of this characterization of normal lexical production systems rely on a variety of kinds of evidence, including formal constraints on processing models, analyses of normal speech errors, language development, and experimental studies of lexical retrieval. Such justifications will be mentioned in passing, but are not systematically pursued here; see other papers in this journal issue, Levelt (1989) and references therein. For our current purposes the relevant set of observations bearing on the adequacy of such a view of lexical retrieval comes from the study of patterns of language pathology, and major features of that evidence are the focus of this discussion.

## 1.2. Loci of lexical failures

Investigators of language disorders have long recognized that failures to produce a target word may have many underlying causes, some quite evidently non-linguistic in nature. In what follows, the deficits to be interpreted are those for which the reporting investigators have reasonable grounds to rule out obvious confounding with sensory or motor limitations.

With respect to the production of a lexical target in a sentence, the following schema provides potential loci of specifically linguistic failure for spoken outputs

(1) Message to lemma representations.
(2) Lemma to word-form representations.
(3) Word forms to phonetic representations for connected speech.
(4) Speech representations to motor representations.

The present discussion focuses on failures of lexical selection, and hence on points (1) and (2); see Butterworth (this volume) for discussion of disorders in the subsequent lexical processing for speech. (See also Caramazza and Miceli, 1990, for consideration of some issues in the structure and control of analogous orthographic output systems.)

### 1.3. A preliminary example

Some early tests of patients assigned to major clinical groupings of the aphasias (Broca's, Wernicke's, conduction, and anomic) on the basis of the Boston Diagnostic Aphasia Examination (BDAE) are illustrative of the principal division of interest here. In work by Goodglass, Kaplan, Weintraub, and Ackerman (1976), these patient groupings were tested for partial knowledge of failed target words by probe questions analogous to those used by Brown and McNeill (1966) in their classic experimental study of tip-of-the-tongue (TOT) states in normal subjects. Goodglass et al. probed for knowledge of the meaning and aspects of word form in their patient groups: the conduction and anomic groups showed the sharpest contrast, with the former showing significant ability to provide the initial sound of the target and the latter showing no evidence of such partial knowledge. Pease and Goodglass (1978) report a complementary finding. They tested the effects of different types of cues in facilitating the recovery of failed lexical targets in a confrontation naming task for anomic, Broca's and Wernike's patients. Patients who failed, for example, to produce the word "hammock" when confronted with a picture of one would then be provided with a series of prompts related to meaning, form or context for the target word. The anomics were overall less impaired than the other two patients groups, but they showed a greater cueing effect for the initial sound/letter cue than did the other two, a result that suggests the availability of lexical meaning but impaired access to the word-form system (e.g., Buckingham, 1979). In brief, the patient group with a striking lack of word-form knowledge in the TOT study was the group most helped by word-form information in the cueing study.

While there are many imponderables in the interpretation of such perform-ances, they testify to a major dissociation of loci of failure in the processes of lexical recovery. Meaning representations of considerable specificity may be demonstrably present and yet the target word not forthcoming. In this respect the apparent parallels to normal speakers' occasional failures of lexical retrieval are compelling. It is a universal fact of normal language experience that lexical form can be gallingly absent despite the lucid subjective presence of exquisite meaning detail. The complementary condition also obtains: there are patients (e.g., jargon aphasics) who generate lexical elements that are well formed but quite without relation to the semantic requirements of the discourse environment. But these facts tell us what needs to be explained, not how to explain it.

Observations of the details of language pathologies are an increasingly important component of the effort to build an extended account of the processing relations between conceptual systems and lexical systems of semantic, syntactic and phonological structure. In following sections, we take up several examples of lexical failure in aphasia that provide some clues to a more developed theory. Two major kinds of evidence are in play: (1) the apparent relations between a target word and an intruding word in an error performance; and (2) accuracy in performance for differing semantic and syntactic word classes on various tasks (e.g., naming, pantomime, picture/word matching, definition) presumed to implicate conceptual to lexical mappings. We will consider the general character of semantic errors in language-disordered groups, some claims for selective semantic losses and for modality-specific semantic losses, and some evidence bearing on selective effects for different syntactic categories.

## 2. Semantic deficits in lexical selection

### 2.1. *The character of semantic errors*

It is fair to say that semantically related word substitution errors are a prominent feature of aphasic speakers' performance. So, for example, semantically related word substitutions are common in Broca's aphasia and in Wernicke's aphasia (Kohn & Goodglass, 1985), they are a characteristic failure in jargon aphasia (usually, though not exclusively, associated with Wernicke's aphasia; Lecours & Rouillon, 1976), and such errors are a defining property of deep dyslexia (Marshall & Newcombe, 1966; Coltheart, 1980). Though all major clinical classes of aphasia patients may display significant incidence of semantic error in lexical selection, they differ strikingly in various other respects. Thus Broca's aphasics characteristically show non-fluent but intelligible speech (sometimes agrammatic), and, compared to Wernicke's aphasics, substantially preserved comprehension capabilities. Jargon aphasia on the other hand is characterized by fluent utterance, with frequent occurrence of meaningless words and phrases, sound substitutions and various word substitutions (including semantic errors and neologisms, i.e., phonologically and morphologically well-formed non-words). Typically, such patients have significant comprehension impairments and do not appear to monitor their own speech for coherence (there is relatively little hesitation and self-correction compared to that observed for most other clinical aphasia groups); their behavior suggests that they are often unaware that listeners do not understand them and that they themselves do not comprehend what is said to them. Deep dyslexics, as a last example, are afflicted with a reading disorder that yields many word substitutions, including a large proportion of meaning-related cases, and, though there is variability here as always, there is evidence that they are aware of their error and that there is greater awareness of semantic error than form error (Patterson, 1978). These and other sorts of contrast in collateral performance features certainly suggest potential differences in the nature of the semantic error processes that should be explored (see sections 2.3 and 3.1). Nonetheless, on initial consideration, the errors from different patient groups often look much the same. And one must attend to the similarities this suggests as well as to the likely differences suggested by the diversity of associated symptoms. Some examples of semantic substitutions from Broca's aphasics are given in (1), some from deep dyslexics in (2), and some from a non-fluent and agrammatic patient with a strikingly general semantic error profile in (3):

(1) flower→plant;  dominoes→checkers;  camel→desert;  palette→easel; noose→rope; label→paper (oral naming performance; from Kohn & Goodglass, 1985)

(2) bush→tree;  antique→vase;  uncle→nephew;  tulip→crocus;  March→ August;  robin→bird;  comfort→blanket (oral reading performances; from Coltheart, 1980)

(3) arm→finger;  truck→van;  lobster→shrimp;  helicopter→airplane; apple→peach; dophin→whale; sock→gloves; bed→couch (oral naming performance; from Hillis, Rapp, Romani, & Caramazza, 1989)

Such aphasic errors may be compared to semantic substitution errors made by normal speakers. A number of investigators have reported on the general properties of word substitution errors as reflected in error corpora for normal spontaneous speech and writing (see, for example, Fay & Cutler, 1977; Fromkin, 1971; Garrett, 1980; Harley, 1984; Hotopf, 1980). Just as was suggested earlier with respect to normal TOT states, it is a significant, though unsettled, question what relation holds between such normally occurring errors and those found in various pathological language conditions. On the surface, one could certainly say of the meaning-related aphasic errors that they look qualitatively like normal meaning-based word substitutions. Though the basis for comparison is not fully detailed or quantitative, the incidence of, for example, synonymic and antonymic relations, and the role of coordinate and associative relations in meaning-related aphasic errors seems roughly comparable to those in normal errors (see, for example, Kohn & Goodglass, 1985, or Hillis et al., 1989; see Garrett, in press, for a report of error subtypes within semantic substitutions for normal speakers). However, there are potentially interesting differences. These include constraints of grammatical category (see the discussion in section 3.1) and the role of category hierarchy effects (subordinate/superordinate relations).

The matter of relations between subordinate and superordinate lexical terms requires comment (even though I believe the data from language disorders is presently inconclusive). These are implicated for instances in which a superordinate term displaces one of its subordinates. Such a performance is related to what Levelt (1989) has called the "hypernym problem"; for example, ANIMAL is a hypernym of HORSE and PLANT of FLOWER (in general, if $W_1$ entails $W_2$, then $W_2$ is a hypernym of $W_1$). Levelt asks, given that the conceptual conditions of a target word are satisfied by its hypernym, why the hypernym is not regularly retrieved rather than the correct (subordinated) target? Search processes incorporating a categorial hierarchy would confront this problem and would require some mechanism to suppress the hypernym and ensure the selection of the subordinate target. Malfunction of such a retrieval system might be expected to yield hypernym substitutions. In normal speech, however, a substitution like "plant" for "oak" or "meat" for "sausage" is a rare event, perhaps in fact a non-event when the putative cases are carefully examined (Hotopf, 1980). Either such errors are very uncommon or they are not readily detectable in the observable behavior of normal speakers. But what about hypernym substitutions as a pathological language condition?

There is some evidence implicating a hierarchical conceptual organization in aphasic naming disorders based on evidence that lexical failures in aphasia (e.g., Hillis et al., 1989; Warrington, 1975; Warrington & Shallice, 1984) and particularly in Alzheimer's disease (Martin, 1987; Schwartz, Nolan, & Saffran, 1985) may show loss of specific lexical distinctions in the presence of well-preserved superordinate category information; for example, patients in a visual naming task may show frequent failure to retrieve or to discriminate the names of the members of a semantic category, but are accurate in assigning the same category exemplars to their appropriate superordinate category label. (See also section 2.2 for related evidence.) Such conditions might lead one to expect hypernym substitutions in dementia and aphasia. And indeed, for Alzheimer's patients, such naming errors have been reported (Martin & Fedio, 1983; but see Bayles, Tomoeda, & Trosset, 1990). One might try to construe some of the circumlocutory speech of anomics as an illustration of such a tendency – there, general terms are "substituted" for specific ones to a very substantial extent; and there are scattered examples in reports of aphasic errors in naming tasks (e.g., "plant" for "flower" in Kohn & Goodglass, 1985; "bird" for "robin" in Hillis et al., 1989), though such errors are not prominent in the aphasia reports.

A significant concern here – one not easily evaluated on available evidence – is the extent to which the (possibly frequent) hypernym errors in dementia and those in aphasia should be treated as a database that will support inferences about normal retrieval structure, that is, whether they are like the fluent involuntary substitutions of normal speakers (for whom hypernym substitutions are not well attested), or whether they are like the voluntary substitutions that normal speakers make when they realize they cannot readily recover a target word. Similarly for the circumlocutory speech of anomics, or perhaps for the apparent examples of hypernym substitutions one finds in aphasia reports. Where such substitutions are more akin to the voluntary search for alternative ways to express a recalcitrant idea or "trading for time" while one seeks the correct target, they have little import for the analysis of the hypernym problem.

But, if one accepts such cases as errors, how might they relate to the retrieval process? Levelt (1989, chapter 6) argues on several grounds for a lexical retrieval system incorporating parallel featural tests, perhaps organized as linked decision tables (e.g., as in Miller & Johnson-Laird, 1976), with table-internal tests made in parallel and table-to-table transfer a serial process; tables correspond to specific "semantic fields". Such a system might readily accommodate the apparent loss of discriminative capacity internal to fields in the face of preserved superordinate category information; the former might represent the compromise of the parallel feature tests for lexical selection and the latter the organization of table transfer relations in such a system. Moreover, the difference in mechanism for the two types of lexical relations might be appealed to in an account of the rarity of hypernym errors in normal language usage.

As a final note on the requirements for comparing normal and aphasic word substitution errors, we must bear in mind that normal substitution errors are a heterogeneous lot in their own right and their precise decomposition into types is a theoretically freighted issue. There is general agreement on a broad classification into meaning-based, form-based, and environmentally triggered lexical substitution errors (e.g., Garrett, 1988), but there are important issues of disagreement about the underlying mechanisms that result in the surface error distribution (Dell & Reich, 1981; Harley, 1984; Stemberger, 1985) and these will ultimately figure in any detailed comparison of normal and aphasic word substitution errors. In particular, the relation between meaning-based and form-based errors in aphasia is not a systematically explored problem. There are certainly case reports of patients who show an almost exclusive predilection for semantic error, one of which we will take note of in later discussion (Hillis et al., 1989), and there are suggestive general observations that can be made concerning the evolution of symptoms in jargon aphasias. However, precise examinations of the evidential base for an interaction between form processing and meaning processing (e.g., of the sort proposed in Dell's (1986) network model) are not extensive for lexical substitutions in aphasic speech. (See Bloch (1986), and Schwartz, Saffran, & Dell (1990) for a more general evaluation of a jargon case and its import for interactive processes. See also Hillis and Caramazza (1990) for an interesting recent discussion of an interaction between output systems for form and occurrences of meaning-related substitutions in one case study.) For errors in reading, there are data compatible with such interactions: in deep dyslexia, word substitutions based on meaning and substitutions based on visual form are both common, and errors in which these two factors are simultaneously present are fairly frequent; in two reports (Shallice & Coughlan, 1980; Shallice & McGill, 1978) the incidence of such mixed errors exceeded chance estimates derived from base rates of meaning and form errors in the patients studied (see also Hinton & Shallice, 1989). A number of complex analysis problems (e.g., choice of indices of form and meaning similarity) as well as examination of possible performance differences across dyslexic patient types will be required before the significance of this for normal models of speaking and reading can be determined.

A related and particularly difficult issue concerns the role of attentional and memory factors in normal error processes. There is excellent reason to identify certain of the lexical error processes in normal language performance with failures of attention and/or the working memory systems that control discourse (e.g., the "environmental intrusion errors"; Garrett, 1980; Harley, 1984). How those factors may enter into aphasic error performance is largely unknown, though it is certain that they are of considerable significance. We will set this and related issues aside for now, noting only that one obvious class of aphasic errors to which the normal environmental error processes might be linked are lexical perservations. (See Buckingham, 1985, for a useful discussion of several aspects of aphasic preservation in the context of normal production processes.)

## 2.2. Semantic field effects

There is an accumulating body of observation on the occurrence of selective impairments for semantically related sets of lexical items. These are cases which document a loss of capacity to produce lexical targets in specific semantic domains, such as terms for concrete (as compared to abstract) reference, or terms referring to living (as compared to non-living) things, and even losses so specific as color terms, or food terms. What is the inventory of such types and what is their implication for lexical selection processes?

Various clinical reports of such phenomena were made in the years prior to the more aggressive recent pursuit of the possibility that such effects might exist. Goodglass et al. (1966) analyzed the naming performance of a substantial body of cases grouped into major clinical classes and reported apparent selective impairments, both for preservation and loss, in categories of objects, actions, numbers, letters, and color terms. They suggested on this basis that selective lexical impairment might be a rather general feature of aphasic compromise of language function.

Warrington and Shallice (1984) reviewed evidence for category-specific losses, citing a number of earlier clinical accounts indicating such effects; in that paper they reported their own study of four patients who showed semantic field deficits. Several subsequent publications have reported additional cases that affirm and extend the findings reported there (see, for example, Damasio, 1990; Shallice, 1988). Warrington and Shallice's objectives were twofold. One was to document selective semantic losses and the other was to examine the relation of such losses to modality of performance. We will take up the first matter here and discuss the second in section 2.4.

There are, broadly speaking, two sorts of conceptual/lexical categories that have been reported to show selective loss or preservation. These are cases that show compromise of a higher featural contrast (concrete/abstract, living/non-living or animate/inanimate), and cases that show compromise of lower-level categories like body parts, colors, food, animals, plants, fruit, vegetables. Since the two sorts of losses sometimes occur in the same patients, it may be difficult to sort out just which is responsible for a reported experimental contrast showing different levels of success with a given set of lexical or picture stimuli. Nonetheless, there seem to be a sufficient number of instances of such failures to be confident that both sorts exist even if there is some doubt about the exact boundaries of the effects. We will consider several examples.

Warrington (1975) reported a case study showing greater loss for concrete than for abstract terms for auditory comprehension, and subsequently (1981) reported a case with similar semantic impairment, this time for visual representations. Warrington and Shallice (1984) also report that one of four patients in their study showed significantly poorer performance for concrete terms as compared with abstract terms.

Within the domain of concrete terms, Warrington and Shallice also reported for their four patients that performance for the category "living things" was much poorer than the inanimate objects category in two modalities (picture naming and description, word definition). Note that the category of "living things" was quite heterogeneous (e.g., parrot, daffodil, snail, ostrich, eel, duck, wasp, crocus, spider) including plants, animals, birds and insects. Two of these patients also showed a clear loss for "food" terms (as compared with inanimate object terms) in both visual and auditory modes.

Young, Newcombe, Hellawell, and DeHaan (1989) report a case study showing a deficit for the category living things for two tests (generation of exemplars for a category; category membership decision) including a response time measure. They compared typicality effects in the living and non-living categories; controls showed similar typicality effects in both categories, while the patient showed strong differences for the two classes.

For these reports, and most cited later, some of the contrasts in performance levels are more than just "statistically significant" – differences are sometimes quite large. For a few patients and categories, performance on an affected category may be at 10% success with most other categories showing success rates that are normal or near normal. Moreover, some of the reports show such dissociations to be stable in repeated testing across significant time periods.

There are other features of testing for such differences that implicate alternative accounts, of course. How general are the results with respect to the descriptive categories used? And what correlated variables might be contributing to performance? In Warrington and Shallice, for example, several different sets of stimuli were used in repeated tests spanning many different lexical items and pictures. Word frequency was controlled in most comparisons and conclusions are not likely to be compromised by that variable. Familiarity is also not a particularly persuasive alternative explanation: foods were a "lost" category and those items were judged more familiar than some of the preserved category exemplars. These and similar factors have role in lexical processing and must be carefully examined in any putative case of selective impairment for conceptual or lexical categories, but overall they do not seem to provide a satisfactory alternative account of all the available observations.

Another possibility for an alternative account was raised by Humphries and Riddoch (1987). They suggested that the apparent loss of semantic categories (e.g., "animals", "fruits and vegetables") might reflect differences in the difficulty of processing between that class and preserved ones. The concern is that there may be a higher degree of overlap among the perceptual representations for animals, for example, than for the representations of members of contrasting categories and that this factor may have an impact on the information-processing demands associated with various of the testing procedures. They report some observations of patient performance consonant with this view (Riddoch & Humphries, 1987).

Without denying the existence of such effects, there seem good grounds not to attribute the major features of at least some category-specific effects to them. One way to evaluate this is in terms of the kinds of items used to test for the categories. While the narrow category "animals" (i.e., four-legged beasts with hairy exteriors) may be a plausible candidate for such an effect, it seems not at all plausible with respect to the "living things" category tested by Warrington and Shallice and by some other investigators (which as noted, included items so disparate as parrots, snails and daffodils). The perceptual similarity issue is important, but by itself does not satisfactorily cover the ground given the character of the several different classes for which there is now some evidence of selective loss. There is, moreover other evidence indicating a complementary loss and preservation of given categories. Warrington and McCarthy (1983) report a selective loss (for the auditory modality) for inanimate object terms while flowers, foods and animal names were preserved. This is the reverse of the pattern reported in Warrington and Shallice. Similarly, there are reports of both preservation (Dennis, 1976) and loss (Goodglass & Budin, 1988; McKenna and Warrington, 1978) of body parts terms. More sharply focused on this point is a report by Hillis and Caramazza (1991). They tested two patients with the same materials and demonstrated a double dissociation for the animal category. This result documents in a convincing way the earlier claims that a given category may show both selective preservation and selective loss and makes processing complexity accounts of the selective effects, whether conceptual or perceptual, difficult to sustain.

At this point, it is useful to consider a case report by Hart, Berndt, and Caramazza (1985) of a selective deficit for the categories "fruits" and "vegetables". Again frequency and familiarity were not the relevant factor – the patient succeeded with relatively rare exemplars outside these categories and failed on the common elements from within. Failure for these categories was consistent across a range of tasks (picture identification, tactile naming, naming from descriptions, and picture sorting by category), thus apparently indicating a conceptual deficit for these categories. But a striking feature of this report shows the problem is not conceptual compromise per se, but instead a compromise of the link between conceptual representations and lexical items. These failures were specific to test conditions that did not provide the name for a target concept. When the patient was given the names instead of pictures or descriptions as input, there was clear success on the full range of tasks. The patient showed a clear understanding of the classifications of the target words and detailed knowledge of the objects they refer to. The link from names to conceptual structure was functional. But the links from both sensory and linguistic descriptions were not.

General conceptual and linguistic resources were available and perceptual processing was adequate to contact those resources except in the semantic categories fruits and vegetables. Some specialized aspect of the representational processes in the impaired modalities might be suspected, and an interpretation in terms of modality-specific semantic processing considered (see section 2.4). A problem with such a solution for this case lies in the report that naming from *verbal description* was also impaired. This latter observation must be stressed. It shows that even verbal input conditions that lack the name were compromised and thus that the link from modality-neutral conceptual representations is compromised. It appears that the deficit lies in a category-specific system for retrieving a lexical label from a conceptual representation whether perceptually or linguistically generated. In the terms we are using here, this is a failure of effective correspondence between message substructures and the conceptual descriptions in lemma representations that govern lemma access, and the failure must be at the lemma level. Lemma representations appear to be the only recourse for describing both the semantic character of the loss and its restriction to specific semantic fields while at the same time maintaining satisfactory performance in the affected domains for general inferential tasks triggered by the name input.

A semantic field may be described as a set of lemmas with some specified and functional similarity among their conceptual representations. The utility of such fields may be related to the requirements for rapid evaluation of lexical alternatives in the language production processes, one aspect of which concerns us in section 2.3. In normal processing, semantic field effects may be seen in patterns of spontaneous lexical errors. These are errors that have been discussed as failures of lemma access (Garrett, 1988; Levelt, 1989). We will therefore supplement the preceding observations with a brief comment on connections between these and the apparent category-specific effects in aphasia.

For normal word substitution errors, semantic field effects are readily apparent and intuitively compelling. A substantial proportion of the word substitution errors that involve meaning-related pairs may be organized into clusters that correspond to natural categories, many of which are similar in character to those discussed for selective deficits in aphasia. One example that well illustrates this is the field of "body part" terms. The terms in this set are for the most part morphologically simple and are part of the common production vocabulary of ordinary English speakers, and, as noted earlier, have been reported to show selective preservation and loss in aphasia. It is a useful set not only because of its salience, but also because the relations among the terms fall into subfields within the larger semantic set: head, torso, and limb. Normal word substitution patterns strongly reflect the overall field boundary and the subfield structure within it. So, in a set of 32 substitutions (taken from three different error corpora) in which the target word is a body part term, there are no field external terms as error words (Garrett, in press). Subfield effects also seem to be present: 80% of the error pairs are within subfields. Other semantic fields in the normal error corpus show similar well-developed boundaries.

Note that the convergence of field effects indicated by aphasic loss and those indicated in the normal error patterns is best in the lower-level category sets (e.g., food, fruit, vegetable, body parts, color). The higher-order featural contrasts (abstract/concrete; living/non-living) do not have an obvious counterpart in the normal errors (though, not surprisingly, the concrete/abstract contrast is rarely violated in meaning-related substitution patterns). This may suggest that an alternative description should be assigned to the observations ascribed to those contrasts – i.e. those particular patterns of aphasic loss implicate some focus not equivalent to a semantic field.

The force of the claim that a concrete/abstract "feature" is implicated in the aphasic error patterns may, in any event, be somewhat problematic. Ideally, if sets defined by a concrete/abstract featural contrast were impaired, all concrete instances should show a problem relative to all abstract ones, but this does not appear to be the typical case. For example, in the Warrington and Shallice report, this contrast co-occurs with the animate/inanimate contrast, and the patient data indicate that both inanimate concrete and abstract terms were preserved. The extent to which the abstract/concrete contrast may be the product of the compromise of other more specific fields needs consideration, as does the possibility that it is the reflection of a correlated ("non-descriptive") aspect of the cognitive architecture (see section 2.4).

The support for a living/non-living contrast is clearer, however, since some reports of loss grouped living things together quite comprehensively – animals, fish, birds, insects, and plants. Warrington and Shallice suggest that the basis for this category distinction may lie in the processing roles of *functional* and *sensory* feature descriptions (which they further link to the notion of modality-specific systems of semantic representation). Functional description is taken to be not generally relevant for living things but crucial for (inanimate) artifacts. It is a plausible suggestion, but may need to be tailored a bit to cover the full body of observations (viz., some animals do have functional roles; conversely, some inanimate objects do not – artifacts do, but natural objects generally do not). And, again, whether this or the other higher-level contrasts ought to be thought of in featural terms within a representational system, or explained otherwise, and in a different way from the account of the lower-level contrasts remains an interesting open issue.

There are, in fact, some normal error instances that suggest higher-level feature changes; for example, wheel → foot (Garrett, in press). Such examples seem to involve an analogical relation between target and intrusion. For this error example, Warrington and Shallice's suggestion may be apt. If selective impairments for the category living things are properly captured by a featural analyses that contrasts "functional" and "perceptual" descriptions, then a crossover from one of these domains to the other might, in normal performance, reflect a failure of that classificatory decision in the presence of partial correspondences for featural descriptions at lower levels. If, for example, the perceptual description of animates within the living things category includes something like [capable of motion], and [limbs/means for locomotion], the extension from "wheel" for automobile to "foot" for a person is a plausible conflation in mapping from concept to lemma representation. A number of the cases of cross-field substitutions with an analogical flavor might be so described (e.g., "speed" for "temperature" in an action description for an oven; "awake" for "open" in the description of a restaurant; "years" for "yards" in a measure expression).

We should also note the relation of this characterization of the living/non-living contrast to findings by Flores d'Arcais and Schreuder (1987) with reference to visual object recognition. They distinguish P(erceptual) features and F(unctional) features as a means of accounting for patterns of lexical and picture priming in normal subjects. Flores d'Arcais and Schreuder connect the differences in priming effects of P features and F features to distinct components of the conceptual system that affect both visual object processing and lexical processing. Whether this is treated as two aspects of a common central processing system, as Flores d'Arcais and Schreuder do, or as the manifestation of two separate semantic systems, as Warrington and Shallice are inclined to do, the findings provide added evidence of the salience of this contrast.

In sum: there are some clear field effects in the aphasic errors; they involve some interesting classes that have conceptual plausibility, and they connect to similar phenomena in a normal speaker's patterns of speech errors. Moreover, there is some compelling indication for a difference in the relations between lexical (lemma) representations and conceptual representation and those between conceptual and perceptual representations (i.e., the Hart et al. findings). In the next section, we extend our enquiry to some questions about the different ways in which semantic errors may arise.

## 2.3. Causes of semantic error

An issue that directly affects our assessment of the import of a given aphasic error pattern is the probable assignment of the failure to one or more of the component processes that comprise the production and comprehension systems. Most accounts of semantic error have focused on the conceptual semantic system(s) or their relation to lexical representations. And the most natural account of semantic errors has seemed to most investigators to be some compromise of semantic systems themselves or some breakdown in the mechanisms that connect concepts to lexical items. For the most part, such accounts have not distinguished lexical representations of meaning from lexical representations of form (the lemma/word form distinction); or, in complementary spirit, have not distinguished semantic properties of lexical items from the conceptual representation of those properties (viz., the concept/lemma distinction). On the working account we are pursuing here, there are two general loci of potential failure that could give rise to semantic errors: conceptual impairment and various aspects of lemma processing (i.e., conceptual to lemma mapping, lemma representation failure, and lemma to form mapping). To these, Caramazza and Hillis (1990) add a third: word-form output system failure. We will consider these options in the context of observations of aphasic error patterns.

The relevance of conceptual and lemma impairments is obvious; the third option requires expansion. Caramazza and Hillis (1990) raise this issue in the context of observations of semantic error in two patients (RGB and HW) whose conceptual competence was demonstrably intact but who nevertheless made frequent semantic errors in reading and oral picture naming. They argue that patients, such as these, whose semantic errors are restricted to one or two task domains, and whose performance shows preserved comprehension, do not have a semantic processing problem. (In particular, they would argue that there is no need to postulate a modality-specific semantic impairment – a point of discussion that we will take up in section 2.4.) The alternative account they propose for these cases is that they have an output system problem, and that the failure of the phonological or orthographic systems to generate output permits a (possibly normal) pattern of semantic processing to reveal itself in error performance. The core assumption is that spreading activation from the target word to its neighbors at the semantic level makes semantically related words more available for output. A second factor in this argument is that alternative paths to correct naming (and hence to an inhibition of the semantically based erroneous response) must be blocked; so, in particular, for oral reading, print-to-sound conversion routes should be unavailable. Patients RGB and HW met these criteria – they generated frequent semantic errors for spoken output, demonstrated intact conceptual competence for performance in other modalities, and were quite unable to read non-words (i.e., to exploit a non-lexical print-to-sound conversion); on these grounds, Caramazza and Hillis ascribe their failure to output system compromise. By way of contrast, they also cite the case of a patient (KE) who showed a consistent pattern of semantic failures for lexical processing across all task domains, including those spoken and written word/picture-matching tasks that do not require a lexical output (Hillis et al., 1989). The source of KE's errors is therefore plausibly conceptual.

An essential feature of the explanation offered by Caramazza and Hillis is the activation of multiple lexical candidates in the production process that underlies these patients' performances. Such multiple activation might be seen either as a part of the impairment or as a part of the normal production process. The occurrence of semantically related word substitutions in normal speaker's error performances might be taken as evidence for the latter view; there is also some more direct evidence for the activation of multiple lexical candidates in normal production processes provided by lexical and phrasal blends (e.g., Fromkin, 1971; Garrett, 1980); for example, cases like "evoid" for evade/avoid or "sleast" for slightest/least. Such blends are of corresponding grammatical category (they are candidates for the same output slot in the intended utterance) and almost uniformly strongly synonymic. Constraints on blends and substitutions do differ in some respects, and these may reflect differences in processing that arise during or after lemma activation. However the detail of that issue may be settled, it is plausible on grounds of normal error processes including both blends and substitutions to assume the activation of multiple lexical candidates at the stage of message to lemma processing.

We should note at this juncture that the mechanism that gives rise to multiple candidates may involve semantic activation spreading, but need not. Other possibilities exist. It might be argued that a normal feature of lexical selection in production is the consideration of multiple lexical candidates – possibly as a consequence of the way in which the production system deals with the existence of multiple ways to express a given proposition. For example, Levelt's (1989) discussion of lemma selection characterizes it as (partly) determined by the emergence during message construction of message fragments that correspond to the conceptual representations specified in lemma representations. Depending on the detail of lemma and message matching procedures, it is possible that more than a single lemma will match the partial representation, indeed, it seems quite likely that several lemmas of a semantic field may match a message fragment, with these being distinguished only by the emergence of additional conceptual structure, or in some cases by the features that are associated with the pragmatic objectives of the message being formulated. There is a question, presently unanswered, of what constitutes the substructure of a message for which it is appropriate to initiate lemma retrieval. It is at least possible that the answer to this is not perfectly disciplined, being partly determined by what portions of the message structure have already been associated with a lemma and in part by the order in which message structures develop. An issue intimately connected with this would involve the (potential) constraints on the use of a message fragment in more than a single lemma-matching operation.

Under the sorts of circumstances we have just been discussing, or those associated with semantic spreading, a failure of the output system to generate a target word form could readily occur in the context of alternative lexical candidates, and the relation of these alternatives to the target would be the same as cases in which no output failure had occurred. Therefore, for aphasic errors traceable to such causes, whether by reason of the compromise of output systems as Caramazza and Hillis suggest or for another reason, a correspondence might be expected between the aphasic errors and patterns of relations seen in normal errors. This is a matter for which we have little systematic evidence at present, although, as earlier remarked, the impression to be derived from informal inspection of examples suggests a potentially interesting degree of correspondence.

To this question of assessing causal factors in aphasic patients' semantic errors, we might also apply the logic suggested by Levelt's (1989) analysis of associative cases of meaning substitutions. He reported some evidence that associatively connected but not (merely) semantically/conceptually related words showed frequency effects in substitution errors (higher-frequency forms tending to displace lower-frequency forms). Levelt's reasoning was applied to distinguish relations between lemmas from conceptual relations as error causes, but may be applied in the Caramazza and Hillis case as well. If, as they suggest, some meaning errors reflect the relative availability of word forms – as opposed to the processes that relate conceptual structure to lexical representations – one might expect more frequent forms to displace less frequent ones – or, perhaps, in terms of the mechanism suggested by Caramazza and Hillis, that the failure rate for target words should be greater for lower-frequency items (their activation levels are lower); and in complementary fashion, the intrusion rate for error words activated by semantic spreading should be greater for higher-frequency items (their activation levels are higher). The latter such effects are not supported for the semantic field substitutions considered in the study of semantic substitutions discussed in section 2.2 (Garrett, in press). There was no significant tendency for higher-frequency field members to replace lower-frequency ones or for the displaced words to come more often from lower-frequency strata. This would indicate, with the possible exception of the associatively related cases cited by Levelt, that the error mechanism for normal word substitutions is not the mechanism suggested for patients RGB and HW in the Caramazza and Hillis report, that is, the normal substitution errors would arise from processes specific to conceptually driven lemma selection rather than as an indirect consequence of word-form failures. Note, however, that semantic errors that do arise via the word-form system should show frequency effects and other evidence implicating word-form representations. Caramazza and Hillis did report that frequency influenced the error rate for RGB – fewer semantic errors were made for high-frequency targets than medium-frequency targets.

There is, however, a fly in this theoretical ointment, and it is the presence of selective semantic losses in RGB. Selective failures of the sort discussed in section 2.2 are not good candidates for the indirect error induction process we are considering here. Which phonological representation fails should, on our working assumptions and on Caramazza and Hillis's model, be unrelated to their semantic category. There is no reason to cross-classify *word forms* by semantic class and considerable reason not to, given the manifest semantic independence of the robust patterns in form-related word substitution errors in normals (Fay & Cutler, 1977; Garrett, 1975, 1980) and experimental demonstrations of the staged application of meaning and form relations in retrieval (Schriefers, Meyer, & Levelt, 1990). Thus, the fact that patient RGB showed category-specific effects in his semantic substitution errors poses a serious question. The only apparent answer lies in connecting the failure of a semantic category with lemma representations (which have linkages to word-form representations as part of their content). We are barred on the argument of Caramazza and Hillis from invoking a conceptual deficit for the category-specific errors (RGB's performance on word–picture matching and written naming was normal for this class). But, semantically specific lemma failure would be possible with preservation of conceptual competence. This puts a different light on the picture since the word-form system's failure to produce an output is not causal on this story; that is, it does not result from structure intrinsic to the word-form system itself. Note that this move will, while avoiding the postulation of semantic categories in the output lexicon, make the word-frequency effects discussed earlier problematic, since on the current evidence frequency does not have a strong impact on message-driven lemma processing.

A further, and quite instructive, problem remains. The most general version of a lemma account would assume that the semantic and syntactic content of lemma representations is compromised. But, we are apparently barred from such a conclusion in RGB's case: written naming is unimpaired in this patient – only oral naming performances yielded semantic errors. On the view that full lemma representations are compromised for the affected categories, all lemma-mediated retrieval tasks should be impaired. Two options suggest themselves. First, one might try to rationalize the successful written performance by an appeal to the slower rate of written naming responses and to the availability of error correction mechanisms not available for the spoken modality. Second (and perhaps not independently), one might specify the deficit in an even more limited way: the deficit might lie only with the aspect of lemma representations that provides their linkage to word-form representations. Note that in order to adopt this option one is required to presume direct, and *independent* mappings from lemmas to orthographic representations for writing and from lemmas to phonological and phonetic representations for pronounciation; that is, phonological word-form representations do not mediate the former (see, for example, Shallice, 1981). Without further evidence, a lemma account as compared with an output systems account cannot be decided.

## 2.4. Modality-specific semantic failures

The account in section 2.3 distinguished three loci for semantic word substitutions in the interaction between the message system, lemmas, and the word-form output system, See Rapp and Caramazza (1991) for review and discussion of related issues. There is yet another suggestion for the "fractionation" of these systems, this one at the semantic conceptual level itself.

Modality-specific failures of language performance (Shallice, 1988; Warrington & Shallice, 1984) have been interpreted as indicating separate semantic systems associated with different modalities. What is the empirical base for this interpretation? There seem to be two arguments. One relies on consistency of failure within as compared to between modalities of test (i.e., within-modality test/retest correlations for items vs. cross-modality correlations), with the most striking such instances being modality-specific semantic category losses. The other relies on demonstrations of preserved semantic competence in the impaired modality; that is, stimuli for which the system fails to produce an appropriate lexical output may nevertheless support a significant non-lexical demonstration (e.g., detailed mime performance) of intact knowledge. (Note: I am here using "modality" to distinguish language and various non-language systems.)

Selective semantic category losses in a subset of test modalities is a potentially powerful argument for modality-specific semantics; that is, the demonstration would be that the modality of performance was linked to the nature of the semantic loss, as if, for example, only animate objects were absent for picture-naming tasks but were present for naming responses to written definitions of words. This argument is only as good as the case for the claim that it is the functional classification of the objects or events that unites them in their susceptibility to error. If the afflicted set is equally well described by a common core of perceptual attributes, the force of the claim for a semantic system is diminished. Similarly for paradoxical mime or classification performances in the affected modality: the argument has force to the extent that the preserved performance goes beyond the acknowledged representations intrinsic to the perceptual or motor functions of the performance system, or to the extent that performance is not triggered by some non-semantic associative link between featural details of the items in the stimulus set and another set of representations not in the impaired modality.

Several examples of patterns of impairment have been cited in discussions of this issue. We need to look at some of the different types of argument to assess the status of these claims. Let us first consider some specific cases that concern the claim for preserved capacity in the impaired modality.

Denes and Semenza (1975) report a patient (PWD) whose naming for visual, tactile, and olfactory stimuli was very accurate, but who showed a significant deficit in naming environmental sounds. However, PWD could match sounds with appropriate pictures of sound sources in a four-choice decision task. An interpretation in terms of modality-specific semantics would hold that the failed modality for naming – audition – has an independent representational system that expresses relations between auditory events and visual experience, thus permitting associations of sound and picture that do not depend on the (impaired) system that mediates relations between non-linguistic auditory events and language.

What does such a pattern require us to say? The spoken naming output process is clearly intact and the relation between the naming system and a non-language auditory processing system clearly impaired; relations between visual coding of an auditory sound source (say the picture of a whistle) and auditory coding of sound is, however, functional, as are relations between pictures and words. But given these latter two links, the matter of a modality-specific semantic capacity is moot. The picture has access to both sound and name representations. We are not required to presume more than that the sound stimulus alone has impaired access to central processes.

While the sound alone does not support an analysis that will distinguish a name, that failure tells us nothing about the capacity of a picture stimulus to evoke information concerning characteristic sounds associated with an object or event. The patient may be unable to say, upon hearing a whistle sound, that it is a whistle, but when the picture of the appropriate source is presented, he presumably can say "well, it must be a whistle". The picture and the sound both have access to conceptual representations and they converge.

Notice that if the picture did *not* elicit correct naming, we would have some evidence (though not conclusive) that the picture processing was blocked from central semantic systems, and the successful association of picture and sound would more plausibly be attributed to a separate representational system (holding sound representations and some coding for the visual properties of their generators); the picture/sound match might then be cited as the basis for claiming significant structure in a modality-specific cognitive system.

Consider another example, that concerns mime performance, with two patients displaying complementary losses: Beauvois, Saillant, Meinninger, and Lhermitte (1978) report that their patient RG showed good auditory and visual naming, but very limited tactual naming. He could, however, mime the use of the objects he could not name from tactual inputs. Lhermitte and Beauvois (1973) report that their patient JF showed auditory and tactual naming superior to visual naming; visual inputs were not named or were misnamed, but mime for visual targets was successful.

In both instances we must ask what performance base the mime requires. On the face of it, for a patient like JF, the visual information elicits a description that is associated with an appropriate motor system representation, so we are not dealing in a set of perceptual object schema attributes, but in some cross-modal association of sensory and motor schemata. And, similarly for the tactual naming failure with mime success since it requires a relation between haptic and motor responses. In either case, the association of the miming gestures with the visual representation or the tactual representation may reflect general conceptual competence, a domain-specific relation, or brute association. Which?

The first question always to be posed concerns what such a patient reports of his or her subjective awareness of the identity of the object. This is crucial to the evaluation of the kind of representation that is driving the mime performance. If the subject claims knowledge of the object's identity, no modality-specific conclusion can be drawn (i.e., it would be like a conventional anomic attack in a normal person). If the patient denies knowledge of an object being palpated – that is, says "I don't recognize this" – and is then asked to mime its use or is tested in a tactile test of object association and succeeds, while still denying knowledge of the identity of the objects being palpated, one might, depending on the test, be entitled to a claim that some modality-specific associative performance has been demonstrated.

What would constitute "semantic competence" in the tactual system? If just a list of sensory predicates, it is a limited form that permits association of sensory input with stored representations – some necessary conditions for object identity could be stipulated. If we assume "semantic" capacity, one expects the representations, just as with words (and their auditory, visual, tactile representations) to lead to inferential processes that will connect the different representations in ways that are veridical. In the case of words, we don't put that part of the work at the level of the form representations – it is done via links to the meaning representations for words. Presumably, the same holds for the tactile array – they must be linked to some representational system, by the hypothesis at issue, modality specific, that will support semantically relevant behavior. If a subject could not name (i.e., denies knowledge of identity) a spoon or cup from its feel, access to the verbal information about relations between cups and spoons is presumably blocked. If that patient could then match cup and spoon (which are, presumptively, not themselves particularly similar tactually,) as a pair in a triple, such as spoon/cup/jar, one might be inclined to credit the tactile representational system with a significant inferential capability. In the instant case, Riddoch and Humphries (1987) report that a patient who failed at tactual naming and succeeded at miming failed a tactual association task. From one such failure, of course, we cannot discount the possibility of a future success that would satisfy these conditions.

Hillis et al. (1989) discussed the case of patient KE in examining semantic impairments. This patient showed consistent failure across a range of semantic tasks in different processing domains, indicating by Hillis et al.'s argument, the compromise of an "amodal lexical semantic component" that mediates performance in all motor and sensory domains. Such a case is presented as contra the "multiple semantics" hypothesis. Hillis et al. explore the nature of KE's impaired performance as a way to test the viability of a modality-neutral account of performance patterns that have been offered in support of modality-specific semantics. Paradoxical mime success is, for example, claimed to be non-semantic, that is, to be the result of features of modality-specific perceptual representations that are linked to the amodal semantic store. This account is offered for KE's failures with lexical inputs compared to success with perceptual inputs (e.g., the word "fork" was not distinguished from "spoon", but the picture of a fork produced an appropriate spearing motion – one inappropriate to a spoon).

Hillis et al. say the "cornerstone of this argument is the demonstration of intact semantic processing in the impaired modality" – correct miming or correct forced choice matching are the indices of semantic success. Question: what sort of representations are required to support such performances? Hillis et al. argue that the necessary level of knowledge is not semantic but is perceptually based. They observed that words have no information intrinsic to the objects they name – everything must come from the stored representation; but pictures and objects do have task-relevant information for mime performance or for discrimination and matching tasks (e.g., the parts of an object can be linked to conceptual structure – parts of words cannot). (See Caplan, 1992, for a related discussion.) We will return to the question of what the data from mime performance or category matching should be like to support a claim for modality-specific semantic capacity.

The preceding remarks concern ways in which performance in the impaired modality may suggest semantic competence. Contrast that with the other kind of argument for modality-specific semantics: the specificity of the losses relative to modality. Consider two hypothetical cases – one with a general loss of naming in a single modality and one with a specific loss in a single modality.

A. Visual naming fails quite generally (i.e., poor performance across all semantic classes), but miming is available and tactile naming succeeds well.
B. Visual naming fails specifically (i.e., poor performance just for animal or food terms), but mime and tactile naming succeed for the failed categories.

In case A, we may simply argue that there is a problem with naming mechanisms as they relate to the modality of input (e.g., visual object descriptions ↛ conceptual/name representations; naming output system is intact (tactile naming demonstrates this). The potential problem for an amodal semantic account will be to explain any demonstration of conceptual competence that can be offered for the failed modality (e.g., mime or successful picture sorting) – how can the appropriate structure for sorting be available, and not be sufficient to access the lemma system to provide the name? This is just the problem discussed in the preceding paragraphs.

In case B, we can say that there is a problem with the relation between the conceptual class and the naming representation; the naming machinery for that modality of input (visual object representations) is shown to be intact by the good performance on other categories than, for example, food. Thus names for food concepts are shown to be available in other modalities but not accessible from the visual representational system. The visual object representation link conceptual structure for food objects is weak; we know that the conceptual representation for food is *not* weak because of its satisfactory status in other modalities of performance. And we know that the concept to food–lemma links are not weak because they succeed, for example, for definitional inputs. The question then becomes one of interpreting the claim that the visual object representation to food concept links are weak. What does such a claim mean? If the modality-neutral conceptual representations are not impaired, it places the difficulty in the visual object representation system, and that requires that one distinguish such a category in that very representational system. But it does *not* indicate how that class is to be distinguished (viz., by accidental properties that have no compelling semantic force, or by representational features that may be plausibly linked to interpretation). Is it semantics? A priori, one cannot say. The answer lies in the nature of what must be spanned to represent the empirically certifiable cases of failure that motivate the assignment of the class label "objects for which food terms are appropriate".

In Warrington and Shallice (1984) the main supporting point for the modality-specific claim in the four patients reported there was that consistency of response in two of the patients tested was greater within than between modalities. The category deficits, however, showed up across modality. In the Warrington cases (1975, 1981) semantic class losses were modality specific, and similarly for the

Warrington and McCarthy report (1983); other cases in which semantic category losses were restricted to one or two modalities have been reported (e.g., Young et al., 1989; Caramazza & Hillis, 1990). These include the concrete/abstract contrast and subversions of the living/non-living contrast (e.g., animate/inanimate). Alternative accounts of some of the specific classes have been proposed, and the matter is by no means a settled one. There do seem cases, like that of the living/non-living contrast in which it is rather difficult to formulate a satisfactory non-conceptual description. The generality and reliability of such cases will in major part determine a preferred account.

Let us consider this problem a bit more generally. The existence of multiple "modes of thought" (visual images, kinesthetic codes, sequential structure, propositional structures) cannot be doubted even if the precise nature of the representations and processes associated with each is not established. Levelt (1989) puts this problem of modes of thought in the context of message construction. Message representations are necessarily propositional, and hence the conceptual systems that construct messages must provide for a translation of any non-propositional information into a propositional format; all modes must be translated into the propositional mode to the extent they can be talked about. Note that this position does not preclude direct translations between various of the non-propositional modes of thought, and these procedures for moving from one class of representations to another need not be propositional. Thus, Levelt's formulation is compatible with (though it does not require) the existence of modality-specific "semantic" systems. Production of a linguistic description is what forces a modality-neutral propositional representation.

How might this apply to the gestural evidence we considered earlier? Evidently the normal gestural repertoire we use in speaking has some global iconic properties, but these are not sufficient to support the detailed pantomime performances that are relevant to the "non-verbal" evaluations of language comprehension that figure in some assessments of aphasic performance. The processes that support a language user's ability to emulate on verbal command the motor schemata that would be engaged by real test objects or situations are not well understood. But it is clear that the mediation of the inferential system that constructs pre-verbal messages is a necessary component. A correspondence between the interpretation of the verbal commands and the representations that drive the gestural system must be established. It is, however, an open question where the "semantic" work that yields an appropriate performance is done.

Quite apart from the problem of gestural analysis, a significant range of information processing that might be described as "semantic" has been argued to take place within the visual domain (e.g., some of the processes that yield object recognition, mental rotation, relative size judgments, relative location judgments, and the rather complex interactions between language and visual problem-solving strategies suggested by Johnson-Laird, 1983). The interesting point, upon which a plausible exercise of a claim for "semantic competence" would depend is which, if any, of these capacities are preserved or impaired in a patient who presents with, for example, "optic aphasia" (and thus cannot name objects visually presented that can be named for tactile presentation, but can "gesture appropriately" for visual presentations that do not elicit the correct name). If the patient could produce a real range of semantically significant behavior in the name-deficient modality, one would be inclined to credit the modality-specific processing with something akin to what we mean by "semantic processing". The number and kind of tests for such capacity in language-impaired patients must be greater than what is currently available to reach a firm conclusion.

## 3. Syntactic category effects

The material in the preceding section examined aspects of the relation between meaning representations and lexical retrieval failures. In this section we consider some evidence that bears on the role of the other major feature of lemma representations, their syntactic description. There are two major classes of effect to be considered in reports of language disorders: those associated with differences in the failure rate for retrieval of nouns, verbs and adjectives – "open class" vocabulary; and those associated with failures of retrieval for minor grammatical category elements – "closed class" vocabulary.

### 3.1. Closed class retrieval failure

There are a number of reasons to distinguish open class and closed class retrieval problems as representing two species of error. This holds both in terms of patterns of aphasic failure and in terms of normal lexical processing for production. We will not review the evidence from normal performance here, but see Garrett (1980, 1988), Dell (1990), and Bock (1989) for a range of evaluations of the case for such a distinction in normal processing models.

The observations from aphasia that indicate some language-processing deficits specific to closed class vocabulary are for the most part familiar, but nevertheless striking in a number of ways. These include features of agrammatism, paragrammatism and deep dyslexia (see, for example, Saffran, Schwartz, & Marin, 1980, for an influential early discussion). Though our focus is on production, it is well to keep in mind that the relevant observations, particularly for agrammatism, include both comprehension and production performances. Agrammatism is, in the first instance, a disorder of production – the speech of such aphasics is notably deficient in the superficial marking for the phrasal organization of sentences and has been dubbed "telegraphic" as a way of describing its elided forms, with much reduced use of both bound and free grammatical morphemes. The effort to determine links between such production failures and certain comprehension limitations often observed in agrammatic patients (e.g., Caramazza & Zurif, 1976; Linebarger, Schwartz, & Saffran, 1983; Zurif, 1990) generated a number of quite interesting and important studies of that deficit that may suggest certain conclusions about the characteristic production failures.

Comprehension and production must be linked in many ways, but direct inference from a given structural failure for production to a claim for similar failure for comprehension is unwarranted (e.g., Miceli, Mazzucci, Menn, & Goodglass, 1983). Moreover, it is also clear that even in the common case where agrammatic production *is* associated with comprehension limitations, those limitations may not represent a straightforward generalization of the closed class retrieval failure evidenced in the agrammatic production pattern. There are now a number of demonstrations that agrammatics are sensitive to well-formedness constraints on the distribution of closed class elements even though they show the comprehension limitations characteristic of the disorder (Linebarger et al., 1983; Saddy, 1990; Schwartz, Linebarger, Saffran, & Pate, 1987; Shankweiler, Crain, Gorrell, and Tuller, 1989). Such recognition results show a detailed ability to use information about closed class constraints for well-formedness judgments *even* when there is compromised ability to interpret the same sentences. Thus, we must accept that the reduced presence of closed class elements in the output of agrammatic aphasics can reflect other limitations than a general failure to use the closed class information in specifically syntactic processes.

Though the preceding observations make it clear that one should approach claims about the relation between comprehension and production failures with utmost caution, perhaps it is not too adventurous to speculate that these two problems in agrammatism may implicate the same level of interaction among processing components. The locus of failure indicated by the comprehension studies is in the mapping from syntactic representations to interpretations – the phrasal analyses of sentences and their associated logical representations are not, for whatever reasons, successfully linked with the conceptual representations of message structures. If one applies that global conclusion to the analysis of production failures, one may be led to prospect for evidence that agrammatic failures in production reflect some limitation on appropriate semantic constraint for lemma retrieval and the associated processes of phrasal construction for language output, including the phrasal role of closed class elements. So, for example, major phrasal types might be represented and the distributional constraints on the appearance of closed class elements in phrasal structures available, but meaning contrasts within closed class sets compromised. Since the characteristic closed class failure for agrammatism is omission, such a compromise of closed class retrieval is difficult to evaluate; there is not that much to go on, but there are two or three straws in the wind.

This way of describing an underlying problem with agrammatic production seems to converge with the description of another major class of deviant production performances involving closed class vocabulary – that of paragrammatism. Paragrammatism is often observed in the speech of Wernicke's aphasics. The speech output is fluent and superficially well formed prosodically and syntactically. There are, however, numerous lexical substitutions in both open and closed class that violate semantic constraint. In extreme cases the speech may be uninterpretable. Paragrammatics often have comprehension problems, and it is at least plausible to describe the inappropriate use of both open and closed class vocabulary as a loss of the ability to select those elements that correspond to the target meaning – they have a message-to-lemma mapping problem. For present purposes, it is relevant that in paragrammatism the minor category boundaries are respected. That is, substitution appears to be within categories – pronouns substitute for other pronouns, prepositions for prepositions, connectives and qualifiers for other elements of the same subclasses (see, for example, Butterworth & Howard, 1987).

It is in this respect that there is some evidence for similarities between paragrammatic and agrammatic performance. Grodzinksy's (1984) report of agrammatic performance in Hebrew is relevant. In languages like Hebrew and Arabic, the different morphemes of a polymorphemic word are not independently pronounceable – as they are in a language like English with linear ordering of morphemes affixed to a base. In languages with non-linear morphology, the phonological components of morphemic constituents are discontinuous and the stem form cannot be uttered without its affixal elements. This presents a pretty puzzle to a Broca's aphasic in Hebrew: omission of the closed class elements is not an option. Grodzinsky's observation is that there are frequent incorrect substitutions within the inflectional subclasses. A possibly related observation is reported by Kolk (1987; Kolk, Van Grunsven, & Keyser, 1985). In tasks in which agrammatic speakers were required to generate closed class forms – a "forced production" situation – he reports frequent substitution errors; these substitutions are within closed class subcategories – agrammatic errors and paragrammatic errors are similar in at least that respect. More strongly, Butterworth and Howard (1987) have argued that both agrammatic patterns of omission and paragrammatic patterns of substitution were present in the speech of the fluent aphasics of their study.

One may wish to consider the possibility that the structural and lexical failures in agrammatism and paragrammatism have some common factors – which may be manifest in the processes that map from message representation to sentence form, with the processes of lemma retrieval as an integral part of that link. I do not suggest that typical agrammatic Broca's aphasics do not differ in important ways from typical paragrammatic Wernicke's aphasics. The differences that lead to their different clinical classifications are evident enough. But from that it does not follow that there can be no significant overlap in their language-processing problems. For example, the differences in fluency and in awareness and self-monitoring are striking, but neither of these need be linked directly to the limitations of structural or processing capacity that impair their language production and comprehension, even though both might affect the character of their surface language behavior in various ways (see, for example, Kolk, 1987, for one discussion). The particular suggestion entertained here is that some aspect of the processes that express message constraints on closed class selection may be compromised in both groups. That compromise does not implicate open class elements in the same measure for agrammatics as for paragrammatics. (See Butterworth & Howard, 1987, for a related discussion.)

The constraint of grammatical subcategories on closed class substitution patterns in both agrammatism and paragrammatism is the principal empirical observation that suggests a common factor. There are many subclasses of the closed class elements, and because the classes are small and syntactically distinct their intersubstitution within subcategory contrasts quite sharply with a simple overall category constraint. One way to highlight and extend this observation is to contrast the agrammatic and paragrammatic patterns with that of closed class reading failures in deep dyslexia. This is also a condition in which closed class failure is prominent. The reading errors by deep dyslexics are sometimes described in terms of a category hierarchy, with fewest errors observed in reading concrete nouns and the highest error rate for reading closed class elements, with verbs and adjectives falling between. Closed class failure is prominent, as it is for agrammatism. Indeed, it is the case that many deep dyslexics are agrammatic speakers, but as Coltheart (1980) points out, deep dyslexic reading performance is not always associated with agrammatic speech; the locus of failure may well be different for the two impairments. The most pertinent observation is that, for reading words in isolation, there is clear and frequent failure of closed class grammatical *sub*category correspondence in deep dyslexic errors. So, one sees prepositions being read as modals, pronouns as conjunctions, quantifiers as determiners, etc. (see examples in Coltheart, 1980). And these are, of course, reading errors that may be associated with failures of a second-stage retrieval or transcoding operation rather than failures of some aspect of a lemma mapping operation. It is significant that when deep dyslexics are required to read text rather than isolated words, success in reading closed class elements is somewhat improved and there is some evidence for constraint of grammatical category on substitutions. This suggests two routes to the production of closed class items: one that involves lemma access and is mediated by the recovery of phrasal structure, and one that depends on connections between orthographic representations and phonological representations, including, but not necessarily limited to, grapheme-to-phoneme conversion. The latter system(s) is, by the emprical observations just cited, not constrained by the syntactic structure of the closed class vocabulary.

We note in passing the possibility that this performance feature might also express a guessing system for the deep dyslexics – they recognize failure to contact a closed class entry when reading an isolated word, and just guess, but do so unconstrained by anything but the gross category – no phrasal information is present. Notice that no new claim about special storage of closed class elements in an undifferentiated set is required for this hypothesis. If the normal retrieval of such elements in recognition is constrained by local phrasal geometry, absence of such information might well yield an error signal if the alternative route through orthographic conversion were blocked, and that error signal could invoke the guessing strategy.

Some suggestions have been made about normal retrieval for closed class elements that relate to these observations of agrammatic and paragrammatic speech. Certain features of normal speech errors suggest the hypothesis that open and closed class words are recruited by different retrieval processes in normal language production (Garrett, 1975, 1980). On that hypothesis, open class retrieval and phrasal construction are carried out in related but distinct processes, and the retrieval of closed class elements is identified with the recovery of the surface phrasal configurations for sentences; that is, the closed class forms, both bound and free, are asserted to be features of the representation of phrasal planning frames used to integrate the systematic phonological representations of sentences. Arguments for modification of one aspect of that proposal have been made. Lapointe and Dell (1989) have argued that only bound forms are associated with planning frames and that free forms in the closed class inventory are separately recovered. This invites, but does not require, identifying the retrieval mechanisms of open class and closed class free forms. (See Bock, 1989, for an experimental test of one version of the hypothesis that closed class free forms are associated with phrasal frames.)

If some version of the original hypothesis could be sustained, the association of closed class forms with the phrasal planning for pronunciation might provide a way to account for the features of agrammatic and paragrammatic production discussed above. In the general terms of contrasts between closed class and open class elements, both impairments may yield phrasal structures whose defects can be dissociated from the open class content items that appear in those frames. Note: this is not to claim that open class elements are unaffected in agrammatic or paragrammatic performance, but only that mechanisms for such defects may be distinguished in significant ways from those for closed class elements. For example, Lecours (1982) reviews a number of case reports and experiments that show compromise of open class performance that contrasts with intact closed class performances in aphasia, observing, for example, that phonemic paraphasias and neologisms seem restricted to the open class. He suggests that such contrasts may hold both for bound and free closed class forms.

In this connection we should also note that Butterworth and Howard (1987) have reported that the incidence of neologisms – which one may take as one index of open class failure – is unrelated to the incidence of paragrammatic errors (both open and closed) in their speech samples. They interpret this and the existence of paragrammatisms that are not readily analyzable as word substitutions as an argument against a lexical retrieval account of paragrammatism. However, barring the requirement that every error in the paragrammatic speech of fluent aphasic be attributable to a single cause, the fact that some errors occur (e.g., lexical anticipations or perseverations; resumptive pronouns) that are not simple substitutions really does not impugn a lexical account of a major portion of closed class failures in paragrammatism. Moreover, there is a great difficulty in actually identifying errors as *not* representing a lexical failure. The case is a bit easier if one insists that each error must be recoverable by a single lexical replacement. But even in that perhaps overstringent case, a number of the errors presented in their paper as constructional errors could, by substitution at another locus in the sentence than the one they chose, be rendered grammatical with a single lexical change. Finally, we should bear in mind that more than one sort of lexical account may be considered. The one they argue against is apparently at the form retrieval level rather than at the lemma level and the phrase building that is associated with lemma recovery. We will turn to another such option in the discussion of Levelt's model of lexical recovery and phrasal construction.

A related but somewhat different proposal for the indirect access of closed class vocabulary has been described by Levelt (1989). For example, in prepositions, he distinguishes those retrieved directly at lemma level and those retrieved indirectly; that is, by being specified in the entry for another lemma. This latter retrieval device applies in a number of similar cases. The activation of such items is not conceptually mediated, but is done by indirect means associated with the syntactic construction of phrases. For example, the lemma for AUX is not directly driven conceptually, but determined by conditions of tense, aspect, mood. Such cases contrast with modals, which on Levelt's account are directly activated conceptually. The treatment of modals is different from that of other auxiliary elements; and similarly there is different treatment for the two sorts of preposition forms as well. All these elements would fall within the closed class and be given uniform treatment on the speech-error-motivated hypothesis of distinct open and closed class retrieval processes. Levelt's treatment distinguishes within this class. The available evidence for aphasic production performance with the closed class does not give us clear evidence to determine if the more restricted treatment of indirect access in Levelt's proposal could be made to capture the relevant contrasts of agrammatic and paragrammatic closed class performance. One might try to find a convergence of Levelt's proposal and the proposal based on speech error analyses by applying the one (Levelt's) at lemma access and the other at the level of phonological interpretation of surface phrasal structures. Either could accommodate the preservation of closed class subcategories for semantically inappropriate substitutions, but the locus of the agrammatic and/or paragrammatic production deficit would be assigned to different aspects of sentence-building processes. We will return to this matter in the context of our discussion of aspects of major category retrieval limitations to be taken up next.

## 3.2. Major category contrasts

A factor in semantic substitutions for which there is little to go on in aphasia reports is the effect of major grammatical category constraints on aphasic word substitutions. In normal errors, correspondence of grammatical category for target and error words is a very powerful constraint. This is consonant with – though it does not demand – the characterization of such semantic substitutions as failures of lemma selection. But, for aphasic errors of semantic substitution, this constraint is difficult to evaluate since so much of the data arises from reading and picture-naming tasks in which the grammatical category of the target is constrained by the elicitation procedure as well as by whatever language-processing steps are required for generation of the response. In reading tasks where grammatical category is varied, published examples of errors in aphasic performance seem responsive to the constraint (e.g., Caramazza and Hillis, 1991). The observation that the paragrammatic speech of some fluent aphasics is substantially well formed with respect to major lexical and phrasal categories is an indication that the frequent word substitutions that occur in such disorders are matched in grammatical category (i.e., target and error correspond). But detail is lacking on this point and it will require additional observation.

There are some features of aphasic language performance, however, that are persuasively related to major category contrasts. One example comes from two case studies by Caramazza and Hillis (1991), and the other, more general finding, from a contrast in the performance of agrammatic and anomic aphasics.

The report by Caramazza and Hillis bears on this general issue and indicates that a selective impairment of verbs may be observed in cases with no semantic impairment – comprehension performance is unimpaired and the lexical impairment is modality specific. They report two patients: one (patient HW) who showed greater impairment for verbs than for nouns in oral output only, and a second (patient SJD) who showed such an impairment in written output only. They interpreted their findings as evidence for the redundant marking of grammatical category in the representations for phonological and orthographic output systems. Note that these findings of impaired performance specific to grammatical category are not obviously associated with the same causes as those discussed below for the contrast in agrammatic and anomic patients. Both HW and SJD showed impairment of verbs relative to performance for nouns, and both are characterized as fluent aphasics. In the contrast of agrammatic and anomic performance, the non-fluent agrammatics show impaired verb performance.

Two related studies (Miceli, Silveri, Villa, & Caramazza, 1984; Zingeser & Berndt, 1990) demonstrate a contrast in the processing of nouns and verbs in a number of different tasks, and most interestingly it is evidence for a double dissociation – superior performance for nouns compared to verbs in one aphasic group and just the reverse in a contrasting group. These two groups are anomic aphasics and agrammatic Broca's aphasics.

The experimental evaluations noted are responsive to a history of clinical reports of differences in the performance of agrammatics and anomics vis à vis verbs and nouns, with agrammatics observed to display impaired verb production – manifest again by the occurrence of few verbs in their speech and by the nominalization of verb forms in context for which verbs would normally be used. Similarly, the circumlocutory speech of anomics and associated word-finding difficulty seem associated with the noun class. This difference in apparent lexical impairments may be linked to the poor sentence-level performance of agrammatics and to the unimpaired sentence structures for anomics whose difficulty is with nouns, a point taken up below.

The Zingeser and Berndt study of five agrammatics and four anomics (based on BDAE) used several different tasks (picture naming, naming to definition, action description, elicited narrative) to assess performance for target words that were form class unambiguous, frequency and length-matched nouns and verbs. This experiment represents an English language version of the earlier Miceli et al. experiment, in which Italian aphasics' performance was studied. There the noun–verb categories are marked by affixation. In the English language version, this contrast is based on frequency of use of the words selected for the experimental tasks.

For the naming and description tasks, the patterns showed agrammatics to be more impaired for verbs than for nouns, and anomics showed the reverse pattern. For the connected speech task, the ratio of N to V showed the same general pattern: anomic N/V ratio (.78) = controls (.93), but agrammatics were sharply different – N/V ratio = 2.08. The pattern of results was the same in both the Italian study and in the English language study. Note that the depressed verb performance for agrammatics in both a picture-naming task and definitional tasks shows that it is not an effect peculiar to the use of an elicitation procedure more suited to nouns than to verbs, that is, a "picture-naming effect".

Miceli et al. argue against a syntactic processing account of the verb deficit in agrammatism on grounds that the verb deficit shows up in deep dyslexics (who are typically agrammatic). This observation depends on assuming that syntactic processing is not required in the reading aloud failures for isolated verbs (and closed class items) typical of those patients. However, it is worth recalling that the performance of deep dyslexics with both closed class and open class reading may reflect different causal factors than their picture naming or descriptive speech. Miceli et al. also argue that the closed class failures and the verb deficit are unrelated – some patients may show one without the other (i.e., some agrammatic speakers show a normal verb/noun ratio).

The general thesis they advance for these contrasts is that it is a lexicon problem. Miceli et al. note that the correct nominalizations for verbs that are often produced by agrammatics are evidence that the conceptual capacity for the semantic distinctions carried by problematic lexical items is retained. Though specifically conceptual compromise may be unlikely as the source of these differences, no clear case can be made from these data as to whether they arise from a semantic-to-lexical mapping failure or elsewhere in the lexicon.

Zingeser and Berndt suggest that the noun/verb differences they observed between agrammatic and anomic patients may be related to sentence construction processes. This is based on the central role in sentence organization provided by verbs – the argument structures and subcategorization frames associated with verbs are in a quite reasonable sense the major basis for the syntactic organization of sentences. The suggestion fits the observations that agrammatics, who display difficulty with the interpretation and fluent production of syntactic structures, are the same aphasic group who show impaired performance with verbs, and in complementary fashion, anomics, who show normal verb profiles, also seem to have normal control of syntactic structure.

We can make a more specific case for this suggestion by considering Levelt's model of syntax generation: certain substructures in messages correspond to lemmas; which fragments of messages are so interpretable and the order in which their components are elaborated in message construction will determine the lexicalization of messages. And that in turn will have an impact on the syntactic expression of the message in a system like the one proposed by Levelt in which access to constructive syntactic routines is via the lemma representations recovered from tests for correspondence of message substructures and a lemma's conceptual description.

Consider anomia in this light. If it were at the level of lemma retrieval, it should interfere with phrasal construction. But such does not appear to be the case – phrasal construction in anomia is apparently normal. Hence, the locus of anomic failure is more plausibly placed at the word-form retrieval level; the evidence for anomic performance noted in section 1.1 is consonant with that view.

What about agrammatism? In the productions of agrammatics, we do have evidence of failures in the phrasal construction process, and by the line of argument we are considering, one might opt for a characterization of agrammatism as, at least in part, an impairment of the lemma retrieval process. Notice, as argued earlier, this might also have as an indirect consequence the impairment of production for certain of the closed class vocabulary elements, that is, those which are recovered by indirect retrieval (by specification from lemma representations rather than by direct conceptual nomination).

As a final point, we should briefly consider the role of frequency in accounts of the grammatical category effects we have reviewed. There is clearly more than frequency at issue in all these contrasts. In the noun/verb case, the experimental results showing complementary effects were frequency controlled and cannot be plausibly attributed to some general tendency for higher-frequency vocabulary elements to better survive neurological impairment. Such general accounts also fare poorly when applied to other grammatical category contrasts.

It has been suggested that in some or all of the performance the contrasts for open and closed class vocabulary in both normal (e.g., Dell, 1990) and in aphasic language are the consequence of the very substantial frequency differences between the classes. Though this is most certainly a hypothesis that deserves continuing and careful examination for any particular performance difference proposed to depend on such categorial differences, it is difficult to see how it can be made to satisfy the full range of reported dissociations. So, for example, homophonic open class/closed class word pairs (e.g., bee/be, wood/would) have been reported to show opposite patterns of success for Broca's and Wernicke's aphasics (Marin, Saffran, & Schwartz, 1976), with the former succeeding better with the open class version and the latter with the closed. Ellis et al.'s report of a case study showing no difference for a Wernicke's patient reading frequency-matched open and closed class words indicates that frequency may play a role in such cases; that is, the apparent intactness of closed class vocabulary in Wernicke's patients may reflect the greater frequency of those elements. But that observation does not address the dissociation of effect in the two patient groups. One may, of course, simply argue that the paragrammatic and agrammatic difficulties with closed class elements are quite unrelated and that frequency protects closed class in Wernicke's and not in Broca's. If so, the relations between paragrammatic compromise and agrammatic compromise of closed class will require other accounts.

In general, for many closed class observations, frequency accounts pose an inconsistency. When one observes that frequency has a powerful effect on a lexical performance – for example, anomic failures are more noteworthy for lower-frequency items, these are open class effects: closed class items that show impaired performance in agrammatism and paragrammatism are higher in frequency than the open class elements that show a retrieval advantage relative to lower-frequency open class words. This pattern for frequency is also present in deep dyslexic failure with closed class elements. Here again, the most frequent elements in the language show the lowest performance levels but only if they are closed class; for open class elements, frequency is correlated with sparing. Such frequency effects on lexical performance must be stated in terms of open and closed class categories.

## 4. Summary

There are diverse effects of aphasic performance that implicate the effectiveness of lexical retrieval processes. The processes that recover individual lexical items under conceptual control have a detailed substructure that distinguishes the semantic and syntactic aspects of lexical description from their abstract phonological description. More precisely, the indications from the aphasic patterns of disturbance are that the lemma level is necessary as an interface between phonological representation and conceptual representation. The recovery of lemma representations appears to be susceptible to impairment independent of the compromise of conceptual structure. That impairment could represent a defect either of the representation of specific lemmas or of the processes that are responsible for determining the correspondence relations between a lemma's conceptual representation and substructures of the message. No good basis to distinguish these two possibilities suggests itself from the available data. The relation between the semantic features of lemma representation and the syntactic features is similarly obscure on the aphasic evidence. It is clear enough that losses that reflect grammatical category membership are identifiable and that the detail of their patterning is consistent with the general character of normal processing model distinctions. In many instances, however, the evidence concerning grammatical category effects is fragmentary and the basis for distinguishing such effects from correlated conceptual level compromise not readily found.

In general, it seems rather clear that the study of language impairments intersects issues in the study of normal processing in detailed ways that are significant for deciding unsettled processing questions. There are, therefore, a number of problems for which we may expect focused study of language impairment will contribute to our better understanding of the models that are being developed for normal language processing performance.

## References

Bayles, K., Tomoeda, C., & Trosset, M. (1990). Naming and categorial knowledge in Alzheimer's disease: The process of semantic memory deterioration. *Brain and Language, 39*, 498–510.

Beauvois, M., Saillant, B., Meininger, V., & Lhermitte, F. (1978). Bilateral tactile aphasia: A tacto-verbal dysfunction. *Brain, 101*, 381–401.

Bloch, D. (1986). *Defining the speech production impairment in a case of Wernicke's neologistic jargon aphasia: A speech error analysis*. PhD dissertation, University of Pennsylvania.

Bock, J.K. (1989). Closed class immanence in sentence production. *Cognition, 31*, 163–186.

Brown, R., & McNeill, D. (1966). The tip of the tongue phenomenon. *Journal of Verbal Learning and Verbal Behavior, 5*, 325–337.

Buckingham, H.W. (1979). Linguistic aspects of lexical retrieval disturbances in the posterior fluent aphasias. In H. Whitaker & H.A. Whitaker (Eds.), *Studies in neurolinguistics* (Vol. 4, p. 269). New York: Academic Press.

Buckingham, H.W. (1985). Preservation in aphasia. In S. Newman & R. Epstein (Eds.), *Current perspectives in dysphasia*. Edinburgh: Churchill Livingstone.

Butterworth, B. (1980). Some constraints on models of language production. In B. Butterworth (Ed.), *Language Production, Vol. 1: Speech and Talk* (pp. 423–459). London: Academic Press.

Butterworth, B. (1985). Jargon aphasia: Processes and strategies. In S. Newman & R. Epstein (Eds.), *Current perspectives in dysphasia*. Edinburgh: Churchill Livingstone.

Butterworth, B., & Beatty, G. (1978). Gesture and silence as indicators of planning in speech. In R. Campbell & G.T. Smith (Eds.), *Recent advances in the psychology of language: Formal and experimental approaches*. New York: Plenum Press.

Butterworth, B., & Howard, D. (1987). Paragrammatisms. *Cognition, 26*, 1–37.

Caplan, D. (1992). *Language: Structure, processing and disorders*. Cambridge, MA: MIT Press, Bradford Books.

Caramazza, A. (1988). Some aspects of language processing revealed through analysis of acquired aphasia: The lexical systems. *Annual Review of Neurosciences, 11*, 395–421.

Caramazza, A., & Hillis, A. (1990). Where do semantic errors come from? *Cortex, 26*, 95–122.

Caramazza, A., & Hillis, A. (1991). Lexical organization of nouns and verbs in the brain. *Reports of the Cognitive Neuropsychology Laboratory, 90-10*, Johns Hopkins University.

Caramazza, A., & Miceli, G. (1990). The structure of graphemic representations. *Cognition, 37*, 243–297.

Caramazza, A., & Zurif, E. (1976). Dissociation of algorithmic and heuristic processes in language comprehension: Evidence from aphasia. *Brain and Language, 3*, 572–582.

Coltheart, M. (1980). Deep dyslexia: A review of the syndrome. In M. Coltheart, K. Patterson, & J. Marshall (Eds.), *Deep dyslexia*. London: Routledge and Kegan Paul.

Damasio, A.R. (1990). Category related recognition deficits as a clue to the neural substrates of knowledge. *Trends in Neuroscience, 13*, 95–98.

Dell, G. (1986). A spreading activation theory of retrieval in sentence production. *Psychological Review, 93*, 283–321.

Dell, G. (1990). Effects of frequency and vocabulary type on phonological speech errors. *Language and Cognitive Processes, 5*, 313–349.

Dell, G., & Reich, P. (1981). Stages in sentence production: An analysis of speech error data. *Journal of Verbal Learning and Verbal Behavior, 20*, 611–629.

Denes G., & Semenza, C. (1975). Auditory modality-specific anomia: Evidence from a case of pure word deafness. *Cortex, 11*, 401–411.

Dennis, M. (1976). Dissociated naming and location of body parts after left anterior temporal lobe resection: An experimental case study. *Brain and Language, 3*, 147–163.

Fay, D., & Cutler, A. (1977). Malapropisms and the structure of the mental lexicon. *Linguistic Inquiry, 8*, 505–520.

Flores d'Arcais, G.B., & Schreuder, R. (1987). Semantic activation during object naming. *Psychological Research, 49*, 153–159.

Flores d'Arcais, G.B., Schreuder, R., & Glazenborg, G. (1985). Semantic activation during recognition of referential words. *Psychological Research, 47*, 39–49.

Fromkin, V. (1971). The non-anomalous nature of anomalous utterances. *Language, 47*, 27–52.

Fromkin, V. (1987). The lexicon: Evidence from acquired dyslexia. *Language, 63*, 1–22.

Garrett, M.F. (1975). The analysis of sentence production. In G. Bower (Ed.), *Psychology of learning and motivation* (Vol. 9, pp. 133–175). New York: Academic Press.

Garrett, M.F. (1980). Levels of processing in sentence production. In B. Butterworth (Ed.), *Language production, Vol. 1: Speech and talk* (pp. 177–210). London: Academic Press.

Garrett, M.F. (1988). Processes in language production. In F. Newmeyer (Ed.), *Linguistics: The Cambridge survey, Vol. III: Language: psychological and biological aspects*. New York: Cambridge University Press.

Garrett, M.F. (in press). Lexical retrieval processes: Semantic field effects. In E. Kittay & A. Lehrer (Eds.), *Frames, fields and contrast*. Hillsdale, NJ: Erlbaum.

Goodglass, H., & Budin, C. (1988). Auditory comprehension deficit for body parts, colors, numbers, and letters. *Neuropsychologia, 26*, 67–78.

Goodglass, H., Kaplan, E., Weintraub, S. & Ackerman, N. (1976). The tip-of-the-tongue phenonomenon in aphasia. *Cortex, 12*, 143–153.

Goodglass, H., Klein, B., Carey, P., & Jones, K. (1966). Specific semantic word categories in aphasia. *Cortex, 2*, 74–89.

Grodzinksy, Y. (1984). The syntactic characterization of agrammatism. *Cognition, 16*, 99–120.

Harley, T. (1984). A critique of top down independent models of speech production: Evidence from non-plan-internal errors. *Cognitive Science, 8*, 191–219.

Hart, J., Berndt, R., & Caramazza, A. (1985). Category specific naming deficit following cerebral infarction. *Nature, 316*, 439–440.

Hillis, A., & Caramazza, A. (1990). Mechanisms for accessing lexical representations for output: Evidence from a category-specific semantic deficit. *Reports of the Cognitive Neuropsychology Laboratory, 90-7*, Johns Hopkins University.

Hillis, A., & Caramazza, A. (1991). Lexical organization of nouns and verbs in the brain. *Nature, 349*, 788–790.

Hillis, A., Rapp, B., Romani, C., & Caramazza, A. (1989). Selective impairment of semantics in lexical processing. *Reports of the Cognitive Neuropsychology Laboratory, 41*, Johns Hopkins University.

Hinton, G., & Shallice, T. (1989). Lesioning a connectionist network: Investigations of acquired dyslexia. *Technical report CRG-TR-89-3*, Department of Computer Science, University of Toronto.

Hotopf, W. (1980). Semantic similarity as a factor in whole-word slips of the tongue. In V. Fromkin (Ed.), *Errors in linguistic performance: Slips of the tongue, ear, pen and hand* (pp. 97–109). New York: Academic Press.

Humphries, G., & Riddoch, M. (1987). On telling your fruit from your vegetables: A consideration of category specific deficits after brain damage. *Trends in Neurosciences, 10*, 145–148.

Humphries, G., & Riddoch, M. (1988). On the case for multiple semantic systems: A reply to Shallice. *Cognitive Neuropsychology, 5*, 143–150.

Johnson-Laird, P. (1983). *Mental models: Towards a cognitive science of language, inference, and consciousness*. Cambridge, MA: Harvard University Press.

Kohn, S.E., & Goodglass, H. (1985). Picture naming in aphasia. *Brain and Language, 24*, 266–283.

Kolk, H. (1987). A theory of grammatical impairment in aphasia. In G. Kempen (Ed.), *Natural language generation: New results in artificial intelligence, psychology and linguistics*. Dordrecht: Martinus Nijhoff.

Kolk, H., Van Grunsven, M., & Keyser, A. (1985). Agrammatism as a variable phenomenon. *Cognitive Neuropsychology, 2*, 347–384.

Lapointe, S., & Dell, G. (1989). A synthesis of some recent work in sentence production. In G. Carlson and M. Tanenhaus (Eds.), *Linguistic structure in language processing*. Dordrecht: Kluwer.

Lhermitte, F., & Beauvois, M. (1973). A visual-speech disconnection syndrome. *Brain, 96*, 695–714.

Lecours, A.R. (1982). On neologisms. In J. Mehler, F. Walker, M. Garrett, S. Franck (Eds.), *Perspectives on mental representation*. Hillsdale, NJ: Erlbaum.

Lecours, A.R., & Rouillon, F. (1976). Neurolinguistic analysis of jargonaphasia and jargonagraphia. In H. Whitaker & H.A. Whitaker (Eds.), *Studies in Neurolinguistics* (Vol. 2). New York: Academic Press.

Levelt, W.J.M. (1989). *Speaking: From intention to articulation*. Cambridge, MA: MIT Press.

Linebarger, M., Schwartz, M., & Saffran, E. (1983). Sensitivity to grammatical structure in so-called agrammatic aphasics. *Cognition, 13*, 361–392.

Marin, O., Saffran, E., & Schwartz, M. (1976). Dissociations of language in aphasia: Implications for normal function. *Annals of the New York Academy of Sciences, 280*, 868–884.

Marshall, J. (1986). The description and interpretation of aphasic language disorder. *Neuropsychologia, 24*, 5–24.

Marshall, J., & Newcombe, F. (1966). Syntactic and semantic errors in paralexia. *Neuropsychologia*, 4, 169–176.

Marshall, J., & Newcombe, F. (1973). Patterns of paralexia: A psycholinguistic approach. *Journal of Psycholinguistic Research*, 2, 175–199.

Martin, A. (1987). Representation of semantic and spatial knowledge in Alzheimer's patients: Implications for preserved learning in models of amnesia. *Journal of Experimental and Clinical Neuropsychology*, 9, 191–224.

Martin, A., & Fedio, P. (1983). Word production and comprehension in Alzheimer's disease: The breakdown of semantic knowledge. *Brain and Language*, 19, 124–141.

McKenna, P., & Warrington, E. (1978). Category-specific naming preservation: A single case study. *Journal of Neurology, Neurosurgery, and Psychiatry*, 41, 571–574.

Miller, G.A., & Johnson-Laird, P. (1976). *Language and perception*. Cambridge, MA: Harvard University Press.

Miceli, G., Mazzucci, A., Menn, L., & Goodglass, H. (1983). Contrasting cases of Italian agrammatic aphasia without comprehension disorder. *Brain and Language*, 19, 65–97.

Miceli, G., Silveri, M.C., Villa, G., & Caramazza, A. (1984). On the basis for the agrammatics' difficulty in producing main verbs. *Cortex*, 20, 207–220.

Patterson, K. (1978). Phonemic dyslexia: Errors of meaning and the meaning of errors. *Quarterly Journal of Experimental Psychology*, 30, 587–607.

Pease, D., & Goodglass, H. (1978). The effects of cueing on picture naming in aphasia. *Cortex*, 14, 178–189.

Rapp, B.C., & Caramazza, (1991). A. Lexical deficits. In M. Sarno (Ed.), *Acquired aphasia*. Orlando: Academic Press.

Riddoch, M., & Humphreys, G. (1987). Visual object processing in optic aphasia: A case of semantic access agnosia. *Cognitive Neuropsychology*, 4, 131–185.

Saddy, J.D. (1990). *Investigations into grammatical knowledge*. PhD dissertation, Massachusetts Institute of Technology.

Saffran, E., Schwartz, M., & Marin, O. (1980). Evidence from aphasia: Isolating the components of a production model. In: B. Butterworth (Ed.), *Language production, Vol. 1: Speech and talk* (pp. 221–241) London: Academic Press.

Schwartz, M. (1987). Patterns of speech production deficit within and across aphasia syndromes: Application of a psycholinguistic model. In: M. Coltheart, G. Sartori, & R. Job (Eds.), *The cognitive neuropsychology of language*. London: Erlbaum.

Schwartz, M., Linebarger, M., Saffran, E., & Pate, D. (1987). Syntactic transparency and sentence interpretation in aphasia. *Language and Cognition*, 2, 85–113.

Schwartz, M., Nolan, K., & Saffran, E. (1985). Anomia in dementia: Studies in the semantics of object concepts. Unpublished manuscript, University of Pennsylvania.

Schwartz, M., Saffran, E., & Dell, G. (1990). *Comparing speech error patterns in normals and jargon aphasics: Methodological issues and theoretical implications*. Unpublished MS, Academy of Aphasia presentation, Baltimore, MD, October 1990.

Shallice, T. (1988). *From neuropsychology to mental structure*. Cambridge, UK: Cambridge University Press.

Shallice, T. (1981). Phonological agraphia and the lexical route in writing. *Brain*, 104, 413–429.

Shallice, T. & Coughlan, A. (1980). Modality specific work comprehension deficits in deep dyslexia. *Journal of Neurology, Neurosurgery and Psychiatry*, 43, 866–872.

Shallice, T., & McGill, J. (1978). The origins of mixed errors. In J. Requin (Ed.), *Attention and performance, Vol. 7*. Hillsdale, NJ: Erlbaum.

Shankweiler, D., Crain, S., Gorrell, P., & Tuller, B. (1989). Reception of language in Broca's aphasia. *Language and Cognitive Processes*, 4, 1–33.

Stemberger, J.P. (1985). An interactive action model of language production. In A. Ellis (Ed.), *Progress in the psychology of language*. Hillsdale, NJ: Erlbaum.

Warrington, E. (1975). The selective impairment of semantic memory. *Quarterly Journal of Experimental Psychology*, 27, 635–657.

Warrington, E. (1981). Concrete word dyslexia. *British Journal of Psychology*, 75, 175–196.

Warrington, E., & McCarthy, R. (1983). Category specific access dysphasia. *Brain*, 106, 859–878.

Warrington, E., & Shallice, T. (1984). Category specific semantic impairments. *Brain*, *107*, 829–854.

Young, A., Newcombe, F., Hellawell, D., & DeHaan, E. (1989). Implicit access to semantic information. *Brain and Language*, *11*, 186–209.

Zingeser, L.B., & Berndt, R.S. (1990). Retrieval of nouns and verbs in agrammatism and anomia. *Brain and Language*, *39*, 14–32.

Zurif, E. (1990). Language and the brain. In D. Osherson (Ed.), *An invitation to cognitive science*, *Vol. 1: Language* (pp. 177–199). Cambridge, MA: MIT Press.

# 6

# Investigation of phonological encoding through speech error analyses: Achievements, limitations, and alternatives*

Antje S. Meyer

*Max-Planck-Institute für Psycholinguistik, Postbus 310, NL 6500 AH Nijmegen, Netherlands; and Catholic University Nijmegen, Comeniuslaan 4, POB 9102, 6500 HC Nijmegen, Netherlands*

Meyer, A.S., 1992. Investigation of phonological encoding through speech error analyses: Achievements, limitations, and alternatives. Cognition, 42: 181–211.

*Phonological encoding in language production can be defined as a set of processes generating utterance forms on the basis of semantic and syntactic information. Most evidence about these processes stems from analyses of sound errors. In section 1 of this paper, certain important results of these analyses are reviewed. Two prominent models of phonological encoding, which are mainly based on speech error evidence, are discussed in section 2. In section 3, limitations of speech error analyses are discussed, and it is argued that detailed and comprehensive models of phonological encoding cannot be derived solely on the basis of error analyses. As is argued in section 4, a new research strategy is required. Instead of using the properties of errors to draw inferences about the generation of correct word forms, future research should directly investigate the normal process of phonological encoding.*

## Introduction

The formulation of an utterance can be broken down into two components, namely the generation of the meaning and syntactic structure of the utterance on the one hand, and the creation of its form on the other hand (see, for example,

*I am very grateful to Andrew Crompton, Aditi Lahiri, Pim Levelt, and two anonymous reviewers for helpful comments on an earlier draft of this paper. In addition, I would especially like to thank Lyn Frazier and Harry van der Hulst for extensive discussions of the issues considered in this paper. Requests for reprints should be sent to A.S. Meyer, Max-Planck-Institute for Psycholinguistics.

Butterworth, 1980, 1989; Fay & Cutler, 1977; Fromkin, 1971; Garrett, 1976, 1982, 1988; Kempen & Huijbers, 1983; Levelt, 1989). The present paper is concerned with the second of these components, which will be called phonological encoding. Phonological encoding is defined as the set of processes creating the form of an utterance on the basis of syntactic and semantic information. It includes the retrieval of stored word forms from the mental lexicon, the determination of the rhythmical structure and intonation contour of the utterance, and the creation of a phonetic representation, which is taken to be the input to the articulatory component.

The available evidence about phonological encoding stems mainly from analyses of sound errors. Naturally, there is considerable variation in the results of analyses performed by different researchers on different corpora and in different languages. However, there are certain core properties of sound errors that have been discovered in many corpora. The discussion of the error evidence in section 1 will focus on these regularities and their interpretation (for more comprehensive reviews of the findings see, for instance, Levelt, 1989, or Shattuck-Hufnagel, 1983, 1987). In section 2, two prominent models of phonological encoding will be described, which are largely based on speech error evidence, namely Shattuck-Hufnagel's scan-copier (Shattuck-Hufnagel, 1979, 1983, 1987) and Dell's spreading activation model (Dell, 1986, 1988).

In section 3, it will be shown that in spite of the large number of error analyses that have been carried out, it has not been possible to characterize in detail which form representations speakers create or how they create them. It is, for instance, still unknown, whether speakers create a single phonological representation for each word or several representations, and what the planning units are out of which these representations are constructed. In addition, contrary to what has often been maintained, sound errors only provide very limited evidence about the process of phonological encoding.

There are a number of methodological reasons for the fact that error analyses have only been partially successful. It is, for instance, difficult to establish exactly how often different types of errors arise because they differ in how likely they are to be detected by listeners and because many errors can be classified in several ways. However, as will be shown, even if these problems are minimized, speech error analyses can still not provide more than a global characterization of phonological encoding.

It appears that in order to gain a better understanding of phonological encoding, a new research strategy should be adopted. So far, most researchers have taken a highly data-driven approach, working up from properties of errors to explanations of the generation of error-free speech. A more fruitful strategy for future research might be to start from a working model of correct phonological encoding, to derive new hypotheses about the generation of correct speech from the model, and to devise methods to test them empirically. How such a working model could be attained and tested is discussed in section 4.

## 1. Evidence from sound errors

Sound errors are utterances that deviate from the speaker's intention in the placement or identity of one or more phonological segments not corresponding to a complete morpheme of the target utterance (see (1) to (7)). Some sound errors, such as (1) and (2), are most naturally described as exchanges of segments or segment clusters. Examples (3) and (4) can be analysed as incomplete exchanges. In (3), which is a sound anticipation, [l] replaces [r] and is repeated in its target position. In (4), which is a perseveration, [g] appears in its target position and replaces the onset of the following word. In all of these errors, the sounds of words are ordered incorrectly, taking positions that were meant for other sounds. In addition to such ordering errors, there are so-called non-contextual errors, which cannot be explained by reference to the immediate utterance context. Some sound substitutions (such as (5)) and many additions (such as (6)) and deletions (such as (7)) belong to this category.[1]

(1)  *h*eft *l*emisphere (left hemisphere)
(2)  *fl*eaky *squ*oor (squeaky floor)
(3)  a *l*eading list (a reading list)
(4)  gave the *g*oy (gave the boy)
(5)  a trans*g*ormational rule (a transformational rule)
(6)  enjoy*d*ing it (enjoying it)
(7)  split bain (split brain)

A large number of analyses of sound errors have been carried out. Two general questions have guided most of these analyses, namely, first, how the speakers' representations of word forms can be characterized and, second, how these representations are retrieved or constructed. In this section, I will review what sound errors reveal concerning these issues.

An important property of sound errors is that they are almost always phonetically well formed (e.g., Boomer & Laver, 1968; Wells, 1951). Errors rarely yield illegal sound sequences, and misplaced sounds are usually phonetically accommodated to their new environment, or the environment is accommodated to the intruding sound following the rules of the language in question (Berg, 1987; Fromkin, 1971, 1973; Garrett, 1976, 1980; Stemberger, 1983a, 1985a). For instance, when an English stop consonant moves from a word-initial to a word-internal position or vice versa, it loses or acquires aspiration, as appropriate for its new environment (Fromkin, 1973). When a syllable-final voiced consonant is replaced by a voiceless one or vice versa, the length of the preceding vowel is adjusted accordingly (Shattuck-Hufnagel, 1985a). To give a final example, when, as in (8), the first segment of a noun changes from vowel to consonant or vice versa, the preceding article is modified accordingly.

---

[1]Unless indicated otherwise, the errors stem from the Appendix to Fromkin (1973).

(8)  *a m*eeting arathon (an eating marathon)

Linguistic theory distinguishes between a fairly abstract phonological representation of a word and a more detailed phonetic representation (e.g., Browman & Goldstein, 1986; Chomsky & Halle, 1968; Mohanan, 1986). The phonetic well-formedness of sound errors shows that they arise before the phonetic form of the utterance is created and before illegal sound sequences are edited out or changed (but see Stemberger, 1985a). Thus, speakers apparently construct both phonological and phonetic representations of utterances; and most sound errors arise during, and provide evidence about, the creation of the former representation.

It should be noted that not all sound errors are phonetically well formed. Ill-formed sequences regularly occur in tongue-twister experiments (Butterworth & Whittaker, 1980), and also, at least occasionally, in spontaneous speech (Buckingham & Yule, 1987; Fromkin, 1973; Hockett, 1967; Stemberger, 1983a). A possible reason why they appear to be so rare is that listeners often fail to notice violations of phonetic rules (see, for instance, Marslen-Wilson & Welsh, 1978, or Warren, 1970, for experimental results supporting this supposition; see also Cutler, 1981). The occurrence of phonetically ill-formed errors can either be explained by assuming that these errors arise at the phonological level, but that the processes that modify or delete ill-formed sequences have failed to apply, or that they arise during later planning processes.

The mere fact that sound errors regularly occur allows for an important conclusion about the process of phonological encoding. Apparently, word forms are not retrieved from the mental lexicon as fully specified units, but are constructed by selecting and combining certain sublexical units. If they *were* retrieved as single entities having no internal structure, errors involving parts of words could not arise.

The units out of which phonological representations are created can be determined by classifying the error units, that is, the sounds and sound sequences by which errors deviate from intended utterances. The most frequent error units are single segments, accounting for 60–90% of the errors. Another large class of error units, appearing in approximately 10–30% of the errors, are sequences of two adjacent segments, either two consonants, or a vowel and a consonant (see, for instance, Berg, 1985, 1988; Boomer & Laver, 1968; Fromkin, 1971; Nooteboom, 1969; Shattuck-Hufnagel, 1983; Shattuck-Hufnagel & Klatt, 1979). Thus, word forms are apparently composed out of phonological segments and possibly certain segment sequences.[2]

---

[2]A number of studies have investigated whether some segments are more likely to be involved in errors than others, and whether certain classes of segments are "weak", that is, replaced more often than replacing others, while other classes are "strong", that is, replace other segments more often than being replaced. Though the evidence is not entirely clear, there do not seem to be any particularly error-prone, or strong or weak segments (e.g., Shattuck-Hufnagel & Klatt, 1979). In a speech error elicitation experiment, Levitt and Healy (1985) observed that high-frequency segments were more likely to replace low-frequency segments than the reverse.

Apparently, the representations of word forms capture not only which segments, but also which phonological features the words include. Evidence for the representation of phonological features comes from two sources. First, there are errors like (9) that are best described as movements of individual features. Such feature errors are not observed very frequently; probably less than 5% of all sound errors are feature errors (e.g., Berg, 1985; Fromkin, 1973; Shattuck-Hufnagel, 1983; Shattuck-Hufnagel & Klatt, 1979), but they occur often enough to require an explanation. Second, interacting segments in sound errors show a strong tendency to share more features than expected on the basis of a chance estimate (Fromkin, 1971; García-Albea et al., 1989; Garrett, 1975; Nooteboom, 1969). In most sound errors, the displaced and displacing segments differ by only one feature. This phonemic similarity effect is observed in interactions of consonants as well as in interactions of vowels. The features shared most frequently by interacting consonants are manner and voice (see Berg, 1985; Kupin, 1982; MacKay, 1970; Nooteboom, 1969; Shattuck-Hufnagel & Klatt, 1979). In vowel errors the feature tense is more likely to be shared than backness (Shattuck-Hufnagel, 1986). The fact that vowels almost always interact with vowels and consonants with consonants (e.g., Fromkin, 1971; Garrett, 1975; MacKay, 1970) can also be seen as an instance of the general tendency of errors to involve similar segments, though there are other accounts for this finding (see below).[3]

(9) glear plue sky (clear blue sky)

Recently, it has been argued that sound errors involve smaller planning units than segments or features. Using electromyography, Mowrey and MacKay (1990) traced the motor activity during the production of tongue-twisters. As expected, they found some variation in the motor patterns associated with different realizations of one and the same correct utterance. However, there was much more variability in the patterns associated with errors. For instance, analyses of deletions of [l] in "Bob flew by Bligh Bay" showed that in most cases there were still traces of the motor activity associated with [l] at the moment when it should have been pronounced. Similarly, in most [l]-additions, stronger or weaker traces of the motor activity typically associated with [l] were registered, but not the full activity pattern. Thus, at the motor level sound errors do not seem to be all-or-none, but graded events.

One interpretation of these findings is that the error units are phonological segments, as has traditionally been assumed, and that the competition of

---

[3]The phonemic similarity effect is one of a number of similarity biases in sound errors. Another similarity bias is the repeated phoneme effect. Two segments that are followed or preceded by identical segments are far more likely to interact with each other than two segments that are followed or preceded by different segments (see, for example, MacKay, 1970). This effect has been found for vowel and consonant errors. It is strongest when identical segments are direct neighbours of the interacting segments, but it is also obtained from more remote identical segments (Dell, 1984; Shattuck-Hufnagel, 1986; Stemberger, 1990).

phonological forms affects the planning at subsequent levels using smaller planning units. An alternative hypothesis, favoured by Mowrey and MacKay, is that sound errors do not arise at the phonological level, but at a lower planning level, and that they are not transpositions of complete segments or features, but of units controlling small sets of motor units. On this account, the main reason why sound errors usually appear to be segmental errors is that the articulatory irregularities that can be discovered by means of electromyography are not noticed by listeners. On the basis of the available data it is not possible to decide between these hypotheses.

In addition to the segmental and subsegmental structure, the word forms speakers create also capture the syllabic structure of the words. Complete syllables rarely function as error units, probably in less than 5% of all sound errors (e.g., Shattuck-Hufnagel, 1983), but there is evidence from a number of other sources to support the representation of syllabic structure. First, when error units comprise two or more segments, these segments practically always belong to the same syllable. There are no errors in which the error unit includes the last segment of one syllable and the first segment of the next syllable. Moreover, the segments of complex error units usually belong to the same syllable *constituent*. A syllable can be divided into an onset, which comprises the pre-vocalic segments, and a rhyme, which includes the remaining segments. The rhyme can further be divided into a vocalic nucleus and a post-vocalic coda. By far the most common complex error units are onset clusters (see (10)), but complex nuclei (see (11) and (12)) are also regularly found. Second, the segments constituting complex syllable constituents of the target words typically stay together in errors. There are errors, such as (13)–(15), in which only one segment of an onset cluster or a complex nucleus is displaced (see Stemberger, 1983b; Stemberger & Treiman, 1986), but such cases are less frequent than replacements of complete complex constituents (Shattuck-Hufnagel, 1983, 1986; but see Kubozono, 1989, for counter-evidence from Japanese errors). Occasionally, errors are observed in which the error unit includes nucleus and coda (i.e., the rhyme), or onset and nucleus of a syllable (Nooteboom, 1969; Shattuck-Hufnagel, 1983). By contrast, there are no errors in which two segments belonging to different complex syllable constituents form an error unit. For example, the second consonant of an onset cluster and the following vowel never form an error unit (for other evidence on the psychological reality of syllable constituents see Fowler, 1987; Treiman, 1983, 1984, 1986).

(10) *sl*oat *thr*itter (throat slitter)
(11) s*er*p is s*ou*ved (soup is served)
(12) h*o* bl*ai*rer (hair blower) (from Shattuck-Hufnagel, 1986)
(13) s*p*rive for perfection (strive for perfection)
(14) c*ar*n – corn cobs (from Stemberger, 1983b)
(15) they [m*uy*] – they may be moving (from Stemberger, 1983b)

Additional evidence for the coherence of syllable constituents in errors stems from analyses of word blends and haplologies. Word blends are combinations of words, which are typically related in meaning (see (16)–(18)). MacKay (1972) found that in blends of polysyllabic words the breakpoint tends to fall between rather than within syllables (see (16)). If breaks occur within syllables, they tend to fall between syllable constituents, most often between the onset and the rhyme, as in (17). By contrast, errors like (18), in which the segments of a single onset cluster are separated from each other, are rare.

(16) recoflect (recognize/reflect)
(17) Irvine is quite clear (close/near)
(18) what shromkin said (she/Fromkin)

Haplologies are errors in which parts of intended utterances are missing (see (19)–(22)). As Crompton (1982) has pointed out, the missing part usually corresponds to one or more complete syllables (as in (19)) or syllable constituents (as in (20) and (21)). However, a complex syllable constituent does not function as a unit in *all* deletion errors. In some errors, such as (22), only one segment of a complex constituent is missing (see Stemberger & Treiman, 1986).

(19) tremenly (tremendously)
(20) shrig souffle (shrimp and egg souffle)
(21) it is too dailed (detailed)
(22) below the gottis (glottis)

Another piece of evidence for the representation of syllabic structure is a positional constraint on complete and incomplete sound exchanges (see examples (23)–(25)), described by Boomer and Laver (1968) in the following way:

> Segmental slips obey a structural law with regard to syllable-place; that is, initial segments in the origin syllable replace initial segments in the target syllable, nuclear replace nuclear, and final replace final. (p. 7)

(23) *m*ell *w*ade (well made)
(24) b*u*d b*e*gs (bed bugs)
(25) go*d* to see*n* (gone to seed)

This syllable-position constraint is observed in the majority of sound errors in the English, German, Spanish, and Dutch corpora that have been analysed (Fromkin, 1971, 1973; García-Albea et al., 1989; MacKay, 1970; Motley, 1973; Nooteboom, 1969; Shattuck-Hufnagel, 1983, 1987; Stemberger, 1982; but see Abd-El-Jawad & Abu-Salim, 1987, on Arabic and Kubozono, 1989, on Japanese errors). The description of certain errors as sound exchanges implies that the segments' positions are specified independently of the segments themselves (see also Fry, 1969; Garrett, 1975). If there were no independently defined positions, one would expect that each of the two displaced segments could be inserted anywhere in the utterance, independently of the position of the other displaced segment. Instead, each segment is confined to the position vacated by the other segment involved in the exchange. An explanation for the observation that the interacting segments usually stem from corresponding syllable constituents is that the positions to which segments are assigned correspond to syllable constituents, and that each segment is marked as eligible for association to one type of syllable constituent (e.g., Baars & Motley, 1976). Accordingly, most models of phonological encoding assume that during the creation of word forms a set of phonological segments is retrieved, syllable frames are created, whose positions correspond to syllable constituents, and the segments are associated to the syllable constituents.

Recently, however, Shattuck-Hufnagel (1985b, 1987, this volume) has pointed out that most evidence for the positional constraint stems from errors involving word onsets. Shattuck-Hufnagel (1987) found that 66% of all consonant errors in her corpus occurred in word-onset position, whereas only 33% of all consonants in normal adult speech appear word-initially. The preference for word-onset positions was more pronounced for ordering errors (i.e., sound anticipations, perseverations, and exchanges) than for non-contextual errors; 82% of the misorderings and 43% of the non-contextual errors occurred in word-onset position. In most ordering errors, the interacting segments or clusters both stem from a word-onset position (Shattuck-Hufnagel, this volume; see also Fromkin, 1977; Garrett, 1975, 1980; but see García-Albea et al., 1989, for counter-evidence from Spanish errors). Thus, the segments of a word onset have a higher error rate than segments of other word positions, and they prefer to interact with each other rather than with word-internal or word-final segments. In analyses of hearing errors, it has been found that the edges of words, especially the beginnings, are perceived more accurately than the middle parts (Browman, 1978; Garnes & Bond, 1980; see Cohen, 1980, for the results of a shadowing study). Thus, errors in word onsets are probably more likely to be detected than errors in other word positions, but given the magnitude of the word-onset effect it is unlikely to be due exclusively to a listener bias.[4]

Shattuck-Hufnagel's analysis raises the question of whether it is necessary to assume both a word-based and a syllable-based constraint, or whether the movements of segments can be captured by reference to word position alone. Evidence bearing on this issue could come from errors involving word-internal and word-final segments. However, as such errors are scarce, there is little information about error rates and preferred interactions. It has been claimed that syllable onsets are more error prone than codas (e.g., MacKay, 1970), but it is

---

[4]What makes the word-onset effect particularly intriguing is that in sound errors word onsets are particularly vulnerable, whereas in malapropisms and TOT states they are more likely to be correct than segments in other word positions (e.g., Browman, 1978; Brown & McNeill, 1966; Fay & Cutler, 1977; Rubin, 1975).

uncertain whether this still holds once word onsets are excluded from analysis. An important observation is that vowels usually interact with other vowels and consonants with other consonants (see, for instance, Fromkin, 1971; Garrett, 1975; MacKay, 1970). This tendency *can* be explained by reference to syllable frames, in which the positions for onsets, nuclei, and codas are marked. However, it also suffices to assume the existence of frames that do not represent syllables, but include positions reserved for vowels and positions reserved for consonants (see Stemberger, 1990). This confines vowels and consonants to vocalic and consonantal positions, respectively, but it does not rule out interactions between onset and coda segments. A third possibility is to attribute the tendency of vowels and consonants to interact with segments of the same class to the general preference of segments to interact with phonologically similar rather than with dissimilar segments. No counts seem to be available of how often word-internal and word-final consonants move from their target positions to corresponding positions in new syllables, or how often they assume different syllable positions. If there is no syllable-position constraint, but only a word-onset constraint, frames could be postulated that include one distinguished position, the word onset, followed by an undifferentiated set of positions for the remaining segments of the word, or possibly by a sequence of consonantal and vocalic positions. Given frames divided into onset and "remainder", it would not be necessary to assume the existence of syllable frames.

In considering this hypothesis, however, other evidence should be taken into account. One relevant observation has already been discussed above, namely the tendency of complex syllable constituents to function as units in errors. Unfortunately, this evidence, like the evidence concerning the positional constraint, stems largely from errors involving word onsets. Another observation supporting the assumption of syllable frames is that sound errors are systematically affected by the stress pattern of the words in which they appear. Two trends can be distinguished. First, segments of stressed syllables are more likely to be involved in errors than segments of unstressed syllables.[5] Second, a segment prefers to move from its target syllable to a syllable with the same stress value rather than to a syllable with a different stress value; that is, a segment from a stressed syllable tends to move to a new stressed syllable and a segment from an unstressed syllable to a new unstressed syllable (e.g., Boomer & Laver, 1968; Fromkin, 1971, 1973; Garrett, 1980; Nooteboom, 1969; Shattuck-Hufnagel, 1983).[6]

The interpretation of these findings is complicated by the fact that the syllable

---

[5]This finding might in part be due to the fact that errors in stressed syllables are more likely to be detected than errors in unstressed syllables (see Browman, 1978; Garnes & Bond, 1980).

[6]In an analysis of German within-word errors, MacKay (1971) found that segments from stressed syllables were more likely to replace segments from unstressed syllables than the reverse, in particular when the unstressed preceded the stressed syllable (see also Berg, 1990). However, this finding was not replicated for English errors of the same type (Shattuck-Hufnagel, 1983).

carrying the main stress is often also the first syllable of the word. In monosyllabic words this is necessarily the case, but it also holds for many polysyllabic words. For instance, in Shattuck-Hufnagel's (1987) corpus, 60% of the polysyllabic words involving an error were stressed word-initially. Shattuck-Hufnagel (1985b, 1986) examined whether segment movement could be better predicted by reference to the word position or the stress value of the target syllable. She concluded that for movement of onset consonants word position was the more influential factor, but that stress also had a significant effect. By contrast, for vowel movement, stress was the more influential factor. Vowels of stressed syllables were more vulnerable than vowels of unstressed syllables, and both types of vowels preferentially moved to syllables with the same stress value as their target syllable (see also Berg, 1990; Shattuck-Hufnagel, this volume).

These findings show that the stress pattern of the utterance is represented at the moment when a sound error arises. In current linguistic theory, stress is usually taken to be carried by syllables, not by segments (see, for instance, Liberman & Prince, 1977). This view is also supported by speech error evidence. When vowels move from stressed to unstressed syllables or vice versa, the stress pattern of the utterance is usually maintained (see, for instance, Berg, 1990; Fromkin, 1971; Shattuck-Hufnagel, 1986; Stemberger, 1983a), indicating that stress value is not a property of a vowel itself, but of the position it takes. If stress values are linked to syllables, it is difficult to explain the effects of stress on sound errors without assuming that the syllabic structure of the utterance is represented. Hence, indirectly, the effects of stress support the assumption that the frames to which segments are associated in phonological encoding capture the syllabic structure of the words.

To summarize, though the results of the large number of speech error analyses performed by different investigators on different corpora by no means match in all details, there are a number of findings that have been replicated in many studies and that have led to important conclusions about phonological encoding. First, the fact that sound errors arise at all shows that word forms are assembled out of smaller units, rather than being retrieved from the mental lexicon as single entities. Second, the phonetic well-formedness of the errors indicates that they arise during the creation of a phonological representation, rather than during phonetic encoding or articulation. Third, given that the majority of error units can best be described as segments or segment sequences, the units out of which phonological representations are created are probably segments and maybe certain segment clusters. Fourth, the phonemic similarity effect and the occurrence of feature errors show that the subsegmental structure of words is also represented. Fifth, the fact that segments often exchange positions in errors indicates that the positions must be specified independently of the segments that fill them. Finally, the tendency of complex syllable constituents to function as coherent units in errors, the syllable-position constraint, and the effects of stress on movement errors suggest that the syllabic structure of the utterance is represented at the moment when sound errors arise. One should, however, keep in mind that much of this evidence stems from analyses of errors involving word onsets, and that much less is known about the movement patterns and coherence of segments outside the word onset. In the next section, it will be shown how these generalizations are fleshed out in two models of phonological encoding, namely in the models proposed by Shattuck-Hufnagel (1979, 1983, 1986, 1987) and Dell (1986, 1988; for related models see Berg, 1988; Harley, 1984; MacKay, 1982, 1987; Stemberger, 1985b).

## 2. Models of phonological encoding

### 2.1. Shattuck-Hufnagel's scan-copier

Shattuck-Hufnagel (1979, 1983, 1986) assumes that during phonological encoding an ordered set of sublexical units is associated to the ordered positions of independently created syllable frames. Because speech errors do not provide conclusive evidence about the representation of complex syllable constituents, two versions of the model are proposed. In one, word forms are created out of segments, segment sequences, and zero segments. Syllables have three slots each, corresponding to the syllable constituents onset, nucleus, and coda. Each slot accepts a single segment, a segment sequence, or a zero segment as insert. Zero segments take the onset or coda positions of syllables that begin or end in vowels. In the other version of the model, there are no units corresponding to segment sequences, but only units corresponding to single segments and zero segments. Complex syllable constituents are represented as sequences of two or three segments. The syllable frame includes a separate slot for each segment.

The model presupposes the generation of the syllable frames for a stretch of speech, probably a phrase, and the retrieval of the corresponding ordered set of sublexical units. It describes the association of the segments to the positions of the syllable frames. A scan-copier is proposed, which selects the correct insert for each slot from the set of retrieved units and copies the units into the slots. This is done sequentially, proceeding slot-by-slot and unit-by-unit from the beginning of the utterance to its end. As soon as a given unit has been inserted into a slot, it is marked by a check-off monitor as "used". A second monitor inspects the developing representation and deletes or edits sequences that are likely to be the result of errors, such as sequences in which a particular segment is repeated several times.

Sound errors arise when slots are filled by wrong units, and the monitor fails to notice this. In a sound exchange, a unit is inserted into a slot too early, and the segment that should have taken that slot is inserted into the slot that was meant to be filled by the anticipated segment. Both segments are correctly checked off as "used" as soon as they have been associated to a position. Anticipations and perseverations are more complex errors in that they involve not only wrong placements of segments, but also failures of the check-off routine. In an anticipation, a unit is erroneously inserted into a slot preceding its target slot, is not checked off, and is inserted again into the appropriate slot. Similarly, a perseveration occurs when a unit is inserted into its target slot, is not checked off, and is later inserted again into another slot. The model correctly predicts that most sound errors are segmental errors, as segments and possibly certain segment sequences are the sublexical units out of which word forms are composed. The model cannot explain the occurrence of feature errors.

In order to explain the syllable-position constraint on sound errors, it is assumed that the positions of the syllable frames are labelled as onset, nucleus, and coda positions and that the sublexical units are labelled correspondingly as onset, nucleus, and coda units. A segment that may appear in two syllable positions (such as English stop consonants) is represented twice with different labels. In filling a given syllable position, the scan-copier only considers units that are marked as appropriate for that type of position. Thus, in correct utterances and in errors, each segment can only be linked to one type of position. In order to explain why a segment preferentially moves to a syllable with the same stress value as its target syllable, Shattuck-Hufnagel (1983) suggests that slots and inserts might not only be marked as to their positions in the syllable, but also as belonging to stressed or unstressed syllables. It should be noted that the labelling of segments and positions is only necessary to account for the constraints on movements of segments in errors, but not to explain the ordering of segments in correct utterances. As segments and positions are already ordered before they are linked to each other, and as the association is a left-to-right one-to-one mapping process, no additional information is necessary to link the sublexical units to correct positions.

Important observations that Shattuck-Hufnagel's (1979, 1983) original model cannot explain are the heightened error risk of word onsets and their tendency to interact with each other rather than with segments outside word onsets. However, a recent extension of the model includes an account of these findings (Shattuck-Hufnagel, 1987). In order to create a well-formed utterance, the speaker must integrate information about word forms and syntactic information, as they jointly determine the stress pattern and rhythm of the utterance. In Shattuck-Hufnagel's extended model, the insertion of sublexical units into positions of frames is part of the process by which lexical and syntactic information are combined. First, a frame is created with two positions for each word, one for the word onset and one for the "rest of the word". As the metrical structure of an utterance only depends on "rests of words", but not on word onsets, "rests of words" are associated to their positions before onsets. The most common type of error arising during this process is that an onset unit is linked to the onset position of a wrong word. In the next processing step, a frame is created with segment-sized positions, and the segments of the words become available and are associated to these positions. During this process, all segments of a word are about equally likely to be involved in errors.

The separation of the word onset from the rest of the word provides for an explanation of the word-onset effects in errors, but it is not particularly plausible linguistically. For the determination of the metrical structure of an utterance, not only word onsets, but all syllable onsets are irrelevant (see, for instance, Selkirk, 1984). If metrically relevant information is to be processed first, syllable rhymes should precede onsets. Yet, in Shattuck-Hufnagel's model the complete "rest of the word", including rhymes and word-internal syllable onsets, is associated to its position before the word onset.

## 2.2. *Dell's spreading activation model*

In Dell's (1986) model, as in Shattuck-Hufnagel's, word forms are generated by inserting sublexical units into the slots of independently created frames. But whereas Shattuck-Hufnagel's model presupposes the availability of the sublexical units to the scan-copier, Dell's model describes their retrieval within a spreading activation framework.

The linguistic units participating in phonological encoding are morphemes, syllables, rhymes, segment clusters, segments, and features. The nodes representing these units are connected to form a hierarchical structure, in which each unit is linked to its constituents. As in Shattuck-Hufnagel's model, segments and clusters are marked as onset, nucleus, or coda units. Again, there are zero-segments, which take the onset or coda position in syllables beginning or ending in a vowel.

The nodes are processing units, which can be activated to a greater or lesser extent. The links between the units are bidirectional. When a particular unit is activated, it spreads some of its activation to all units to which it is connected, and these units in turn feed part of their activation back to the unit that activated them in the first place. Activation decays over time so that unbounded spreading of activation from one node to all other nodes of the network is avoided.

When the form of a monosyllabic morpheme is created, activation spreads from the morpheme node to its syllable node, and from there to the corresponding segment and cluster nodes, which become gradually more and more highly activated. At the same time, a syllable frame with ordered onset, nucleus, and coda slots is created. After a certain time interval, these slots are filled by whatever onset, nucleus, and coda units are the most highly activated. Provided that no error occurs, these are the units that are being activated by the morpheme whose form is to be created. The three slots of the frame are filled in parallel. Upon their insertion into the frame, the selected units are tagged as being part of the phonological representation, and their activation level is reduced to zero so that they will not be immediately selected again. However, as the tagged units are still receiving some activation from activated superordinate and subordinate nodes, their activation quickly rebounds from zero and then gradually decays.

The syllables of polysyllabic morphemes are encoded in succession. For each syllable, the syllable frame is created and filled by suitable segments. From the activated morpheme node, activation spreads in parallel to all of its syllable nodes and to the corresponding segments and clusters. In addition, the first syllable node initially receives an extra boost of activation. Because of this additional activation, its segments and clusters become more strongly activated than all other segments and clusters and are therefore selected when the syllable frame is to be filled for the first time. Then the activation levels of the first syllable and its segments and clusters are set to zero, and the second syllable starts to receive extra activation. When the syllable frame is to be filled for the second time, the segments of the second syllable emerge as the most highly activated units and fill the slots, and so on, until all syllables of the morpheme have been encoded.

Dell (1988) has recently outlined a modification of his model, which instead of one syllable frame with the slots onset, nucleus, and coda, assumes several frames (called wordshapes, as only monosyllabic words are considered). These frames are sequences of C- and V-slots and are of variable length. A word node activates not only a set of segments, as in the earlier version of the model, but also a wordshape. From the wordshape, activation flows to so-called phoneme category nodes. The CVC-wordshape, for example, connects to the phoneme category nodes for pre-vocalic consonants, vowels, and post-vocalic consonants. The phoneme category nodes in their turn activate all segments of their respective categories. Thus, the segments of a word receive activation via two routes, directly from the word node and via the wordshape and phoneme category nodes. As soon as a segment reaches a selection threshold, it is selected as part of the phonological representation. The assumption of several types of frames is linguistically more plausible than the assumption of only one type because differences in the syllabic structure of various words can be represented and because it is not necessary any more to postulate zero-segments as fillers for onset and coda positions of syllables that begin or end in a vowel. In the new version of the model, such syllables simply do not have onset or coda positions.

Sound misorderings arise when segments or clusters are the most highly activated units of their categories at the wrong moment and are therefore associated to incorrect positions. For example, an anticipation like (26) occurs if the onset of the second word is more highly activated than that of the first word at the moment when the syllable frame is to be filled for the first time. Similarly, a perseveration like (27) occurs if the onset of the verb is still more highly activated than that of the noun when the noun is to be phonologically encoded. Such irregularities in the activation of segments can arise because each unit in the mental lexicon connects to many others from which it receives variable amounts of activation. Usually, the input from the morpheme level is strong enough to override these random influences so that correct segments are selected in the right order, but sometimes wrong segments win out, and errors arise.

(26) *h*inch hit (pinch hit)
(27) gave the *g*oy (gave the boy)

Many properties of sound errors are explained in similar ways in Dell's as in Shattuck-Hufnagel's model. Errors are usually phonetically well formed because they arise during the creation of a phonological representation and thus before the phonetic form of the utterance is specified. The main error units are segments and certain segment sequences because these are the units that are selected and combined to form phonological representations. Feature errors cannot be explained, but there is an account for the phonemic similarity effect on segmental errors: phonologically similar segments have links to identical feature nodes, through which they activate each other so that their activation levels become similar and they become more likely to be confused with each other than dissimilar segments that do not activate each other via shared subordinate nodes. The syllable-position constraint on movements of segments is explained, as in Shattuck-Hufnagel's model, by the assumption that a segment is labelled according to the position it may take. No account is offered for the effects of word onset on sound errors.

## 3. Limitations of speech error analyses

Typically, speech errors are not analysed because they are particularly interesting or important as such, but because they are assumed to reveal how correct speech is created. Section 1 discussed a number of properties of sound errors and the inferences about normal phonological encoding they invite. In section 2, it was shown how these inferences are fleshed out in two models of phonological encoding. Despite numerous investigations of sound errors and the existence of speech-error-based models of phonological encoding, it will be argued here that the creation of utterance forms is not well understood. Moreover, it seems unlikely that it will be understood unless new research methods are employed.

Understanding phonological encoding would imply, among other things, knowledge of the structure and content of the representations of utterance form that speakers create. Using the results of sound error analyses, certain aspects of these representations can be broadly characterized, but many important questions remain unanswered. For example, given that complex syllable constituents function as units in most, but not all errors, it cannot be decided whether they are represented as single entities, or as segment sequences, or perhaps in both ways. We also know little about the representation of phonological features. The phonemic similarity effect on segmental errors indicates that words are represented in terms of their features as well as in terms of their segments. But the radically different rates of segment and feature errors suggest that segments and features are represented in different ways. To give a final example, little is known about the frames to which the segments are associated; the available evidence does not reveal whether there are only syllable frames, or only word frames, or perhaps both types of frames.

Why has it not been possible to specify word forms in more detail? In section 1, two important methodological problems of speech error analyses were mentioned. One problem is that the diagnosis of sound errors depends on listener judgments. This is a problem because some errors probably have higher detection rates than others (e.g., Cutler, 1981; Ferber, 1991). For instance, it is likely that errors in word onsets and in stressed syllables are noticed more easily than errors in other word positions. A second problem is the notorious ambiguity of errors (see also Cutler, 1988). For example, many displacements of segments can either be characterized as movements from a given syllable position to a corresponding position in another syllable, or as movements from a given word position to a new word position of the same type. Listener strategies and the ambiguity of errors conspire to conceal the true distribution of different error types in speech production.

A third problem is that certain classes of errors that one would need to analyse in order to obtain a more complete picture of phonological encoding are hardly ever observed. Speakers must create representations of the intonation contour and stress pattern of their utterances, and they must construct phonetic representations. But errors of stress, intonation, or phonetic encoding are seldom observed (e.g., Cutler, 1980; Fromkin, 1977). One possibility is that speakers rarely commit these types of errors; an alternative is that such errors do, in fact, regularly occur, but that listeners usually do not notice them. As mentioned, there is experimental evidence suggesting that listeners might often fail to notice violations of phonetic rules (Cutler, 1981; Marslen-Wilson & Welsh, 1978; Warren, 1970). Cutler (1980) has pointed out that if a speaker places stress on the wrong word, the focus of the sentence will be affected; but unless this has dramatic pragmatic consequences, the listener will not notice an error, but will understand the utterance to mean something slightly different from what was intended by the speaker. For similar reasons, errors of intonation might appear to be rare. If a wrong intonation contour is applied to a sentence, the listener might misunderstand the speaker (e.g., as being ironic instead of sincere) rather than noticing a speech error.

There are ways of minimizing these problems. By using taped corpora instead of transcripts, listener strategies can be minimized, and reasonable samples of unambiguous errors can be obtained by collecting large error corpora. An efficient way of acquiring speech error corpora is to induce errors in experimental settings, for instance by using the SLIPS procedure introduced by Baars et al. (1975),[7] or by asking subjects to produce tongue-twisters, such as "She sells sea shells on the sea shore" (see, for instance, Butterworth & Whittaker, 1980; Kupin, 1982; Levitt & Healy, 1985; Shattuck-Hufnagel, 1987, this volume). Problems of such techniques are that some of the normal planning processes might be omitted or altered and that the articulation might be more difficult than in spontaneous speech. Therefore, the results of error induction experiments must always be validated by comparison to the results of analyses of errors in spontaneous speech.

On the basis of further analyses of large reliably registered error corpora it should be possible to obtain estimates of the relative frequencies of different classes of errors and to answer some of the open questions concerning the nature of the representations of utterance forms. For instance, it can probably be determined how likely the segments of a complex syllable constituent are to stay together in errors or to be separated from each other and how often segments outside word onsets move from their target positions to corresponding versus different positions in new syllables. Such distributional data are necessary to decide whether the frames to which the segments are associated encode the syllabic structure of the utterance. Whether substantial corpora of errors involving stress and intonation and of phonetic errors can be collected, and what can be learned from such corpora, remains to be seen.

In order to understand phonological encoding we must not only find out *which* form representations are constructed, but also *how* they are constructed. It must be determined which functionally different planning processes are to be distinguished and how these processes are coordinated with each other in time. Sound errors allow for a rough estimate of the relative order of certain planning processes. For instance, the effects of syllable position and stress on displacements of segments show that the syllabic structure of an utterance is generated before, or at about the same time as the segments are retrieved and ordered. Similarly, the phonetic well-formedness of most errors indicates that the phonetic

[7] In SLIPS experiments, subjects are presented with series of word pairs. On most trials, no overt reaction is required, but occasionally a word pair is accompanied by an auditory signal prompting the subject to say the word pair aloud. Such target word pairs are preceded by a series of biasing pairs designed to induce particular errors. For instance, if the target pair "deal back" is preceded by "big dumb", "bust dog", and "bet dart", subjects are likely to make the onset exchange error "beal dack" (example from Dell, 1988). This paradigm has been widely used to test output biases, such as the tendency of sound errors to result in existing words or syntactically well-formed sequences of the language (Baars & Motley, 1976; Baars et al., 1975; Motley & Baars, 1976; Motley et al., 1981, 1983), but also to investigate the repeated phoneme effect (Dell, 1984) and properties of onset cluster errors (Stemberger & Treiman, 1986).

form of an utterance is specified after its segments have been assigned to positions in word or syllable frames.

However, to build a satisfactory model, far more detailed information about the time course of various processes is required. The results of additional error analyses might firmly establish the existence of both word and syllable frames, but they will not reveal whether the two types of frames are created at the same time or, as Shattuck-Hufnagel (1987) has proposed, at different times. Similarly, even if we know exactly how often segment and feature errors arise, we still cannot decide whether the segmental and subsegmental structures of words are created in parallel or in succession. To give a final example, speech errors show that segments are associated to positions in planning frames, but they reveal nothing about the time course of this process. Shattuck-Hufnagel (1983) assumes that the association is a strictly serial process, proceeding position by position from the beginning to the end of the utterance. By contrast, in Dell's model (1986), the segments within a given syllable can be associated to their positions in any order, but the positions of successive syllables must be filled in sequence. These assumptions have important implications for other features of the models. In Shattuck-Hufnagel's model, the order of a word's segments must be stored in the mental lexicon; whereas in Dell's view, the order of the segments within a syllable is not stored, but established when the segments are associated to the ordered slots of syllable frames. Speech errors do not tell us anything about the time course of the association of segments to positions, nor do they reveal whether the order of segments within syllables is stored in the mental lexicon or generated during phonological encoding.

A model of phonological encoding should not only describe the temporal coordination of various planning processes, but should also specify their functions. Unfortunately, speech errors do not provide any functional information. Sound errors reveal that word forms must be created out of smaller units, but not why this is necessary. Given that there is only one correct phonological representation for each word, one might expect word forms to be stored and retrieved as units without internal structure. The function of the mapping of segments to positions in frames is also unknown. Both Dell (1986) and Shattuck-Hufnagel (1979, 1983) assume that it serves to establish the appropriate surface order of segments. However, in Shattuck-Hufnagel's model the segments are already ordered before the association, so it is unclear why they should be ordered again. Other functions have been ascribed to the mapping process, for instance, that it might be part of the transfer of information from a lexical to a phrasal processor (Shattuck-Hufnagel, 1987), or that it might be necessary to create surface phonological forms out of stored lexical representations (Levelt, 1989). Sound errors do not convey which of these hypotheses, if any, is correct.

To explain certain properties of errors, other processes have been postulated whose functions are also quite obscure. For instance, connectionist models assume that activation spreads not only from higher to lower-level units (i.e., from words to syllables, segments, and features), but also back from lower- to higher-level units (e.g., Dell, 1985). This explains a number of characteristics of sound errors, such as the phonemic similarity effect on segmental errors, but it is not clear what the function of the upward spread of activation could be. One can speculate about it. For instance, there might only be one lexicon for language production and comprehension, and upward connections might be crucial for the comprehension process. But speech errors do not provide any evidence in support of this, or any other, functional hypothesis.

To sum up, analyses of sound errors are usually carried out on the assumption that errors provide evidence about the representations of utterance forms and the way they are generated. However, so far only a very broad characterization of certain parts of the form representations has been achieved. Maybe some properties of the representations can be further specified on the basis of additional evidence. However, in the light of what has been achieved so far, it seems unlikely that sufficient evidence will ever be obtained from speech errors to characterize all levels of representation, including, for instance, the representations of intonation and stress. Furthermore, errors provide little evidence about the planning processes involved in phonological encoding, revealing little about the temporal coordination of different processes and nothing about their functions. Thus, it appears that the evidence that can be gained from speech errors is far more limited than has often been assumed.

## 4. Implications for future research

In order to understand phonological encoding a new research strategy seems to be required. The main strategy pursued so far has been to start from existing speech error corpora and to construct theories that are tailored to account for the characteristics of errors, but that are also supposed to explain phonological encoding in error-free speech. As we have seen, a number of important properties of sound errors have indeed been accounted for; but we still do not understand the normal process of phonological encoding very well, mainly because sound errors fail to provide the necessary evidence. It might be more fruitful to use as a starting point a working model of correct phonological encoding, to derive new hypotheses from that model, and to find ways to test them empirically. The evolving theory should be tailored to explain normal phonological encoding, but it should, ideally, also explain the properties of errors. Thus, instead of a highly data-driven approach that relies on one type of evidence and primarily aims at the explanation of a fairly infrequent type of behaviour, namely errors, a more theory-driven approach is advocated that can draw on many different types of data and aims directly at the explanation of the true object of arguing, the generation of correct speech.

How could a working model of phonological encoding be derived? There is little psycholinguistic evidence on which such a model could be based, but there is a large body of relevant linguistic research. Detailed theories of lexical representations have been proposed (e.g., Clements, 1985; Clements & Keyser, 1983; Goldsmith, 1976; Halle & Mohanan, 1985; McCarthy, 1979; Prince, 1983; Selkirk, 1984; van der Hulst, 1984, 1989; van der Hulst & Smith, 1986). In addition, there are theories on the derivation of the stress pattern and rhythm of utterances (e.g., Gussenhoven, 1984; Kaisse, 1985; Nespor & Vogel, 1986; Pullum & Zwicky, 1986; Selkirk, 1984) and descriptions of the intonation contours of various languages and their conditions of application (e.g., Bolinger, 1985; Cruttenden, 1986; Hart & Collier, 1975; Liberman & Pierrehumbert, 1984). Finally, there is ample phonetic evidence on the acoustic realization of intonation contours and stress patterns (e.g., Collier & Gelfer, 1983; Cooper & Paccia-Cooper, 1980; Cooper & Sorensen, 1981; Fujimura, 1981; 't Hart et al., 1990; Nakatani et al., 1981; Ohala, 1978). Obviously, phonological and phonetic theories are not processing theories, but they can contribute to such theories by offering hypotheses about the representations speakers might create.

Given that linguistic theories do not entail hypotheses about the generation of representations, the processing assumptions of a working model of phonological encoding must be independently motivated. Levelt (1989) has recently proposed a model that is much wider in scope than the speech-error-based models discussed in this paper. It not only specifies the retrieval of stored phonological forms, but also the creation of phonological words and phrases, the generation of stress patterns and intonation contours, and the selection of articulatory commands. The model's structural assumptions are largely linguistically motivated, whereas its processing assumptions are based primarily on psychological considerations. A central assumption of the theory is, for instance, that speakers generally attempt to minimize their memory load. Therefore, representations are created in a piecemeal fashion, and partial representations are handed over to the following processor as soon as possible. According to the theory, speakers do not construct and store the phonological representation of an entire complex sentence before starting to determine its phonetic form and to select appropriate motor commands. Instead, phonetic encoding and articulation begin as soon as possible, maybe as soon as the first phonological word of the utterance has been created. A second consequence of the strategy of minimizing memory load is that, in creating representations, speakers rely as much as possible on local information rather than looking far ahead. For instance, when assigning stress to a particular word, speakers probably consider the stress pattern of preceding words, the lexical stress pattern of the word under consideration and maybe of the following word, but most of the time they do not look further ahead than that.

How could such a working model of phonological encoding be tested? Given the complexity of the process under consideration, it is unlikely that one method can be found that can be employed to address all these questions. Most likely, a variety of methods must be used to investigate different aspects of phonological encoding. A number of suitable techniques are described below.

First, much can be learned about phonological encoding from analyses of spontaneous speech. As mentioned, there is an extensive linguistic literature on the phonological and phonetic properties `of utterances. However, linguistic research has primarily investigated which types of utterances are permissible, universally or in particular languages. The empirical evidence often stems from a small group of trained speakers, who carefully read out a set of words or sentences. By contrast, surprisingly little is known about the characteristics of spontaneous speech. For instance, certain types of Dutch sentences can be pronounced with a particular intonation contour, the so-called "hat" pattern, which is characterized by the maintenance of a high pitch level between two pitch accents ('t Hart & Collier, 1975). Speakers *can* apply this intonation contour, but they need not do so in order to produce well-formed utterances. Similarly, English speakers can adjust the stress patterns of words to avoid clashes of stressed syllables (saying, for instance, *síxteen ábstract páintings* instead of *sixtéen abstráct páintings*), but it has been shown that they rarely do so (Cooper & Eady, 1986; see also Kelly & Bock, 1988).

Analyses of spontaneous speech reveal which of the options existing in a given language speakers typically take and allow for certain inferences about the underlying representations of utterance forms. For instance, it can be determined whether speakers regularly produce utterances whose intonation contours are best described as "hat" patterns, or utterances in which the lexical stress patterns of words are altered to avoid stress clashes. In addition, certain inferences can be drawn about the speaker's planning processes. In particular, it can be established whether certain postulated processes, like the creation of "hat" patterns or stress adjustment, take place at all and which information speakers take into consideration when performing them. For example, one might find that speakers create "hat" patterns, but only if the syllables carrying pitch accent are not separated from each other by more than a certain number of syllables or words. This would suggest that the processor takes some of the following context of a word into account when determining its pitch level, but that its preview is limited to a certain stretch of speech.

An alternative to the study of spontaneous speech is to analyse utterances elicited in experiments in which subjects describe pictures, answer questions, paraphrase sentences, or recall sentences or texts from memory. An obvious advantage of the experimental approach, compared to analyses of spontaneous speech, is that the structure of the speakers' utterances can be systematically varied, as well as the linguistic and non-linguistic factors that are expected to affect utterance forms. A disadvantage is that some of the planning processes taking place in spontaneous speech might be altered or not take place at all.

Therefore, it is important to validate the results of utterance elicitation studies by comparing them to the results of analyses of spontaneous speech.

Another way to study phonological encoding is to test how long it takes speakers to generate certain types of utterances. Utterance initiation times provide evidence about the time course of the generation of utterances, since they reveal which planning activities are completed before utterance onset and which are executed afterwards. In one group of experiments, the difficulty of semantic and phonological encoding of different parts of utterances was varied, and it was tested which of these manipulations would affect utterance initiation times (Kempen & Huijbers, 1983; Levelt & Maassen, 1981; Lindsley, 1975, 1976). The results of these studies have led to the conclusion that speakers plan utterances further ahead on the semantic than on the phonological level; however, they do not tell us exactly how far ahead they plan on either level. In further research, it could be tested more systematically whether the difficulty of semantic and phonological encoding of words appearing in various sentence positions affects sentence initiation times. On the basis of such results it could be determined which sentence fragments are semantically and phonologically encoded before sentence onset.

Additional evidence concerning the issue of advance planning in sentence production comes from experiments by Ferreira (1991), who studied sentence initiation times and pauses when subjects reproduced sentences of varying length and syntactic complexity from memory (see also Balota et al., 1989; Sternberg et al., 1978).[8] She found that the initiation times for sentences like *The big and hairy dog went to the pond that's next to the museum* depended on the number of phonological words in the subject of the sentence and, given a constant number of phonological words, on the syntactic complexity of the subject noun phrase. By contrast, the complexity of the object did not affect the initiation times but instead the probability and duration of pre-verbal pauses. Ferreira assumed that sentence initiation times and pause durations depended on the difficulty of translating the semantic–syntactic structures of the sentences into phonological representations. On this assumption, her results suggest that the size and nature of the sentence fragment that speakers phonologically encode before utterance onset do not correspond to a certain number of syllables or words, but are defined by the structure of the sentence. The available results do not reveal which aspect of sentence structure is relevant; that is, whether the encoded fragment is a

---

[8]Some evidence about when speakers plan different parts of a sentence can be gained from analyses of hesitations and pauses in spontaneous speech (e.g., Butterworth, 1980; Cooper & Paccia-Cooper, 1980; Ford & Holmes, 1978; Garrett, 1980; Gee & Grosjean, 1983; Goldman-Eisler, 1968; Kowall et al., 1985; van Wijk, 1987). However, as the distribution and durations of pauses and hesitations are determined by a number of factors, such as the speaker's communicative intentions, syntactic and semantic influences, and the difficulty of various planning processes, it is difficult to obtain evidence suitable to answer questions concerning phonological encoding.

syntactic unit (i.e., the subject) or a prosodic unit (i.e., a phonological or intonational phrase). Further experiments using the same paradigm should address this issue.

Utterance initiation times have also been analysed to investigate the time course of phonological encoding of individual words. Meyer (1991) ran a series of experiments, in which subjects first learned sets of word pairs, such as *dog–cat*, *prince–king*, *thief–cop*. On each test trial, the first member of one of the pairs (e.g., *dog*) was presented, and the subject named the second member of the pair (e.g., *cat*) as quickly as possible. The stimulus materials consisted of two types of sets. In so-called *heterogeneous* sets the response words were unrelated in form, whereas in *homogeneous* sets they had one or more segments in common. The shared segments either corresponded to the syllable onset (as in the above example) or to the rhyme (as in *boy–man*, *car–van*, *skin–tan*).

Naming times were shorter in the homogeneous than in the heterogeneous sets when the response words shared the onset, but not when they shared the rhyme. In the shared-onset condition, the subjects presumably created and retained a phonological representation of the redundant part of the response words, and on each trial only appended the non-redundant part of the word to it. This took less time than creating the complete phonological representations of the response words. In the shared-rhyme condition, such a strategy could apparently not be applied. However, in experiments using disyllabic response words, stronger facilitatory effects were obtained in homogeneous sets in which the response words shared the entire first syllable than in sets in which they only shared the word onset. In preparing for the response words, the subjects apparently could not deviate from the order in which words are normally encoded, which is in a left-to-right manner. In other words, the results suggest that the onset of a syllable must be phonologically encoded before its rhyme. In other experiments using the same paradigm it was shown that successive syllables of a word are likewise encoded sequentially, according to their order in the word (Meyer, 1990).

In order to obtain convergent evidence for the claim that word forms are created in a left-to-right fashion, Meyer and Schriefers (in press) tested this hypothesis again, using a picture–word interference paradigm. The subjects saw pictures of common objects, which they named as quickly as possible. Again, utterance initiation times were the main dependent variable. Together with the pictures, interfering words (IWs) were presented, which were either phonologically related or unrelated to the picture names. For each picture there were two related IWs. The two related IWs for pictures with monosyllabic names had the same onset and nucleus, or the same nucleus and coda as the picture names. The two related IWs for pictures with disyllabic names shared the first or second syllable with the picture names. In addition, the relative timing of picture and IW presentation was varied. The IWs were either presented so that the segments they shared with the picture names began exactly at picture onset, or so that the shared segments began slightly before or after the picture onset.

The effect of the phonological relatedness of IWs and picture names depended on the timing of the IW presentation and on the word positions of the shared segments. When the IWs were presented so that the critical segments began before picture onset, utterance initiation times were shorter in the related than in the unrelated condition, provided that the shared segments appeared word-initially (i.e., corresponded to the onset and nucleus of monosyllabic words and to the first syllable of disyllabic words). By contrast, when the IWs were presented later, facilitatory effects were obtained in the related condition regardless of the word position of the shared segments. Presumably, when an IW was presented, its phonological representation in the mental lexicon was activated for a certain time period. When some of the segments of the IW were also included in the target, the selection of these target segments was facilitated, provided that this process took place soon enough after the presentation of the IW. A likely reason why the effect of shared word-initial segments appeared before the effect of shared word-final segments is that the encoding of the ends of words began later than the encoding of their beginnings. Thus, these results support the conclusion from Meyer's (1990, 1991) experiments that onset and rhyme of a syllable, as well as successive syllables of a word, are phonologically encoded in succession.

Because the effects of many different types of phonological relationships can be tested, the paradigms used by Meyer and by Meyer and Schriefers may be useful tools for further research on phonological encoding. The available results suggest that the onset of a syllable is encoded before its rhyme. In further experiments it should be tested whether there are smaller units within these syllable constituents that are encoded in succession, and in which order different parts of morphologically complex words are encoded. In addition, evidence could be gained about the types of representations speakers create. It could, for instance, be tested whether the naming responses in a picture–word interference experiment are facilitated by IWs that do not share any segments with the target names, but include the same number and types of syllables. This would indicate that subjects create representations of the syllabic structure of the words they are about to say. In a similar way it could be tested whether the representations capture which phonological features words are composed of.

Finally, phonological encoding can be investigated by means of so-called production priming experiments (see Dell & O'Seaghdha, this volume, for a review). In such experiments, subjects prepare for a certain word, phrase, or sentence. Depending on a cue presented after the preparation interval, they either have to produce the prepared utterance, or to change plans and do something else, like reading a new word or classifying a new stimulus as a word or non-word. It is tested how quickly subjects can switch from the planned to the new reaction. As the relationship between the two responses can be freely varied, this paradigm can be used for many different purposes.

Dell & O'Seaghdha (this volume) carried out production priming experiments to investigate the span of advance planning in sentence production. Their subjects prepared to say sentences, such as *The boxer removed the coat*. After a preparation interval, they either saw an asterisk and recited the sentence, or they saw a new stimulus (e.g., *coal*), which they named or, in a different experiment, classified as word or non-word (see also Levelt et al., 1991, for a similar methodology). Dell and O'Seaghdha found systematic reaction time differences between new words that were phonologically related to one of the words in the prepared sentence and new words that were unrelated to the words in the sentences. The direction of the difference (facilitation vs. inhibition in the related compared to the unrelated condition) depended on whether the new word was related to a word appearing at the beginning or at the end of the sentence. As Dell and O'Seaghdha argue, this suggests that at utterance onset, beginning and end of a sentence are in different states of preparation. Most likely, the phonological representation of the beginning of the sentence has been completed, whereas the representation of the end is only beginning to be activated.

Like the method used by Ferreira (1991), the response-priming paradigm can be used to test which parts of utterances are phonologically encoded before speech onset. In order to explore when non-initial parts of sentences are phonologically encoded, new words can be presented at different moments during the articulation of a sentence rather than before utterance onset. In addition, by varying the type of relationship between the new word and the critical word in a prepared utterance, it can be determined which properties of word forms (e.g., their segmental or subsegmental structure, their stress pattern, or syllable structure) have been retrieved. For instance, Meyer and Gordon (1985) asked subjects to prepare for syllable pairs, such as *up–ub*, which shared the vowel and differed in their codas. The new response required on some test trials was to say the syllables in reversed order. Meyer and Gordon found that it took subjects longer to initiate the new response when the final consonants of the syllables shared the feature voicing or place of articulation than when this was not the case. As they argue, this suggests that the representations of the syllables include specifications of their phonological features and that segments with shared features inhibit each other (see also Yaniv et al., 1990).

To summarize, the most common approach in the study of phonological encoding has been to start from sound errors and to construct a theory that primarily explains the properties of errors, but is also supposed to explain phonological encoding in error-free speech. This strategy has led to important insights about phonological encoding, for instance to the conclusion that word forms cannot be retrieved as units from the mental lexicon, but must be constructed out of certain sublexical units, that phonological segments are important planning units, and that frames are built to whose positions the segments are associated. Yet, it appears that no more can be expected from analyses of sound errors than a global characterization of the representations of utterance forms speakers create. Moreover, sound errors reveal very little about how these representations are constructed.

For the further investigation of phonological encoding a new research strateg seems to be more promising, which is to directly investigate the normal process o phonological encoding rather than taking the detour via error evidence. It wa illustrated in this section how one might proceed. The starting point could be working model of phonological encoding. So far, little psycholinguistic researcl has been specifically directed at phonological encoding, but there is a large bod of linguistic evidence suggesting hypotheses about the speaker's representations c utterance forms. Hypotheses about how these representations could be con structed can be deduced from general psychological principles.

A number of different ways of empirically testing such a model were discusse above. Important evidence can be obtained by analysing the phonological an phonetic properties of utterances produced spontaneously or in laboratory se tings. Such analyses reveal what the products of the speaker's planning activitie are and permit certain inferences about the corresponding representations an planning processes. Additional evidence can be gained from chronometric studies for instance from analyses of utterance initiation times and from productio priming studies.

As the existing methods will certainly not suffice to address all issues arising i the study of phonological encoding, new methods must be developed. I woul expect that in research on phonological encoding, as in other areas of psycho linguistics, methodological and theoretical developments will go hand in hand that is, that once researchers become interested in those aspects of phonologica encoding about which speech errors fail to provide evidence, they will also fin ways to empirically investigate them.

# References

Abd-El-Jawad, H., & Abu-Salim, I. (1987). Slips of the tongue in Arabic and their theoretica implications. *Language Sciences*, *9*, 145–171.

Baars, B.J., & Motley, M.T. (1976). Spoonerisms as sequencing conflicts: Evidence from artificiall elicited errors. *American Journal of Psychology*, *89*, 467–484.

Baars, B.J., Motley, M.T., & MacKay, D.G. (1975). Output editing for lexical status in artificiall elicited slips of the tongue. *Journal of Verbal Learning and Verbal Behavior*, *14*, 382–391.

Balota, D.A., Boland, J.E., & Shields, L.W. (1989). Priming in pronunciation: Beyond patter recognition and onset latency. *Journal of Memory and Language*, *28*, 14–36.

Berg, T. (1985). Is voice suprasegmental? *Linguistics*, *23*, 883–915.

Berg, T. (1987). The case against accommodation: Evidence from German speech error data. *Journa of Memory and Language*, *26*, 277–299.

Berg, T. (1988). *Die Abbildung des Sprachproduktionsprozesses in einem Aktivationsflußmodel. Untersuchungen an deutschen und englischen Versprechern.* [The representation of the proces language production in a spreading activation model: Studies of German and English speech errors.] Tübingen: Niemeyer.

Berg, T. (1990). The differential sensitivity of consonants and vowels to stress. *Language Sciences*, *12*, 65–84.

Bolinger, D. (1985). *Intonation and its parts: Melody in spoken English*. London: Edward Arnold.

Boomer, D.S., & Laver, J.D.M. (1968). Slips of the tongue. *British Journal of Disorders of Communication*, *3*, 2–12.

Browman, C.P. (1978). *Tip of the tongue and slip of the ear: Implications for language processing*. UCLA Working Papers on Phonetics, No. 42. University of California, Los Angeles.

Browman, C.P., & Goldstein, L.M. (1986). Towards an articulatory phonology. *Phonology Yearbook*, *3*, 219–252.

Brown, R., & McNeill, D. (1966). The "tip of the tongue" phenomenon. *Journal of Verbal Learning and Verbal Behavior*, *5*, 325–337.

Buckingham, H.W., & Yule, G. (1987). Phonemic false evaluation: Theoretical and clinical aspects. *Clinical Linguistics and Phonetics*, *2*, 113–125.

Butterworth, B. (1980). Some constraints on models of language production. In B. Butterworth (Ed.), *Language production: Vol 1. Speech and talk* (pp. 423–459). London: Academic Press.

Butterworth, B. (1989). Lexical access in speech production. In W. Marslen-Wilson (Ed.), *Lexical representation and process* (pp. 108–135). Cambridge: MIT Press.

Butterworth, B., & Whittaker, S. (1980). Peggy Babcock's relatives. In G.E. Stelmach & J. Requin (Eds.), *Tutorials in motor behavior* (pp. 647–656). Amsterdam: North-Holland.

Chomsky, N., & Halle, M. (1968). *The sound pattern of English*. New York: Harper & Row.

Clements, G.N. (1985). The geometry of phonological features. *Phonology Yearbook*, *2*, 225–252.

Clements, G.N., & Keyser, S.J. (1983). *CV-Phonology: A generative theory of the syllable*. Cambridge, MA: MIT Press.

Cohen, A. (1980). Correcting of speech errors in a shadowing task. In V.A. Fromkin (Ed.), *Errors in linguistic performance: Slips of the tongue, ear, pen, and hand* (pp. 157–163). New York: Academic Press.

Collier, R., & Gelfer, C.E. (1983). Physiological explanation of FO declination. In M.P.R. Van den Broecke & A. Cohen (Eds.), *Proceedings of the Tenth International Congress of Phonetic Sciences* (pp. 354–360). Dordrecht: Foris.

Cooper, W.E., & Eady, S.J. (1986). Metrical phonology in speech production. *Journal of Memory and Language*, *25*, 369–384.

Cooper, W.E., & Paccia-Cooper, J. (1980). *Syntax and speech*. Cambridge, MA: Harvard University Press.

Cooper, W.E., & Sorensen, J.M. (1981). *Fundamental frequency in sentence production*. New York: Springer.

Crompton, A. (1982). Syllables and segments in speech production. In A. Cutler (Ed.), *Slips of the tongue and language production* (pp. 663–716). Berlin: Mouton.

Cruttenden, A. (1986). *Intonation*. Cambridge, UK: Cambridge University Press.

Cutler, A. (1980). Errors of stress and intonation. In V.A. Fromkin (Ed.), *Errors in linguistic performance: Slips of the tongue, ear, pen, and hand* (pp. 67–80). New York: Academic Press.

Cutler, A. (1981). The reliability of speech error data. *Linguistics*, *19*, 561–582.

Cutler, A. (1988). The perfect speech error. In L.M. Hyman & C.S. Li (Eds.), *Language, speech, and mind* (pp. 209–223). New York: Cumm and Helm.

Dell, G.S. (1984). Representation of serial order in speech: Evidence from the repeated phoneme effect in speech errors. *Journal of Experimental Psychology: Learning, Memory, and Cognition*, *10*, 222–233.

Dell, G.S. (1985). Positive feedback in hierarchical connectionist models: Applications to language production. *Cognitive Science*, *9*, 3–23.

Dell, G.S. (1986). A spreading activation theory of retrieval in sentence production. *Psychological Review*, *93*, 283–321.

Dell, G.A. (1988). The retrieval of phonological forms in production: Test of predictions from a connectionist model. *Journal of Memory and Language*, *27*, 124–142.

Fay, D., & Cutler, A. (1977). Malapropisms and the structure of the mental lexicon. *Linguistic Inquiry*, *8*, 505–520.

Ferber, R. (1991). Slip of the tongue or slip of the ear? On the perception and transcription o naturalistic slips of the tongue. *Journal of Psycholinguistic Research*, *20*, 105–122.

Ferreira, F. (1991). Effects of length and syntactic complexity on initiation times for prepared utterances. *Journal of Memory and Language*, *30*, 210–233.

Ford, M., & Holmes, V.M. (1978). Planning units in sentence production. *Cognition*, *6*, 35–53.

Fowler, C.A. (1987). Consonant–vowel cohesivenesss in speech production as revealed by initial an final consonant exchanges. *Speech Communication*, *6*, 231–244.

Fromkin, V.A. (1971). The non-anomalous nature of anomalous utterances. *Language*, *47*, 27–52

Fromkin, V.A. (1973). Introduction. In V.A. Fromkin (Ed.), *Speech errors as linguistic evidence* (pp 11–45). The Hague: Mouton.

Fromkin, V.A. (1977). Putting the emPHAsis on the wrong sylLAble. In L.M. Hyman (Ed.), *Studie in stress and accent* (pp. 15–26). Southern California Occasional Papers in Linguistics. Vol 4 Department of Linguistics, University of Southern California, Los Angeles.

Fry, D. (1969). The linguistic evidence of speech errors. *BRNO Studies of English*, *8*, 69–74 (Reprinted in V.A. Fromkin (Ed.) (1973), *Speech errors as linguistic evidence* (pp. 157–163) The Hague: Mouton.)

Fuijmura, O. (1981). Temporal organization of articulatory movements as a multi-dimensional phrasa structure. *Phonetica*, *38*, 66–83.

García-Albea, J.E., del Viso, S., & Igoa, J.M. (1989). Movement errors and levels of processing i sentence production. *Journal of Psycholinguistic Research*, *18*, 145–161.

Garnes, S., & Bond, Z.S. (1980). A slip of the ear: A snip of the ear? A slip of the year? In V.A Fromkin (Ed.), *Errors in linguistic performance: Slips of the tongue, ear, pen, and hand* (pp 231–239). New York: Academic Press.

Garrett, M.F. (1975). The analysis of sentence production. In G.H. Bower (Ed.), *The psychology c language and motivation* (Vol. 9, pp. 133–175). New York: Academic Press.

Garrett, M.F. (1976). Syntactic processes in sentence production. In R.J. Wales & E. Walker (Eds.) *New approaches to language mechanisms* (pp. 231–256). Amsterdam: North-Holland.

Garrett, M.F. (1980). Levels of processing in sentence production. In B. Butterworth (Ed.), *Languag production: Vol 1. Speech and talk* (pp. 177–210). New York: Academic Press.

Garrett, M.F. (1982). Production of speech: Observations from normal and pathological language us In A.W. Ellis (Ed.), *Normality and pathology in cognitive functions* (pp. 19–76). Londo Academic Press.

Garrett, M.F. (1988). Processes in language production. In F.J. Newmeyer (Ed.), *Linguistics: Th Cambridge Survey. Vol. III: Psychological and biological aspects of language* (pp. 69–96 Cambridge: Harvard University Press.

Gee, J.P., & Grosjean, F. (1983). Performance structures: A psycholinguistic and linguistic appraisa *Cognitive Psychology*, *15*, 411–458.

Goldman-Eisler, F. (1968). *Psycholinguistics: Experiments in spontaneous speech*. London, New Yor Academic Press.

Goldsmith, J. (1976). An overview of autosegmental phonology. *Linguistic Analysis*, *2*, 23–68.

Gussenhoven, C. (1984). *On the grammar and semantics of sentence accents*. Dordrecht: Foris.

Halle, M., & Mohanan, K.P. (1985). Segmental phonology of modern English. *Linguistic Inquiry*, *1 57–116.

Harley, T.A. (1984). A critique of top-down independent levels of speech production: Evidence fro non-plan-internal speech errors. *Cognitive Science*, *8*, 191–219.

Hart, J.'t, & Collier, R. (1975). Integrating different levels of intonation analysis. *Journal Phonetics*, *3*, 235–255.

Hart, J.'t, Collier, R., & Cohen, A. (1990). *A perceptual study of intonation*. Cambridge, U Cambridge University Press.

Hockett, C.F. (1967). Where the tongue slips there slip I. *To honor Roman Jakobson: Vol. 2*. Th Hague: Mouton. (Reprinted in V.A. Fromkin (Ed.) (1973). *Speech errors as linguistic eviden* (pp. 93–119). The Hague: Mouton.)

Kaisse, E.M. (1985). *Connected speech: The interaction of syntax and phonology.* New York: Academic Press.

Kelly, M.H., & Bock, J.K. (1988). Stress in time. *Journal of Experimental Psychology: Human Perception and Performance, 14,* 389–403.

Kempen, G., & Huijbers, P. (1983). The lexicalization process in sentence production and naming: Indirect election of words. *Cognition, 14,* 185–209.

Kowall, S., Bassett, M.R., & O'Connell, D.C. (1985). The spontaneity of media interviews. *Journal of Psycholinguistic Research, 14,* 1–18.

Kubozono, H. (1989). The mora and syllable structure in Japanese: Evidence from speech errors. *Language and Speech, 32,* 249–278.

Kupin, J.J. (1982). *Tongue twisters as a source of information about speech production.* Bloomington: Indiana University Linguistics Club.

Levelt, W.J.M. (1989). *Speaking: From intention to articulation.* Cambridge, MA: MIT Press.

Levelt, W.J.M., & Maassen, B. (1981). Lexical search and order of mention in sentence production. In W. Klein & W. Levelt (Eds.), *Crossing the boundaries in linguistics: Studies presented to Manfred Bierwisch* (pp. 221–252). Dordrecht: Reidel.

Levelt, W., Schriefers, H., Vorberg, D., Meyer, A.S., Pechmann, T., & Havinga, J. (1991). The time course of lexical access in speech production: A study of picture naming. *Psychological Review, 98,* 122–142.

Levitt, A.G., & Healy, A.F. (1985). The roles of phoneme frequency, similarity, and availability in the experimental elicitation of speech errors. *Journal of Memory and Language, 24,* 717–733.

Liberman, M., & Pierrehumbert, J. (1984). Intonational invariance under changes in pitch range and length. In M. Aronoff & R.T. Oehrle (Eds.), *Language and sound structure: Studies in phonology presented to Morris Halle by his teacher and students* (pp. 156–233). Cambridge, MA: MIT Press.

Liberman, M., & Prince, A. (1977). On stress and linguistic rhythm. *Linguistic Inquiry, 8,* 249–336.

Lindsley, J.R. (1975). Producing simple utterances: How far to we plan? *Cognitive Psychology, 7,* 1–19.

Lindsley, J.R. (1976). Producing simple utterances: Details of the planning process. *Journal of Psycholinguistic Research, 5,* 331–351.

MacKay, D.G. (1970). Spoonerisms: The structure of errors in the serial order of speech. *Neuropsychologia, 8,* 323–350.

MacKay, D.G. (1971). Stress pre-entry in motor systems. *American Journal of Psychology, 84,* 35–51.

MacKay, D.G. (1972). The structure of words and syllables: Evidence from errors in speech. *Cognitive Psychology, 3,* 210–227.

MacKay, D.G. (1982). The problem of flexibility, fluency, and speed–accuracy trade-off in skilled behavior. *Psychological Review, 89,* 483–506.

MacKay, D.G. (1987). *The organization of perception and action: A theory for language and other cognitive skills.* New York: Springer.

Marslen-Wilson, W.D., & Welsh, A. (1978). Processing interactions and lexical access during word recognition in continuous speech. *Cognitive Psychology, 10,* 29–63.

McCarthy, J. (1979). *Formal problems in Semitic phonology and morphology.* Doctoral dissertation, MIT, Cambridge, Massachusetts (distributed by Indiana University Linguistics Club, Bloomington).

Meyer, A.S. (1990). The time course of phonological encoding in language production: The encoding of successive syllables of a word. *Journal of Memory and Language, 29,* 524–545.

Meyer, A.S. (1991). The time course of phonological encoding in language production: Phonological encoding inside a syllable. *Journal of Memory and Language, 30,* 69–89.

Meyer, A.S., & Schriefers, H. (in press). Phonological facilitation in picture–word interference experiments: Effects of stimulus onset asynchrony and types of interfering stimuli. *Journal of Experimental Psychology: Learning, Memory, and Cognition.*

Meyer, D.E., & Gordon, P.C. (1985). Speech production: Motor programming of phonetic features. *Journal of Memory and Language, 24,* 3–26.

Mohanan, K.P. (1986). *The theory of lexical phonology.* Dordrecht: Reidel.

Motley, M.T. (1973). An analysis of spoonerisms as psycholinguistic phenomena. *Speech Monographs*, 40, 66–71.

Motley, M.T., & Baars, B.J. (1976). Laboratory induction of verbal slips: A new method for psycholinguistic research. *Communication Quarterly*, 24, 28–34.

Motley, M.T., Baars, B.J., & Camden, C.T. (1981). Syntactic criteria in prearticulatory editing: Evidence from laboratory-induced slips of the tongue. *Journal of Psycholinguistic Research*, 5, 503–522.

Motley, M.T., Baars, B.J., & Camden, C.T. (1983). Experimental verbal slip studies: A review and an editing model of language production. *Communication Monographs*, 50, 79–101.

Mowrey, R.A., & MacKay, I.R.A. (1990). Phonological primitives: Electromyographic speech error evidence. *Journal of the Acoustical Society of America*, 88, 1299–1312.

Nakatani, L.H., O'Connor, J.D., & Aston, C.H. (1981). Prosodic aspects of American English speech rhythm. *Phonetica*, 38, 84–106.

Nespor, M., & Vogel, I. (1986). *Prosodic phonology*. Dordrecht: Foris.

Nooteboom, S.G. (1969). The tongue slips into patterns. In A.G. Sciarone, A.J. van Essen, & A.A. van Raad (Eds.), *Nomen: Leyden Studies in Linguistics and Phonetics* (pp. 114–132). The Hague: Mouton.

Ohala, J.J. (1978). Production of tone. In V.A. Fromkin (Ed.), *Tone: A linguistic survey* (pp. 5–39). New York: Academic Press.

Prince, A. (1983). Relating to the grid. *Linguistic Inquiry*, 14, 19–100.

Pullum, G.K., & Zwicky, A.M. (1988). The syntax–phonology interface. In F.J. Newmeyer (Ed.), *Linguistics: The Cambridge Survey. Vol. I: Linguistics: Foundations* (pp. 255–280). Cambridge, UK: Cambridge University Press.

Rubin, D.C. (1975). Within word structure in the tip-of-the-tongue phenomenon. *Journal of Verbal Learning and Verbal Behavior*, 14, 392–397.

Selkirk, E. (1984). *Phonology and syntax: The relation between sound and structure*. Cambridge, MA: MIT Press.

Shattuck-Hufnagel, S. (1979). Speech errors as evidence for a serial-order mechanism in sentence production. In W.E. Cooper & E.C.T. Walker (Eds.), *Sentence processing: Psycholinguistic studies presented to Merrill Garrett* (pp. 295–342). Hillsdale, NJ: Erlbaum.

Shattuck-Hufnagel, S. (1983). Sublexical units and suprasegmental structure in speech production planning. In P.F. MacNeilage (Ed.), *The production of speech* (pp. 109–136). New York: Springer.

Shattuck-Hufnagel, S. (1985a). Segmental speech errors occur earlier in utterance planning than certain phonetic processes. *Journal of the Acoustical Society of America*, 77 (Suppl. 1), S84–85.

Shattuck-Hufnagel, S. (1985b). Context similarity constraints on segmental speech errors: An experimental investigation of the role of word position and lexical stress. In J.L. Lauter (Ed.), *Proceedings of the conference on the planning and production of speech in normal and hearing-impaired individuals: A seminar in honor of S. Richard Silverman. ASHA Report*, 15, 43–49.

Shattuck-Hufnagel, S. (1986). The representation of phonological information during speech production planning: Evidence from vowel errors in spontaneous speech. *Phonology Yearbook*, 3, 117–149.

Shattuck-Hufnagel, S. (1987). The role of word-onset consonants in speech production planning: New evidence from speech error patterns. In E. Keller & M. Gopnik (Eds.), *Motor and sensory processes of language* (pp. 17–51). Hillsdale, NJ: Erlbaum.

Shattuck-Hufnagel, S., & Klatt, D.H. (1979). The limited use of distinctive features and markedness in speech production: Evidence from speech error data. *Journal of Verbal Learning and Verbal Behavior*, 18, 41–55.

Stemberger, J.P. (1982). The nature of segments in the lexicon: Evidence from speech errors. *Lingua*, 56, 43–65.

Stemberger, J.P. (1983a). *Speech errors and theoretical phonology: A review*. Bloomington: Indiana University Linguistics Club.

Stemberger, J.P. (1983b). The nature of /r/ and /l/ in English: Evidence from speech errors. *Journal of Phonetics*, 11, 139–147.

Stemberger, J.P. (1985a). *Phonological rule ordering in a model of language production.* Bloomington: Indiana University Linguistics Club.

Stemberger, J.P. (1985b). *The lexicon in a model of language production.* New York: Garland Publishing.

Stemberger, J.P. (1990). Wordshape errors in language production. *Cognition, 35,* 123–157.

Stemberger, J.P., & Treiman, R. (1986). The internal structure of word-initial consonant clusters. *Journal of Memory and Language, 25,* 163–180.

Sternberg, S., Monsell, S., Knoll, R.L., & Wright, C.E. (1978). The latency and duration of rapid movement sequences: Comparisons of speech and typewriting. In G. Stelmach (Ed.), *Information processing in motor control and learning* (pp. 117–152). New York: Academic Press.

Treiman, R. (1983). The structure of spoken syllables: Evidence from novel word games. *Cognition, 15,* 49–74.

Treiman, R. (1984). On the status of final consonant clusters in English syllables. *Journal of Verbal Learning and Verbal Behavior, 23,* 343–356.

Treiman, R. (1986). The division between onsets and rimes in English syllables. *Journal of Memory and Language, 25,* 476–491.

van der Hulst, H. (1984). *Syllable structure and stress in Dutch.* Dordrecht: Foris.

van der Hulst, H. (1989). Atoms of segmental structure: Components, gestures and dependency. *Phonology, 6,* 253–284.

van der Hulst, H., & Smith, N. (1986). An overview of autosegmental and metrical phonology. In H. van der Hulst & N. Smith (Eds.), *The structure of phonological representations. Part I* (pp. 1–45). Dordrecht: Foris.

Van Wijk, C. (1987). The PSY behind PHI: A psycholinguistic model for performance structures. *Journal of Psycholinguistic Research, 16,* 185–199.

Warren, R.M. (1970). Perceptual restoration of missing speech sounds. *Science, 167,* 392–393.

Wells, R. (1951). Predicting slips of the tongue. *Yale Scientific Magazine, 26,* 9–30. (Reprinted in V.A. Fromkin (Ed., 1973), *Speech errors as linguistic evidence* (pp. 82–87). The Hague: Mouton.)

Yaniv, I., Meyer, D.E., Gordon, P.C., Huff, C.A., & Sevald, C.A. (1990). Vowel similarity, connectionist models, and syllable structure in motor programming of speech. *Journal of Memory and Language, 29,* 1–26.

# 7

# The role of word structure in segmental serial ordering*

Stefanie Shattuck-Hufnagel

*Speech Communication Group, Research Laboratory of Electronics, Massachusetts Institute of Technology, Cambridge, MA, USA*

Shattuck-Hufnagel, S., 1992: The role of word structure in segmental serial ordering, Cognition, 42: 213–259.

*To test the hypothesis that similarity in position within the syllable provides an adequate description of the position constraints on segmental interaction errors in American English, five error elicitation experiments were carried out using sets of tongue-twisters based on pairs of confusable target consonants. Interaction errors increased when the two target segments shared position in the word onset, or before a stressed vowel, suggesting that these factors play an active role in the normal phonological encoding process.*

## Introduction

This paper reports evidence from error elicitation experiments for a word structure effect in segmental serial ordering during speech production planning for utterances in American English. Recent models of the phonological aspects of speech production planning, reflecting the re-emergence of the syllable in phonological and phonetic theory, have focused on that unit as the organizing framework for segmental serial ordering (Dell, 1986; Levelt, 1989; MacKay, 1987; Shattuck-Hufnagel, 1983, 1987). The proposal that syllables provide the organizing frame has been supported with arguments from the position similarity constraint on spontaneous speech errors, where initial segments interact with other initial segments but not with segments in non-initial positions. However, the evidence from spontaneous speech is also compatible with another unit: the word. The error elicitation experiments described in this paper were designed to test the

*The support of NIH Grant NS-043320-20, and useful comments from Merrill Garrett, the late Dennis Klatt, and Pim Levelt on earlier versions of this paper are gratefully acknowledged.

hypothesis that syllable structure alone can account for position constraints on interaction errors between target segments of an utterance, by determining whether the influence of larger elements like the word can be discerned in segmental error patterns.

*Observations from spontaneous errors*

Almost every error analyst has made the observation that *interaction errors* between target segments are not random, but are constrained by a number of factors. Interaction errors include *exchanges* ("a *sh*irt as *sk*ort as yours" for "*sk*irt as *sh*ort"), and other errors like *anticipatory substitutions* ("a la*tch* di*tch* effort" for "la*st* di*tch* effort") and *perseveratory substitutions* ("Cotton *P*otch Rag" for "Cotton *P*atch Rag"). The arguments in this introduction will be based on exchanges, since they provide the strongest evidence for the existence of an organizing frame separate from its segmental contents; see Shattuck-Hufnagel (1979) for supporting arguments.

Factors that have been found to influence segmental interaction errors collected from spontaneous speech include phonological similarity, frequency of use in the language and, in corpora collected from speakers of American English and related languages, the position of the segment in a larger unit (Berg, 1987; Boomer & Laver, 1968; Dell, 1986; Fromkin, 1976; MacKay, 1970; Nooteboom, 1967; Shattuck-Hufnagel, 1979; Stemberger, 1983; and others). The position constraint is usually described as a tendency for an initial segment to interact with another initial segment, but not with a final segment, and vice versa. For example, Fromkin (1971) cites Boomer and Laver's claim that

> segmental slips obey a structural law with regard to syllable place; that is, initial segments in the origin syllable replace initial segments in the target syllable, nuclear replace nuclear, and final replace final.

Fromkin notes that her own data from a corpus of errors in American English show the same pattern. Nooteboom (1969), looking at errors in Dutch, MacKay (1970), looking at errors in German, and others make similar observations. The MIT–Arizona corpus of errors collected from American English speech (Garrett, 1975) shows the same pattern, as reported for example in Shattuck-Hufnagel (1979): "of 211 between-word phoneme exchange errors ... all but 4 take place between phonemes in similar positions in their respective syllables." Some further examples will illustrate the point:

initial: . . . a *t*erry *ch*art . . . (*ch*erry *t*art)
        *M*ait a *w*inute! (*W*ait a *m*inute!)
final: Ouch, I have a sti*ck* ne*ff*. (sti*ff* ne*ck*)
        This isn't gree*p* gra*ne* season, is it? (gree*n* gra*pe*)

Absolute initial position and absolute final position are not the most appropriate descriptive terms, as can be seen in errors like the following:

"Did the grass clack?" (glass crack)
"sprit blain' (split brain)

Since segments in structurally parallel (rather than serially identical) locations interact, the position constraint can be recast in terms of the theory of syllable structure, in which the initial consonants form the onset, the vocalic (or most sonorant) portion the nucleus, and the final consonants the coda. In these terms, onset consonants interact with consonants in parallel positions in other onsets, but not with codas, etc.

Note, however, that in these examples the target segment pairs occupy parallel positions both in their words *and* in their syllables. Thus, they do not distinguish between the word and the syllable as the larger constraining unit. Although most researchers have focussed on the syllabic interpretation, the observations are compatible with either a word-based or a syllable-based position similarity constraint.

### The position similarity constraint in planning models

The distinction is an important one, because this constraint contributes substantively to many proposed models of production planning. For example, in spreading activation models of segmental serial ordering, activation spreads in a network with separate nodes for syllable onset and syllable coda allophones of each segment (Dell, 1986, discussed in Levelt, 1989). Moreover, the framework that guides the selection process during serial ordering is made up of syllables, each with its onset, nucleus and coda. Evidence for this aspect of the model is drawn directly from the position similarity constraints observed in spontaneous speech errors.

Analogously, the position similarity constraint provides evidence for the frameworks invoked in frame-and-filler models. These models propose that the phonological processing representation includes a framework of segmental slots structured into larger units, and that this framework is represented separately from the segments that will eventually become associated with it (Shattuck-Hufnagel, 1983). According to arguments based on the position similarity constraint, the target slots or locations are not an undifferentiated string; instead, they are structured into larger phonological units. The question is, what are these larger units? Are they syllables, or are they morphemes or words? (It is not clear exactly what the most appropriate description of this alternative unit is; we will use the term "word" as a shorthand reference for the class of possible constituents larger than the syllable.)

*Problems in interpreting data from spontaneous errors*

There are two reasons why the distribution of errors in collections from spontaneous speech does not clarify the nature of the larger frame unit. The first arises
from the hierarchical embedded structure of words and syllables, mentioned
above. This problem is particularly acute for errors in monosyllabic words, which
make up a substantial proportion of the segmental errors in the MIT–Arizona
corpus. Here, the position of a segment in its word and in its syllable are
identical, so position similarity does not distinguish between the two proposed
framework units.

The second reason is an additional position constraint, one that reflects a
position *preference* for the location of an error (separate from the position
*similarity* of two interacting segments). In collections of errors in American
English, there is a striking predominance of word-onset consonants, while consonants in other positions in the word are substantially under-represented. For
example, Fromkin (1976) reported that in a corpus of segmental exchange errors
in the UCLA corpus, 73% involved word-initial segments. Similarly, Shattuck-
Hufnagel (1987) noted that of 187 consonant exchange errors in the MIT–Arizona
corpus, 88% involved pairs of word-onset segments. This predominance of
word-onset position was found even for exchanges in polysyllabic words, which
distinguish between the word-based and the syllable-based hypothesis. Here, the
proportion of consonant exchanges that involved word onsets was 91%, even
though only 19% of the consonants in polysyllabic words occur in this position
(Shattuck-Hufnagel, 1987). Other error types also showed a preference for
word-onset locations, although the asymmetry was not as strong.

This predominance of word-onset segments among interaction errors is in itself
some evidence for the role of the word as a unit in the framework structure. But it
is complicated by still another factor: most words of English carry lexical stress on
their first syllable. Does the predominance of errors among word-onset consonants simply reflect the common value of lexical stress for their syllables?

A few critical cases in the MIT–Arizona corpus, involving words without initial
stress, suggest that shared word onset position can evoke errors between pairs of
segments whose syllables differ in lexical stress:

*m*ath review→ *r*ath *m*eview
*sh*oulder *s*eparation→ *s*oulder *sh*eparation
*c*ult of *p*ersonality→ *p*ult of *c*ursonality
*f*orm-*p*ersuasive garments→ *p*orm-*f*ersuasive . . .
*n*ode of *R*anvier→ *r*ode of *N*anvier

But since most words of English are either monosyllabic or stress initial, most
consonantal interaction errors involve segments that are located both in the onset
of a word *and* in the onset of a lexically stressed syllable. As a result, it is difficult

to determine which of these two factors is influencing the distribution of errors. Thus the question about the position similarity constraint can be expressed in this way: is syllable position similarity an exhaustive description of the structural constraints on interacting segments? Or, must an adequate model invoke word position and/or lexical stress?

*An experimental approach*

To answer the question about the role of the word, what is needed is a set of target utterances in which pairs of confusable syllable-onset segments appear in two contrasting structural conditions:

– both segments appear in word-onset position, versus
– one segment appears in word onset position while the other does not.

For example, for the target pair /p/–/f/, the utterance

(1) The *p*eril is a *f*ad

places both /p/ and /f/ in word-onset position, while the utterance

(2) To re*p*eat is to *f*ail

places only one of the two target segments in word-onset position; the other is word medial. If the number of errors in stimuli like (1) exceeds the number of errors in stimuli like (2), it will suggest that the position of a target segment in its word must be taken into account in models of the segmental serial ordering process. On the other hand, if the two types of stimuli elicit errors at a similar rate, it will suggest that there is no need to invoke the word, because the syllable (or the syllable plus its lexical stress) can provide an adequate description of the position similarity constraint on segmental interaction errors. The argument here reflects the assumption that when two target segments share a common value along a dimension that influences the selection of segments, they are more likely to interact in an error than two segments that do not share such a common value. The experiments ask the question: which one of the several dimensions shared by most interacting segments evokes the larger number of segmental interaction errors? In other words, the method compares the degree of preference among different types of position similarity.

In utterances (1) and (2) above, both of the target segments /p/ and /f/ appear in lexically stressed syllables. Consequently, results from these utterances will not reveal anything about the role of stress in determining segmental interaction errors. To evaluate the role of this factor, we need another kind of comparison, holding word position constant and varying stress. For example, consider an utterance like

(3) The *p*arade is on *f*oot

where the syllables of /p/ and /f/ differ in their lexical stress. If stimuli like (1) elicit more errors than stimuli like (3), it will suggest that lexical stress cannot be ignored as a determinant of segmental interaction patterns. Finally, as a control, consider an utterance of the form

(4) So the ri*pp*le will *f*ade

where /p/ and /f/ differ both in word position and in the lexical stress of the following nucleus. Comparison of such patterns with those in (2) and (3) will provide an additional means of evaluating the role of shared word position and shared stress.

In summary, the aim was to discover, by means of error elicitation experiments, whether shared position in the syllable and/or shared lexical stress of the syllable can provide an adequate account of the constraints on segmental interaction errors, or whether it is necessary to invoke the influence of a larger unit like the word. In other words, which of the possible position similarity constraints is doing the work?

## Experiment 1: Word position, syllable position and lexical stress

*Method*

### Stimuli

The stimuli were based on pairs of target segments that were highly confusable, as shown by their high frequency of interaction errors in the MIT–Arizona corpus (Shattuck-Hufnagel & Klatt, 1979; the experiments are described briefly in Shattuck-Hufnagel, 1985a, 1987). For each pair of target segments, for example /p/–/f/, a quadruple set of four tongue-twisters was developed, each consisting of a list of four words in the following order:

bisyllable, monosyllable, monosyllable, bisyllable

In the first twister of each quadruple set, the target consonants shared word-onset position, syllable-onset position and the lexical stress of their respective syllables. For example, a Type 1 twister for /p/–/f/ was

*p*arrot *f*ad *f*oot *p*eril
Type 1: Both word position and stress position same

In the second twister for this quadruple set, the two target segments shared word position, but they did not share lexical stress; for example, /f/ appeared in lexically stressed syllables but /p/ did not, as in

*p*arade *f*ad *f*oot *p*arole
Type 2: Word position same, but not stress position

In the third twister, the two target segments shared position in the onset of a stressed syllable, but they did not share word position. For example, /f/ appeared in word-onset position but /p/ did not, as in

re*p*eat *f*ad *f*oot re*p*aid
Type 3: Stress position same, but not word position

Finally, in the fourth twister the target segments shared neither word-onset position nor lexical stress; /f/ appeared in word-onset position in the lexically stressed syllable, while /p/ appeared in non-word-onset position before an unstressed syllabic nucleus, as in

ri*pp*le *f*ad *f*oot ra*p*id
Type 4: Neither word position nor stress position same

Note that in this last twister there is some question as to the syllable position of the word-medial /p/ at the point when segmental errors occur, because of issues associated with ambisyllabicity. In all other cases the target segments appear in the syllable onset, so that this experiment does not directly test the role of syllable position similarity. This issue is addressed further in the general discussion at the end of the paper.

In each of the four twisters of a quadruple set, there is a third consonant that appears in onset position, like the /r/ in these four examples. This third consonant, as well as in most cases the two monosyllabic words, were the same for all four twisters of a given quadruple set, in an attempt to keep the elicitation context as similar as possible. For all but a few of the 384 words used, the stressed vowels of the four target words in a twister were different. The final consonants of the two monosyllabic words were always different, but the final consonants of the bisyllabic words were not controlled.

The 12 pairs of confusable target consonants that were used to construct the stimuli are shown in Table 1. For some pairs, it was possible to construct more than one set of four twisters, so that the total number of stimulus quadruple sets was 24, and the total number of individual twisters was 96. The 24 quadruple sets are given in Appendix A. Occasionally it was necessary to use a non-optimal word like a last name, or an obscure lexical item; speakers were familiarized with these words in the instructions.

*Task*

The speaker's task was to read each tongue-twister aloud three times, and then recite it from memory three times, for a total of six utterances per twister. The reading condition was included as a partial check on the possibility that errors were taking place in memory rather than in production planning per se. Since the

Table 1.    *Pairs of confusable target consonants used to generate the stimuli for Experiment 1*

| Target segment pair | Number of quadruple sets |
|:---:|:---:|
| f/p | 4 |
| r/l | 4 |
| b/g | 3 |
| l/y | 2 |
| b/p | 2 |
| m/n | 2 |
| r/w | 2 |
| d/g | 1 |
| p/k | 1 |
| l/n | 1 |
| d/t | 1 |
| j/d | 1 |
| 12 | 24 |

stimuli were in the speaker's field of vision throughout the reading condition, little memory burden was imposed. If the pattern of errors is similar for the reading and recall conditions, it might be inferred that the determining factor was operating during production planning itself, which is a common processing stage for both conditions, rather than in a separate memory buffer not directly related to the planning process.

Speakers were instructed that the variable of interest was not whether they could recall the twister, but rather how they produced it when they did recall it. Thus, they were free to consult the written stimulus as often as needed between renditions in order to accomplish this goal. Freedom to re-read the stimulus lessened the stress on the speakers, and helped to ensure that the errors were produced during the production planning process rather than as the result of confusions in memory.

No attempt was made to control speaking rate, other than by instructing the speakers to speak a little faster than they normally would. For most speakers, this injunction soon lost its force, and they reverted to their preferred comfortable speaking rate.

### Presentation

Each twister was typed horizontally on a 3 × 5-inch index card. Each twister card was followed by a card for an intervening distractor task unrelated to this experiment, which involved the generation and repetition of sentences. The sentence generation task served as a rest from the sometimes stressful twisters, and ensured that the anecdotally reported tendency for errors to increase geometrically during the course of repeating a difficult string was prevented from disrupting the production of the subsequent tongue-twister.

It was presumed that if a speaker produced all four twisters for a given quadruple set, he or she would be so well practiced for that pair of target segments as to no longer make an appreciable number of errors. Based on this assumption, presentation was designed so that each speaker produced only two of the four twisters for most stimulus sets. That is, for 20 of the 24 quadruple sets, each speaker produced Types 1 and 2 for half of the stimulus sets, and Types 3 and 4 for the other half, in a counterbalanced design. To shed some light on whether errors *would* become rare if speakers produced all four twisters of a quadruple set, the remaining four quadruples were produced entirely by the same speakers; half of the speakers produced two of them, and the other half the remaining two. Thus, each speaker produced a total of 48 of the 96 stimuli, in a series of two half-hour experimental sessions separated by several days.

Speakers were seated in an acoustically attenuated room about 10 inches from an Altec 684B microphone. Recordings were made on a Presto 800 Studio tape recorder for later transcription.

*Subjects*

The 20 speakers who participated in this experiment were native speakers of American English, between the ages of 18 and 30, right-handed, and without known speaking or hearing difficulties. All were members of the MIT community who had volunteered to serve as paid subjects in speech experiments. Half were male and half were female.

*Transcription*

The recorded utterances were played back on a Sony TC-800B tape deck over Sony MDR-V6 earphones, and transcribed by the author. Utterances containing errors were reviewed many times, and transcription was only considered complete when all six utterances had been re-heard without a change in the transcription record. Criteria for labeling events as interaction errors in the sense of this experiment were stringent: utterances which sounded "odd", non-fluent or simply ambiguous were noted, but not transcribed as interaction errors.

Some additional decisions were made about which of the dysfluencies transcribed as errors by these criteria would be counted as interaction errors between pairs of target segment. Included in the count were full complete exchanges and substitutions, as well as errors in interrupted, corrected utterances, like "parade fad put---foot parole". Also included were errors which occurred during correction attempts. Exchanges were counted as two separate errors. If an error was interrupted immediately after the target segment, as in "parade [p]---pad foot parole", the error was included as a segmental error, even though the error unit might have been a CV– (e.g. *pi*d) or CVC (e.g., *pit*) if completed. This decision reflected the fact that CV– and CVC units were rare among completed errors in these experiments, while single-segment error units were very common. Also included were instances in which one or more segments not contiguous to the target segment were replaced in the target word, as in "parade *pab* foot parole" (for "parade *fad*..."). Not included were errors with completed CV-, -VC or larger error units (even if these units included an error in the target segment), unintelligible dysfluencies, interaction errors between non-target-pair segments, no-source substitutions, and instances in which the audible information was too sparse to permit entirely reliable identification of the segment (largely cases of stop closure without release).

After transcription, all interaction errors between pairs of target segments (e.g., /p/ and /f/ in the examples above) were tabulated; these were called Expected Errors. In addition, interactions between one member of the target pair and the third onset consonant in the stimulus (e.g., /r/ in the examples above) were tabulated, either as Unexpected Between-Word Errors like "pa*f*ade *r*ad" for "parade *f*ad", or as Unexpected Within-Word Errors like "*p*ereet" for "*r*epeat".

## Results

In interpreting the results of this experiment it is helpful to consider the relationships among the stimuli shown in Table 2. For example, comparing Both stimuli with Stress stimuli will reveal the effect of shared word position, because this is the factor that distinguishes these two stimulus types. Similarly, comparing Both stimuli with Word stimuli will show the effect of shared stress position. Comparisons with the Neither stimuli are less informative, because of the possibility that target pairs in these stimuli differed in their syllable position.

The distribution of expected interaction errors between pairs of target segments elicited during the production of 23 040 words elicited in this experiment are shown in Table 3. Overall, only 1.6% of the words contained interaction errors

Table 2.  *Position differences and similarities between locations of target segment pairs in the four types of stimuli*

| Stimulus type | Word position | Stress position | Syllable position |
|---|---|---|---|
| Both Positions Same ( *peril fad*...) | same | same | same |
| Word Position Same ( *parade fad*...) | same | *different* | same |
| Stress Syllable Position Same (re*peat fad*...) | *different* | same | same |
| Neither Position Same (ri*pple fad*...) | *different* | *different* | ???? |

Table 3.  *Number of interaction errors between pairs of target consonants elicited by four stimulus types in Experiment 1*

| Type 1<br>Both Same<br>(*peril fad*...) | Type 2<br>Word Position Same<br>(*parade fad*...) | Type 3<br>Stress Syllable Position Same<br>(*repeat fad*...) | Type 4<br>Neither Same<br>(*ripple fad*...) |
|---|---|---|---|
| 182 | 130 | 55 | 14 |

between target segments, suggesting that repeating a twister six times does not cause the speech production mechanism to break down to an unnatural degree.

The first comparison to look at is the number of errors elicited by the Both Positions Same stimuli and the Stress Syllable Position Same stimuli. When both syllable position and stress position are held constant, significantly more errors occur between segments that share word position (*peril fad*...) than between segments that do not (*repeat fad*...), 182 versus 55, using the square root of (npq) as an estimate of sigma, $p < .01$.

This difference suggests that word structure plays a role in determining which of the target segments of an utterance are likely to interact with each other in errors. That is, if we compare target pairs that share word-onset position, syllable position *and* stress, with those that share only syllable position and stress, the extra similarity of shared word-onset position is associated with a significant increase in the interaction error rate.

The second comparison of interest is between Word Position Same stimuli and Stress Position Same stimuli. In this direct comparison between the effectiveness of shared word-onset position versus shared stress position, Word Position Same stimuli (*parade fad*...) provoke more than twice as many errors as Stress Position Same stimuli (*repeat fad*...), 130 versus 55, significant with $p < .01$. That is, shared position in the word onset increases the likelihood of an interaction error (even for two segments that do not have stress in common) more than shared lexical stress increases the likelihood of error for two segments that do not have word-onset position in common. It appears that models which ignore the role of word structure in the serial ordering of segments cannot adequately describe the distribution pattern of segmental interaction errors.

An additional observation of interest is that where segment pairs share neither word nor lexical stress position, they only rarely interact in errors in this experiment (i.e., in Type 4 stimuli, Neither Position Same, e.g., "*ripple fad*..."). Apparently the mere presence of phonologically similar segments in the target words of an utterance, without other structural factors in common, is only a weak determinant of segmental interaction patterns.

Finally, the fact that more errors occur for Both Positions Same stimuli than for Word Position Same stimuli indicates that lexical stress similarity plays a role in constraining segmental errors. Otherwise, one would expect no increase in the number of interaction errors when lexical stress similarity is added to word-onset position similarity. Since the number of errors for the Both Positions Same stimuli (peril fad...) is significantly greater than the number for the Word Position Same stimuli (parade fad...), 182 versus 130, $p < .01$, it appears that similarity of the lexical stress level of the nuclei following the two target consonants increases the likelihood of an interaction error between them.

*Discussion*

The observation that both word position and the lexical stress level of the syllable constrain the error patterns for onset consonants raises the question: where in the production processing mechanism do each of these two factors play a role? If the effects of word-onset position and lexical stress of the syllable are independent, then the error rate in stimuli where both are operating can be predicted using the product of the correct production rates in the two sets of stimuli which explore each factor separately (Levelt, personal communication). Using this method, the number of errors predicted for the Both Position Same stimuli if word position and stress are independent is 170, and the number of errors observed is 182; this difference is not significant ($\chi^2$ with one degree of freedom, $p < .05$). Thus, the results of Experiment 1 provide no evidence for the claim that the two factors shown here to affect consonant interaction errors (i.e., shared word-onset position and shared lexical stress level in the following syllabic nucleus) interact. That is, the data so far offer no support for any claim about whether these factors operate at the same point in the production planning process or not. We will return to this observation in the discussion of subsequent experiments.

Analysis of the four quadruple sets for which all four twisters were produced by the same speakers showed that their error pattern was similar to those where two twisters were produced by one group of speakers and two by another group. This finding was taken into account in improving the design for Experiment 2 below, where speakers produced all four twisters of their quadruple sets.

While the results of Experiment 1 clearly support the claim that word structure must be taken into account in models of the segmental serial ordering process for speakers of American English, they raise a number of questions. For example, are four-word tongue-twisters an appropriate speech stimulus for testing hypotheses about normal spontaneous speech planning? Do the results vary when speakers are asked to produce grammatically well-formed phrases, as has been found in other elicitation experiments? Does the word-onset constraint arise during the process of lexical access? These questions are addressed in Experiments 1(a) to 1(c), which employ stimuli based on the words used in Experiment 1.

**Variations on Experiment 1: (a) Phrases; (b) Sentences; (c) Non-words**

*Experiment 1(a): Stimulus words embedded in phrases*

The phrasal elicitation experiment was embarked on for two reasons: (1) to provide stimuli that are structured somewhat more like the utterances of normal speech; and (2) to control for the possibility that segmental error patterns might differ for lists versus phrases, as suggested by results from a separate series of experiments using monosyllabic stimuli (Shattuck-Hufnagel, 1987). In those experiments, proportionally fewer errors occurred among the final segments of CVC words when they were produced in grammatically well-formed phrases, as compared to when they were produced in word lists: 23% of total errors in phrases versus 56% in lists.

A new set of stimuli was developed in which the four words of each word-list twister of Experiment 1 were embedded in short phrases, in their original order:

Type 1P (Both word position and stress position same):
  Make the *p*arrot a *f*ad and the *f*oot is in *p*eril
Type 2P (Word position same but not stress position):
  The *p*arade is a *f*ad and the *f*oot has *p*arole
Type 3P (Stress position same but not word position):
  To re*p*eat is a *f*ad and on *f*oot you re*p*ay
Type 4P (Neither word position nor stress position same):
  Call the ri*p*ple a *f*ad and the *f*oot can be ra*p*id

Locally, each of the four phrases in one of these twisters is grammatically well formed, although the resulting sentences are sometimes semantically anomalous. (Stimuli for Experiment 1(a) are given in Appendix A.) The task, presentation, subject pool, recording and transcription were unchanged from Experiment 1, except that each typed phrasal twister took up two lines on the 3 × 5-inch card rather than one.

Results for both the list condition (Experiment 1) and the phrase condition (Experiment 1(a)) are shown in Table 4.

Table 4. *Number of interaction errors between pairs of target consonants, elicited by list stimuli (Experiment 1) and phrase stimuli (Experiment 1(a))*

|  | Both Same | Word Position Same | Stress Syllable Position Same | Neither Same |
|---|---|---|---|---|
| Experiment 1 (lists) | 182 | 130 | 55 | 14 |
| Experiment 1(a) (phrases) | 202 | 134 | 59 | 15 |

In both experiments, significantly more interaction errors occurred between pairs of segments that shared position in the word onset (Both Position Same) than between pairs that did not (Stress Syllable Position Same), syllable position and stress being equal. As before, these results support the claim that some aspects of word structure play a role in segmental serial ordering.

Other aspects of the results for phrasal twisters parallel those for the list stimuli used in Experiment 1. For example, the number of errors in the Both condition, where similarity of word position and lexical stress are both at work, are not significantly greater than is predicted by the operation of each factor separately ($\chi^2$ with one degree of freedom, $p < .05$).

### Additional observations, Experiments 1 and 1(a)

*Unexpected errors.* Recall that each twister built around a pair of confusable target consonants like /p/–/f/ also contains a third onset consonant, like the /r/ in the Stressed Syllable Position Same stimulus "*r*epeat *f*ad *f*oot *r*epaid". In a number of cases, this segment interacts in an error with a member of the target segment pair. This can happen in two ways:

(1) in Between-Word errors like
   *f*epeat *r*ad foot repaid (for "*r*epeat *f*ad...")
   or
   pa*f*ade *r*ad foot repaid (for "pa*r*ade *f*ad...")

where the /r/ unexpectedly interacts with the target segment /f/ that begins one of the monosyllabic words; or:

(2) in Within-Word errors like
   pe*r*eet fad foot repaid (for "*r*epeat...")
   or
   pi*rr*el fad foot repaid (for "*r*ipple...")

where the /r/ unexpectedly interacts with the target segment /p/ within the same bisyllabic word.

The distribution of the Between-Word Unexpected errors for Experiments 1 and 1(a) is shown in Table 5. (The column headings refer to the positions of the two interacting segments in the unexpected error, and thus do not correspond to the original stimulus types. For example, Unexpected Word Position errors occur between word onset consonants in Stress Position Same stimuli like "repeat fad foot repaid", that put the original pair of target segments /p/–/f/ in the same stress position. This error would be listed under Unexpected Word Position in the table, although it occurred in a Stress Position Same stimulus.)

Like Expected errors, Unexpected errors are most likely to occur when the two target segments share position in the word onset. This observation lends compel-

Table 5.   *Number of unexpected between-word interaction errors elicited by list stimuli (Experiment 1) and phrase stimuli (Experiment 1(a))*

|  | Unexpected Both Position Same | Unexpected Word Position Same | Unexpected Stress Syllable Position Same | Unexpected Neither Same |
|---|---|---|---|---|
| Experiment 1 (lists) | 24 | 25 | 11 | – |
| Experiment 1(a) (phrases) | 45 | 44 | 14 | – |

ling support to the claim that shared word-onset position increases the tendency of consonants to interact in segmental errors in these experiments, since the segment pairs involved here are phonemically dissimilar compared to the original target pairs. On a simple three-way categorization of manner, place and voicing, the target segment pairs differed by an average of only 1.2 features out of 3, while the segment pairs involved in unexpected errors have a mean difference of 2.3. This indicates that even phonemically dissimilar segments can be drawn into interaction errors if they share position in their respective word onsets.

The second type of Unexpected Error occurs within the word, and involves an interaction between the other member of a target segment pair and the third onset consonant. Unlike the Between-Word Unexpected errors, which occurred in both iambs and trochees, the Within-Word errors occurred mostly in iambic words like "morraine" and "relate" (73 errors for Experiments 1 and 1(a) combined), rather than in trochaic words like "moral" and "really" (14 errors in both experiments). Examples include substitutions like "*me*moan" for "bemoan", "*de*dew" for "bedew", and "*be*buse" for "bemuse"; exchanges like "*me*rote" for "remote" and "*Re Loy*" for "LeRoy", and additions like "ra*c*roon" for "racoon". In many cases it was not possible to tell whether the error was an interaction between two consonants in the word, or an omission of the initial unstressed syllable, because the speaker stopped after the first consonant, as in "f---suffuse". In the 1984 count of the MIT–Arizona corpus, the small number of within-word exchanges contained both segment pairs that shared syllable position (e.g., "They had recurrent relyngeal..." (laryngeal), and "He's a tegevarian" (vegetarian)), and segment pairs that did not (e.g., "It could injure the shif" (fish), and "The question about spoke..." (scope)). Since the number of Within-Word Unexpected errors produced in this experiment is too small to provide reliable evidence, and since these errors do not bear directly on the question of whether or not word structure governs the position similarity of between-word interaction errors, we will not analyze them further here.

*Reading versus recall.* The reading condition was included in the experimental design for Experiments 1 and 1(a) to provide some indication of the error pattern when minimal short-term memory storage was required. Presumably, while the speakers had the written version of the stimulus in front of them, the memory load was minimal. Results for the reading and recall conditions are compared for Experiments 1 and 1(a) in Table 6.

The patterns are similar for the reading and the recall conditions: (a) target segment pairs that share word position (as well as syllable position and stress) interact more than three times as often as those that share only syllable position and stress; and (b) target pairs that share word onset position, but differ in stress, interact more than twice as frequently as pairs that differ in word position but share stress. This similarity in the distribution of errors for the two speaking conditions, reading and recall, supports the view that the interaction errors in these elicitation experiments are occurring during the production planning process which is common to them both. It is likely that the smaller number of errors in the Reading condition reflects the fact that it included the first three renditions of each twister by the speaker; the Recall condition, made up of the 4th, 5th and 6th renditions, might be expected to have a higher error rate if tongue-twisters become progressively more difficult to articulate with each successive utterance.

*Across subjects.* The variability in error elicitation rate across subjects in these experiments is very striking. For example, the most error-prone speaker in Experiment 1 produced 41 errors (error rate 3.6%), while the least error-prone produced 1 error. In view of this variability, it is of interest to test for the reliability of the effect across different speakers. The first step is to evaluate the hypothesis that there is a non-random pattern in the distribution of errors across the four conditions of Both Positions Same, Word Position Same, Stress Syllable Position Same and Neither Position Same. Using Friedman's two-way analysis of variance for rank order data, corrected for ties (of which there were many, for the speakers with very low error rates), all four sets of speakers (two sets of 10 in Experiment 1 and two different sets of 10 in Experiment 1(a)) were found to show a significant departure from random distribution of errors across the four conditions, with $p < .01$ (Siegel, 1988). Since not all subjects produced the same utterances for each target pair (in each experiment, 10 speakers produced two of

Table 6. *Number of interaction errors between target pairs of consonants elicited by list stimuli (Experiment 1) and phrase stimuli (Experiment 1(a)) in reading and recall conditions*

| | Experiment 1 (lists) | | | | Experiment 1(a) (phrases) | | | |
|---|---|---|---|---|---|---|---|---|
| | Both | Word | Stress Syllable | Neither | Both | Word | Stress Syllable | Neither |
| Reading | 49 | 33 | 16 | 3 | 58 | 49 | 17 | 5 |
| Recall | 133 | 97 | 39 | 11 | 144 | 85 | 42 | 10 |
| Total | 182 | 130 | 55 | 14 | 202 | 134 | 59 | 15 |

the conditions and another 10 produced the other two for any given quadruple set of twisters), it was difficult to test which differences were reliable across speakers. We will return to this question in the discussion of Experiment 2, which was designed in part to eliminate this problem.

*Across stimulus sets.* Variability in number of errors elicited was also substantial across quadruple sets of twisters; in Experiment 1, the largest number of errors was 35, elicited by the target pair /r/–/w/ with /b/, and the smallest was 0, elicited by /d/–/t/ with /f/. Using Friedman's two-way analysis of variance for rank-order data corrected for ties, the results for 24 quadruple sets show a significant departure from random distribution across the four types of stimuli with $p < .05$. Analysis of which differences are responsible for the significance will be postponed until Experiment 2.

*Non-word-onset consonants.* It is interesting to compare the results for word-medial consonants in Experiment 1, where the words were spoken in lists, and in Experiment 1(a), where they were embedded in short grammatically structured phrases. This manipulation did not significantly affect the number of errors in word-medial consonants; that is, the error rate for target segments in word-medial position was very similar in the two experiments: 55 versus 59 for Stress Syllable Similar stimuli and 14 versus 15 for Neither. This stands in sharp contrast to the behavior of another category of non-onset consonants, those in final position in CVC words. When these words are embedded in phrasal tongue twisters like

"From the leap of the note to the nap of the lute"
and
"It's the peal of the tone from the pan on the tool"

their final consonants are differentially protected against errors in comparison with those same words when they are produced in lists like "leap note nap lute" and "peal tone pan tool" (Shattuck-Hufnagel, 1987). That experiment used only CVC target words, so it was not possible to say whether the protective effect of phrases extends to all consonants outside the word onset, or just to final consonants. The fact that the word-medial consonants in the phrasal stimuli of Experiment 1(a) are not differentially protected against errors by the phrasal context seems to suggest that the protective effect of phrasal structure does *not* apply to all segments outside the word onset, but only to those in certain positions. Note, however, that a word-medial error in the present experiments would necessarily involve an interaction across word position, that is, an interaction with a consonant in a word onset or a word coda, since there was only one medial consonant type in each twister stimulus. This cross-position circumstance may be the reason for the failure of phrasal contexts to reduce the error rate in non-word-onset consonants, via a floor effect.

*Distribution of errors across the four words of the stimulus*

If the large number of errors in Word Position Same stimuli like "parade fad foot parole" arose primarily from errors in the prosodically weak word-onset segment /p/, it would suggest a model of the error process in which the prosodically strong segment from the stressed syllable, here /f/, systematically replaces the prosodically weaker /p/. This, however, is not the case. Figure 1 shows the distribution of errors across the four words of each twister, for Word Position Same stimuli and Both Positions Same stimuli (like "peril fad foot parrot") for Experiments 1 and 1(a).

If we define a segment located in the onset of a lexically stressed syllable to be in some sense strong, then two aspects of this distribution argue against a model in which strong segments replace weak ones. First, strong segments (like the /p/'s in "peril" and "parrot") are replaced by /f/ at least as often as the weaker ones (like the /p/'s in "parade" and "parole"). Thus, weak segments are not especially susceptible to interaction errors; instead, strong–strong interactions are no less likely than weak–strong. Second, prosodically strong segments are replaced by weaker segments at least as often as vice versa. That is, for the Word Position Same stimuli:

– weaker /p/ replaced by stronger /f/ or equivalent = 127 errors
– stronger /f/ replaced by weaker /p/ or equivalent = 139 errors

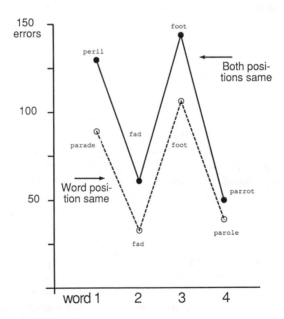

Figure 1.    *Error rate by word position in the stimulus (Experiments 1 and 1(a) combined).*

These results argue for a model in which errors occur by mis-selection among similar candidate elements, rather than by strong segments overwhelming weak ones.

*Experiment 1(b): A sentence generation task*

One disadvantage of Experiments 1 and 1(a) is that the task of repeating tongue-twisters that are provided by the experimenter, even those with a phrasal form, could be regarded as a special speaking situation in which processing may differ significantly from normal speech production planning. Thus, this task may not provide the best possible test of the hypothesis that word structure constrains the segmental interaction errors that occur during the processing associated with normal speech production. The phrasal stimuli of Experiment 1(a) move somewhat toward natural speech structures, but an even more persuasive test would be provided by a sentence generation task, in which the speaker creates an utterance based on the four words of the twister stimulus.

In Experiment 1(b), speakers were presented with each four-word list stimulus from Experiment 1 (e.g., parade fad foot parole, repeat fad foot repaid), and asked to generate a sentence that used the four words in the order given. All 24 quadruple sets (96 twisters) from Experiment 1 were used. The 40 speakers were divided into two groups: 20 speakers produced Type 1 and Type 3 stimuli for half of the quadruple sets and Type 2 and Type 4 stimuli for the remaining half, while the remaining 20 speakers produced the remaining stimuli. Since the words in a twister were often unrelated in meaning, the sentence was not required to have a high likelihood of being uttered in the real world, but it had to be complete and grammatically well formed.

This sentence generation experiment served as the distractor task in two sessions from an unrelated speaking experiment. Each speaker generated a sentence for 48 of the 96 four-word twisters (24 in each half-hour session), and repeated it aloud three times. Thus, both the nature of the utterance (a self-generated sentence), the number of speakers (40) and the number of utterances per stimulus provided by each speaker (3) differed from Experiment 1. Otherwise, presentation, subjects, recording and transcription, as well as the total number of utterances produced, were as in the earlier experiment.

The distribution of interaction errors involving the target segment pairs is shown in Table 7. Although the experimental designs of the two earlier experiments are not strictly identical, their results are included for comparison.

Like the results of earlier experiments that employed lists and phrases read aloud and recited from memory, these sentence generation results show that pairs of consonants that share lexical stress are significantly more likely to interact in errors when they both occur in word-onset position (Both Positions Same condition) than when one is a word onset and one is not (Stress Syllable Position

232    S. Shattuck-Hufnagel

Table 7.    *Number of interaction errors elicited in a reading + recall task using lists (Experiment 1) and using phrases (Experiment 1(a)), and in a sentence generation task (Experiment 1(b))*

|  | Both Same | Word Same | Stress Syllable Same | Neither |
|---|---|---|---|---|
| Experiment 1 (lists; reading plus recall) | 182 | 130 | 55 | 14 |
| Experiment 1(a) (phrases; reading plus recall) | 202 | 134 | 59 | 15 |
| Experiment 1(b) (sentence generation) | 134 | 72 | 30 | 7 |

Same condition). This finding supports the claim that word structure plays a role in constraining segmental interaction errors in the more natural speaking conditions of sentence generation. The earlier finding of a reliable effect of stress similarity is also replicated in the results of Experiment 1(b).


*Experiment 1(c): Non-word stimuli*

In all of the experiments described so far, word-onset consonants appear to be particularly susceptible to segmental interaction errors. One possible account of this finding is that the planning during which these errors occur is related to the process of selecting lexical items. This is a reasonable suggestion, on the assumption that onset segments play a significant and distinct role in the lexical selection process for speech production. This assumption is supported to some degree by observations of the tip-of-the-tongue phenomenon, where speakers sometimes report they know the first few segments of a word even if they cannot retrieve the entire item (Brown & McNeill, 1966). To test this possibility, we designed a set of non-word stimuli based on the segmental structure of the real-word stimuli used in Experiments 1, 1(a) and 1(b). The non-words were created by replacing non-target-pair segments in selected real-word stimuli with different segments, e.g.:

parade fad foot parole→perash fide fote perimm
repeat fad foot repaid→rapeen fide fote ropabe

This transformation was carried out for the 16 most error-prone quadruple sets of twisters from Experiment 1, but only for their Word Position Same and Stress Syllable Position Same forms (starred in Appendix A); stimuli from the Both and Neither conditions were discarded. The 32 new non-word twisters, as well as their

32 original real-word versions, were produced by 10 subjects in two half-hour sessions. Half of the real-word and half of the non-word forms were included in each session. Presentation, task, subject pool, recording and transcription were otherwise as in Experiment 1.

Results of this experiment, comparing error distributions for real-word and non-word stimuli for the same speakers, as well as results for the different set of speakers who produced the same 16 real-word stimuli in a different design in Experiment 1, are shown in Table 8. The tendency for expected interaction errors to occur in word-onset consonants is, if anything, greater for non-words than for real words (284 errors vs. 122).

Unexpected Between-Word errors, involving an interaction between one of the target pair and the third onset consonant of the stimulus, show at least as large an asymmetry in favor of errors between word-onset consonants for the non-words as for the words in this experiment. The same asymmetry was observed in the earlier experiment using real words and different speakers, as can be seen in Table 9. These observations for both Expected and Unexpected interaction errors make it less likely that the word-onset effect is related to the process of lexical selection,

Table 8.    *Number of interaction errors elicited by real-word and non-word list stimuli*

|  | Word Position Same | Stress Syllable Position Same |
|---|---|---|
| Real words (Experiment 1, 32 original stimuli, different subjects, included for comparison only) | 86 | 41 |
| Real words (Experiment 1(c), 32 original stimuli) | 122 | 99 |
| Non-words (Experiment 1(c), 32 new stimuli) | 284 | 101 |

Table 9.    *Number of unexpected between-word interaction errors elicited by real-word and non-word list stimuli*

|  | Word Position Same (16 stimuli) | Stress Syllable Position Same (16 stimuli) |
|---|---|---|
| Unexpected errors in real-word stimuli (Experiment 1) | 19 | 6 |
| Unexpected errors in real-word stimuli (Experiment 1(c)) | 27 | 7 |
| Unexpected errors in non-word stimuli (Experiment 1(c)) | 83 | 4 |

since it is improbable that the segments of non-words are retrieved by lexical look-up, at least in models in which lexical retrieval is separate from phonological encoding. We will return to this issue in the discussion below.

It is interesting to note that though the number of interaction errors among word-onset consonants is substantially larger for non-words than for real words, the number of errors among stress-syllable-onset consonants is nearly identical for real word and non-word stimuli (99 vs. 101 errors between target segments). This difference between the behavior of word-onset pairs and stressed-syllable-onset pairs could arise in one of several ways. First, the word-onset errors could be occurring in short-term memory, which can reasonably be expected to be weaker for non-words than for real words. But as we have seen, results in both the Sentence Generation task in Experiment 1(b) and the Reading/Recall comparison in Experiments 1 and 1(a) suggest that this is not the case. A second possible account is that we are dealing with two kinds of production planning errors: one type that occurs between pairs of word-onset consonants and another involving consonants that need not be located in word-onset position. On this view, the finding that one set of errors is significantly affected by the status of the stimulus as a real word, while the other is not, raises the possibility that word-onset errors and stress-syllable-onset errors reflect two different aspects of the planning process. We will return to this question in the discussion below.

### Experiment 2: A new design and new stimuli

Since the variability from speaker to speaker and from stimulus set to stimulus set in earlier experiments was substantial, and since by the design of those experiments not all the stimuli in a quadruple set were produced by the same speakers, it seemed advisable to repeat the experiment with a new design, and a new set of stimulus words and target segments. Stimuli took the form of word lists, just as in Experiment 1, but several changes were made in both the nature of the stimuli and their presentation to the speaker, for a stronger experimental design.

(1) A balanced number of two stimulus sets was used for each target pair of segments, as shown in Table 10. (The stimuli are given in Appendix B.)

(2) A different word order was used, to test for the generality of the results. While words in the stimuli in Experiment 1 appeared in the order bisyllable, monosyllable, monosyllable, bisyllable, stimuli in Experiment 2 took the form monosyllable, bisyllable, bisyllable, monosyllable. Thus, a quadruple set of twisters for the target pair /p/–/f/ with /s/ took the following form:

Both Positions Same: *p*ack *f*ussy *f*ossil *p*ig
Word Position Same: *p*ad *f*orsake *f*orsee *p*ot
Stress Position Same: *p*in su*ff*use suf*f*ice *p*et
Neither Position Same; *p*od so*f*a su*ff*er *p*eg

Table 10. *List of target consonant pairs used to construct stimuli for Experiment 2*

| Target pair | Number of quadruple sets |
|:---:|:---:|
| w/r | 2 |
| n/m | 2 |
| p/f | 2 |
| p/k | 2 |
| l/r | 2 |
| y/l | 2 |
| d/j | 2 |
| b/g | 2 |
| t/d | 2 |
| p/b | 2 |
| sh/s | 2 |
| g/d | 2 |
| 12 | 24 |

(3) Different pairs of monosyllabic words were used for each of the four twisters of a quadruple set, in contrast to Experiment 1, where the same pair of monosyllables was used for all four twisters.

(4) The same speakers produced all four twisters for any given quadruple set, instead of two twisters being produced by half the speakers and two by the other half. Ten speakers produced one of the two quadruple sets for each target pair of segments, and ten speakers produced the other.

Otherwise, task, presentation, subject pool, recording and transcription were as in Experiment 1.

*Results*

The distribution of interaction errors between target segment pairs across the four stimulus types is shown in Table 11. Although this combination of stimuli and

Table 11. *Number of interaction errors between target consonants elicited by list stimuli of Experiment 2 (expected errors between target pair; unexpected errors between one member of target pair and third onset consonant)*

| | Both Positions Same | Word Position Same | Stress Syllable Position Same | Neither Position Same |
|:---|:---:|:---:|:---:|:---:|
| Expected errors | 253 | 132 | 75 | 26 |
| Unexpected between-word errors | 58 | 21 | 4 | 1 |

speakers elicits more errors than in Experiment 1 (486 vs. 381, or errors in 2.1% vs. 1.6% of the words), the results clearly replicate the finding that substantially more interaction errors occur between target segment pairs located in their respective word onsets (Both and Word Position), than between segment pairs that are merely in syllables with the same stress (Stress Syllable Position). This result holds for Expected as well as Unexpected Between-Word errors. Thus, the finding that shared word-onset position increases the likelihood of an interaction error is robust for an entirely new set of stimulus words arranged in a different rhythmic configuration.

### Significance across speakers and stimulus sets

Like Experiment 1, Experiment 2 showed a wide variation in error rate from speaker to speaker, from 64 errors by the most error-prone speaker to 6 for the least. Using Freidman's two-way analysis of variance for rank order data, corrected for ties, we found that the distribution in the four conditions is significantly different from random across speakers, with $p < .05$. Since all four stimulus types for each target pair were produced by the same speakers, it was possible to explore further where this non-random aspect of the distribution is located, looking at each subpart of the experiment (consisting of 10 speakers producing 48 stimuli in quadruples built around 12 target consonant pairs) separately. There are six comparisons to be made among the four conditions, and the results for both subparts of the experiment are the same. Using the one-tailed test and setting the significance level at $p < .05$, the rank order sums of the following types of stimuli are reliably different across the 10 speakers in each subpart:

> Both versus Neither
> Both versus Stress
> and
> Word Position versus Neither

In visual terms, these can be specified as the following comparisons along the scale from Both (largest number of errors) to Neither (smallest number of errors):

```
Both     Word Position Same     Stress Same     Neither
X ------------------------------------------X
X ----------------------------X
               X-----------------------X
```

For the other three comparisons of rank order, differences did not reach significance with $p < .05$. These comparisons include Both versus Word Position, Word Position versus Stress, and Stress versus Neither, pairs which are fewer than three positions apart on the scale. Critically, Stress Position Same stimuli are ranked reliably lower than Both Positions Same stimuli. Since what distinguishes Both stimuli from Stress Syllable stimuli is the fact that target segment pairs share word-onset position in the Both stimuli, this result indicates that shared position in the word onset leads to more interaction errors, all other things being equal.

In an attempt to assess informally whether the larger number of errors produced by error-prone speakers would show more clearly that the number of errors elicited across the four conditions was ordered as Both > Word > Stress > Neither, the rank orders for all 40 speakers in Experiments 1 and 2 were examined. Fifteen of the 40 showed the B–W–S–N ordering, and of the remaining 25 most differed by a tie or a reversal between Word and Stress, or between Stress and Neither. However, of the 20 speakers who produced the largest number of errors, only 9 showed the B > W > S > N pattern, suggesting that high-error-rate speakers do not necessarily reveal the pattern more reliably. Thirty of the 40 speakers produced more errors with Word-Position than with Stress-Position stimuli; 4 were tied and 6 produced more Stress-Position errors. Although these observations are consistent with the possibility that target segments sharing word-onset position are more likely to be drawn into an interaction error than target segments sharing stress, they do not unequivocally support this claim.

A similar problem arises for the reliability of the B > W > S > N ordering across stimuli. Again using Freidman's two-way analysis of variance corrected for ties, and analysing each subpart of the experiment separately (where each subpart consists of errors from 10 speakers producing quadruple sets for 12 target pairs), we find that the claim of a non-random distribution across the four conditions is supported with $p < .05$. But the only reliable difference across stimuli for both parts of the experiment is Both versus Neither. In addition, Word versus Neither is significant for the first subpart, and Both versus Word and Both versus Stress are significant for the second. These equivocal results suggest that any claims about the relative power of the two position constraints in conditioning elicited segmental speech errors would be premature, despite the consistent finding of 1.5–2.5 times as many errors for the Word Position Same stimuli as for the Stress Syllable Position Same stimuli.

*Interaction between the two position factors*

It has been argued that if two factors can be shown to interact in determining behavior, it is likely that they operate at the same point in processing. In other words, if two factors operating together produce more errors than would be expected based on the effectiveness of each factor separately, we can infer that those two factors are represented at the same point in the planning process. Using the product of the observed error rates for the Word Position and Stress Syllable Position stimuli separately to estimate the expected error rate for the Both Positions stimuli, we find that the 253 errors elicited in the Both condition in Experiment 2 significantly exceed the expected value ($\chi^2 < .001$, one degree of freedom).

This result differs from the finding of no significant interaction in Experiment 1. Several factors may account for this difference. First, the error rate may be substantially affected by characteristics of the individual words in the twister stimuli. It is possible that the words in the Both stimuli in Experiment 1 were such that their onset segments were more confusable than those in Experiment 2. The picture is not clarified by two further observations: (1) there was no interaction between the word onset and stress factors in Experiment 1(a), which used the same words as Experiment 1, but placed them in phrases; and (2) the interaction is significant in Experiment 1(b), which used the same words for a sentence generation task ($\chi^2 < .001$, one degree of freedom).

A second possible account relies on inter-speaker differences in error rate. Since error rates vary widely from speaker to speaker and from one quadruple set to another, it is possible that more error-prone speakers were assigned the more error-prone stimuli for certain conditions. This seems unlikely to account for the difference between Experiment 1 and Experiment 2, however, since the larger number of Stress Same stimulus errors in Experiment 2 could only have increased the expected probability of errors for Both stimuli, making it more difficult to demonstrate an interaction between the word onset and stress factors. Yet it is this experiment that shows the interaction.

Since the design of Experiment 2 compares the error rate across the four twister types for the same speaker, and Experiment 1 does not, some argument can be made for accepting Experiment 2's results showing an interaction between the two factors as more conclusive on the question, particularly since one of the three experiments using the earlier set of stimuli, the Sentence Generation task in Experiment 1(b), also showed the interaction. In any case, the interaction between the two factors in two of the four relevant experiments reported here raises the possibility that similarity in word position and in stressed syllable position together can increase the likelihood of an interaction error beyond the sum of the two effects acting separately, at least under some circumstances.

## General discussion

The results of the five error elicitation experiments described in this paper clearly support the claim, hinted at by evidence from spontaneous speech errors, that segmental serial ordering errors made by speakers of American English are constrained by at least one aspect of word structure, that is, position in the word onset. Specifically, the experimental results show that more interaction errors occur where the two target segments share position in the word than where they do not. This result shows that word structure information has not been eliminated from the processing representation at the point where segmental ordering errors occur.

In addition, there is appreciable evidence for a second position similarity constraint, which we have described in terms of lexical stress: more errors occur with shared stress than without it. In the discussion that follows, we will examine the nature of these constraints more closely for any light they might shed on the role of syllable structure, and then address the question of how both factors might participate in a model of the phonological planning process. We will argue that the results of these experiments do not provide unequivocal evidence for the role of the syllable per se in speech production processing. In other words, although the syllable may in fact be an active representational unit in production planning, constraints on segmental interaction errors can be accounted for without it.

## The syllabic view and an alternative

One of the most noticeable aspects of the error patterns across the four types of twisters in these experiments is that errors occur rather freely between pairs of consonants which occur in syllable onset position, that is, in Both, Word and Stressed Syllable stimuli. In contrast, errors rarely occur in the Neither stimuli, like "ri*pp*le *f*ad *f*oot ra*p*id", where /f/ is syllable initial but it is not clear that /p/ is.

One possible interpretation of this pattern of results is that two segments simply cannot interact in an error unless they share a common syllable position. On this view, other factors, such as shared word position and stress, may increase the likelihood of an interaction between segments in parallel syllable positions, but the error will not be possible unless the syllable-position constraint is met. (Arguments about the role of the syllable, and of syllabic constituents like the onset, rhyme, nucleus and coda, as error *units* abound in the literature; we will not summarize them here because we are focussing on the role of these supraseg-mental structures as a framework that guides the processing of smaller units, rather than on their possible role as elements which might themselves undergo serial ordering.)

The view that shared syllable position is a *sine qua non* for segmental interaction is consistent with the experimental results, but it is not required in order to account for them. Note that in all three of the stimulus structures that elicit substantial numbers of errors, the propensity for interactions could be accounted for on the basis of a factor other than the syllable. In Word Position Same stimuli, of course, the targets share position in the word onset. And in Stress Position Same stimuli they not only share lexical stress; they also occupy parallel positions in a potential organizational unit based on phrasal prominence. For all of the stimuli in these experiments, except for the sentence generation experiments, speakers generally chose to produce the lexically stressed syllables with what might be called a pitch accent (i.e., a perceptually salient pitch obtrusion drawn from the repertoire of such patterns in American English and associated with syllables in patterns defined over a prosodic unit called the intonational phrase; see Pierrehumbert, 1980). Thus, each lexically stressed syllable could be thought of as beginning a "phrasal foot". If we define this foot-like unit as a prosodically strong syllable followed by its succeeding weaker syllables, including (in the phrasal stimuli) reduced monosyllabic function words, then segments that share position in the onset of a lexically stressed syllable also, in these production experiments, share position in the onset of this constituent. Thus, Stress Position Same stimuli like

(re)*p*eat / *f*ad / *f*oot re-/-*p*aid
(To re)*p*eat is a / *f*ad and the / *f*oot is re-/-*p*aid
*p*in su-/-*ff*use su-/-*ff*ice / *p*et

place their target consonant pairs in the onset of each "phrase-level foot". Further analysis of individual utterances would be required to determine whether a similar prosodic pattern was followed in the sentence generation experiment, which provoked a similar pattern of interaction errors.

In any case, there is an alternative to the syllable-position view, equally well supported by the experimental evidence, which would explain the apparent pervasiveness of syllable-position similarity in interaction errors as a consequence of the fact that the target pairs of consonants are either word-initial, associated with stress, or both. On this account, although syllable structure might be represented within the foot, it would not constrain error patterns; only position in the foot would influence interaction errors. In the strong form of this account, any of the foot-medial consonants in one foot could interact with any of the foot-medial consonants in another foot, subject to the word-based position similarity constraints of the kind demonstrated in the experiments described above.

One of the roadblocks to adopting this view that constraints on segmental interaction errors can be accounted for without reference to syllable structure arises from interaction errors in polysegmental word onsets. As we have seen in errors like "sp*r*it b*l*ain" for "split brain", the position constraints within complex onsets are not expressed in terms of absolute serial order, but rather in terms of parallel structural locations in the syllable. However, this apparent necessity for syllable structure could result from quite a different factor, that is, the propensity of phonologically like segments to interact with each other. Since the types of segments that can occur in each structural location in the onset have much in common, the constraint may be imposed by phonological (rather than structural) similarity.

A second roadblock to adopting the non-syllabic view is the question of why word-onset consonants should form a separate structural subunit, if this does not come about as a reflection of syllable structure across the entire word. However, the requisite substructure

[onset consonants] + [rest of word]

is suggested by certain error patterns in spontaneous speech. The arguments are presented in Shattuck-Hufnagel (1987); they rely on examples from word blends (e.g., "clish" or "*cl*am" + "*fi*sh", "prubble" for "*pr*oblem" + "*tr*ouble") and a relatively rare form of error in which the [onset consonants] remain in place but the [rest of the word] exchanges (e.g., "H*aire* and Cl*oward*" for "Howard and Claire", "the *anguage* of l*acquisition*" for "the acquisition of language").

Since word-onset consonants can always be described as syllable onsets, the critical evidence to distinguish between syllable-based and non-syllable-based views of position similarity constraints lies in the pattern of errors among consonants that are not word initial. If syllable-onset consonants showed a tendency to interact with each other even when they were not in the word onset or stressed syllable (e.g., "a com*b*ination re*p*air"), it would demonstrate that the syllable per se imposes constraints on the interaction of segments in errors, beyond word and stress similarity. A similar conclusion would be warranted if syllable coda consonants interacted whether or not they were in word-final position. Unfortunately, the present experiments do not bear on this question, and the small number of interaction errors between non-onset consonants in corpora of errors from spontaneous speech in American English, combined with the fact that many such errors involve word-final segments, has made it difficult to address this issue with the data at hand.

Whether or not syllable structure plays a role, it is clear that the process of serially ordering the segments of candidate lexical items is constrained by both word-onset position and stress. How might these two factors, as well as the interaction between them suggested by the present experiments, be incorporated into a model of the phonological planning process?

## A model of phonological planning

One indisputable fact about utterances is that they contain at least two kinds of phonological information: that which specifies the segmental identity of their words, and that which specifies their prosody at the phrasal level and other levels. The necessity of integrating these two kinds of information is illustrated by the fact that they often find their expression in the same acoustic parameters, as when the duration of a vowel reflects its tenseness or laxness, its lexical stress value and its location at an intonational phrase boundary (Klatt, 1979). How might such an integration process operate? And in particular, how might the process operate in such a way as to permit the mis-ordering of phonological segments whose order is already specified in the lexicon, and to show the influence of both word structure and stress? A likely candidate for this integration process is the mechanism which is responsible for the serial ordering of segments. Before turning to the question of how to model this mechanism, we will summarize the arguments for adopting a serial ordering model that explicitly posits a planning frame.

## The need for a planning frame

Several models of the segmental serial ordering process have appeared in the literature. Many of them have in common the assumption that the phonological planning process involves the creation of a phonological representation specific to the utterance being planned, prior to the articulation of the utterance. In other words, some form of segmental selection process precedes the process of articulation, and is guided by representations which are both broader in extent and more abstract than the neuromuscular instructions for articulation. (These larger representations need not encompass the entire utterance by the time the speech musculature begins to operate, but the part of the representation which is relevant to a particular portion of the utterance is generated in advance of the execution of that portion.) This type of model contrasts sharply with another possible view, which holds that the planning process is exactly analogous to traversing a pathway through a series of nodes in a network which represent the elements of an utterance, where activating a node means executing the articulatory instructions contained in that node.

We reject this latter view, and favor the hypothesis that a planning representation is generated prior to and separate from the articulatory execution process, for two reasons. First, as Lashley (1957) and countless others have remarked, the occurrence of two-part exchange errors in speech strongly suggests the existence of some kind of planning framework: that is, a representation of the utterance, separate from the phonological elements it contains, that extends beyond the segment being produced at any one time. Both the anticipatory and the place-holding aspects of exchanges support this claim. Second, a model in which selection of an element equals its articulatory execution requires a very large number of representations of each element in the language, since the phonetic shape of each element varies substantially (and systematically) with many syntactic, lexical, and prosodic factors.

The purport of this second argument can be easily seen in a simple example. Consider the utterance of a child asking his father to open a can of soda: "Pop a pop, poppa?" Although the phonological segments of this utterance repeat several times, the details of their acoustic and articulatory shapes will vary substantially in the different locations in the utterance. For example, the F0 of the three /a/ vowels will be very different, according to the location of pitch accents and boundary tones; the duration of the pre-boundary noun "pop" will be longer while the "pop-" in the bisyllabic word "poppa" will be shorter; the pre-stressed /p/ in "poppa" will have more aspiration then the pre-unstressed /p/, etc. In the selection-as-execution view, there is no mechanism for generating these differences other than by selecting among pre-existing nodes in a network, so one must postulate a separate node for each such systematic distinction among the /a/ segments and for each one among the /p/ segments that is not determined by the physiology of the speech mechanism. The potential size of this set of nodes for each phonological element is very large; see Klatt (1976) for a discussion of the factors that influence the acoustic phonetic shape of a segment.[1] Moreover, if the acoustic correlates of some of these distinctions vary continuously, rather than being distributed in discrete categories, selection among pre-stored elements will not provide a felicitous model for their production.

We find these points to form a persuasive argument for the generation of an abstract utterance-specific representation of the utterance, which can embody the relevant differences among various occurrences of a segment as the result of the application of processes or rules. Evidence that the planning process can impose phonetic adjustments appropriate to the segments introduced into new contexts by exchange errors (e.g., the adjustment of vowel durations when exchanges introduce voicing errors in post-vocalic consonants, Shattuck-Hufnagel, 1985b), also supports the existence of an abstract utterance-specific representation of phonological shape (e.g., one in which vowel durations have not yet been determined).

## Selected examples of frame-based models

Several current models postulate such a representation. For example, Shattuck-Hufnagel (1987) proposed a word-based framework to guide the serial ordering of phonological segments from a short-term store of lexical candidates for the utterance, by means of a scan-copier mechanism. In that model, the organizing frame is established in order to work out the prosodic structure of the utterance. Thus, word-onset consonant slots in the organizing frame were distinguished from locations in the rest of the word: because they are not required for the assignment of prominence, they can undergo selection for a location in the frame at a later time than the segments in the rest of the word, which *are* required for stress assignment. Word onsets form a special set of planning elements, addressed later in the serial ordering process, and can easily become mis-selected for each other. No other suprasegmental structure was envisioned within the word frames, which consist of partial specifications for the word-onset consonants followed by a string of C and V slots. This model now appears inadequate, since the experimental

---

[1]A similar argument for abstract processing representations of phonological information from an articulatory point of view appears in MacNeilage (1970).

results described above suggest that stress also plays a role in constraining interaction errors between phonological segments.[2]

A second model, proposed by Dell (1986), 'views the process of serially ordering phonological segments into an utterance-specific frame in the context of a spreading activation model. Here the processing framework consists of canonical syllables made up of onsets, nuclei and codas. This framework guides the selection of segments from a network of phonological segment nodes, which are not specific to the target words for the utterance but encompass all the segments of the language. The segmental level of this network contains separate representations of onset and coda versions for each consonant that can occur in both positions. Serial ordering errors occur when an alternative node of the appropriate structural type has a higher level of activation than the node for the target segment. This model also appears insufficient; it does not account for the predominance of word-onset and stress-associated consonants among interaction errors, because all syllable onsets are equivalent in the processing frame.

Finally, Levelt (1989) has proposed an explicit and thoroughly worked out three-step process of phonological encoding that combines aspects of both these approaches. In his model, prosodic planning and the generation of word form are closely interwoven; each depends on aspects of the other. Lexical entries are first spelled out as stems and affixes with stress patterns, then as individual segments in the onset, nucleus, and coda slots of syllable frames, and finally as syllable-based instructions which will govern the articulators after a number of adjustments related to the prosody of the phrase. These syllable-based articulatory instructions are envisioned as a set of overlapping and interacting gestures, a view which has much in common with the articulatory phonology of Browman and Goldstein (1986). Although this model implicitly leaves room for a word position constraint, the spell-out process unfolds across the segments of one word at a time, which means that the constraints of word position and stress similarity are not explicitly invoked.

*Incorporating word- and stress-position constraints*

How might the word-position and stress constraints be incorporated into these models? We will assume for the purposes of this discussion that syllable structure per se is not represented, even though this issue is far from settled. We will also assume, as almost every error investigator has done, that the factors that constrain interaction errors play an active role in normal processing representations.

To invoke a position similarity constraint in a spreading activation model that contains separate nodes for segments that appear in different positions, one need only strengthen the connections among nodes that share that position dimension,

[2]See also Sussman (1984).

so that activation in one such node can increase the activation levels in other similar nodes. It appears that it will be necessary to incorporate word structure, at least in the form of separate nodes for word-onset consonants, into the organizational frame (currently syllable-based), and to postulate a set of word-onset-specific segmental nodes in the network. Similar adjustments could be made to incorporate the stress constraint, and some provision would need to be made for the interaction of these two constraints, if it occurs.

How might the two similarity factors of word position and stress be incorporated in a scan-and-copy model? The essence of this model is that the organizing frame provides the instructions for scanning a particular class of segments in the buffer that contains the segments of the lexical candidates for the utterance. Thus, possible intruding elements are restricted to the segments in the class being scanned, rather than including any segment in the language network that can attain a high enough level of activation. That is, in spreading activation models every segment in the language has a finite probability of intruding on every target segment in a given utterance, while in scan-and-copy models the set of possible interactions is limited to pairs of segments among those specified by the lexical items that have been selected during the planning for this particular utterance, and more specifically, to the subset of those segments specified by the scan instructions for a particular location in the planning frame. These scan instructions are presumably sometimes sketchy enough to permit mis-selection. Within the to-be-scanned subset, the probability of mis-selection by the scanner can be influenced by other shared representational factors. (Of course, seemingly non-interaction errors like "*p*lime the tree" for "climb the tree" do occur; in a scan-copy model, their source is presumed to be an unexpected entry in the short-term lexical candidate store, like "play in" for this error. An unexpected lexical item may be selected because of its close association with one of the target items, by its occurrence in the visual or auditory field of the speaker, etc.)

To see how a scan-and-copy model might incorporate both the word-position and stress effects, as well as their possible interaction, consider the planning process for the utterance in Figure 2: "Pitch the tent." Here, we assume earlier processing analogous to that proposed in Garrett (1982) and particularly in Levelt (1989), where surface structure and intonational meaning have served as input to the prosody generator, along with a limited transfer of metrical information about the lexical candidates (e.g., number of syllables, location of lexical stress). The processing representation now consists of two parts: an organizing prosodic frame, and a set of candidate content word items from the lexicon. The organizing frame is made up of prosodic units, each of which contains one or more prosodically prominent syllables (where "prominent" is defined at the phrasal level). In addition, the boundaries of lexical items are marked, left over from the syntactic/morphological structure on which the prosodic structure has been imposed. (The function-word elements are shown as spelled out, for convenience.

**Utterance:  "Pitch the tent"**

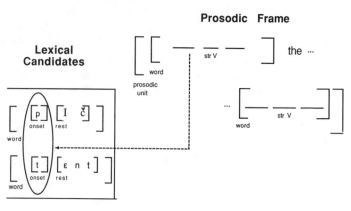

Figure 2.    *Phonological encoding components.*

Evidence from segmental errors suggests that the grammatical morphemes or function words that define the syntactic shape of an utterance do not participate in the same kind of segmental serial ordering processes as content-word morphemes. For example, segmental serial ordering apparently does not apply to inflectional affixes, as shown by the rarity with which they participate in segmental interaction errors, and also by such affix-isolating errors as

You have to use ro*p* ro*k*es (ro*ck* ro*pes*)
... zo*d*ing and co*ne* enforcement (zo*n*ing and co*de*)
I couldn't hel*f* la*pp*ing (hel*p* lau*gh*ing)

where the segments share final position in their respective lexical morphemes although not in their surface words. See Garrett (1980) for discussion.)

In contrast, the second component of the planning representation, that is, the short-term store of candidate content-word lexical items, marks these two kinds of information (word boundaries and prominence) in a different way. Since each entry in the table is a single lexical item, the locations of word boundaries are automatically available. In addition, word-onset consonants are marked off as a special subset, since they were not needed during the process of determining prosodic prominence. (For example, they play no role in determining the levels of lexical stress on various syllables of a word.) Finally, the lexical candidate representation includes the metrical structure involved in the earlier process of marking lexical stress.

Serial ordering of the segmental information from the lexical candidates can now occur under the guidance of the prosodic frame, since the critical information is available (though in different forms) in both representations. For example, in scanning for a segment to fill a word-onset slot in the frame, the scan-copy mechanism isolates all the word-onset segments in the buffer, which are already represented as separate from the rest of the word, and then scans across the candidate segments in this set. The experimental suggestion of an interaction between stress and word position suggests that, within this scan set, lexical stress is one of the factors determining similarity between candidate segments. Thus when two onset segments share lexical stress, there is higher probability of mis-selection between them.

Conversely, in scanning for a segment to fill a pre-prominence slot in the prosodic frame, the scan-copy mechanism isolates all the stress-associated consonants in the buffer, because only lexically stressed elements can associate with phrasal prominence. (We will not deal here with the complexities introduced by the phenomenon of "stress shift", as in "MassaCHUsetts" versus "MAssachusetts MIRacle", except to note that stress can only shift to an unreduced vowel. This means that a scan set based on a stress-shifted frame might have to include all of the segments before unreduced vowels. Alternatively, stress shift may occur at a later processing stage, after phonological encoding is complete.) Within *this* scan set, position of the segment in the word onset is one of the factors that determines similarity. In this case, when two stress-associated segments occur in their respective word onsets, there is a higher probability of mis-selection between them. Note that separate scan sets are hypothesized here only for word-onset and stress-associated consonants. Other possible scan sets include stressed vowels and word-final consonants. Segments not included in specific scan sets will be serially ordered left to right from the lexical candidate representation, and will thus not participate in between-word errors.

A reasonable expansion of this model would include a partial specification, in the prosodic frame, of the information that identifies the segments destined for each slot, to direct the scanner to the right target segment. This partial segmental specification will have been transferred from the short-term lexical store to the frame at an earlier processing stage, and ensures that the scanning operation normally selects the correct segment without error. Although analyses of speech errors have not yet been applied to the problem of what the partial specification might look like, error patterns suggest that it almost certainly distinguishes consonants from vowels. In addition, it is not unreasonable to suppose that it includes the information necessary for the processing that determines lexical stress for the candidate lexical items in the short-term store, either by computation or by a process of association between retrieved segments and stress pattern. The characteristic of transferring information from the lexical candidates to the planning frame in several separate processing steps is drawn directly from Levelt's (1989) model.

*Further discussion of the revised scan-and-copy model*

The provision for lexical stress processing in the short-term store may provide a partial answer to a puzzling difference that is emerging between the phonological error patterns of Spanish and American English. Del Viso, Igoa, and Garcia-Albea (1989) have analyzed a corpus of more than 3600 errors in Spanish, and have found no evidence for a word-position similarity constraint on segmental interaction errors: 68% of their errors occur between pairs of target segments in different word positions, and among 137 errors involving syllable-initial segment pairs of segments only 11% also shared word-onset position (p. 20). In contrast, they do find evidence to support a syllable-position similarity constraint. Since the word stress patterns of Spanish are more regular and predictable than those of English, it may be that the step of transferring lexical candidates to a short-term store where their stress patterns can be worked out is unnecessary in Spanish. In that case, word-onset consonants would not need to be treated in any special way.[3]

Although this model with its prosody-based frame hypothesizes considerably more structure in the planning representations than did previous models, and is therefore less parsimonious, it provides potential answers to several questions. The first is how to account for the increase in errors for word-onset-position segments in the nonsense words in Experiment 1(c). If the nonsense words enter the short-term store of "lexical" candidates directly from a text-to-sound process, rather than via lexical access, then they do not bring with them all of the information that a lexical item brings. As a result, their onset consonants may be even less tightly tied to the rest of the word than are the onset consonants of an existing lexical item. In this case, there will be an increased probability of mis-selection among these elements for the onset slot of the wrong non-word. In contrast, since segments outside the word onset receive no special treatment in the short-term store, they will be treated similarly in real words and non-words. Thus, once stress has been assigned, pre-stress consonants will participate in errors at the same rate for both types of stimulus items, just as they did for the Stressed-Syllable Position Same stimuli in Experiment 1(c).

A second question to which this model (and other models based on prosodic planning) provides an answer is: why do the segments of a word, whose order must be defined in the lexicon, undergo misordering at all? The answer is found in the fact that two separate representations must be integrated: a set of lexical candidates which has undergone lexical processing, and a planning frame for phrasal prosody processing. This integration is accomplished in several steps, one of which involves the serial transfer of segmental information from one of these structures to the other. During this process, mis-ordering of segments can occur.

Finally, the model provides a hint of the solution to a puzzle raised by the

[3]See also Crow (1991) for related findings in elicitation experiments with French speakers.

preliminary findings reported in Shattuck-Hufnagel (1987), showing that phrasal structure protects final-position segments against interaction errors to some extent. This observation is particularly interesting in view of the rarity of final-position errors in corpora collected from spontaneous speech, which is normally (if imperfectly) structured into phrases rather than lists. Why should final consonants be protected by phrasal structure? If the prosody-based planning framework for sentences and phrases is based on constituents larger than the word, then word-final segments may be less likely to be isolated as a separate scan set. For word-list stimuli, with less complex prosody, word-final segments may be more likely to serve as a separate scan set.

**Conclusion**

The results of five error elicitation experiments clearly show that pairs of word-onset consonants tend to interact in segmental speech errors more often than pairs of consonants in two different word positions. Similarly, more errors occur between pairs of consonants that share stress, than between pairs that do not. The word-onset effect suggests that the word (or at least the word onset) must be incorporated into descriptions of the processing representations that guide segmental serial ordering during phonological encoding for speech production. The stress effect suggests that some such provision must also be made for the representation of stress. Models which rely solely on syllable position to capture the constraints on segmental error interactions will fail to capture significant aspects of the data. These observations lend support to planning models in which word-onset consonants as well as stress-associated consonants are identifiable to the serial ordering processor.

The results leave open the question of whether or not syllable position constraints per se also play a role in determining either the similarity of interacting pairs of segments (as is suggested by the rarity of interactions between onsets and codas in between-word errors from spontaneous speech) or the preferred location for interaction errors. They also do not reveal whether word-position, stress-association or syllable-position constraints operate at locations other than the onsets of words and other constituents. Further experimental investigation will be necessary to determine precisely what role these suprasegmental structures play in the phonological encoding process.

At this point, even after twenty years of error investigation, the sum total of what we know about the factors that influence segmental interaction errors severely underdetermines our models of the highly complex speech planning process. As a result, we can neither propose nor eliminate detailed models with much confidence. However, our understanding of the distinctions and similarities among error types and the factors which influence them is increasing, and we can begin to hope that this kind of evidence, as it accumulates, will show that the mechanisms by which errors can fragment words are not only small in number, but also directly reflective of the important processing mechanisms for normal error-free speech planning. To this end, we need to look more carefully at distinctions like the ones that have emerged in these experiments. For example, do the factors of word-onset position similarity and lexical stress similarity interact, or not? Why do these two factors differ in their effect on errors in non-words? Does the overwhelming finding of parallel syllable positions for segments that interact in errors mean that this parallelism is a *sine qua non* for such errors, or can it be accounted for in terms of other factors, like word position and stress? What are the facts about position similarity constraints on errors involving segments which are neither word-onset nor stress-associated? As we begin to explore these issues, in analyses of both spontaneous and elicited errors, we will form a clearer picture of both the major components and the details of the phonological planning process.

## Appendix A: Stimuli for Experiments 1, 1(a), 1(b) and 1(c)

*Experiment 1* used the four content words in each phrase as a list.
*Experiment 1(a)* used the phrasal stimuli as given here.
*Experiment 1(b)* used the four content words in each phrase as the basis for a sentence generation task.
*Experiment 1(c)* used non-word versions of the 32 starred word and stress stimuli.

B = Both word and stress positions of two target segments same
W = Word positions of two targets same but stress positions different
S = Stress positions of two targets same but word positions different
N = Neither word positions nor stress positions of two targets same

1. p/f; r

       B – It's a peril when fad takes a foot from the parrot
       W – The parade is a fad and on foot gets parole*
       S – You repeat like a fad and your foot gets repaid*
       N – You can ripple a fad but on foot it's more rapid

2. f/p; g

       B – It was figgy to pat when the pun was a fogger
       W – To forgive make a pot and the pun will forgo*
       S – Don't guffaw when old Pat makes a pun on gaufrette*
       N – My new gopher can pat with a pun that is goofy

3. p/f; l

> B – From the palace the fame had a fib for Miss Polly
> W – How polite is the fame of the fib to police
> S – Your lapel has the fame and the fib of LaPointe
> N – If the lipid brought fame then the fib brought a leaper

4. f/p; d

> B – With a fiddle a pin took a poke on the foredeck
> W – It's foredone that the pin cannot poke or foredoom*
> S – You defy me the pin and I'll poke to defend*
> N – In a duffle the pin had to poke for a daffy

5. r/l; p

> B – You can ripple a load but a lot is more rapid
> W – You repeat quite a lot and your load gets repaid*
> S – The parade is a load and a lot of parole*
> N – It's a peril to load such a lot for the parrot

6. r/l; m

> B – If the rumor should lag take a lick at some roaming
> W – Don't remove what may lag if the lick seems remote
> S – A morass does not lag when you lick a moraine
> N – For a moral don't lag what you lock but don't marry

7. l/r; j

> B – It's a legend to rig for a rack has no logic
> W – He's legit with his rig but the rack has largesse*
> S – It's July and the rug cannot rock the Gillette*
> N – Give the jello a rug and a rock to the julep

8. l/r; b

> B – If the lubber can run we can root for a label
> W – If Labatt does not run we can root for LaBelle
> S – The balloon did not run from the root of ballet
> N – With a belly the run on the root will not ballot

9. b/g; r

> B – Make the berry a gun with the gas in the barrel
> W – You berate with a gun though the gas is bereft*
> S – You rebuff with a gun and you get to rebuild*
> N – Do a ribbon and gun ever get to a rebate?

10. b/g; 1

> B – From the belly a gun will not get me a ballot
> W – The balloon had no gun and could get the ballet
> S – Old LaBatt who is gone will not get to LaBelle
> N – When the lubber is gone we can get him a label

11. g/b; f

> B – Make my gopher a bet on the ban that is goofy
> W – He'll guffaw on a bet and he'll ban the gaufrette*
> S – To forgive make a bet that the ban will forgo*
> N – It is figgy to bet when the ban was a fogger

12. l/y; k

> B – In the local a yen gets his yacht for some liquor
> W – This locale has a yen for a yacht by LaCoste*
> S – You collect if you yawn but not yet said Colleen*
> N – Go to college and yawn but not yet for the killer

13. l/y; r

> B – If the laurel has yin it's not yet for Sir Larry
> W – To LaRue goes the yin though as yet there's LeRoy*
> S – I relate to the yin though we yet can rely*
> N – We can rally for yin but not yet for the really

14. b/p; m

> B – We are booming to pack with our pig down in Beaumont
> W – We bemoan that you pack since the pig can bemuse*
> S – I misbook when I pack with the pig for McBay*
> N – He said maybe the pack has a pig for the marble

15. b/p; d

> B – Any bundle you pat leaves a pot for the bedding
> W – We bedeck when we pat the new pot and bedew
> S – They'll disbar with a pat if you pop the debate
> N – The debit can pat if the pop is a double

16. m/n; r

> B – For a moral don't nag and it's Nick who will marry
> W – The morass cannot nag when you nick a moraine
> S – You remove when you nag and say Nick is remote
> N – There's a rumor to nag when it's Nick who is roaming

17. m/n; b

    B – He said maybe the nick has some nog for the marble
    W – I misbook when I nick from the nog for McBay*
    S – You bemoan Father Nick when a nog can bemuse*
    N – They are booming where Nick took his nog down to Beaumont

18. r/w; b

    B – If the ribbon is wan it's too wet for a rebate
    W – The rebuff was too wan since it's wet to rebuild*
    S – You berate though I'm wan and my wit is bereft*
    N – Make the berry a win and it's wet in the barrel

19. r/w; l

    B – We can rally to win but it's wet for a really
    W – I relate to the win though it's wet to rely*
    S – It's LaRue who has won from the wit of LeRoy*
    N – For the laurel was won by the wit of Sir Larry

20. d/g; b

    B – When the debit you've got leaves a gap you can double
    W – To disbar what you've got is a gap to debate
    S – We bedeck what we've got and the gap we bedew
    N – Did the bundle he got have a gap for some bedding?

21. k/p; l

    B – In a college a pen has no pot for a killer
    W – They collect for the pen with the pot of Colleen*
    S – The locale has a pen and a pot from LaCoste*
    N – In the local a pen gets a pot for your liquor

22. l/n; p

    B – There's a lipid whose name gives a nib to a leaper
    W – My lapel had a name and a nib from LePointe
    S – How polite is the name of the nib to police
    N – In the palace the name had a nib for Miss Polly

23. d/t; f

    B – In a duffle the tin had to talk to the daffy
    W – You defy me the tin and I talk to defend*
    S – It's foredone that the tin gave a talk to foredoom*
    N – On the foredeck of tin do not talk of the fiddle

24. j/d; l

>    B – Give the jello a dog and a dock to the julep
>    W – It's July and the dog wants to dock the Gillette*
>    S – It's legit not to dig but the duck has largesse*
>    N – It's a legend to dig for a duck has no logic

## Appendix B: Stimuli for Experiment 2

1. w/r; p

>    B – watt rapid reaper wed
>    W – wet repeat repine was
>    S – win peruse parade wool
>    N – wig pirate peril weak

2. w/r; d

>    B – wet riddle radar witch
>    W – wick redeem reduce wag
>    S – web derive direct whelp
>    N – watch derrick during wit

3. n/m; l

>    B – nub mileage melon node
>    W – need molest malign nut
>    S – nod lament LeMay note
>    N – nag loamy limit nick

4. n/m; r

>    B – knock merit Moorish nag
>    W – neat marine mirage nod
>    S – note remind remiss nap
>    N – nick rhymer Roman nape

5. p/f; s

>    B – pack fussy fossil pig
>    W – pad forsake forsee pot
>    S – pin suffuse suffice pet
>    N – pod sofa suffer peg

6. f/p; l

    B – food pollen polo fib
    W – fig pollute police folk
    S – fog lapel LaPorte fang
    N – fun leaper loopy foam

7. p/k; m

    B – pip camel comma pub
    W – pit command commence pug
    S – pan McCoy macaw put
    N – pass mocha mica push

8. k/p; t

    B – cuss petty potter cash
    W – can partake perturb calm
    S – cog toupee tapu cad
    N – come topic taper kin

9. l/r; k

    B – loss racket wrecking lush
    W – lope racoon recant lob
    S – lot carafe carouse lip
    N – line courage carat long

10. l/r; f

    B – lib refuge raffle lop
    W – lid reform refer lot
    S – lack Farrar Farouk log
    N – leg forest ferret lock

11. y/l; t

    B – yon latter lettuce yam
    W – yes LaTour LaTache Yaz
    S – yoke Tulane Talat yip
    N – year tailor tulip yew

12. y/l; p

    B – yard leopard lupin yon
    W – yen lapel LaPonce yacht
    S – yap pollute police yet
    N – young pillow pilot yam

13. d/j; r

    B – dig Jared gerund deck
    W – dash Gerard giraffe dose
    S – dot reject rejoice deed
    N – doubt rajah rigid dude

14. j/d; l

    B – jazz dollar daily Jude
    W – joy delight delay Joe
    S – jam LeDuce LeDorr job
    N – jock lady ladder jug

15. b/g; l

    B – bite gully gallop bid
    W – bin galumph galoot bad
    S – bop lagoon legate butt
    N – beak laggard luggage bit

16. g/b; l

    B – gum bellow bailer gong
    W – go belong believe guy
    S – get LeBon LeBar good
    N – gas labor libel gosh

17. t/d; r

    B – tick dory during tug
    W – tin deride derail tomb
    S – tub redeem reduce top
    N – tag riddle riding talk

18. t/d; b

    B – tin debit dabble tong
    W – ton debate debut tall
    S – toss bedeck bedab tiff
    N – Tom Buddha body tan

19. p/b; r

    B – pad barren boring pot
    W – pick barrage bereave peg
    S – pit rebel robust poke
    N – pig robin robot pack

20. p/b; k

    B – pour bacon buckle pow
    W – pin becalm because pot
    S – pal caboose kabob pair
    N – pat cable cabbage pod

21. sh/s; l

    B – shy salad saline shore
    W – shove salute saloon shop
    S – shot LaSalle Lausanne shad
    N – sham lasso lesson ship

22. sh/s; p

    B – shag supper soapy shock
    W – show superb support shire
    S – shot persuade pursue shad
    N – shine parcel person sham

23. g/d; l

    B – gob dally darling gaff
    W – get delight delay gone
    S – Gus LaDine LeDouce gig
    N – gate ladder leading gas

24. g/d; t

    B – guess dative detour gash
    W – Gus detain deter gaff
    S – gulp today to-do golf
    N – give tidal Tudor gab

# References

Berg, T. (1987). The case against accommodation: Evidence from German speech error data. *Journal of Memory and Language, 26*, 277–299.

Boomer, D.S., & Laver, J.D.M. (1968). Slips of the tongue. *Journal of Disorders of Communication, 3*, 2–12. (Reprinted in Fromkin, V.A. (Ed.) (1973). *Speech errors as linguistic evidence* (pp. 120–131). The Hague: Mouton.)

Browman, C., & Goldstein, L. (1986). Towards an articulatory phonology. *Phonology yearbook, 3*, 219–252.

Brown, R., & McNeill, D. (1966). The "tip of the tongue" phenomenon. *Journal of Verbal Learning and Verbal Behavior, 5*, 325–337.

Crow, C. (1991). A comparison of elicited speech errors in monological and bilingual speakers of French and English. Doctoral thesis, University of Texas at Austin.

Dell, G.S. (1986). A spreading activation theory of retrieval in sentence production. *Psychological Review*, *93*, 283–321.

Del Viso, S., Igoa, J., & Garcia-Albea, J. (1989). Moverment errors and levels of processing in sentence production. *Journal of Psycholinguistic Research*, *18*, 145–161.

Fromkin, V.A. (1971). The non-anomalous nature of anomalous utterances. *Language*, *47*, 27–52. (Reprinted in V.A. Fromkin (Ed.), (1973). *Speech errors as linguistic evidence* (pp. 215–242). The Hague: Mouton.)

Fromkin, V.A. (1976). Putting the emPHAsis on the wrong sylLABle. In L. Hyman (Ed.), *Studies in stress and accent* (pp. 15–26). Los Angeles: University of Southern California.

Garrett, M.F. (1975). The analysis of sentence production. In G. Bower (Ed.), *Psychology of learning and motivation* (Vol. 9, pp. 133–175). New York: Academic Press.

Garrett, M.F. (1980). The limits of accommodation: Arguments for independent processing levels in sentence production. In V.A. Fromkin (Ed.), *Errors in linguistic performance: Slips of the tongue, ear, pen and hand* (pp. 263–272). New York: Academic Press.

Garrett, M. F. (1982). Production of speech: Observations from normal and pathological language use. In A.W. Ellis (Ed.), *Normality and pathology in cognitive functions* (pp. 19–76). London: Academic Press.

Klatt, D.H. (1976). Linguistic uses of segmental duration in English: Acoustic and perceptual evidence. *Journal of the Acoustical Society of America*, *59*, 1208.

Klatt, D.H. (1979). Synthesis by rule of segmental durations in English sentences. In B. Lindblom & S. Ohman (Eds.), *Frontiers of speech communication research* (pp. 287–300). New York: Academic Press.

Lashley, K.S. (1951). The problem of serial order in behavior. In L.A. Jefferess (Ed.), *Cerebral mechanisms in behavior* (pp. 112–136). New York: Wiley.

Levelt, W.J.M. (1989). *Speaking: From intention to articulation*. Cambridge, MA: MIT Press.

Nooteboom, S. (1967). Some regularities in phonemic speech errors. *Annual Progress Report, Institute for Perception Research IPO*, *2*, 65–70.

Nooteboom, S. (1969). The tongue slips into patterns. In A.G. Sciarone, A.J. van Essen, & A.A. van Raad (Eds.), *Nomen Society, Leyden studies in linguistics and phonetics* (pp. 114–132). The Hague: Mouton. (Reprinted in V.A. Fromkin (Ed.) (1973). *Speech errors as linguistic evidence* (pp. 144–156). The Hague: Mouton.)

MacKay, D. (1970). Spoonerisms: The structure of errors in the serial order of speech. *Neuropsychologia*, *8*, 323–350. (Reprinted in V.A. Fromkin (Ed.) (1973). *Speech errors as linguistic evidence*. The Hague: Mouton.)

MacKay, D. (1987). *The organization of perception and action: A theory for language and other cognitive skills*. New York: Springer.

MacNeilage, P.F. (1970). Motor control of serial ordering of speech. *Psychological Review*, *77*, 182–196.

Pierrehumbert, J.B. (1980). The phonology and phonetics of English intonation. Doctoral dissertation, Massachusetts Institute of Technology, Cambridge, MA.

Shattuck-Hufnagel, S. (1979). Speech errors as evidence for a serial order mechanism in sentence production. In W.E. Cooper & E.C.T. Walker (Eds.), *Sentence processing* (pp. 295–342). Hillsdale, NJ: Erlbaum.

Shattuck-Hufnagel, S. (1983). Sublexical units and suprasegmental structure in speech production planning. In P.F. MacNeilage (Ed.), *The production of speech* (pp. 109–136). New York: Springer.

Shattuck-Hufnagel, S. (1985a). Context similarity constraints on segmental speech errors: An experimental investigation of the role of word position and lexical stress. In J. Lauter (Ed.), *On the planning and production of speech in normal and hearing-impaired individuals: A seminar in honour of S. Richard Silverman* (pp. 43–49). ASHA Reports 15.

Shattuck-Hufnagel, S. (1985b). Segmental speech errors occur earlier in utterance planning than certain phonetic processes. *Journal of the Acoustical Society of America*, *77*, S1, 84–85.

Shattuck-Hufnagel, S. (1987). The role of word onset consonants in speech production planning: New evidence from speech error patterns. In E. Keller & M. Gopnik (Eds.), *Motor and sensory processing in language*. Hillsdale, NJ: Erlbaum.

Shattuck-Hufnagel, S., & Klatt, D.H. (1979). The limited use of distinctive features and markedness in speech production: Evidence from speech error data. *Journal of Verbal Learning and Verbal Behavior, 18,* 41–55.

Siegel, S., & Castellan, N.J. Jr. (1988). *Nonparametric statistics for the behavioral sciences.* New York: McGraw-Hill.

Stemberger, J.P. (1983). Speech errors and theoretical phonology: A review. Bloomington, IN: Indiana University Linguistics Club.

Sussman, H.M. (1984). A neuronal model for syllable representation. *Brain and Language, 22,* 167–177.

# 8

# Disorders of phonological encoding*

Brian Butterworth

*Department of Psychology, University College London, Gower Street, London WC1E 6BT, UK*

Butterworth, B., 1992. Disorders of phonological encoding. Cognition, 42: 261–286.

*Studies of phonological disturbances in aphasic speech are reviewed. It is argued that failure to test for error consistency in individual patients makes it generally improper to draw inferences about specific disorders of phonological encoding. A minimalist interpretation of available data on phonological errors is therefore proposed that involves variable loss of information in transmission between processing subsystems. Proposals for systematic loss or corruption of phonological information in lexical representations or in translation subsystems is shown to be inadequately grounded. The review concludes with some simple methodological prescriptions for future research.*

## Introduction

Normal speakers quite frequently make mistakes producing the intended sound of a word. They might, for example, say "corkical" instead of "cortical", or "prostitute" instead of "Protestant", or "Fats and Kodor" instead of "Katz and Fodor", or "shrig souffle" instead of "shrimp and egg souffle" (Fromkin, 1973, Sections B, Q, C and V). Estimates of the incidence of such errors from recordings of normal conversation vary from 1.6 errors per 1000 words (Shallice & Butterworth, 1977) down to 62 (segment errors and haplologies) in approximately 200 000 words of the London–Lund corpus (Garnham, Shillcock, Brown, Mill, & Cutler, 1981). In studies of aphasic speakers, these errors are called "literal" or "phonemic" paraphasias, and some, but not all, aphasic patients may make far more errors than normal speakers, although no comparable statistics for aphasic conversation are available. However, one patient described by Pate, Saffran, and Martin (1987) produced between 3% and 67% of phonemic paraphasias in

*The author would like to thank the following people for helpful comments on the first draft of this paper: Pim Levelt, David Howard, Lindsey Nickels, Wendy Best and Carolyn Bruce.

spontaneous speech, with the variation depending on the length of the target (3% for one-syllable words, 67% for four-syllable words.) In picture-naming tests, which may be different in important ways from free speech, Howard, Patterson, Franklin, Morton, and Orchard-Lisle (1984) found that a sample of 12 patients produced between 0% and 14% of phonemic errors[1] in 1500 naming attempts per patient. Classically, frequent paraphasias in the patient's speech, combined with an impairment of repetition, has been the hallmark of a syndrome known as *conduction aphasia*. More recent research distinguishes repetition (short-term memory) capacity from the ability to reproduce accurately even single words (Shallice & Warrington, 1977).

It might be presumed, a priori, that sources of normal slips of the tongue are different from aphasic paraphasia; that aphasics, by hypothesis, suffer a deficit in one or more of the processes that lead from the thought to its expression in speech, whereas normals, by definition, do not suffer deficit. (See Caramazza, 1986, for the elevation of this definitional convenience into a metaphysical principle.)

To identify a *disorder* or deficit responsible for phonemic paraphasias, one needs to do two things. First, find a *consistent* pattern of deviation from the phonological norm in the responses of patients studied on a case-by-case basis: a small, but consistent deviation may be lost in group means, and even a large one may be cancelled out by an equally significant (interesting) deviation in the opposite direction. Second, show how these responses might result from a deficit to one or more subsystems of a proposed model of normal phonological encoding. Although we have models of the normal processes whose main features, if not well established, are at least widely held, the burden of this essay will be that the evidence currently available is inadequate for identifying specific disorders of phonological encoding, despite claims to the contrary, since the prerequisite of individual *consistent deviation* has rarely been satisfied in the existing studies.

By the term "phonological encoding" (henceforth PE), I shall mean those processes that intervene between ascertaining that there is a (single) word in the mental lexicon that can express the lexical intention or plan and the full phonetic description that realizes it. Of course, further processes will be required to turn this description into a motor plan for articulation, but these will not be dealt with here.

Intuitively, PE of a known word entails accessing a stored representation of the sound of that word, what I shall term the phonological lexical representation

---

[1]Howard et al. (1984) were interested primarily in the variability of the ability to retrieve the target name, rather than in phonemic errors as such; they therefore treated single-segment deviations from the target as correct naming responses. Two deviations are required for the response to be counted as a phonemic paraphasia. Deviations that resulted in real words were treated as word substitution errors.

(PLR) ("lexeme" in Kempen and Huijbers' (1983) terminology). PLR has to contain sufficient information to specify, for the word in its intended speech context: (1) the syllabic structure of the word; (2) the stress pattern of the word; and (3) the segmental contents of the syllables. I leave aside entirely the question as to whether the PLR is an "underlying" or a "superficial" phonological representation (but see Caplan, 1987, for arguments in favour of an underlying representation). Following a number of authors, I will assume that these three types of information are represented separately (see Levelt, 1989, chapter 9, for a review). A set of processes must then *translate* the information stored in the PLR into the phonetic representation appropriate to the current speech context that is ultimately passed on to the articulators. Encoding subsystems "spell out", in Levelt's (1989) useful term, information in a PLR. One can think of a PLR as containing phonological information in a condensed or abbreviated form, which requires elaborating before it can be deployed by later processes. Elaboration may involve adding information on the basis of general rules of phonology, which the (normal) speaker may be assumed to know. For example, it may involve generating allophonic variants appropriate to the current syllabic context, like lengthening a vowel before a voiced obstruent. Unfortunately, we have insufficient evidence to be precise about how this spelling out might work. Allophonic variation may already be explicitly encoded in the PLR. PLRs may also be underspecified in a more technical sense; that is, some phonetic features will systematically not be represented in the PLR so that, for example, the consonant following /s/ in *start* will be marked for place but voicing is left unspecified, and is represented instead by an archiphoneme /T/ that could be realized as either /t/ or /d/. Other types of underspecification in underlying lexical representations have been suggested in phonological theory (e.g., Archangeli, 1985; Kiparsky, 1982), and some of the ideas have been recruited to explain normal speech errors (Stemberger & Treiman, 1986) and aphasic paraphasias (Beland, 1990).

I shall follow several authors (Levelt, 1989, chapters 8 and 9; Shattuck-Hufnagel, 1987) in assuming that translation processes have the form of a slot-and-filler device. The slots are defined jointly by spelling out the syllabic structure (how many syllables, and their form) and spelling out the prosodic structure – the stress (and pitch, where relevant) of each syllable. Information about the segmental content is spelled out and inserted into the appropriate slots. (This account is a considerable simplification, as well as a slight modification, of Levelt's in several ways, and the reader is urged to consult his book for a fuller description of the processes that might be at issue.)

The reader may also note similarities between the slot-and-filler model, and an earlier model proposed by Shaffer (1976). In this model, a "structural representation", derived from lexical representations, contains coordinated information concerning syllabic position and segments, where segments are designated by abstract symbols, called the "name" of the segment. A translation device converts names to featural descriptions of each segment on a level-by-level basis; that is, each name at the syllable-initial level is translated, then each name at the nucleus level, then each name at the coda level. The results of the translation process are called the "command representation". The level constraint ensures that error interactions between syllables are confined to homologous syllable positions (which is the normal pattern of interaction errors in spontaneous speech). The priority (or other temporal differences) of initial position translation may be related to the predominance of syllable (and word)-initial interactions (Shattuck-Hufnagel, 1987, this issue). In effect, this model, like the slot-and-filler model, takes two sources of information – syllable structure and segment identity – and combines them into a structured, featural description of the segments in their syllable positions as commands to the motor system. (See Butterworth & Whittaker, 1980, for a critical discussion of Shaffer's model.)

I have assumed, so far, that PE begins with the PLR; however, there is evidence to suggest that an earlier stage in word retrieval makes use of phonological information. A number of authors (e.g., Butterworth, 1980, 1989; Fromkin, 1971; Garrett, 1984; Kempen & Huijbers, 1983; Levelt, 1989) have argued that word retrieval takes place in two separate stages: the retrieval of an abstract representation, called a "lemma" by Kempen and Huijbers (1983) and Levelt (1989), from a separate lexicon of such representations, called a "semantic lexicon" by Butterworth (1980, 1989) since it is claimed that these items are organized semantically so that each semantic input specification is paired with a "phonological address". According to Butterworth (1980, 1981, 1989) these representations provide a phonological address (Garrett's, 1984, "linking address") for locating PLRs in the "phonological lexicon" where items are organized according to their phonological properties. According to Butterworth (1981) and Garrett (1984) information about the form of the intended word can be recovered from the addresses themselves since the addresses are systematically linked to phonological characteristics, like number of syllables, initial segment, etc. The address locates a PLR in a multidimensional phonological space in which similar-sounding words will be at neighbouring addresses. Information from the address can be used when a lexical search fails to locate a PLR in the phonological space, as for example in the tip-of-the-tongue state. Here the word itself is inaccessible but the speaker is nevertheless able to report at least some phonological features correctly, especially first segment and number of syllables (Brown & McNeill, 1966). These states are explained in the following way: the lemma has been successfully retrieved, along with the phonological address. When the PLR proves inaccessible, the speaker can recover information from the address which can then be reported to the experimenter, or used to generate candidates by guessing the missing information.[2] We will return to specific deficits of addressing in section 3 below.

I differ from Levelt (1989) in not considering here the morphological structure of the planned word. I shall assume without argument that word forms for known words are not derived on-line from morphemic components. This is not to say that morphology is unrelated to the phonological form of a word (cf. Kiparsky, 1982), nor that the rules for derivation and inflexion are unknown to the speaker, nor even that a PLR contains no morphological information, but only that information about morphology and lexical rules are deployed just when word search fails to retrieve a PLR meeting the retrieval specification – the phonological address.[3]

This outline account, presented diagrammatically in Figure 1, leaves open many details, some of which will be discussed below.

*Control processes*

An important point to note is that each subsystem in translation is served by a control process which, inter alia, retrieves information from an earlier subsystem as indicated by a directional arrow, and that the transmission of information from one subsystem to another is subject to transmission loss. A control process checks the output of the subsystem it serves. I assume that it does this by running through the process twice and comparing the results. (See Butterworth, 1981, for further explication.)

*Back-up*

I also assume that control processes provide access to back-up devices that can be invoked when things go wrong. One way this may happen in PE is for default values of phonological parameters to be generated when information cannot be

[2]Later processes, which I shall not discuss here, deal with other aspects of the precise phonetic realization in context of the filled slots: for example, overall properties of the output due to register, like rate of speech, volume, across-the-board phonetic features, like the palatalization of solidarity in Basque (Corum, 1975, cited by Gazdar, 1980) or dismissive or sarcastic nasalization in some English and American dialects, or sentence-final lengthening. Accounts of resyllabification processes – like "John is" to "John's" for informal talk or the dropping of word-final post-vocalic /r/ in British English and some American dialects – are arguably a systematic part of the translation from PLR, though some forms, like epenthetic vowels and liaison in French, seem to be later processes, in part at least, pragmatically conditioned like the former examples.

[3]A defence of this position can be found in Butterworth (1983). The use of morphological rules by an aphasic patient to construct new forms when search fails is described in Semenza, Butterworth, Panzeri, and Ferreri (1990).

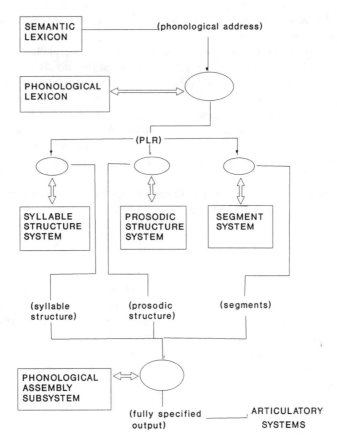

Figure 1.    *Outline model of phonological encoding processes. The operation of this model can be best illustrated by stepping through the encoding of the word* tenant, *and the paraphasia* /'semənt/. *(See section 1.1 for further details.)*

   1. *A phonological address is retrieved from the SEMANTIC LEXICON and can be thought of as an* n*-tuple defining a location in the PHONOLOGICAL LEXICON; for example,* ⟨2, 3, 6 ...⟩. *It will have as neighbour, say,* tennis *at* ⟨2, 3, 7 ...⟩. *The generation of both target and paraphasia are held to start with the retrieval of the correct address.*

   2. *The PHONOLOGICAL LEXICON associates the address with a PLR (phonological lexical representation) that contains information as to how* tenant *should be pronounced – the segments it contains, and its syllable and prosodic structures. For reasons that are explained in section 1.1, the PLR for* tenant *has not been corrupted in store.*

   3. *This information is spelled out by dedicated, independent systems for SYLLABLE STRUCTURE, PROSODIC STRUCTURE and SEGMENTS. For the correct output,* tenant, *all the information in the PLR is correctly spelled out. For* /'semənt/, *syllable and stress information may be fully available, though defaults could yield similar outcomes, but it is assumed that some or all of the information about the first consonant has been wholly or partly lost in transmission; the segment system generates a default segment,* /s/, *either from scratch, or from residual information about place of articulation, with manner information lost.*

retrieved from the PLR. Thus, if a syllable specification is unavailable, then a default pattern is generated – for example, CVC; if a stress pattern is unavailable, then perhaps the (English) default strong–weak for a two-syllable word will be generated; or if a segment value is unavailable, a default segment is generated, though it is unclear on what basis: perhaps, only unmarked segments are generated, or in the case where some but not all features of the segment are available, then an unmarked version consistent with the available features is constructed. We will consider these possibilities below.

A further point is that the phonological assembly subsystem (PASS) can contain the phonological description of more than one word; this appears necessary to explain errors with source in another word, like segment and feature movements ("heft lemisphere", "capsy tag"; Fromkin, 1973), word blends ("shromkin" – "she" + "Fromkin") and environmental contaminants ("ungutted frish" from planned "fish" and heard "fresh"; Harley, 1990).

This model has many features in common with the interactive activation model proposed by Dell (1989). Words are linked to phonemes for output via direct links and via a wordshape network specifying the syllabic structure. This mirrors the slot-filling idea. One could develop the analogy between links and addresses, and explore the possibility that explicit checking can be modelled as feedback activation. In any event, little of what is said here will discriminate between these modelling frameworks. (See Butterworth, 1989, and Levelt, 1989, chapter 9, for further discussion of these issues.)

One omission from our model, and from others discussed, is how non-words are intentionally generated. Non-words are important methodologically, since they permit us to assess whether brain damage has disturbed the translation processes themselves since PLRs are not implicated. Typical tests deploy the reading or repetition of non-word stimuli. I shall assume that the processes of reading and repetition generate phonological information in the same format as PLRs – a list of segments, a syllable structure outline and a stress pattern – which can be spelled out by the relevant systems and assembled by PASS. This has some plausibility given that a novel stimulus may become a genuine lexical entry; however, a definitive account of non-word generation awaits further investigation.

---

4. *These are then assembled by the PHONOLOGICAL ASSEMBLY SUBSYSTEM, which fits the segments into slots in a prosodically specified syllable structure. Thus the initial /t/, or the default /s/, is fitted into the onset position of the strong first syllable. The fully specified output needs to include all relevant information for the ARTICULATORY SYSTEM.*

*The control processes, indicated by ovals, enable the generation of default information from the associated systems, or elsewhere, in the event that relevant information is missing from the PLR. For further explanation, see text.*

## 1. Deficits of phonological lexical representations versus deficits of translation

The most basic and apparently the most straightforward issue is whether a phonological error arises as the result of a corrupted stored PLR or as a malfunction in the translation processes, in particular whether the malfunction is due to some impairment in one of the translation processes.

I shall begin by looking at five kinds of study that try to address this issue. The outcome will be, I am afraid, rather dull from a theoretical perspective. To the extent that a deficit can be identified, it lies not in the systematic, or even unsystematic, corruption of information in the PLRs; it is simply one of *noise in transmission* from PLRs to the translation, so that translation processes have to spell out specifications with variable, perhaps random, holes in them. Picturesque-ly, we could contrast seeing a hill through swirling mist – the hill is still there but the features are only intermittently visible (transmission loss) – with a word written in washable ink that has had water splashed on it (loss or corruption in storage).

The methodological moral I shall draw is equally trite, and moreover, rather old. In 1926, the British neurologist, Henry Head wrote:

> It is not a sufficient test to hold up some object and ask the patient to name it; at one time he may be able to do so, at another he fails completely. No conclusion can be drawn from one or two questions put in this way; his power of responding must be tested by a series of observations in which the same task occurs on two or more occasions. (1926, Vol. 1, p. 145)

To determine the source of an error or phonological encoding, it is necessary to observe in each patient several attempts to say the same word, for example by testing the patient several times with the same naming stimuli; in addition, it is necessary to see whether comparable errors are made on words alike and unalike in the theoretically relevant respects. To take an (imaginary) example: does patient X always say "chee" instead of "tea", and "sip" instead of "ship", but is correct on "toast" and "sap"? Or does he say "fis" instead of "fish" *and*, in general, always says /s/ instead of /ʃ/, in the manner of the child Amahl, whose developing phonology is described by Smith (1973)? That is to say, are there *item-specific* errors which show up on just some words with a particular feature, or are there *feature-specific* errors that apply to all words (and non-words) with a particular feature? In the case of Amahl, the contrast, in production, between /s/ and /ʃ/ had not yet developed.

### 1.1. An example of the difficulties of identifying the locus of an error

Because phonological representation and processes are implicated in, and link, lexical representations to phonetic plans for output, the presence of a speech error may be difficult to interpret with respect to candidate processes and representations. For example, a jargon aphasic patient, DJ, produced ['semənt] instead of the target, *tenant* (Butterworth, 1985). Single phoneme substitution paraphasias are not uncommon in aphasic speech (e.g., Fry, 1959), nor indeed in normal speech (e.g., Shattuck-Hufnagel & Klatt, 1979), yet a definitive locus in the production system is uncertain. DJ may have a corrupted lexical representation for *tenant* in which the initial /t/ has been replaced by an initial /s/; or the /t/ may have lost elements of featural specification, in the PLR, so that only something like [−sonorant, +coronal] remains to specify the initial segment and additional features will need to be generated, in this case incorrectly; or the initial phoneme /t/ has just been lost in its entirety, yet syllabic structure clearly indicates that an initial consonant is required; or, like normal errors, where loss of information at the level of PLR is not usually an option, something has gone wrong translating the PLR /t/ into the phonetic plan; or some arthric or praxic difficulty prevents /t/'s, or stops more generally, being properly articulated.

To eliminate some of the candidate interpretations, one needs to see what other types of error the patient makes; in particular, one needs to see whether the patient makes the same error every time he or she tries to produce the target.

In the case of DJ and *tenant* we do have some relevant data. DJ was a publican, working as the tenant of a brewery, a fact he was at pains to convey, since a tenant, who holds a lease on the pub, has a different, and, in DJ's view, a higher, status than a mere manager who simply operates the pub for a salary. Five examples, in two sessions, of his attempts to produce *tenant* in spontaneous conversation were recorded, and are reproduced in example (1):

(1) ['emnənt ... 'semənt ... 'tenənt ... 'tenəmən ... 'təneit]

Each attempt came from a separate sentence, so the sequence cannot be regarded as *conduite d'approche* (see section 1.2). Taking the incorrect attempts as a whole, one can see that each segment, /t, e, n, ə, n, t/, is produced in its correct word position at least once, and no error is produced more than once; and one attempt was fully correct. It is reasonable to suppose, therefore, that the PLR of the word has not suffered permanent corruption, neither through the replacement of a target segment by an intrusion, nor by the loss of a phonetic feature on one or more of the segments. Leaving aside arthric or praxic problems, from which DJ did not suffer, some problem in translating an intact PLR into a phonetic plan seems the most likely explanation, though the variability of error forms precludes proposing a specific locus in the translation process. The most likely account is that on each attempt to say the word some of the information about the segments was lost in transmission, but in a rather unsystematic, perhaps random, way. (This is not, of course, to say that DJ had a fully preserved vocabulary that sometimes got scrambled in his attempts to talk, but only that for this target the translation explanation appears the most consistent with the evidence so far presented.)

A similar analysis can be adduced for the syllabic structure of the PLR: in three examples it corresponds to the target – ['semənt, 'tenənt, 'tɜneit] – while the other two show distinct error types. In ['emnənt] the structure of the syllable CVC$CVCC rather than CVC$VCC, with stress remaining on the first syllable and in ['tenəmən], we find an additional epenthetic weak syllable, and a final syllable reduced from CVCC to CVC, though the first syllable is like the target. It is plausible to interpret this pattern also as due to variable loss in transmission from an intact PLR.

Without an examination of other attempts to say the same word the translation account of the original error, ['semənt], for this patient would not have been adequately grounded. In the case of normal speech errors, we are entitled to assume that the target PLR is intact, unless there are good grounds for thinking otherwise, as there are for Sheridan's character, Mrs Malaprop.

Of course, we were fortunate in finding several examples of the same identifiable target in free speech. This permitted the inference of loss of information from one intact PLR to the translation processes. However, if only one PLR resulted in this pattern of errors, then a reconsideration of this inference would be needed. To see whether other words suffered the fate of "tenant", we tested D. on a picture-naming task in two separate sessions one month apart. Overall, he named three pictures in Session 1 that he was unable to name in Session 2, and five pictures in Session 2 that he could not name in Session 1. The paraphasic errors indeed showed a similar pattern to the *tenant* example:

(2)  Target: eskimo
        Session 1: ['esiməu]
        Session 2: ['æstiməu]
      Target: hedgehog
        Session 1: ['dɪdʒɒg]
        Session 2: [ɪg, ɒs, 'hɪdʒɒg, 'egɒg], H–E–
      Target: jacket
        Session 1: ['dʒækə, dʒæk]
        Session 2: ['dʒækə], zipper, [zɪpəweiz]

Although we found evidence that he knew all the segments of *hedgehog*, the other two examples show different errors on each occasion, as would be expected if there was variable loss in transmission, but the errors do not contain in sum the whole segmental specification of the target. Perhaps with further trials the remaining segments would have emerged (/k/ in *eskimo*, /ɪt/ in *jacket*). With only two trials it is hard to say. However, in most studies of phonological encoding there is only one trial for each word presented as evidence, which means that, at best, the pattern across different errors remains the only evidence to identify the locus of the deficit.

## 1.2. Evidence from successive attempts

One interesting exception comes from a study by Joanette, Keller, and Lecours (1980) of a familiar aphasic symptom, *conduite d'approche*, in which the speaker makes successive attempts to say an intended word, in contrast to our study of DJ, which analysed separate attempts at the same word. (See also Kohn, 1984, for a similar analysis of a single case.) Joanette et al. noted that for French-speaking Broca, Wernicke and conduction aphasics, successive approximation tended to approach the target pronunciation. The only example they offer is:

(3) target: /krejõ/ (crayon)
approximations: /kreb . . . krevõ . . . krejõ/
(Transcriptions as in the original.)

They argue that because approximations tend toward the target, this indicates a degree of control by the patient over what we have called the translation process. The control consists of an awareness of error (in comparison with the target) and the availability of a "monitor" to modify the output. It is perhaps significant that the strongest trend towards accuracy was found in the conduction aphasics, where comprehension is typically more intact than in the other two groups, suggesting the involvement of comprehension processes in monitoring, along the lines indicated by Levelt (1989). However, for this to be established one would need correlations on a patient-by-patient basis between the degree of comprehension ability (especially for single words) and the incidence of errors corrected, as well as with the trend of the approximations. A further interesting finding is that the trend disappeared in conduction aphasics for a non-word repetition task and was very weak for a real-word repetition task (data were not available for the other groups). These patients are partly defined by poor repetition ability, and at least some will have especial difficulty in maintaining a phonemic trace of the input. This suggests that the approximations are based on a comparison between the attempts and the representation of an internally generated lexical target.

Since conduction aphasics appear to end up on or very close to the target, it is reasonable to suppose that the target PLR is more or less intact, so that the comparison term which the monitor is using to assess attempts will be correct, but that some aspect of the translation process is malfunctioning, at least on occasion. For the other groups, this interpretation is less clear, and it may be that more severely impaired patients do indeed suffer corruption or loss of stored PLRs, though whether for all words, or some category of words (e.g., low-frequency words) cannot be inferred from the data Joanette et al. present. One useful analysis that they might have done would have compared, say, the word frequency of those targets where the approximations show a trend toward the target with the frequency of those which do not show this trend.

In any event, these data also suggest that one aspect of the encoding cycle – the PLR – can be intact while the translation processes sometimes fail to spell out the information therein contained. One problem here is that although translation occasionally fails, overwhelmingly it seems to work satisfactorily, producing the intended output. Again, occasional loss of PLR information in transmission to the translation processes is indicated.

## 1.3. Variability and consistency in naming errors

To separate storage deficits of PLRs from translation impairments, a minimal requirement is to know whether particular words usually lead to phonemic errors in a given patient and whether there are some aphasics who characteristically produce phonemic errors. This requires testing and retesting a group of patients on the same words on several occasions. A study by Howard et al. (1984) goes some way to answering these questions. Twelve aphasic patients were given a set of 300 pictures to name on three separate occasions, plus another set of 300 different pictures with the same names (plus a test of reading the names). Although subjects were highly consistent in the proportion of names correctly produced in the various tests (correlations by subject, $r > .97$), they were much less consistent on an item-by-item analysis. The contingencies of correct/incorrect on test x and correct/incorrect on test y ranged from .282 to .536. Thus one patient named correctly only 73% of his successes from a previous test, and 38% of his failures. Two pieces of evidence suggest that naming performance depended on an ability to retrieve PLRs of the target: first, for 9 of the 12 patients, accuracy correlated with word frequency, though the correlations were low (from .081 to .340); second, for six patients, there was no correlation between accuracy and word length, and for the others correlations were very low. If the naming deficit were confined to the translation processes, one would expect high correlations with length (since there would then be more opportunities to make translation errors) and purely lexical factors should not be important since the trouble would take place downstream of the successful retrieval of the PLR. Length effects were largely confined to the non-fluent patients, who often suffer arthric and praxic problems in addition to specifically psycholinguistic difficulties.

Howard et al. (1984) also analysed the consistency of the *types* of error made. Four patients made no phonological errors (See footnote 1), while nearly 14% of errors were phonological in two patients (one fluent, one non-fluent), and in general patients were highly consistent in the proportion of phonemic errors from one test to the next (correlation of .933). Thus some patients characteristically make phonemic errors, others do not. Moreover, where a patient makes a phonological error on test 1, he or she will, on average, produce the *identical* error

15% of the time,[4] and another phonological error 10.5% of the time. The remainder were non-responses (44%), correct responses (26%) and semantic paraphasias (4%). None of the responses were unrelated real words (including "malapropisms", see section 2) or neologisms. What is not clear is whether the average conceals some patients in the group who reliably produce identical phonological error responses.

If a patient suffered corruption of stored PLRs, then we would expect identical error responses each time this item was retrieved, *ceteris paribus*. We might also expect that lexical factors would characterize the corrupted items. For example, it may be that infrequent words will be more prone to corruption, as well as to loss or to retrieval delays (Newcombe, Oldfield, & Wingfield, 1965). From Howard et al.'s report, we cannot tell whether infrequent words are more liable than frequent words to phonemic distortion, in particular, to consistent phonemic distortion. Until we know this, we cannot tell, for any patient in the study, whether the phonological errors are due to corrupted PLRs or translation problems or both.

## 1.4. Phonemic errors in reading

A detailed study of one conduction aphasic patient (NU) by Pate et al. (1987) is the most thorough attempt known to the author to assess item-specific consistency of errors. The primary data come from tests of reading, and reading may involve the generation of phonological information by a non-lexical procedure, by mapping graphemes onto phonemes, and this may play a role in the generation, and prevention, of phonemic errors. Nevertheless, Pate et al. claim that NU's reading errors were qualitatively similar to errors found in spontaneous speech. The same words occurred in five different reading contexts, from single words, word blocks and phrases to whole sentences, and responses to some of the words were further presented auditorily in a repetition task. Generally, words that prompted a paraphasia in one test prompted paraphasias in other tests, and words correctly produced in one test were generally correctly produced in others. The number of identical error responses in two test conditions was quite low (11 examples) and

---

[4]It would be interesting to know the probability of producing an identical error when, say, one segment substitution is selected at random from the usual frequency distribution of English segments in the substitution context. For this study, at least two deviations were required for a form to count as a phonemic error, so one would further need to calculate the probability of two segment substitutions resulting in an identical response. There is a further complication: some syllable positions, and some segments, appear more likely to be involved in error than others. (See, for example, Pate et al., 1987, described in section 1.4). It is therefore uncertain whether the identical error responses of Howard et al.'s patients should be treated as candidate corruptions of PLRs or not.

only one word prompted exactly the same error in all five test conditions (diseases /dɪzizə z/ → /dɪsizə z/). The main factor in errors was the length of the target (as it was with Caplan's, 1987, patient RL), and this does not appear an artefact of the greater number of opportunities for error in longer words (again like Caplan's RL).

Like DJ, the various attempts at a target can show different errors, yet jointly realize all the phonological information in the target:

(4) Target: product /pradəkt/
Session 1 /pradək/, Session 2 /pradək/, Session 3 /pradənt, prabən/, Session 4 (omission), Session 5 /pradək/
(Pate et al., 1987, Table 7.)

Notice also that the syllable structure is slightly different in Session 3, though unlike the other attempts is closest to CVC$CVCC structure of the target. (It is difficult to resist the following speculation: suppose NU had spelled out the syllable structure CVC$VC$_i$C and had spelled out /t/ as the final consonant, yet had no segmental information for the content of $C_i$, a likely default filler generated by a back-up device would be something with alveolar feature, for example /n/ or /s/, rather than the /k/ of the target.)

Pate et al. conclude that the striking effects of length on paraphasic errors, combined with the lack of cross-word interaction errors, "reflects a constraint on the amount of phonological information which can be programmed within a unit". That is to say, there is a kind of channel capacity limit to spelling out apparently intact information in PLRs, which is perhaps combined with loss of information in transmission, especially for unstressed material (cf. Caplan's (1987) account of similar length effects in a similar patient).

## 1.5. The generation of phonemic paraphasias and neologisms

Many fluent aphasics produce neologisms. There is no agreed definition of neologism: a single phoneme substitution can lead to the creation of a form not in the dictionary, yet is nevertheless an identifiable distortion of an identifiable target – what is usually termed a phonemic paraphasia – while others bear no apparent relation to the target. The critical point is not how these forms are called, but what account is offered of them. From the framework offered here, the question is, "Can neologisms be explained in terms of a disorder of PE, either as corruptions of stored PLRs or as a systematic malfunctioning of the translation processes?" Unfortunately, most neologisms are nonce occurrences. (Less than 4% of Howard et al.'s (1984) neologistic naming responses were the same on two test sessions). Where they are not, they are stereotypes produced in a wide range of settings for presumably a wide range of targets. These facts reduce the value of repeated testing of the same stimuli. However, something can be learned from the pattern of neologistic production in spontaneous speech.

For those not familiar with neologistic speech, I will offer a brief characterization of the kinds of patient where it most commonly occurs. Neologisms are found in greatest abundance in the speech of "jargon aphasics". This is a term which describes a rather heterogeneous group of speech types and patients (see Butterworth, 1985, for a brief review, and Brown, 1981, for a more extended account). Most neologistic speakers are fluent, with poor comprehension, though the degree of impairment varies widely and is unrelated to the incidence of neologisms (Butterworth & Howard, 1987, p. 27). Usually, perhaps always, they suffer posterior damage and may be considered a subtype of Wernicke's aphasia (Buckingham & Kertesz, 1976). A reasonably accurate extended transcript of a classic case can be found in Butterworth (1979).

According to Butterworth (1979) and Panzeri, Semenza, and Butterworth (1987), non-words have three distinct sources (data from patient KC):

(i) They may be phonemic distortions of the target; e.g. [tʃək] for chair, [dɒkjumən] for doctor.

(ii) They may result from the intrusion of phonemic material from a prior or following word; e.g. "she has to do things [wʌmən] a woman who helps".

(iii) They may be generated by a back-up "device" and bear no relation to any target. Phonemic variants of a device neologism may be used five or six times in different sentential contexts; e.g. [bæklənd . . . bændɪks . . . ændɪks . . . zændɪks . . . lændɒks . . . zæprɪks].

It is argued by Butterworth (1979) that these forms are deployed when there has been a partial or complete failure to retrieve a PLR. For type (i), only part of the target has been retrieved, and a device has to fill in the missing information about syllable structure and segments. For type (ii), the target PLR has not been retrieved, but another word in the plan for the current utterance is active, or available, which in this case has lost some information and the back-up device again fills in the missing information. (Sometimes KC appears to produce a contextual word correctly, but in the wrong place, rather like word-movement errors in normals.) For type (iii), no information is available from the target PLR, or from any other word, and a filler has to be constructed from scratch. If this happens more than once in quick succession, information from the previously constructed neologism(s) can be exploited, hence the sequence of similar-sounding neologisms. A key piece of evidence that Butterworth (1979) used to make this argument is that the pauses before type (iii) were longer than before types (i) and (ii), which in turn were longer than pauses before real words, whether correct or verbal paraphasias, suggestive of search times that depended on the amount of information retrieved. These data are again consistent with the idea that PLRs are uncorrupted in store, but information is lost in transmission to the translation processes.

It is worth noting that the neologisms use the full repertory of phonemes (and no non-English phonemes) in phonotactically legal ways, suggesting that there are no specific deficits in translation. However, given the absence of repeated attempts at the same words, it is also possible that PLRs are corrupted. Certainly, patients like KC suffer word-finding difficulties, and it is likely, but not demonstrated, that some PLRs may be lost, rather than simply being inaccessible. Clearly, further studies of these patients need to be carried out. DJ (Butterworth, 1985; Butterworth & Howard, 1987), who was similar in many respects, showed evidence of variability of accessibility to a target from session to session, but nevertheless he too may have lost vocabulary items. What is critical here is that, on occasion, KC needed to institute translation when no or insufficient phonemic information about the target was available, resulting in forms that were well formed and sometimes quite unrelated to the target. It is implausible to suggest that the PLRs for matches, matchbox, telephone and dial, which were the targets of the neologisms in (iii), were all corrupted so as to yield similar-sounding items.

The claim that neologisms strategically substitute for search failures has been substantiated in a longitudinal study of an Italian jargon aphasic, PZ. Over the course of seven months, the incidence of type (iii) neologisms was drastically reduced, apparently as the result of a developing strategy to avoid contexts in which word search was likely to fail completely. It was argued that stereotyped utterances were increasingly used to avoid search failure. The other types of neologism remained more or less constant.

Another source for neologisms has been suggested by Pick (1931) and Howard et al. (1985). They claim that many are phonemic distortions of a verbal paraphasia (wrong word). Howard et al. report the following examples from their study:

(5) Utterance: /spaidɪd/ from Target: Web via Spider
    Utterance: /ætə/ from Target: Globe via Atlas

Although these examples are well attested and plausibly explained, this account seems unlikely for all the type (iii) neologisms of KC. For our current purposes, these non-word forms do not allow us to distinguish between storage deficits and translational deficits, though they are consistent with the idea that there has simply been loss in transmission of phonemic information from the PLR, in this case the wrong PLR.

## 2. Is there good evidence for specific deficits in translation processes?

In the above brief and selective review, it was argued that there was little direct evidence for corruption of stored PLRs, and that the data presented were compatible with a rather minimalist account of what was going wrong in translation, namely that information from PLRs was "lost in transmission". However, it has often been claimed that aphasic patients suffer more specific disorders of PE. In the next selective and brief review some of these claims are examined. Bear in mind that none of the studies satisfy the basic methodological desideratum of repeated observations of attempts at the same word. Blumstein (1973) has argued that this essentially does not matter:

> Variability in performance is not directly at issue in considering the phonological patterns underlying aphasic performance; i.e. although the quantity of errors may in fact vary from day to day, the direction and types of error should remain qualitatively similar. (1973, p. 22n)

Now it may not matter from the point of view of phonological theory, but it seems to matter when attributing a pattern of errors to a specific processing locus.

## 2.1. Deficits in spelling out segmental structure

In our outline model two subsystems involve segmental information: the subsystem that spells out segmental information in PLR, and the PASS, where segments are inserted into their syllabic slots. We look first at possible evidence for a disorder of reading segmental information from PLR. What might this look like? One possibility is that the subsystem fails to encode certain phonemic distinctions; for example, the voicing feature may be consistently lost, so that all voiced segments come out as unvoiced. More generally, there may be a tendency for marked segments to be produced as unmarked. Of course, without repeated testing of each target, we cannot be confident that the cause of error patterns such as these, should we find them, is to be located in segmental translation or in systematically corrupted PLRs.

In a pioneering study, Fry (1959) analysed the phonemic substitutions in the tape-recorded oral reading of CVC words by one patient. The patient is described as having hesitant speech, with no verbal paraphasias or neologisms, and good comprehension and reading. Nineteen per cent of the responses were phoneme substitution errors (21% of consonant targets and 16% of vowel targets). Errors of place, manner and voicing were found for consonant targets, but with no obvious pattern, except that there appeared to be an unusually high proportion of voicing errors. Some consonants (/ʃ/ and /tʃ/) produced no errors, while /d/ and /v/ produced 43% and 35% respectively. The order of difficulty of consonants was unrelated to the order of difficulty found either in children's errors (Morley, cited by Fry) or in normal adult segment errors (Shattuck-Hufnagel & Klatt, 1979). Although the patient apparently suffered articulatory problems, as evidenced by hesitation and severe difficulties with consonant clusters (which therefore were not tested), this does not seem to account for the pattern of errors. Fry writes:

The most interesting feature of this type of [voicing] error was that the phonemic substitution was complete and hence involved a re-arrangement of the time scheme of a whole word, particularly when a consonant followed a vowel. The patient said /mʌk/ for *mug*, for example, with appropriate vowel length for its voiceless consonant... Much more is involved here than the failure to make the larynx work when required; the whole organisation of the syllable has to be changed... It was not that at the level of articulation he merely made a poor attempt at the correct phoneme. (1959, p. 57)

In a study of 17 aphasic patients, Blumstein (1973) found that overall patients were able to use the full inventory of American English phonemes. In contrast to Fry, the patients' overall probability of an error on a phoneme was inversely related to the phoneme's frequency of occurrence. It may be that some patients were unsystematic in this respect, like Fry's patient; unfortunately individual patient data are not presented. Different types of aphasia – Broca, Wernicke and conduction – produced similar types and distributions of error types. Although there was a slight tendency for unmarked segments to substitute for marked segments, this did not apply to the conduction aphasics as a group, and may not hold for every patient in the other two groups. It would be interesting to know whether there were some patients for whom this tendency was highly marked, and others who did not show it all. Unlike Fry, Blumstein did not analyse the effects of substitutions on the overall organization of the syllable in which it occurred.

Nespoulous, Joanette, Béland, Caplan, and Lecours (1984) have examined the phonological output of 4 Broca's and 4 conduction aphasics for tendencies to produce unmarked in preference to marked forms. They seem to believe that Blumstein (1973) found no differences between these two groups, and seek to establish more firmly that Broca's do, but conductions do not, have a tendency toward unmarked forms in their errors. They certainly find that Broca's as a group show clearer preferences for certain phonemes as substitutes, with more un-marked responses. However, it is also clear that patients move as readily from the unvoiced (unmarked) to the voiced form as vice versa. At the same time, Broca's are more likely to reduce clusters to single segments (marked to unmarked) than are conduction aphasics, who are as likely to create new clusters in error as to reduce target clusters.

## 2.2. Deficits in spelling out syllabic and prosodic structure

There is very little evidence available here. Pate et al. (1987) found that their patient, NU, was much more likely than chance to omit unstressed syllables than syllables with primary or secondary stress. Moreover, more phonemes were omitted from unstressed syllables than stressed, when word position is controlled. Kean (1977), in a discussion of agrammatic patients, suggested that phonological elements not taking lexical stress were the most prone to omission.

## 2.3. Deficits in assembling segments and syllable structures

It is known from the studies of normal speech errors that phonological distortions are not confined to intrusive substitutions of one or more phonemes; some involve the interaction between two words in the current speech plan – as in segment anticipations, perseverations and metatheses. Are aphasic speakers more prone to these errors? Do they produce different ordering errors? Garrett (1984, p. 189) suggests that an impairment to PASS in conduction aphasics would result in several of the commonly occurring symptoms, including sound-exchange errors.

In Pate et al.'s (1987) study of the reading errors of patient NU, overwhelmingly phonemic movement errors were confined to within-multiword interactions, despite a tested ability to construct phonological phrases appropriately. This effect was checked out in a separate experiment.

In an interesting recent study, Kohn and Smith (1990) analysed the sentence repetition performance of a conduction aphasic, CM. This patient made many segment anticipations and perseverations, but no exchanges. Most of these errors copied a segment so that it replaced a similarly positioned segment, usually the nucleus and/or coda, in the interacting word:

(5) Jane r*oad*→J*oan*
   Nurses tend p*atients*→ /N*ei*, N*ei*/
   Matthew bro*ke* his ankle→ /M*ae*ku, M*ae*k/
(Transcriptions as in the original.)

Now although errors of these types occur in normals, a variety of other types have also been observed in normals, notably exchanges.

Kohn and Smith (1990) offer an explanation of these phenomena which involves a malfunction in a device that "clears" a planning buffer in what we called PASS, so that when the segments from the next PLR come to be inserted into the syllabic slots, some of those slots will still be occupied by segments from the previous word. It is not clear whether the clearing mechanism is more than a terminological variant of Shattuck-Hufnagel's (1987) mechanism that deletes a segment once it has been used: the notional locus is different, to be sure, in the assembled slots rather than in the list of segments to be inserted, but the only data that favours Kohn and Smith's account are the absence of addition errors – that is to say, attempts to insert the correct segment alongside an incorrect segment, to produce a cluster or a new diphthong do not succeed. All interaction errors are simple replacements.

To account for anticipatory errors, it has to be assumed that words are not assembled in strict order of output, and if the predominance of anticipatory errors is evidence, then *typically* words are assembled out of their final utterance order. This may strike the reader as implausible, and certainly independent motivation for this apparently strange way of doing things is needed. For example, one might run an argument to the effect that some particular category of words has priority in PASS, for example, that heads are assembled before modifiers, or that words receiving sentence accent are assembled before others. I know of no good reason to propose this, nor do Kohn and Smith offer an analysis of the data which would allow the reader to investigate such a possibility. Another problem concerns the pattern of phonemic paraphasias that cannot be attributed to movement errors. This is not described, but from the number of sentence stimuli repeated correctly, there appear to be a lot of them. It is possible, at least, that apparent pattern of between-word errors is an artefact of a range of phonemic processes implicated in errors, including exchanges. Within-word exchanges are excluded from the analysis, for example. Further analyses are needed before an interpretation of the locus of these errors can be confidently proposed.

The bottom line, if I understand Kohn and Smith's presentation correctly, is this: (1) between-word interactions are never exchanges, though within-word interactions may be, whereas normal interaction errors produce between-word exchanges routinely (perhaps, predominantly; see Shattuck-Hufnagel, 1987); (2) interactions typically involve the rhyme portion of syllables, whereas normal interactions typically involve onsets (Shattuck-Hufnagel, 1987). In tongue-twisters, the latter pattern is also observed. Butterworth and Whittaker (1980, Experiment 1) asked normal subjects, but including lawyers, to repeat two-syllable items ("mat rat", "pap pack") as quickly as possible. For all types of interaction – anticipations, perseverations and exchanges – rhymes were more often implicated than onsets (though note there are two rhyme positions but only one onset), and perseverations and anticipations were far more common than exchanges. Shattuck-Hufnagel (1982, reported in Shattuck-Hufnagel, 1987) found that the repetition of four-word lists ("leap not nap lute") tended to produce more rhyme interactions than onset interactions, while the same words in a phrasal context ("from the leap of the note to the nap of the lute") showed the opposite pattern of errors, which she attributes to words being "protected" by the phrasal organization provided by the phrasal condition.[5] It is possible that CM has a tendency, for some reason, to treat his output in a more list-like, and less structured manner.

---

[5]Shattuck-Hufnagel's (1982, cited 1987) experiment does not appear to have used the appropriate controls – (a) differs from (b) in more than just the presence of phrasal organization:

(a) leap note nap lute
(b) from the leap of the note to the nap of the lute

Example (b) contains an additional eight unstressed syllables which may act as a buffer between the critical items. The apparent likelihood of interactions between words are conditioned by proximity, and it is possible that the type of interaction is also conditioned by it. Perhaps Shattuck-Hufnagel should have tried strings like (c):

(c) the from leap the of note the to nap the of lute.

## 3. Disorders of phonological addressing

Garrett (1984) suggests that phonological addresses may be impaired, or lost, in anomic conditions, but not in conduction aphasia, and cites as evidence an observation by Goodglass, Kaplan, Weintraub, and Ackerman (1976) that anomics can only produce information about the initial letter of a word they cannot retrieve in 5% of instances, while conduction aphasics can do this on 34% of instances. If, as I suggested above, information from the phonological address can be recovered when search is incomplete, then failure to recover it may indicate loss of the address in the anomic cases. For the conduction aphasics, by contrast, their difficulty seems to occur later, in loss of PLRs or the translation of PLRs into fully assembled output.

Our conception of the speech production system contains a semantic lexicon which associates semantic specifications with phonological addresses for locations of PLRs in the phonological lexicon. This raises a further possibility, namely that the addresses may be corrupted. In our model, a corrupt address would have the following consequences: either the corrupt address locates a blank space in the phonological lexicon, in which case no PLR will be retrieved, or it will locate a neighbouring PLR, which will be similar-sounding, but most likely semantically unrelated.

A relevant case was recently reported by Blanken (1990). The patient, RB, was a fluent anomic patient who managed relatively few content words, and sometimes made phonemic paraphasias and neologisms. He had poor auditory comprehension of single words. On the whole his reading and writing seemed less impaired than the speech modality. The phenomenon that characterized his speech, and has never previously been reported, is a large number of malapropisms, or what Blanken calls "formal paraphasias". These are real words that sound similar to the target but are usually unrelated in meaning. (Some are similar in both sound and meaning.) Examples are:

(6) a.  Schrank (cupboard) → Strand (beach)
    b.  Kreide (chalk) → Kreise (circles)
    c.  Kerze (candle) → Berge (mountains)
    d.  Kasper (Punch) → Kassen (tills)

It is hard to explain these errors in terms of single-segment errors that by chance sound like a real word. If that were the case, one would expect there to be a large, perhaps larger, number of non-word single-segment errors than formal paraphasias. There turn out to be only a few examples of these, and Blanken has calculated that chance errors would not explain his results.

Lack of data on item specificity prevents us ruling out with complete confidence an alternative explanation for the errors in (6). Perhaps RB had obtained the correct address for, say, *Kreide*, but the target PLR /kraidə/ was lost (or seriously damaged); in these circumstances, RB may simply have retrieved its nearest neighbour in the phonological lexicon, *Kreise*. However, although Blanken does not report different attempts at this target, he does offer some relevant indirect evidence. In a repeated naming task, RB was cued with the first phoneme of the target. This manipulation not only improved overall performance (in terms of number of items correct) but also reduced the proportion of formal paraphasic errors (Blanken, 1990, Table 5), suggesting that targets that otherwise led to formal paraphasias were still in store, but not retrieved (or perhaps retrievable) without a cue. The value of cues in aiding retrieval of hard-to-find words has been extensively demonstrated in the aphasic literature (e.g., Howard & Orchard-Lisle, 1984; Howard et al., 1985); and even where explicit cueing does not help, semantic priming may have a sizeable effect on retrieval (Chertkow & Bub, 1990). Thus cueing and priming are useful techniques for establishing loss versus inaccessibility of lexical information. Exactly how the additional phonemic information provided by cueing works is not well understood, but it seems to have both a different time course and other differential effects from priming, where presumably the target PLR receives activation from the prime. It is at least conceivable that cues are incorporated into the phonological address, which would be consistent with our account of the formal errors found in RB.

Examples (6b)–(6d) are interesting in another way: target and response do not show number agreement (singulars become plurals), but like 92% of the examples they do agree in number of syllables, and of these (presumably, Blanken is not clear on this point) 98% agree in stress pattern (the exception involves loan word targets). If, as I suggested above, the phonological lexicon contains full forms rather than roots (or stems), then these outcomes are unproblematic: a near neighbour is selected purely on the basis of the phonological properties of the full form (e.g., Berge). On the other hand, if the phonological lexicon contains roots and affixes separately – in the extreme case where grammatical affixes are part of a separate system in a separate location (e.g. Garrett, 1980) – then it will be hard to explain why, in the examples above, the address does not locate a two-syllable root rather than a one-syllable root, which then gets inflected. Unfortunately, Blanken does not report the likelihood of failure of grammatical agreement between target and response; nor does he report whether agreement failure depends on the structure of the target. So there are some unresolved issues here.

## 4. Conclusion: specific deficits or just more normal errors?

The errors observed in our review of the patient data have been, as far as one can tell, of the same types as those found in normal speech deficits. There is some evidence that certain patients have a predilection for certain types of error; for example, for unmarked over marked segments. However, there is absolutely no evidence as to whether individual normal speakers also have these predilections. Where comparisons between normal and patient errors have been explicitly drawn, the normal data come from the collectivity of errors made by unspecified numbers of different people. Of course, we may find someone not clinically referred, who, like Kohn's patient CM, made anticipatory and perseveratory segment movements, but not segment exchanges. Or, we might find in our control population a speaker whose errors were confined to real words, rather like Blanken's RB. What would we say about such cases? Caramazza (1986) would doubtless have to say that such cases cannot exist (by definition), or that perhaps they are (by definition) neurological cases wandering the streets that ought to have been referred for neurological examination.

The point here is that it is hard to draw inferences about specific deficits if the only data consist of idiosyncratic preferences, often very slight, for one class of normal errors. Taking the studies reviewed above as a whole, the only thing that can be said with any confidence is that in some patients there seems to be loss of information in transmission between one subsystem and another; in which case, *idiosyncratic preferences may reflect the functioning of the back-up systems rather than the normal systems themselves*. There is little evidence that the storage of phonological information in the lexicon, or in the subsystems that spell out lexical entries, is disturbed in any of the patients here discussed; nor is there evidence that the operation of these subsystems has suffered a long-term malfunction. Of course, such things may happen. We just do not have the data to tell, yet.

The data we need should be collected in accordance with the following minimal list of methodological desiderata.

*Item specificity and deficits of storage*

1. Several observations of the production of each target are required.
2. Such tests should be carried out on a patient-by-patient basis.
3. The probability of error for each target should be assessed in relation to known lexical factors, word frequency being the most obvious.

*Feature specificity and deficits of translation*

4. The probability of error should be assessed in relation to the phonological features (characteristics) of the targets. Length, structure and the presence of certain segments are obvious candidates.
5. Non-word repetition (and reading) tests can be used to eliminate lexical, and hence potential storage, deficits. Bear in mind that aphasics, especially conduction

aphasics, may suffer problems at the input end of such tests which will affect repetition of such stimuli.

6. Non-word tests can be designed to assess the involvement of specific phonological features of the targets.

*Articulation versus internal generation of phonology*

7. Tests of phonological judgment – rhyme or homophony, number of syllables or segments, etc. – can be deployed, where the intactness of later, articulatory, processes is in doubt.[6]

# References

Archangeli, D.B. (1985). Yokuts harmony: Evidence for coplanar representation in nonlinear phonology. *Linguistic Inquiry, 16*, 335–372.

Beland, R. (1990). Vowel epenthesis in aphasia. In Nespoulous, J.-L., & Villiard, P. (Eds.), *Morphology, phonology and aphasia* (pp. 235–252). New York: Springer-Verlag.

Blanken, G. (1990). Formal paraphasias: A single case study. *Brain and Language, 38*, 534–554.

Blumstein, S. (1973). *A phonological investigation of aphasic speech.* The Hague, Mouton.

Brown, J.W. (1981). *Jargonaphasia.* New York: Academic Press.

Brown, R., & McNeill, D. (1966). The "tip of the tongue" phenomenon. *Journal of Verbal Learning and Verbal Behavior, 5*, 325–337.

Buckingham, H., & Kertesz, A. (1976). *Neologistic jargon aphasia.* Amsterdam: Swets and Zeitlinger.

Butterworth, B. (1979). Hesitation and the production of verbal paraphasias and neologisms in jargon aphasia. *Brain and Language, 8*, 133–161.

Butterworth, B. (1980). Some constraints on models of language production. In Butterworth, B. (Ed.), *Language production Vol. 1: Speech and talk* (pp. 423–459). London: Academic Press.

Butterworth, B. (1981). Speech errors: Old data in search of new theories. *Linguistics, 19*, 627–662.

Butterworth, B. (1983). Lexical representation. In Butterworth, B. (Ed.), *Language production Vol. 2: Development, writing and other language processes* (pp. 257–294). London: Academic Press.

Butterworth, B. (1985). Jargon aphasia: Processes and strategies. In Newman, S., & Epstein, R. (Eds.), *Current perspectives in dysphasia* (pp. 61–96). Edinburgh: Churchill Livingstone.

Butterworth, B. (1989). Lexical access in speech production. In Marslen-Wilson, W. (Ed.), *Lexical representation and process* (pp. 108–135). Cambridge, MA: MIT Press.

Butterworth, B., & Howard, D. (1987). Paragrammatisms. *Cognition, 26*, 1–37.

Butterworth, B., & Whittaker, S. (1980). Peggy Babcock's relatives. In Stelmach, G., & Requin, J. (Eds.), *Tutorials in motor behavior* (pp. 647–656). New York: Plenum Press.

Caplan, D. (1987). Phonological representations in word production. In Keller, E., & Gopnik, M. (Eds.), *Motor and sensory processes of language.* Hillsdale, NJ: Erlbaum.

Caramazza, A. (1986). On drawing inferences about the structure of normal cognitive systems from the analysis of impaired performance: The case for single-patient studies. *Brain and Cognition, 5*, 41–66.

Chertkow, H., & Bub, D. (1990). Semantic memory loss in dementia of Alzheimer's type. *Brain, 113*, 397–417.

Dell, G. (1989). The retrieval of phonological forms in production: Tests of predictions from a

[6]Feinberg, Rothi, and Heilman (1986) report three patients able to perform similar tasks, though quite unable to vocalize the words involved.

connectionist model. In Marslen-Wilson, W. (Ed.), *Lexical representation and process* (pp. 136–165). Cambridge, MA: MIT Press.

Feinberg, T., Rothi, L., & Heilman, K. (1986). Inner speech in conduction aphasia. *Archives of Neurology*, *43*, 591–593.

Fromkin, V. (1971). The non-anomalous nature of anomalous utterances. *Language*, *47*, 27–52.

Fromkin, V. (1973). Appendix. In Fromkin, V. (Ed.), *Speech errors as linguistic evidence*. The Hague: Mouton.

Fry, D. (1959). Phonemic substitutions in an aphasic patient. *Language and Speech*, *2*, 52–61.

Garnham, A., Shillcock, R., Brown, G.D.A., Mill, A.I.D., & Cutler, A. (1981). Slips of the tongue in the London–Lund corpus of spontaneous conversation. *Linguistics*, *19*, 805–817.

Garrett, M. (1980). Levels of processing in sentence production. In Butterworth, B. (Ed.), *Language production Vol. 1: Speech and talk* (pp. 177–210). London: Academic Press.

Garrett, M. (1984). The organisation of processing structure for language production: Applications to aphasic speech. In Caplan, D., Lecours, A.R., & Smith, A. (Eds.), *Biological perspectives on language*. Cambridge, MA: MIT Press.

Gazdar, G. (1980). Pragmatic constraints on linguistic production. In Butterworth, B. (Ed.), *Language production Vol. 1: Speech and talk* (pp. 49–68). London: Academic Press.

Goodglass, H., Kaplan, E., Weintraub, S., & Ackerman, N. (1976). The "tip of the tongue" phenomenon in aphasia. *Cortex*, *12*, 145–153.

Harley, T. (1990). Environmental contamination of normal speech. *Applied Psycholinguistics*, *11*, 45–72.

Head, H. (1926). *Aphasia and kindred disorders of speech*. Cambridge, UK: Cambridge University Press.

Howard, D., & Orchard-Lisle, V. (1984). On the origin of semantic errors in naming: Evidence from the case of a global aphasic. *Cognitive Neuropsychology*, *1*, 163–190.

Howard, D., Patterson, K., Franklin, S., Morton, J., & Orchard-Lisle, V. (1984). Variability and consistency in picture naming by aphasic patients. In Rose, F.C. (Ed.), *Advances in neurology Vol. 42: Progress in aphasiology* (pp. 263–276). New York: Raven Press.

Howard, D., Patterson, K., Franklin, S., Orchard-Lisle, V., & Morton, J. (1985). The facilitation of picture naming in aphasia. *Cognitive Neuropsychology*, *2*, 49–80.

Joanette, Y., Keller, E., & Lecours, A.R. (1980). Sequences of phonemic approximations in aphasia. *Brain and Language*, *11*, 30–44.

Kean, M.-L. (1977). The linguistic interpretation of aphasic syndromes. *Cognition*, *5*, 9–46.

Kempen, G., & Huijbers, P. (1983). The lexicalization process in sentence formulation. *Cognition*, *14*, 201–258.

Kiparsky, P. (1982). From cyclic phonology to lexical phonology. In van der Hulst, H., & Smith, N. (Eds.), *The structure of phonological representations: Part 1* (pp. 131–176). Dordrecht: Foris.

Kohn, S. (1984). The nature of the phonological disorder in conduction aphasia. *Brain and Language*, *23*, 97–115.

Kohn, S., & Smith, K.L. (1990). Between-word speech errors in conduction aphasia. *Cognitive Neuropsychology*, *7*, 133–156.

Levelt, W.J.M. (1989). *Speaking: From intention to articulation*. Cambridge, MA: MIT Press.

Nespoulous, J.-L., Joanette, Y., Béland, R., Caplan, D., & Lecours, A.R. (1984). In Rose, F.C. (Ed.), *Advances in neurology Vol. 42: Progress in aphasiology* (pp. 203–214). New York: Raven Press.

Newcombe, F., Oldfield, R., & Wingfield, A. (1965). Object naming by dysphasic patients. *Nature*, *207*, 1217–1218.

Panzeri, M., Semenza, C., & Butterworth, B. (1977). Compensatory processes in the evolution of severe jargon aphasia. *Neuropsychologia*, *25*, 919–933.

Pate, D.S., Saffran, E., & Martin, N. (1987). Specifying the nature of the production impairment in a conduction aphasic: A case study. *Language and Cognitive Processes*, *2*, 43–84.

Pick, A. (1931). *Aphasia*. Springfield, IL: Thomas (Translated by J.W. Brown, 1973).

Semenza, C., Butterworth, B., Panzeri, M., & Ferreri, T. (1990). Word-formation: New evidence from aphasia. *Neuropsychologia*, *28*, 499–502.

Shaffer, L.H. (1976). Intention and performance. *Psychological Review*, *83*, 375–393.

Shallice, T., & Butterworth, B. (1977). Short-term memory impairment and spontaneous speech. *Neuropsychologia, 15,* 729–735.

Shallice, T., & Warrington, E.K. (1977). Auditory–verbal short-term memory impairment and conduction aphasia. *Brain and Language, 4,* 479–491.

Shattuck-Hufnagel, S. (1987). The role of word-onset consonants in speech production planning: New evidence from speech error patterns. In Keller, E., & Gopnik, M. (Eds.), *Motor and sensory processes of language* (pp. 17–51). Hillsdale, NJ: Erlbaum.

Shattuck-Hufnagel, S., & Klatt, D. (1979). Minimal use of features and markedness in speech production. *Journal of Verbal Learning and Verbal Behavior, 18,* 41–55.

Smith, N.V. (1973). *The acquisition of phonology.* Cambridge, UK: Cambridge University Press.

Stemberger, J.P., & Treiman, R. (1986). The internal structure of word-initial consonant clusters. *Journal of Memory and Language, 25,* 163–180.

# 9

# Stages of lexical access in language production*

Gary S. Dell

*Department of Psychology, University of Illinois, Urbana, IL 61801, USA*

Padraig G. O'Seaghdha

*Department of Psychology, Lehigh University, Bethlehem, PA 18015, USA*

Dell, G.S., and O'Seaghdha, P.G., 1992. Stages of lexical access in language production. Cognition, 42: 287–314.

*We describe two primary stages in the top-down process of lexical access in production, a stage of lemma access in which words are retrieved as syntactic–semantic entities, and a stage of phonological access in which the forms of the words are fleshed out. We suggest a reconciliation of modular and interactive accounts of these stages whereby modularity is traceable to the action of discrete linguistic rule systems, but interaction arises in the lexical network on which these rules operate. We also discuss the time-course of lexical access in multi-word utterances. We report some initial production priming explorations that support the hypothesis that lemmas are buffered in longer utterances before they are phonologically specified. Because such techniques provide a relatively direct way of assessing activation at the primary stages of lexical access they are an important new resource for the study of language production.*

## Introduction

Many of the current controversies in psycholinguistics concern the temporal properties of language processing. For example, no one disputes that prior context is used in deciding whether a homophone such as /roz/ is a noun or a verb, but

---

*This research was supported by NSF grant BNS-8910546, and NIH grants NS25502 and DC-00191. We thank Linda May, Darryn Andersen, and Julie Owles for their help, and Barbara Malt for comments on an earlier version of the manuscript. Requests for reprints should be sent to Gary Dell.

there is heated debate about when this context is used (see, for example, Burgess, Tanenhaus, & Seidenberg, 1989; Glucksberg, Kreuz, & Rho, 1986; Tabossi, 1988; Van Petten & Kutas, 1987). In general, much of what has been called the modularity question in language processing concerns the time-course of the access and use of various kinds of linguistic and contextual information (Fodor, 1983; Tanenhaus, Dell, & Carlson, 1987). The time-course issue also dominates discussion of the topic of this paper: lexical access in language production. There is little doubt that lexical access involves a mapping between a conceptual representation and a word's phonological form. Similarly, it is universally acknowledged that pragmatic, semantic, syntactic, and phonological information all play a role in achieving this mapping. But difficult questions concerning the time-course of the mapping process remain. When are the various types of linguistic information used? Is their use organized into temporally distinct stages? Or do the various types of information exert their influence throughout the process of mapping from meaning to sound?

Our paper focuses on two aspects of the time-course of access, which we call the *discreteness* and *advance-planning* questions. Both of these questions address the temporal properties of the access of semantic and phonological information during lexical access. The discreteness issue turns on whether semantic information is segregated from phonological information, semantic information being accessed and used at an earlier stage of lexical access than phonological information. The advance-planning question arises in the case of multi-word utterances. At what point is lexical access completed for upcoming words in an utterance? More specifically, how far does planning of the semantic aspect of upcoming words lead that of the phonological aspect?

In order to distinguish the discreteness and advance-planning questions more precisely, we begin with the working assumption that lexical access in production can be roughly divided into two steps. In the first step, *lemma access*, a mapping is achieved between a concept-to-be-lexicalized and a *lemma*, an abstract symbol representing the selected word as a semantic–syntactic entity. In the second step, *phonological access*, the lemma is translated into the word's phonological form. This two-step conception of lexical access has long been a part of language production theory. It has been used to interpret data from the study of normal speech errors (e.g., Dell, 1986; Fromkin, 1971; Garrett, 1975), aphasia (e.g., Butterworth, 1989; Saffran, Schwartz, & Marin, 1980) and a variety of experimental paradigms (e.g., Bock, 1987; Kempen & Huijbers, 1983; Levelt & Maassen, 1981; Levelt et al., 1991; Schriefers, Meyer, & Levelt, 1990).

The discreteness question concerns the nature and time-course of these two steps. The modular two-step hypothesis (Butterworth, 1989; Levelt et al., 1991; Schriefers et al., 1990) contends that lemma and phonological access are non-overlapping stages that operate on different inputs. In particular, semantic but not phonological information is active up to the point of lemma access, but the reverse is true during phonological access. A contrasting view, the interactive two-step hypothesis (Dell, 1986; Harley, 1984; Martin, Weisberg, & Saffran, 1989; Stemberger, 1985) conceives of lexical access in more continuous terms. Activation is predominantly semantic during lemma access, and activation is predominantly phonological during phonological access, but there is some activation of phonological information during lemma access, and some activation of semantic information during phonological access. Typically, this interactive view is implemented through spreading activation.

The distinction between lemma access and phonological access also informs the advance-planning question. Suppose that one were planning a three-word utterance. Let us refer to the lemma of word $n$ as $L(n)$ and to its phonological form as $P(n)$. The advance-planning question concerns the order of accessing lemmas and phonological forms. One possibility, which we call the lemma buffering hypothesis, states that several lemmas are selected before the corresponding phonological forms are filled in. In the simplest version of lemma buffering, the order of the steps might be: $//L(1)\ L(2)\ L(3)\ /\ P(1)\ P(2)\ P(3)//$. That is, the lemmas are all selected first, and the phonological forms are filled in later (see Kempen & Huijbers, 1983). However, because there must be a limit on the number of lemmas that can be buffered, a more plausible version of the lemma buffering hypothesis is that the size of the buffers is related to sentence structure. So, if there were a major structural boundary between words two and three, the step sequence might be: $//L(1)\ L(2)\ /\ P(1)\ P(2)\ //\ L(3)\ /\ P(3)//$. The most distinct alternative to lemma buffering is a word-by-word view in which the phonological form is retrieved sequentially for each lemma: $//L(1)\ /\ P(1)\ //\ L(2)\ /\ P(2)\ //\ L(3)\ /\ P(3)//$. Note that although lemma buffering implies the truth of the two-step hypothesis, it is neutral on the question of whether these steps are modular or interactive.

In the remainder of the paper we review the evidence on the discreteness and advance-planning questions, and introduce some new experiments of our own. We turn first to the discreteness question, which has recently been spotlighted by Schriefers et al. (1990) and Levelt et al. (1991), who used priming techniques to track the time-course of lexical access for single words.

**The discreteness question**

Recently, production researchers have turned to the priming techniques that have been so widely and successfully used to study language comprehension (Bock, 1986, 1987; Levelt et al., 1991; O'Seaghdha & Dell, 1991a, 1991b; O'Seaghdha, Dell, Peterson, & Juliano, in press; Schriefers et al., 1990). In doing so, they have sometimes devised new procedures and sometimes exploited the productive aspects of existing techniques. Thus, Schriefers et al. recently adapted a *picture interference* paradigm (e.g., Glaser & Dunglehoff, 1984; Lupker, 1979) to study the question of the modularity of lexical access in production.

The standard picture interference paradigm involves superimposing an interfering word on a picture-to-be-named. It is called an interference paradigm because presentation of a word usually interferes with picture naming relative to a condition in which the picture alone is presented. Schriefers et al. made one significant change to the standard procedure. Because they were interested in phonological rather than in graphemic effects, they presented the words auditorily. In their experiments, subjects named pictures in the presence of semantically or phonologically related spoken words, or in a variety of control conditions. To examine the time-course of semantic and phonological access, the relative onsets of pictures and words were varied such that the word onset preceded the picture by 150 ms, coincided with it, or lagged it by 150 ms.

Schriefers et al. found evidence of semantic interference, relative to unrelated control words, when the words preceded the pictures, but not in the two later word presentation conditions. In contrast, in the case of phonologically related words, they found facilitation relative to the unrelated condition for the two later word onset conditions, but no effect when the word onset preceded the picture. Thus, they were apparently able to distinguish rather elegantly between an early phase of semantic activation and a later phase of phonological activation.

The presence of semantic interference when the word preceded the picture is in agreement with previous findings with visual word presentation (e.g., Glaser & Dunglehoff, 1984), and thus Schriefers et al.'s conclusions concerning the time-course of semantic activation are likely correct. The mechanism leading to the facilitatory phonological effects is less clear. One possibility derives from the fact that the related words shared initial segments with the picture names. In the late presentation conditions, the conflicting final segments of the interfering words may not have had time to influence processing. As a result, the phonologically related condition may be functionally like an identity priming condition. Alternatively, the effects could be due to some processes that occur after phonological access, such as the kind of auditory–articulatory interactions described by Gordon and Meyer (1984). However, although we are less persuaded by the phonological time-course results than by the semantic ones, the results of Schriefers et al. are generally in accord with a modular two-step view of access.

Some additional evidence which may clarify the nature of phonological priming effects was provided by Levelt et al. (1991), who employed a related but different procedure. As in Schriefers et al., the primary task was to name pictures of concrete objects, and verbal materials were also presented auditorily. However, the auditory items, which occurred on less than one-third of the trials, were word or non-word targets requiring a lexical decision response. On most trials, subjects named the pictures, but on the target trials they made an auditory lexical decision before naming the picture. The targets were presented at a short (73 ms), medium (373 ms), or long (673 ms) delay after the onset of the pictures. As in Schriefers et al., there were unrelated, semantically related, and phonologically related conditions. In addition, Levelt et al. tested a mediated condition where the target was a phonological neighbor of a semantic relative (e.g., picture = *sheep*; semantic relative = *goat*; target = *goal*). According to Levelt et al., interactive spreading activation accounts predict that a priming effect should be observed for both the mediated and directly phonologically related targets, whereas finding phonological activation only in the direct condition would be compatible with a modular account in which phonological activation is confined to a discrete stage and restricted to selected lemmas.

Levelt et al. consistently found inhibitory effects of semantic and phonological relatedness at the short stimulus onset asynchronies (SOAs). However, they found no mediated phonological effect. Also, consistent with Schriefers et al., they found evidence of phonological but not semantic activation at the long delay. But the results contrasted with those of Schriefers et al. in two respects. First, there was no point at which semantic but not phonological activation was observed. The obvious explanation for this is that the targets always lagged the pictures. There was evidently time for phonological activation to occur before the lexical decisions were made, even at the shortest SOA. Secondly, the late phonological effect was inhibitory rather than facilitatory.

This pattern of phonological inhibition in the absence of semantic priming late in the production cycle receives independent confirmation in some recent research of our own (O'Seaghdha & Dell, 1991a). In this research, rather than exploring the time-course of lexical access, we examined a condition in which single words were fully prepared. Our rationale was that this condition provides a clear benchmark for production priming effects. We presented pairs of words at upper and lower locations on a CRT for 1500 ms. Subjects were instructed to read these words. After a 1000-ms blank interval, an arrow appeared, pointing to the former location of one of the words (Figure 1). The arrow was the subject's cue to prepare to say this word, and not the other one which we call the alternate. After 1000 ms of preparation time, one of two possibilities occurred. On two-thirds of the trials an asterisk appeared, signalling the subject to utter the prepared word. On the remaining critical trials, a probe word appeared, and the subject named this target instead of producing the prepared word. The target was related to either the prepared word or the alternate, or it was unrelated to either word. In separate experiments, the relatedness manipulation involved semantic and phonological targets. Just as in the long SOA conditions of Levelt et al., we found inhibition of words phonologically related to prepared words, but no effect for semantically related targets (see Table 1(a)). There was no effect of relatedness to the alternate word for either phonological or semantic targets, indicating that the

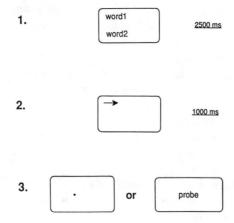

Figure 1.    *The procedure in the single-word preparation experiment of O'Seaghdha and Dell (1991a).*

Table 1.    *Naming latencies to word targets as a function of their relation to prepared utterances*

*(a)  Single-word preparation (choice procedure)*

|  | Semantic target | Form-related target |
|---|---|---|
| Prepared | 538 | 601 |
| Alternate | 543 | 582 |
| Unrelated | 548 | 583 |

*(b)  Sentence preparation (construction procedure)*

|  | Semantic target | | Form-related target | |
|---|---|---|---|---|
|  | Related | Unrelated | Related | Unrelated |
| Passive sentence (critical word early) | 672 | 680 | 728 | 706 |
| Active sentence (critical word late) | 683 | 681 | 702 | 721 |

*(c)  Sentence preparation (reiteration procedure)*

|  | Semantic target | | Form-related target | |
|---|---|---|---|---|
|  | Related | Unrelated | Related | Unrelated |
| Passive sentence (critical word early) | 580 | 607 | 627 | 618 |
| Active sentence (critical word late) | 584 | 599 | 615 | 627 |

phonological effect for prepared words was an effect of preparation, not merely of exposure to the word. Thus, our findings corroborate the results of Levelt et al., using a different procedure and a different response task.[1]

We provisionally interpret the phonological inhibition effect as competition between the discrepant phonological segments of the prepared word (the prime) and the presented word (the target) (O'Seaghdha et al., in press; Peterson, Dell, & Seaghdha, 1989). That is, when planning to produce the target, subjects are influenced by its similarity to the prime. Specifically, there is an increased tendency for segments from the prime to be inserted into the phonological plan of the target. In essence, we believe that the phonological inhibition effect is like the repeated phoneme effect in phonological speech errors (e.g., Dell, 1986). Any similarity between the production plans of activated words increases the chance that contrasting segments will move from one word to another. Thus, the contrasting segments of the prime tend to "slip" into the plan for producing the target. We assume that correction of this tendency incurs a cost in naming time or in any other response that depends on the phonological representation of the target (e.g., Bock, 1987). We also surmise that facilitation rather than inhibition was observed by Schriefers et al. because phonological competition did not arise in their procedure. This could be because no response is required to the words in the picture interference paradigm or because the words were not recognized soon enough to compete. (Similarly, phonological facilitation in production is found in the "implicit primes" task (Meyer, 1990, 1991) in which there is no phonological competition between contrasting segments.) We interpret the absence of a late semantic effect, in agreement with Levelt et al., as indicating a null or negligible level of semantic activation late in the process of producing a single-word utterance.

Because the application of priming techniques to the study of language production is such a recent development, the empirical picture on the discreteness question is still somewhat sketchy. Nonetheless, the framework of language production theory, in combination with the new empirical work, allows us to tentatively identify at least three phenomena to be explained. These are: early semantic activation without phonological activation (Schriefers et al.); the absence of mediated semantic–phonological priming in the presence of both direct semantic and direct phonological priming (Levelt et al.); and the presence of phonological priming in the absence of late semantic priming (all of the studies agree on this point). The first and last observations can be considered as two aspects of the time-course question, so we are left with two primary issues, both of which bear on whether the two steps of lexical access are discrete or continuous. These issues

---

[1]We used a naming task in the reported experiment, but we have obtained similar results with lexical decision (see O'Seaghdha & Dell, 1991a).

are the status of mediated semantic–phonological priming, and the time-course of semantic and phonological activation. Both Schriefers et al. and, more strongly, Levelt et al., favor a discrete, modular, two-step account of lexical access over an interactive spreading activation view, and they argue that the evidence supports the discrete account. However, we have recently argued (Dell & O'Seaghdha, 1991) that the evidence is compatible with a more interactive account, and that that account is to be preferred because of its ability to explain certain speech-error effects. We first outline the structure and motivation of the spreading activation framework, relying for the most part on the model of Dell (1986). Then we will consider how it addresses the mediation and time-course issues we have just identified.

## Lexical activation in an interactive framework

In this section, we adapt the spreading activation model of Dell (1986, 1988, 1990; Dell & Reich, 1981) to address the discreteness question. Like discrete stage models, non-discrete spreading activation models distinguish between semantic–conceptual units, lemma or word units, and phonological units. As shown in Figure 2, the units are organized into a network in which the connections allow for a bidirectional spread of activation between units at adjacent levels. For example, an activated word unit will pass activation downward to phonological units and upward to semantic units. Activation levels are positive real numbers

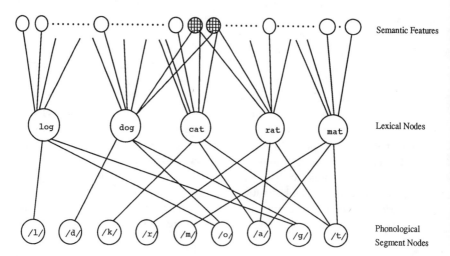

Figure 2.    *Lexical network structure in the spreading activation production model. The figure illustrates the case where two features (highlighted) are shared by the three semantically related lexical nodes. The phonological labels are informal. (From Dell & O'Seaghdha, 1991; copyright 1991 by the American Psychological Association.)*

and are determined by external inputs and a linear activation updating function with a decay factor. As described in Dell and O'Seaghdha (1991), lexical access involves the following six steps:

(1) The semantic units of the concept-to-be-lexicalized receive external inputs.

(2) Activation spreads in an unconstrained fashion throughout the network, as determined by the activation updating function.

(3) The most highly activated word unit is selected. In the case of sentence production, selection entails the linkage of this unit to the developing syntactic frame for the sentence (see, for example, Bock, 1982, 1987; Stemberger, 1985), and is followed by post-selection inhibition, setting the unit's activation to zero (see MacKay, 1987; Shattuck-Hufnagel, 1979).

(4) When the word is ready for phonological encoding, it is given a triggering jolt of activation. For multi-word utterances, which require advance planning, the timing of this external signal is controlled by the syntactic frame slot that the unit is linked to. In the case of a single-word utterance, as in the studies we are currently considering, we assume that the jolt is supplied immediately upon selection.

(5) Activation continues to spread as before, but because of the extra activation of the selected word unit the appropriate phonological units become significantly activated.

(6) The most active phonological units are selected and linked to slots in a constructed phonological wordshape frame, a data structure analogous to a syntactic frame. (Recall that we proposed an account of phonological inhibition effects above in terms of competition. This competition could arise in the filling of the slots of such wordshape frames.)

Much of the motivation of this interactive model lies in its ability to account for a range of speech-error phenomena, particularly the effects of the familiarity of the error string and the similarity of the target and error utterances. Semantic, phonological, and mixed word substitution errors are most relevant here. In these errors, the fact that the substituting and replaced words are very often from the same grammatical class has been taken as evidence that these are lexical rather than segmental errors (see Fay & Cutler, 1977). Phonological word substitutions, or malapropisms, are errors in which a word is replaced by a phonologically related word. For example, if the semantic units for *cat* are active, the word *cat* becomes active, and this, in turn, activates /k/, /ae/, and /t/. These active phonological units then send activation to all words connected to them, for example *mat* in Figure 2. Thus, phonologically related words acquire some activation and one of them may be erroneously selected (step 3). On this view, a malapropism is the result of activation spreading between word and phonological units prior to lexical selection. Semantic word substitutions are explained similarly, except that the competing words are activated by shared semantic features. Thus, *dog* shares some features with *cat* and therefore may compete with it at the selection step. Finally, a mixed error is a word substitution exhibiting both a semantic and a phonological relation (e.g., *start → stop*; *cat → rat*). The important point about mixed errors is that they are much more likely than would be predicted from the independent contributions of phonological and semantic similarity (Dell & Reich, 1981; Harley, 1984; Martin, Weisberg, & Saffran, 1989). Therefore, mixed errors suggest an interactive influence of semantics and phonology in lexical selection.

We now examine the activation levels of words embodying the semantic, phonological, and mixed semantic–phonological relations we have just described, as well as the mediated semantic–phonological relation of Levelt et al., in an implementation of the spreading activation network depicted in Figure 2. The challenge to the spreading activation model is to account for the new empirical data without compromising the attributes that enable it to account for the word substitution errors.

### Simulation of lexical activation levels

Consider how the activation of words exemplifying the relevant relations is simulated in the network depicted in Figure 2. With this model, we can compare the activation of an intended word, *cat*, a phonologically related word, *mat*, a semantically related word, *dog*, a semantically and phonologically related word, *rat*, and a word that is phonologically related to the semantic relative, *log*. We call *rat* the mixed word and *log* the mediated word.

By allowing activation to spread in the network we are simulating steps 1 and 2 of the spreading activation model. The simulation was implemented with the following rules:

(1) *Updating function*: $a(j,t) = a(j,t-1)(1-q) + Input\ (j,t)$

This is the standard linear activation function: $a(j,t)$ is the activation of unit $j$ at time $t$, *Input* $(j,t)$ is the input to $j$, and $q$ is the decay rate.

(2) *Input function*: $Input\ (j,t) = \sum_i w(i,j)a(i,t-1)$

This is the standard weighted sum rule, where $w(i,j)$ is the weight from unit $i$ to unit $j$, all the weights are equal to $p$, $0 < p < 1$, and the summation is over all units.

(3) All connections are bidirectional

We set $p = .1$ and $q = .4$, choosing these settings to keep the overall level of activation within reasonable bounds (Dell, 1986, 1988, 1990; Shrager, Hogg, & Huberman, 1987). By using a single connection weight, $p$, for top-down and bottom-up connections our model has the same degree of "interactiveness" as previous implementations that used interaction to account for the lexical bias effect (the tendency for slips to create words rather than non-words), the repeated phoneme effect (the tendency for sounds in similar environments to exchange), and other errors (Dell, 1986, 1988, 1990).

To enable us to simulate degrees of semantic relatedness, we arbitrarily assigned ten semantic "features" to each lexical concept. In separate simulations, the words semantically related to the intended word *cat* (*dog* and *rat*) shared one, two, or three features with it. Phonologically related words shared two out of three phonological segment nodes. Figure 3 shows activation of all of the word nodes as a function of time. In Figure 3(a), semantically related words share one feature, in Figure 3(b) they share two features, and in Figure 3(c) they share three features. After ten cycles, each figure shows that *cat* attains the highest activation,

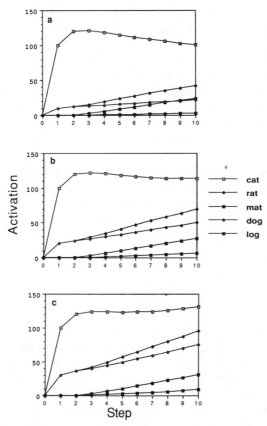

Figure 3.  *Activation of word nodes as a function of time. Panels a, b, and c show the results when one, two, and three semantic features are shared by* cat, rat, *and* dog. *(From Dell & O'Seaghdha, 1991; copyright 1991 by the American Psychological Association.)*

*rat* has the next highest activation, and *log* attains only a small fraction of the activation of *rat*. The semantically and phonologically related words *dog* and *mat* are intermediate to *rat* and *log*, their relative activation levels depending on the number of shared semantic features.

It is easy to show that these activation levels translate into the required pattern of speech errors when a stochastic selection rule (e.g., McClelland & Rumelhart, 1981) is applied (see Dell & O'Seaghdha, 1991). For present purposes, it is sufficient to consider the activation levels. The important result is that there is approximately a tenfold difference in activation levels between the mixed condition (*rat*) and the mediated condition (*log*). This is because in the spreading activation model the mixed condition receives convergent, additive activation from semantic and phonological sources, whereas the mediated condition receives divergent activation in which the contributions of semantic and phonological relations are diluted. In the mixed case, *rat* receives activation from semantic and phonological nodes shared with *cat*. But in the mediated case, *log* receives only phonological activation from the mediating word *dog*, and this activation is scaled down by the relatively weak activation of the mediator. The amount of activation of the mediating condition can be estimated by the activations of the direct semantic (*dog*) and phonological (*mat*) conditions. If *dog* and *mat* are activated to, say, 20% of the level of the intended word *cat*, then *log*'s activation will be on the order of 4% of *cat* ($.2 \times .2$) (see Dell & O'Seaghdha, 1991). Thus, to account for the absence of mediated priming, we are making the strong assumption that competing words are normally not nearly as activated as the target word. Whether this is true or not is difficult to tell since we cannot measure these activations directly. Nonetheless, our account works in the sense that it allows for speech error effects that we attribute to interaction such as mixed errors, but it does not demand that appreciable levels of mediated priming occur. We now consider in more detail the implications of the simulation for the mediated priming issue, and for the time-course of semantic and phonological activation.

### Mediated priming

The first outcome to be explained is the absence of a mediated semantic–phonological priming effect in the Levelt et al. study. Recall that Levelt et al. suggested that the spreading activation model might lose its ability to account for the mixed error effect if the parameters were set in such a way that mediated priming was not observed. In our simulation, activation in the mixed condition was substantial, but in the mediated condition it was quite small. Nonetheless, our spreading activation model does suggest that priming in the mediated condition should be small rather than non-existent. What then is the true status of mediated semantic–phonological priming?

Apart from the Levelt et al. study, the issue of mediated priming has been addressed only in the receptive domain, and primarily for semantic mediation, for example, *lion* priming *stripes* through the mediation of *tiger* (Balota & Lorch, 1986; de Groot, 1983; McNamara & Altarriba, 1988; but see McNamara & Healy, 1988). We note that semantic–phonological mediation appears to involve a better defined manipulation than the semantic mediation studies. Although careful norming procedures were employed in the semantic mediation studies, it may be impossible to provide an entirely satisfactory discrimination between direct and mediated priming within the semantic domain. That is, though the items may have a very low probability of being mentioned as associates, they may nonetheless have some semantic relationship. For example, *sky – color* and *navy – tank* are among the mediated pairs in Balota and Lorch (1986) and McNamara and Altarriba (1988). In addition, several of the targets in these studies were antonyms of the mediating words or bore a contrastive relation to the mediators (e.g., *black – white*; *summer – winter*) and therefore shared many features with them. On our account of spreading activation, for any items that are to some extent directly activated there is convergent activation from the prime and the mediator. Therefore, there could be substantial priming in some cases. These considerations suggest that the mediated priming effect should be smaller in the case of semantic–phonological mediation than in the case of semantic–semantic mediation.

Another factor that may account for Levelt et al.'s null mediated priming effect is their choice of lexical decision as the response task. Balota and Lorch (1986) observed mediated semantic priming in naming but not in lexical decision (see also de Groot, 1983). McNamara and Altarriba (1988) did observe mediated semantic priming in lexical decision, but only under conditions that excluded directly related pairs or that made it difficult to notice whether the pairs were related. This suggests that mediated priming effects may be obscured by the relatedness checking that often characterizes lexical decision (Balota & Lorch, 1986; McNamara & Altarriba, 1988).

Thus, we conclude that mediated semantic–phonological effects should be small, but we leave the determination of just how small to future research. The spreading activation model suggests that there may be a slight effect, whereas the modular two-step account states that there should be none.

*Time-course of semantic and phonological activation*

In accordance with the modular view of lexical access, Schriefers et al. (1990) observed semantic activation early in the process of picture naming when there was no evidence of a phonological effect. Levelt et al. (1991) also argue that their findings are compatible with an early stage of exclusively semantic activation. However, we note that their data do not provide direct evidence of this. Rather, they observed both semantic and phonological effects at the shortest picture–

word asynchrony (73 ms). The claim that there is an early stage of exclusively semantic activation then depends on the reasonable assumption that this stage has been passed at the time of lexical decision even in the short SOA condition. At the other end of the lexical production process, Schriefers et al. (1990), Levelt et al. (1991) and O'Seaghdha and Dell (1991a, 1991b) observed phonological activation in the absence of semantic activation late in the process of producing one-word utterances.

Given these data and our discussion of mediated priming, our general answer to the discreteness question is that the production system is globally modular, but locally interactive (see Dell & O'Seaghdha, 1991). To explain what we mean here, we turn again to the spreading activation model.

*Role of external signals.* In a full-scale model of language production (see Dell, 1986, and our summary above), the scheduling of semantic and phonological activation in the lexical network is strongly influenced by external inputs from modular linguistic rule systems. These signals add greatly to the level of activation of the units receiving them, and thus strongly influence the levels of activation at the different levels of the lexical network. In essence, these signals impose the rule-governed structure of language at each level by determining when a selected unit is realized at a lower level.

If our limited model in Figure 2 were expanded to include external signals, an external signal would come from the conceptual system, as well as from the syntax (which sends a signal to each selected word unit), the phonology (which sends a signal to each selected phonological segment), and the corresponding structural frames at lower levels (e.g., MacKay's, 1987, sequence nodes at the feature and motoric levels).

Consider the following illustration from Dell and O'Seaghdha (1991). Figure 4 shows a simplified network consisting of a single column of semantic, word, phonological, and phonetic/articulatory nodes. Assume that $p = .1$, that $q = .4$, and that a standard external signal of 1.0 is given to the semantic unit. After eight time steps, the lexical node is selected and set to zero, and receives a signal of 1.0 from the syntax. After eight more steps, the phonological node is selected in the same way, a standard signal from the phonology is given to it, and so on. Figure 5 shows the activation levels of the nodes over time. The important feature of the figure is that there is a distinct time-course of semantic and form-related activation. Viewed from a distance one sees a modular system, in which the initial stage involves no phonological activation and where the final stages have next to no semantic activation. Thus, the time-course is globally modular. The sequence of external signals is purely serial and top-down and, with these parameters, the external signals largely determine the time-course of activation. However, the top-down and bottom-up spreading activation process within the lexicon does contribute some local interaction. When most of the activation is at level $N$, there is also some at levels $N + 1$ and $N - 1$. It is this exchange of activation between

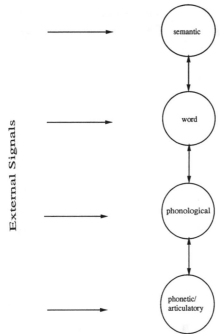

Figure 4. *A simplified network in which external signals are received in sequence by nodes at four representational levels. (From Dell & O'Seaghdha, 1991; copyright 1991 by the American Psychological Association.)*

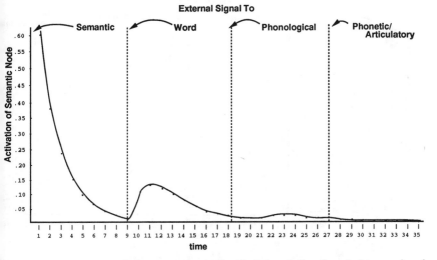

Figure 5. *The activation of the semantic, word, phonological, and phonetic–articulatory nodes of Figure 4 as a function of time. At time steps 0, 9, 18, and 27, external signals of 1.0 are sent to the semantic, word, phonological, and phonetic–articulatory nodes, respectively. (From Dell & O'Seaghdha, 1991; copyright 1991 by the American Psychological Association.)*

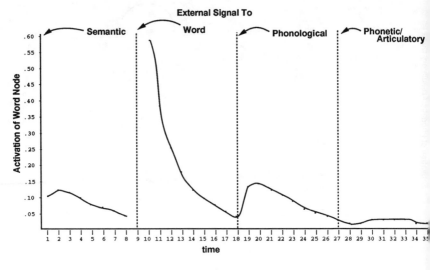

(b)

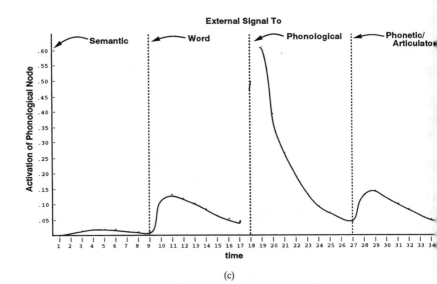

(c)

Figure 5    continued.

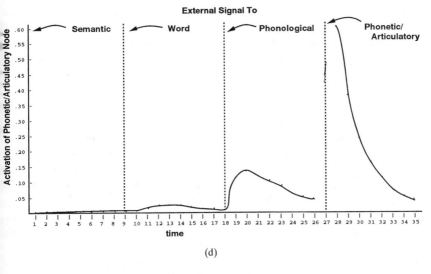

(d)

Figure 5    continued.

nodes at adjacent levels that gives the spreading activation model the ability to account for interactive error effects such as mixed errors.

We conclude that studies of the time-course of the access of single words support the claim that the system is globally modular. This is because linguistic rule systems supply external activation to discrete levels of the lexical network (Dell, 1986; Dell & Reich, 1981). However, this does not mean that interaction within the lexical network can be discounted. Rather, speech errors suggest that interaction in the lexical system allows for the mingling of information from different levels. In the spreading activation model, this mingling is most evident when activation sources converge.

## The advance planning question

Thus far, we have considered the time-course of the production of single words, specifically the question of the discreteness of lemma and phonological form retrieval. Obviously, things become more complex when these issues are addressed in the context of sentence production. We begin by reviewing the rough consensus regarding the components of sentence production that has emerged primarily from the study of speech errors and other dysfluencies in natural and experimental contexts.

Theorists have identified three major stages of production planning: a conceptual, a linguistic, and an articulatory stage (see Levelt, 1989). In the conceptu al stage, a "message" or semantic representation of the utterance is formed. Fo our purposes, this may be viewed as an organized set of propositions standing i relation to a speech act (e.g., inform, request). The goal of the second stage linguistic encoding, is to turn the message into the form of a sentence o sentences. And the goal of the third, articulatory stage is to produce speech. Ou primary focus will be the linguistic encoding stage. Nearly all production theorist agree that linguistic encoding involves the construction of more than one distinc linguistic representation of the utterance (e.g., Bock, 1982; Dell, 1986; Garrett 1975; Kempen, 1978; Levelt, 1989; MacKay, 1982; Shattuck-Hufnagel, 1979 Stemberger, 1985). In keeping with our earlier distinction between lemma acces and phonological access, these theorists agree that there are distinct levels o utterance representation whose basic elements are lemmas and sublexica phonological units. The first level, which is constituted of lemmas, encodes th syntactic structure of the sentence. We refer to it as the syntactic level, though w recognize that it may also encode other kinds of linguistic information and, i fact, may consist of more than one representation. The second level is constitute of phonological segments, and it encodes the phonological forms of lexical items

Thus, the distinction between lemmas and phonological forms that we hav been working with is also critical to distinguishing the syntactic and phonologica representations of sentences. With regard to advance planning, the focus o interest becomes the time-course of the construction of these representations. W introduced this topic earlier in the context of the lemma buffering hypothesi which states that, in sentence production, multiple lemmas must be held i readiness at the syntactic level pending the later activation of corresponding unit at the phonological level. The best evidence on the nature of lemma bufferin comes from the speech errors we have discussed, and from patterns of pausing an hesitation in speech (e.g., Butterworth, 1980; Cooper & Paccia-Cooper, 1980 Ford, 1982; Garrett, 1980; Holmes, 1988). These studies are in agreement that th extent of advance planning at the syntactic level exceeds the extent of planning a the phonological level.

In the case of speech errors, syntactic-level speech errors (e.g., word exchange such as "*The test will be about discussing the class*") span greater distances tha phonological-level errors (e.g., sound exchanges such as "*thollow hud*"). Becaus this suggests that the selection of lemmas can lead the selection of their phonologi cal forms, it indicates some kind of buffering of lemmas. Speech error data als show that most word exchanges and over 90% of sound exchanges involve unit from the same clause (Garrett, 1975). Likewise, hesitations in spontaneous speec often occur at clause boundaries (e.g., Holmes, 1988), and clause boundarie block the application of some phonological rules (Cooper & Paccia-Cooper 1980). Therefore, a good working hypothesis is that the syntactic representation i constructed in clausal units (Butterworth, 1980; Garrett, 1980). That is, lemma within a clause may be simultaneously processed, but those in separate clauses typically are not.

A specific model in which the clausal structure of the utterance determines when lemmas are retrieved has recently been proposed by Levelt (1989). The model distinguishes between the initial activation of lemmas, which occurs as the underlying propositions of the utterance are scanned, and the insertion of lemmas into a syntactic tree. The relevant unit of the initial scanning is the "deep" clause or proposition, and that of the insertion is the "surface" clause.

This model finds support in studies of hesitations in spontaneous and read speech. In spontaneous speech, a hesitation is likely after the matrix verb (*expect* in the examples) when it is followed by either a finite (e.g., *I expect the cat will chase the mouse*) or a non-finite (e.g., *I expect the cat to chase the mouse*) clause (Ford, 1982; Holmes, 1988; see Ford & Holmes, 1978). This result can be seen as reflecting the "deep" clausal organization corresponding to the initial scan component of Levelt's proposal. In read speech, finite clause boundaries attract more pauses than non-finite ones (Holmes, 1988). This sensitivity to surface clausal organization in read speech is exactly what would be expected from Levelt's account on the assumption that reading aloud involves the insertion of lemmas into a syntactic tree, but not the creation and scanning of a propositional representation.

If the clause is the domain of advance planning at the syntactic level, what is the corresponding domain at the phonological level? The speech-error evidence that word exchanges span longer distances than sound exchanges suggests that phonological advance planning is less extensive than the advance planning of lemmas, but it does not identify a domain over which phonological planning operates. At least three hypotheses on the extent of phonological planning warrant consideration:

(1) *The word-by-word hypothesis.* Only the word about to be uttered and the following word are prepared, regardless of the structure of the sentence. This view has the advantage of simplicity and it may be all that is needed in order to accommodate phonological and phonetic rules (Levelt, 1989). That is, the proper phonetic form of a word can be known as long as the phonological forms of only the adjacent words are known.

(2) *The syntactic-structure hypothesis.* Words are phonologically planned in accordance with syntactic units. Given that phonological advance planning should be less extensive than syntactic, the most common proposal has been that phonological forms are retrieved in subclausal chunks corresponding to major syntactic phrases (e.g., Dell, 1986; Garrett, 1975; Lapointe, 1985).

(3) *The prosodic-structure hypothesis.* Several researchers have recently suggested that phonological advance planning may be related to the prosodic structure of the utterance rather than to its syntactic structure (Bock, 1982;

Ferreira, 1991; Gee & Grosjean, 1983; Garrett, 1980; Levelt, 1989; Selkirk, 1984). In prosodic structures, phonological words are concatenated to form phonological phrases which are, prototypically, a content word and any preceding function words. One or more phonological phrases may then constitute an intonational phrase, a level of analysis over which intonational contours are computed. Some studies of pausing have found that the prosodic hierarchy does better than syntactic structure at predicting pauses (Ferreira & Clifton, 1987; Gee & Grosjean, 1983), suggesting that prosodic grouping may also play a role at the syntactic level (see above). For the most part, however, prosodic units such as phonological phrases correspond to syntactic phrases (e.g., subject NPs), and it is therefore very difficult to distinguish between the syntactic and prosodic hypotheses.

At this point, there is simply not enough evidence to make a strong argument for any of the hypotheses concerning either planning of lemmas or planning at the phonological level. What is clearly needed is some way to experimentally assess advance planning of both lemmas and phonological forms. In earlier experimental work on planning in production (e.g., Kempen & Huijbers, 1983; Levelt & Maassen, 1981), researchers measured times to generate utterances while manipulating variables that would likely affect the difficulty of utterance planning at the different levels of processing. This research has helped to make the case for the distinction between concepts, lemmas, and phonological forms. We believe that the production priming techniques used by Schriefers et al. (1990), Levelt et al. (1991), and O'Seaghdha and Dell (1991a) may provide an additional experimental tool for studying the advance planning question, one that has the advantage of providing relatively direct measures of access processes. In the following section, we outline how this could be accomplished, and we present the results of two experiments to illustrate our suggestions.

*Production priming and the advance planning question*

The essentials of the production priming methodology used by Levelt et al. (1991) and O'Seaghdha and Dell (1991a) can be summarized as follows:

(1) The subject view a display whose purpose is to induce the preparation of an utterance.

(2) The subject prepares the utterance.

(3a) On a majority of the trials, the subject simply produces the prepared utterance and the trial ends.

(3b) On critical trials, a target word is displayed. The subject responds to the target and may or may not be required to produce the prepared utterance before the trial ends. The latency and accuracy of responses to targets are the dependent measures of interest.

Thus, production plans serve as primes, and the extent to which the primes influence responses to related targets assesses the extent and nature of the plans. Let us consider some of the experimental options that are available within this general scheme.

## Inducing the preparation of utterances

At least four techniques are available to elicit the preparation of more or less pre-specified utterances:

(1) *Reiteration.* The most obvious procedure is to supply the subject with the content of the utterance, under instruction to produce it on a given cue (e.g., Balota, Boland, & Shields, 1989; Sternberg, Monsell, Knoll, & Wright, 1978). This procedure has the advantage that the utterance to be prepared can be completely pre-specified. However, there are two disadvantages. First, because subjects are merely repeating prescribed materials, we cannot be sure that production processes, particularly higher-level processes, are sufficiently engaged.[2] The second disadvantage is that the eliciting display (e.g., a visual display of a phrase to be repeated) may cause priming that cannot easily be separated from the effects of productive processes. The next procedure addresses this concern.

(2) *Choice procedure.* Here, subjects are given not one but two potential utterances. Then they are cued to prepare one of the two. Because two potential utterances are presented, but only one is prepared, the effect of the eliciting display can be factored out. This was the procedure we used in the experiments mentioned above (O'Seaghdha & Dell, 1991a), and it is related to the response priming procedure of Meyer and Gordon (1985; Gordon & Meyer, 1987).

(3) *Construction.* Many variations are possible under this heading, but their common theme is that subjects are given a set of ingredients together with instructions on how to combine them and are required to produce utterances in keeping with the instructions. For example, in one of the experiments that we report below subjects prepared sentences such as *"The boxer removed the coat"* from a quasi-propositional representation, REMOVE (BOXER, COAT).

(4) *Pictorial displays.* Many production researchers prefer to use pictures as eliciting displays (e.g., Bock, 1986; Levelt et al., 1991; Schriefers et al., 1990). By using carefully selected and normed pictures, it is possible to obtain reasonably consistent descriptions from subjects. The sequence from picture recognition, through sentence formulation and lexical selection, to the phonological specification of an utterance, conforms better to the process of natural language production than the other methods. However, working with pictures necessarily intro-

---

[2]But see Potter and Lombardi (1990) for recent evidence that reiteration of sentences may entail regeneration of utterances from conceptual representations.

duces variability in the utterances and thus limits the practical complexity of the desired utterances to single words or simple phrases or sentences.

## Relations between targets and utterances

One of the greatest advantages of these priming techniques for studying lemma and phonological form retrieval is that one can index different levels of representation by using different prime–target relations. Both Levelt et al. (1991) and Schriefers et al. (1990) were able to track the time-course of lemma and phonological access by comparing phonological and semantic prime–target relations. We also used these relations in the experiments we report below. However, a new wrinkle in our research is that we distinguish between phonological facilitation and phonological inhibition and argue that these may reflect different aspects of lemma and phonological access.

## Choice of task

Two standard tasks, word naming and lexical decision, are widely employed in the priming literature. Naming is the more straightforward of the two tasks; it is both simple and natural. In addition, it involves a production component, and thus to some extent taps into the systems whose representations we wish to investigate. A potential limitation of word naming is that performance may be so fast and skilled that it is largely immune to interference and insensitive to facilitation (Forster, 1981). Lexical decision, in contrast, is more artificial, but has the advantage that priming effects are often larger than in the naming task. For example, Levelt et al.'s (1991) use of auditory lexical decision to track lexical access in production resulted in effects as large as 100 ms. However, there is a potential drawback of using lexical decision in production priming experiments. In contrast to the receptive priming situation where subjects typically merely read the prime and then respond to the target, in a production priming experiment subjects prepare an utterance, but on some fraction of trials are instead required to respond to a target. If the specified response to this target is lexical decision rather than naming, subjects are required to switch tasks as well as responses when the target is presented. This complication would be expected to slow latencies and thus make the task a less direct index of the state of preparation at the moment of target presentation. Therefore we tend to favor the use of naming rather than lexical decision, provided it proves sufficiently sensitive.

## Experiments on sentence production

We have recently completed two experiments investigating the advance planning question using production priming (O'Seaghdha & Dell, 1991b). Both experiments employed naming as the response task. The first involved a construction procedure. On each trial subjects viewed a visually displayed propositional representation of a potential utterance. On half the trials, propositions such as *REMOVE (BOXER, COAT)* were shown, and subjects immediately began to prepare simple past tense declarative sentences, in this case "*The boxer removed the coat*". On the other half of the trials the propositional display contained the word *by*, for example, *REMOVE (BY BOXER, COAT)*. On these trials, subjects were instructed to prepare a passive sentence, "*The coat was removed by the boxer*". Subjects pressed a response button as soon as they had prepared each utterance. Half a second after the button press, the subject either saw an asterisk on two-thirds of the trials, or a target word on the other one-third of trials. The asterisk was simply a signal for the subject to produce the prepared sentence. If a target appeared, the subject named it as quickly as possible. After the subject's naming response, an asterisk appeared and the subject produced the prepared sentence. The target words were designed to tap into the representation of the logical direct object of the prepared sentence (e.g., *COAT*). In the passive condition, the critical word was early in the first phrase of the sentence. In the active condition, it was the last word of the sentence. The target words were either phonologically related to the critical word (*COAL*), semantically related (*SHIRT*), or unrelated. The unrelated target words served as related targets for other sentences tested with other subjects, following standard counterbalancing procedures.

The phonological priming effects (unrelated RT – related RT) revealed a compelling dependence in the planning process (see Table 1(b)). When the critical word was early in the sentence, responses to phonologically related targets were significantly inhibited ($-22$ ms). This result extends the inhibition found in the single-word case (O'Seaghdha & Dell, 1991a), described earlier, to sentences. It is also important in that the critical word in this case is not, strictly speaking, the first word in the sentence. Rather, each sentence began with the determiner *the*. In contrast with this inhibitory outcome, when the critical word was late in the sentence we found a significant facilitatory effect for phonologically related primes ($+19$ ms). So, the phonological relatedness effect is turned around when the critical word is not imminent. We take the difference in phonological priming to reflect a difference in the nature of the sound-based plan for early and late words in an utterance. The harder thing to explain is the nature of this difference. We offer the following tentative interpretation, based on the notion of phonological competition described earlier.

We view the inhibitory effect as indicative of a state in which the access of the phonological form of the prime is complete or nearly complete. Similarity-based competition occurs only when both the identical and the contrasting segments of the prime are present. The identical segments must be there so that the target contacts the representation of the prime. The contrasting segments of the prime must be there to compete with the segments of the target. Thus we argue that, in the passive condition, the phonological planning of the second word in the sentence, *COAT*, was quite advanced.

The facilitatory effect obtained in the active condition, in which *COAT* is the last word in the sentence plan, reflects a lesser degree of planning of the word. In this case, the segments of *COAT* that would contrast with *COAL* are not present in sufficient strength to generate competition. In the absence of this competition, the opportunity arises for facilitation due to similarity to come into play. This might occur through preliminary activation of the initial segments of *COAT* and/or through the mediation of a shared wordshape frame (see Dell, 1986; Stemberger, 1990). We are tempted to conclude that the facilitatory effect indicates a stage in which only lemma access of *COAT* has been effected, whereas the inhibitory effect indexes full phonological access. In fact, this is exactly the case in a model of form-related priming that we have developed to account for the effects of frequency, masking, and homophony in the receptive domain (O'Seaghdha et al., in press; Peterson et al., 1989). However, pending development of an explicit production-oriented priming model, a more conservative conclusion is simply that inhibition indicates a great deal of progress toward a full specification of the critical word's form, whereas facilitation indicates a much lesser degree of preparation.

The results for semantically related targets in the sentence construction experiment were less informative. The effects for the early and late conditions were 8 and −2 ms (see Table 1(b)) and were not significant. Thus, we were not able to contrast semantic and phonological aspects of advance planning in this experiment. We suggested earlier that construction should, in principle, engage production processes more fully than reiteration. However, in this case, the demands of the construction task may have prevented the engagement of semantic processes. Subjects may have been fully occupied by the need to rearrange the words according to the relevant syntactic formulae. A second experiment in which we employed the reiteration procedure instead of construction suggests that this may indeed have been the case.

In this experiment, subjects simply saw the sentences in either the active or passive versions for 1500 ms, and after a blank interval of 1000 ms were presented with either the signal to repeat the sentence or a target word. The results for phonologically related targets mirrored those of the previous experiment – inhibition in the early, passive condition, and facilitation in the late, active condition. But here we found a significant semantic effect as well, 27 and 15 ms for the early and late cases, respectively (see Table 1(c)). Most importantly, the general time-course of the phonological priming effects differed from that of semantic effects as shown by a significant triple interaction of type of relation, relatedness, and sentence structure (active or passive). It appears that position has much less influence on the amount and direction of semantic priming than it did with phonological priming.

This is exactly the result one would expect from the claim that planning at the lemma level exceeds that at the phonological level. The significant semantic and phonological facilitation in the active condition, where the critical word was late, can be taken as evidence of lemma retrieval. We cannot rule out the possibility that there is some phonological activation in this condition, but we can say that phonological activation in the early position is much stronger. Therefore, the kind of phonological access associated with inhibition lags behind lemma retrieval, giving evidence for some kind of lemma buffering.

Earlier, we introduced three contrasting hypotheses of advance planning at the phonological level: the word-by-word, syntactic structure, and prosodic structure hypotheses. However, our experiments do not fully arbitrate between these hypotheses. All three can accommodate a finding that coat in *"The coat..."* is phonologically ready prior to the utterance of *the*. Similarly, all three can deal with the absence of phonological inhibition for a word at the end of a single-clause sentence. The results do place some constraints on the syntactic and prosodic hypotheses, though. They suggest that the advance planning indexed by inhibition does not include a whole clause or an entire intonational phrase. (Subjects typically spoke the sentences in one intonational phrase). Whether the inhibition effect is present only on the next word or on words in the current phonological or syntactic phrase remains to be seen. We are currently studying this question by examining the inhibition effect with a choice procedure. For example, phrases such as *"COAT"*, *"The COAT"*, *"Another COAT"*, *"In the COAT"*, *"Around the COAT"*, *"The big COAT"* and *"The very warm COAT"* can be compared as production primes for *COAL*, in order to examine the effects of additional words with differing prosodic and syntactic characteristics on advance planning within phrases.

## Conclusions

Two questions have guided our inquiry into the time-course of lexical access: the question of the discreteness of the semantic–syntactic and phonological aspects of access, and the question of the extent of advance planning of these aspects. Our conclusions are, for the most part, in agreement with the standard view of production (e.g., Garrett, 1975; Levelt, 1989) in which the production system distinguishes between form-related and meaning-related processes. The reach of advance planning appears to be different for meaning and form, and meaning and form also appear to be separable over the time-course of the retrieval of individual words. Though this evidence tends to favor the idea of discrete stages in production, we believe that a degree of local interaction in the course of lemma and phonological access is necessary to account for mixed semantic–phonological speech errors. These effects can be accounted for entirely by assuming that the phonological and semantic–syntactic representations of words are connected in a lexical network. That is, the interaction is a product of lexical retrieval processes, not of the way that syntactic and phonological rule systems are represented and used.

The empirical focus of our paper has been on a still rather small body of recent research that applies priming techniques to the study of production. A principal advantage of this method is that it has the potential of providing relatively direct measures of activation at more than one level of representation. This potential was exploited by Levelt et al. (1991) and Schriefers et al. (1990) to reveal aspects of the time-course of semantic and phonological activation in the retrieval of single words. Likewise, our own initial studies of sentence production enabled us to discriminate between phonological and semantic levels of advance planning. Thus, the feasibility of using priming techniques to study production appears to be established. Given the level of agreement within the field on the overall architecture of the production system, we expect to see considerable advances in this decade in the detailed exploration of the subtler aspects of the control and coordination of language production.

# References

Balota, D.A., Boland, J.E., & Shields, L. (1989). Priming in pronunciation: Beyond pattern recognition and onset latency. *Journal of Memory and Language, 28*, 14–36.

Balota, D.A., & Lorch, R.F. (1986). Depth of automatic spreading activation: Mediated priming effects in pronunciation but not in lexical decision. *Journal of Experimental Psychology: Learning, Memory, and Cognition, 12*, 336–345.

Bock, J.K. (1982). Towards a cognitive psychology of syntax: Information processing contributions to sentence formulation. *Psychological Review, 89*, 1–47.

Bock, J.K. (1986). Syntactic persistence in language production. *Cognitive Psychology, 18*, 355–387.

Bock, J.K. (1987). An effect of accessibility of word forms on sentence structures. *Journal of Memory and Language, 26*, 119–137.

Burgess, R.C., Tanenhaus, M.K., & Seidenberg, M. (1989). Context and lexical access: Implications of nonword interference for lexical ambiguity research. *Journal of Experimental Psychology: Learning, Memory, and Cognition, 15*, 620–632.

Butterworth, B. (1980). Evidence from pauses in speech. In B. Butterworth (Ed.), *Language production* (Vol. 1, pp. 155–176). London: Academic Press.

Butterworth, B. (1989). Lexical access in speech production. In W. Marslen-Wilson (Ed.), *Lexical representation and process* (pp. 108–135). Cambridge, MA: MIT Press.

Cooper, W.E., & Paccia-Cooper, J. (1980). *Syntax and speech.* Cambridge, MA: Harvard University Press.

Dell, G.S. (1986). A spreading activation theory of retrieval in language production. *Psychological Review, 93*, 283–321.

Dell, G.S. (1988). The retrieval of phonological forms in production: Tests of predictions from a connectionist model. *Journal of Memory and Language, 27*, 124–142.

Dell, G.S. (1990). Effects of frequency and vocabulary type on phonological speech errors. *Language and Cognitive Processes, 4*, 313–349.

Dell, G.S., & O'Seaghdha, P.G. (1991). Mediated and convergent lexical priming in language production: A comment on Levelt et al. (1991). *Psychological Review.*

Dell, G.S., & Reich, P.A. (1981). Stages in sentence production: An analysis of speech error data. *Journal of Verbal Learning and Verbal Behavior, 20*, 611–629.

Fay, D., & Cutler, A. (1977). Malapropisms and the structure of the mental lexicon. *Linguistic Inquiry, 8*, 505–520.

Ferreira, F. (1991). Effects of length and syntactic complexity on initiation times for prepared utterances. *Journal of Memory and Language, 30,* 210–233.

Ferreira, F., & Clifton, C. (1987). *Planning and prosodic structure in sentence production.* Paper presented at the 28th annual meeting of the Psychonomic Society, Seattle.

Fodor, J.A. (1983). *The modularity of mind.* Cambridge, MA: MIT Press.

Ford, M. (1982). Sentence planning units: Implications for the speaker's representation of meaningful relations underlying sentences. In J. Bresnan (Ed.), *The mental representation of grammatical relations.* Cambridge, MA: MIT Press.

Ford, M., & Holmes, V.M. (1978). Planning units and syntax in sentence production. *Cognition, 6,* 35–53.

Forster, K.I. (1981). Priming and the effects of lexical and sentence contexts on naming time: Evidence for autonomous lexical processing. *Quarterly Journal of Experimental Psychology, 33A,* 465–495.

Fromkin, V.A. (1971). The nonanomalous nature of anomalous utterances. *Language, 47,* 27–52.

Garrett, M.F. (1975). The analysis of sentence production. In G.H. Bower (Ed.), *The psychology of learning and motivation* (Vol. 9, pp. 133–175). New York: Academic Press.

Garrett, M.F. (1980). Levels of processing in sentence production. In B. Butterworth (Ed.), *Language production* (Vol. 1, pp. 177–210). London: Academic Press.

Gee, J.P., & Grosjean, F. (1983). Performance structures: A psycholinguistic and linguistic appraisal. *Cognitive Psychology, 15,* 411–458.

Glaser, W.R., & Dunglehoff, F.-J. (1984). The time course of picture–word interference. *Journal of Experimental Psychology: Human Perception and Performance, 10,* 640–654.

Glucksberg, S., Kreuz, R.J., & Rho, S.H. (1986). Context can constrain lexical access: Implications for models of language comprehension. *Journal of Experimental Psychology: Learning, Memory, and Cognition, 12,* 323–335.

Gordon, P.C., & Meyer, D.E. (1984). Perceptual-motor processing of phonetic features in speech. *Journal of Experimental Psychology: Human Perception and Performance, 10,* 153–178.

Gordon, P.C., & Meyer, D.E. (1987). Control of serial order in rapidly spoken syllable sequences. *Journal of Memory and Language, 26,* 300–321.

Groot, A.M.B. de (1983). The range of automatic spreading activation in word priming. *Journal of Verbal Learning and Verbal Behavior, 22,* 417–436.

Harley, T. (1984). A critique of top-down independent level models of speech production: Evidence from non-plan-internal speech errors. *Cognitive Science, 8,* 191–219.

Holmes, V.M. (1988). Hesitations and sentence planning. *Language and Cognitive Processes, 3,* 323–361.

Kempen, G. (1978). Sentence construction by a psychologically plausible formulator. In R.N. Campbell & P.T. Smith (Eds.), *Recent advances in the psychology of language.* New York: Plenum.

Kempen, G., & Huijbers, P. (1983). The lexicalization process in sentence production and naming: Indirect election of words. *Cognition, 14,* 185–209.

Lapointe, S. (1985). A theory of verb form use in the speech of agrammatic aphasics. *Brain and Language, 24,* 100–155.

Levelt, W.J.M. (1989). *Speaking: From intention to articulation.* Cambridge, MA: MIT Press.

Levelt, W.J.M., & Maassen, B. (1981). Lexical search and order of mention in sentence production. In W. Klein & W.J.M. Levelt (Eds.), *Crossing the boundaries in linguistics: Studies presented to Manfred Bierwisch* (pp. 221–252). Dordrecht: Reidel.

Levelt, W.J.M., Schriefers, H., Vorberg, D., Meyer, A.S., Pechmann, T., & Havinga, J. (1991). The time course of lexical access in speech production: A study of picture naming. *Psychological Review, 98,* 122–142.

Lupker, S.J. (1979). The semantic nature of response competition in the picture–word interference task. *Memory and Cognition, 7,* 485–495.

MacKay, D.G. (1982). The problems of flexibility, fluency, and speed–accuracy trade-off in skilled behaviors. *Psychological Review, 89,* 483–506.

MacKay, D.G. (1987). *The organization of perception and action: A theory for language and other cognitive skills.* New York: Springer.

Martin, N., Weisberg, R.W., & Saffran, E.M. (1989). Variables influencing the occurrence of naming errors: Implications for a model of lexical retrieval. *Journal of Memory and Language, 28*, 462–485.

McClelland, J.L., & Rumelhart, D.E. (1981). An interactive activation model of context effects in letter perception. Part 1. An account of basic findings. *Psychological Review, 88*, 375–407.

McNamara, T.P., & Altarriba, J. (1988). Depth of spreading activation revisited: Semantic mediated priming occurs in lexical decisions. *Journal of Memory and Language, 27*, 545–559.

McNamara, T.P., & Healy, A.F. (1988). Semantic, phonological, and mediated priming in reading and lexical decisions. *Journal of Experimental Psychology: Learning, Memory, and Cognition, 14*, 389–409.

Meyer, A.S. (1990). The time course of phonological encoding in language production: The encoding of successive syllables of a word. *Journal of Memory and Language, 29*, 524–545.

Meyer, A.S. (1991). The time course of phonological encoding in language production: Phonological encoding inside a syllable. *Journal of Memory and Language, 30*, 69–89.

Meyer, D.E., & Gordon, P.C. (1985). Speech production: Motor programming of phonetic features. *Journal of Memory and Language, 24*, 3–26.

O'Seaghdha, P.G., & Dell, G.S. (1991a). Production primes: Prearticulatory activation of single words. Manuscript in preparation.

O'Seaghdha, P.G., & Dell, G.S. (1991b). Phonological and semantic indexing of the representations of prepared sentences. Manuscript in preparation.

O'Seaghdha, P.G., Dell, G.S., Peterson, R.R., & Juliano, C. (in press). Models of form-related priming in comprehension and production. In R. Reilly & N.E. Sharkey (Eds.), *Connectionist approaches to language processing*. Hillsdale, NJ: Erlbaum.

Peterson, R.R., Dell, G.S., & O'Seaghdha, P.G. (1989). A connectionist model of form-related priming effects. In *Proceedings of the 11th Annual Conference of the Cognitive Science Society* (pp. 196–203). Hillsdale, NJ: Erlbaum.

Potter, M.C., & Lombardi, L. (1990). Regeneration in the short-term recall of sentences. *Journal of Memory and Language, 29*, 633–654.

Saffran, E.M., Schwartz, M.F., & Marin, O.S.M. (1980). Evidence from aphasia: Isolating the components of a production model. In B. Butterworth (Ed.), *Language production* (Vol. 1, pp. 221–242). New York: Academic Press.

Schriefers, H., Meyer, A.S., & Levelt, W.J.M. (1990). Exploring the time course of lexical access in language production: Picture–word interference studies. *Journal of Memory and Language, 29*, 86–102.

Selkirk, E. (1984). *Phonology and syntax: The relation between sound and structure*. Cambridge, MA: MIT.

Shattuck-Hufnagel, S. (1979). Speech errors as evidence for a serial-order mechanism in sentence production. In W.E. Cooper & E.C.T. Walker (Eds.), *Sentence processing: Psycholinguistic studies presented to Merrill Garrett*. Hillsdale, NJ: Erlbaum.

Shrager, J., Hogg, T., & Huberman, B.A. (1987). Observations of phase transitions in spreading activation networks. *Science, 236*, 1092–1094.

Stemberger, J.P. (1985). An interactive activation model of language production. In W.W. Ellis (Ed.), *Progress in the psychology of language* (Vol. 1, pp. 143–186). Hillsdale, NJ: Erlbaum.

Stemberger, J.P. (1990). Wordshape errors in language production. *Cognition, 35*, 123–158.

Sternberg, S., Monsell, S., Knoll, R.L., & Wright, C.E. (1978). The latency and duration of rapid movement sequences: Comparisons of speech and typewriting. In G. Stelmach (Ed.), *Information processing in motor control and learning* (pp. 117–152). New York: Academic Press.

Tabossi, P. (1988). Accessing lexical ambiguity in different types of sentential context. *Journal of Memory and Language, 27*, 324–340.

Tanenhaus, M.K., Dell, G.S., & Carlson, G. (1987). Context effects and lexical processing: A connectionist approach to modularity. In J.L. Garfield (Ed.), *Modularity in knowledge representation and natural language understanding* (pp. 83–108). Cambridge, MA: MIT Press.

Van Petten, C., & Kutas, M. (1987). Ambiguous words in context: An event-related potential analysis of the time course of meaning activation. *Journal of Memory and Language, 26*, 188–208.

# Language Index

Afrikaans, 54
Arabic, 168, 187

Basque, 265n2

Chinese, 17, 63, 71

Dutch, 10n3, 17, 54, 115, 130, 187,
201, 214

English, 10, 31, 50, 168, 173, 183,
187, 192, 201, 216, 248, 265n2,
273
American, 213, 214, 216, 221, 224,
238, 240, 241, 248, 265n2, 278
British, 265n2

French, 248n3, 265n2, 271

German, 24, 54, 74, 187, 189n6, 214

Hebrew, 168

Italian, 173, 276

Japanese, 186, 187

Spanish, 50, 187, 188, 248

# Name Index

Abd-El-Jawad, H., 187
Abu-Salim, I., 187
Ackerman, N., 145, 281
Allport, D. A., 18
Altarriba, J., 299
Amrhein, P. C., 63, 67, 70, 77, 78, 83, 112, 137
Archangeli, D., 12, 263
Ashby, F. G., 118

Baars, B. J., 2, 18, 19, 188, 197
Bajo, M.-T., 63, 78, 81, 82, 83, 93, 94, 99
Balota, D. A., 202, 299, 307
Balzano, G. J., 69
Bassett, E., 72
Bayles, K., 148
Beattie, G., 2
Beauvois, M., 162
Béland, R., 278
Beller, H. K., 68
Berg, T., 183, 184, 185, 189n6, 190, 191, 214
Berge, 282
Berndt, R. S., 153, 173, 174
Biederman, I., 63
Bierwisch, Manfred, 6, 7, 8, 9, 23–58
Blanken, G., 281, 282, 283
Bloch, D., 149
Blumstein, S., 277, 278
Bock, J. K., 8, 108, 109, 110, 137, 166, 170, 201, 288, 289, 293, 295, 304, 305, 307
Boland, J. E., 307
Bolinger, D., 200
Bond, Z. S., 188, 189n5

Boomer, D. S., 183, 184, 187, 189, 214
Bourne, L. E., 71
Bower, G. H., 115
Boyes-Braem, P., 8, 68, 114
Broca, 145, 146
Browman, C. P., 17, 184, 188, 189n5, 244
Brown, G. D. A., 2, 261
Brown, J. W., 275
Brown, R., 2, 109, 145, 188n4, 232, 264
Brown, W., 62
Bub, D., 3, 282
Buckingham, H. W., 145, 150, 184, 275
Budin, C., 152
Burgess, R. C., 288
Butterworth, B., 2, 3, 12, 14, 19, 108, 109, 144, 145, 168, 169, 171, 182, 184, 196, 202n8, 261–84, 288, 304

Caplan, D., 3, 163, 263, 274, 278
Caramazza, A., 3, 144, 145, 147, 149, 153, 156, 157, 158, 159, 160, 165, 167, 172, 173, 262, 283
Carey, S., 110n1
Carlson, G., 288
Carpenter, E., 76n1
Carpenter, P. A., 46
Carr, T. H., 80, 81, 82
Carson, D., 88
Cattell, J. M., 62
Chambers, S. M., 89
Charniak, E., 117
Chertkow, H., 282

Chiesi, H. L., 66, 72
Chomsky, N., 28, 29, 184
Clark, E. V., 8
Clark, H. H., 5, 40, 46
Clements, G. N., 200
Clifton, C., 306
Cohen, A., 2, 188
Cohen, J. D., 120, 135
Collier, R., 200, 201
Collins, A. M., 7, 64, 82, 90, 110,
    111, 112, 115, 117, 118n4, 120,
    123, 124, 137
Coltheart, M., 146, 147, 169
Cooper, W. E., 200, 201, 202n8,
    304
Cortese, C., 81
Corum, 265n2
Coughlan, A., 150
Crain, S., 167
Cresswell, M., 39
Crompton, A., 17, 187
Crow, C., 248n3
Cruse, D. A., 110
Cruttenden, A., 200
Cutler, A., 2, 96, 109, 128, 147, 159,
    182, 184, 188n4, 196, 261, 295
Czerwinski, M., 80

Dallas, M., 87
Damasio, D., 151
De Groot, A. M. B., 99, 299
De Smedt, K., 111
Deese, J., 2, 65
DeHaan, E., 151
Del Viso, S., 248
Dell, G. S., 9, 11, 12, 17, 18, 41, 52,
    55, 96, 108, 109, 110, 111, 112,
    115n3, 117, 128, 137, 149, 166,
    170, 175, 182, 185n3, 191, 193–
    95, 197n7, 198, 199, 204, 205,
    213, 214, 215, 244, 267, 287–312
Denes, G., 161
Dennett, Daniel, 19n5
Dennis, M., 152
Di Sciullo, A. M., 37
Dik, S. C., 7
Dirkx, J., 68
Dowty, D. R., 27
Dunbar, K., 89, 92, 120

Düngelhoff, F.-J., 2, 63, 69, 71, 77,
    78, 87, 88, 89, 90, 92, 93, 94, 95,
    97, 111, 112, 113, 115, 120, 121,
    125, 126, 127, 132, 136, 290
Durso, F. T., 80, 81, 82
Dwyer, M., 80
Dyer, F. N., 86, 88, 89

Eady, S. J., 201
Egeth, H. E., 63, 95
Ehri, L. C., 89
Ellis, A. W., 94, 175

Faulconer, B. A., 63, 69, 70, 71, 76n1
Fay, D., 96, 109, 147, 159, 182,
    188n4, 295
Fedio, P., 148
Feldman, L. B., 63
Ferber, R., 196
Ferreira, F., 202, 205, 306
Ferreri, T., 265n3
Fiksel, J. R., 115
Flores d'Arcais, G. B., 74, 76, 125,
    155
Flowers, J. H., 88
Flude, B. M., 94
Fodor, J. A., 7, 28, 31n4, 46, 47, 48,
    109, 110, 111, 288
Fodor, J. D., 46, 47, 110
Ford, M., 202n8, 304, 305
Forster, K. I., 308
Fowler, C. A., 186
Fraisse, P., 63, 69, 70, 71, 77, 78
Franklin, S., 18, 262
Frederiksen, J. R., 64
Friedman, A., 71, 228, 236, 237
Fromkin, V. A., 2, 108, 109, 128,
    129, 144, 147, 157, 182, 183, 184,
    185, 187, 188, 189, 190, 196, 214,
    216, 261, 264, 267, 288
Fry, D., 187, 269, 277, 278
Fujimura, O., 200

García-Albea, J. E., 185, 187, 188, 248
Garnes, S., 188, 189n5
Garnham, A., 2, 261
Garrett, M. F., 2, 3, 7, 9, 19, 46, 48,
    52, 96, 108, 109, 110, 111, 128,
    143–76, 182, 183, 185, 187, 188,

189, 202n8, 214, 245, 246, 264, 279, 281, 282, 288, 304, 305, 306, 311
Gazdar, G., 265n2
Gee, J. P., 202n8, 306
Gelfer, C. E., 200
Gentner, D., 47
Gerard, L., 81
Gholson, B., 63
Glaser, M. O., 63, 66, 67, 68, 70, 71, 77, 78, 86, 87, 88, 89, 91, 93, 94, 95, 97, 111, 112, 113, 115, 125, 127, 137
Glaser, W. R., 2, 3, 7, 8, 9, 61–100, 111, 112, 113, 115, 120, 121, 124, 125, 126, 127, 132, 136, 137, 290
Glazenborg, G., 76
Gluck, M. A., 114
Glucksberg, S., 288
Goldman, N., 109, 110
Goldman-Eisler, F., 2, 202n8
Goldsmith, J., 200
Goldstein, L. M., 17, 184, 244
Golinkoff, R. M., 89
Goodglass, H., 145, 146, 147, 148, 150, 152, 167, 281
Goolkasian, P., 88
Gordon, P. C., 205, 290, 307
Gorrell, P., 167
Gray, W. D., 8, 68, 114
Grimshaw, J., 28n3
Grodzinsky, Y., 168
Grosjean, F., 202n8, 306
Gussenhoven, C., 200
Guttentag, R. E., 88, 93, 94, 121

Haith, M. M., 88, 93, 94, 121
Halle, M., 184, 200
Happel, B., 112
Harley, T. A., 8, 18, 111, 128, 147, 149, 191, 267, 289, 296
Harris, P. L., 72, 75
Hart, J.'t, 153, 156, 200, 201
Hay, D. C., 94
Hayes, B., 12, 14n4
Head, Henry, 268
Healy, A. F., 184n2, 197
Hellan, L., 39
Hellawell, D., 151

Hendler, J. A., 117
Hillis, A., 3, 147, 148, 149, 153, 156, 157, 158, 159, 163, 165, 172
Hines, D., 80
Hinton, G., 150
Hjelmslev, L., 40
Hockett, C. F., 184
Hoenkamp, E., 59, 108, 111
Hoffmann, J., 74, 75, 76, 99
Hogaboam, T. W., 71, 73
Hogg, T., 296
Hohle, R. H., 63
Hollan, J. D., 64
Holmes, V. M., 202n8, 304, 305
Hotopf, W., 147, 148
Howard, D., 18, 168, 169, 171, 262, 273, 274, 275, 276, 282
Huberman, B. A., 296
Hudson, P. T. W., 120
Huijbers, P., 3, 108, 109, 112, 137, 182, 202, 263, 264, 288, 289, 306
Humphreys, G. W., 114, 152, 163
Huttenlocher, J., 64, 84, 85, 95

Igoa, J., 248
Irwin, D. I., 63, 69, 77, 79, 81, 82, 93, 99, 125, 127

Jackendoff, R., 5, 7, 27, 31n4, 33, 47
Joanette, Y., 271, 278
Johnson, D. M., 8, 68, 114
Johnson, M. K., 80, 81, 82
Johnson-Laird, P. N., 6, 27, 31n4, 33, 109, 110, 149, 165
Jolicoeur, P., 114, 125
Jones, H. G. V., 109
Jongman, A., 10n3
Juliano, C., 289
Just, M. A., 46

Kaisse, E. M., 200
Kamp, H., 33
Kantowitz, B. H., 68, 87
Kaplan, E., 145, 281
Katz, J. J., 27, 36n7, 91, 95, 125
Kautz, L., 94
Keil, F. C., 137
Keller, E., 271

Kelly, M. H., 137, 201
Kelter, S., 8
Kempen, G., 3, 55, 108, 109, 111,
    112, 137, 182, 202, 263, 264, 288,
    289, 304, 306
Kertesz, A., 275
Keyser, A., 168
Keyser, S. J., 200
Kintsch, W., 46, 110
Kiparsky, P., 27n1, 263, 265
Klapp, S. T., 2
Klatt, D. H., 184, 185, 218, 241, 243,
    269, 277
Klein, G. S., 94
Kleist, H. von, 19
Klimesch, W., 72, 74, 75, 76, 99
Knoll, R. L., 307
Kohn, S. E., 146, 147, 148, 271, 279,
    280, 283
Kolk, H., 168, 169
Kosslyn, S. M., 114
Kowall, S., 202n8
Kramer, P., 68
Kreuz, R. J., 288
Kroll, J. F., 64, 76n1, 85
Kubicek, L. F., 64, 84, 85, 95
Kubozono, H., 186
Kukish, K. S., 89
Kupin, J. J., 197
Kutas, M., 288

La Heij, W., 3, 63, 68, 74, 87, 90, 93,
    94, 95, 97, 99, 111, 112, 113, 115,
    130, 135, 136
LaBerge, D., 87
Lahiri, A., 10n3
Langford, S., 109
Lapointe, S., 170, 305
Larsen, L., 88
Lashley, K. S., 242
Laver, J. D. M., 183, 184, 187, 189
Lecours, A. R., 146, 170, 271, 278
Levelt, W. J. M., 1–20, 43, 48, 49,
    50, 51, 52, 67, 70, 96, 97, 107,
    108, 109, 110, 112, 113, 114n2,
    115n3, 123, 128, 137, 144, 148,
    149, 154, 157, 158, 159, 165, 171,
    172, 182, 198, 200, 202, 205, 244
Levitt, A. G., 184n2, 197

Lhermitte, F., 162
Liberman, M., 190, 200
Ligon, E. M., 63
Lindsley, J. R., 202
Linebarger, M., 167
Loebell, H., 8
Loftus, E. F., 7, 64, 82, 90, 110, 111,
    112, 115, 117, 118n4, 120, 123,
    124, 137
Loftus, G. R., 79
Lombardi, L., 307n2
Lorch, R. F., 299
Lorge, I., 64
Luce, R. D., 118
Lund, F. H., 63
Lupker, S. J., 2, 63, 69, 77, 79, 81,
    82, 88, 90, 91, 93, 94, 95, 97, 98,
    99, 111, 123, 124, 125, 127, 130,
    135, 136, 290
Lyons, J., 110

Maassen, B., 2, 108, 109, 137, 202,
    288, 306
MacKay, D. G., 2, 11, 18, 185, 187,
    188, 189, 191, 213, 214, 295, 300,
    304
MacKay, I. R. A., 185, 186
Maclay, H., 2
MacLeod, C. M., 86, 89, 92, 120
MacNeilage, P. F., 243n1
MacNeill, D., 188
Magee, L. E., 63, 69, 71, 87, 91, 92,
    93, 111, 112, 125, 137
Marin, O. S. M., 109, 166, 175, 288
Marshall, J., 143, 144, 146
Marslen-Wilson, W. D., 184, 196
Martin, A., 148
Martin, N., 18, 19, 261, 289, 296
Mayer, K., 2
Mazzucci, A., 167
McCarthy, J., 200
McCarthy, R., 152, 165
McCauley, C., 79, 80
McClain, L., 95
McClelland, J. L., 41, 117, 120, 298
McCuilough, B., 73, 74, 75, 78, 94,
    99
McEvoy, C. L., 112, 137
McGill, J., 150

McGill, W. J., 118
McKenna, P., 152
McNamara, T. P., 299
McNeill, D., 2, 109, 145, 232, 264
McWeeny, K. H., 94
Mead, R., 121
Meininger, V., 162
Menn, L., 167
Merikle, P. M., 80, 87
Meringer, R., 2
Mervis, C. B., 8, 68, 114
Meyer, A. S., 10, 11, 12, 13, 14, 16,
    52, 96, 109, 159, 181–206, 288,
    293
Meyer, D. E., 79, 85, 205, 290, 307
Miceli, G., 145, 167, 173, 174
Mill, A. I. D., 2, 261
Miller, G. A., 6, 27, 31n4, 109, 110,
    149
Mitchell, R. F., 68
Mohanan, K. P., 184, 200
Monsell, S., 307
Morley, 277
Morris, P. E., 72
Morton, J., 3, 6, 64, 67, 89, 109, 110,
    262
Motley, M. T., 2, 18, 187, 188
Mowrey, R. A., 185, 186
Mulder, M., 112

Nakatani, L. H., 200
Nelder, J. A., 121
Nelson, D. L., 112, 115, 137
Nelson, S. M., 88
Nespor, M., 10n3, 12, 200
Nespoulous, J.-L., 278
Neumann, O., 88, 89, 94
Newcombe, F., 144, 146, 151, 273
Nolan, K., 148
Nooteboom, S., 2, 184, 186, 187, 189,
    214
Norman, D. A., 115

Ohala, J. J., 200
Oldfield, R. C., 2, 64, 109, 273
Olson, D. R., 57, 89
Orchard-Lisle, V., 262, 282
O'Seaghdha, P. G., 9, 11, 18, 109,
    110, 115, 204, 205, 287–312

Osgood, C. E., 2
O'Sullivan, C. S., 81

Paccia-Cooper, J., 200, 202n8, 304
Paivio, A., 64, 65
Palef, S. R., 89, 95
Panzeri, M., 265n3, 275
Parkes, C. H., 7, 48, 110
Parmelee, C. M., 80
Pate, D., 167, 261, 273, 274, 278, 279
Patterson, K., 147, 262
PDP Research Group, 41
Pease, D., 145
Pellegrino, J. W., 66, 71, 72, 73, 75,
    78
Peterson, R. R., 289, 293, 310
Phaf, R. H., 120
Pick, A., 276
Pierrehumbert, J., 200, 240
Pollatsek, A., 115, 127
Posner, M. I., 68, 84, 85, 88, 89
Potter, M. C., 62, 63, 67, 69, 70, 71,
    76n1, 85, 112, 115, 137, 307n2
Prince, A., 190, 200
Proctor, R. W., 94
Pullum, G. K., 200
Purcell, D. G., 80
Pylyshyn, Z. W., 64, 65, 70

Quillian, M. R., 7, 64, 117
Quinlan, P. T., 114

Ragain, R. D., 79
Rapp, B. C., 147, 160
Rayner, K., 95, 96, 97, 98, 115, 120,
    127, 130
Reed, V. S., 112, 137
Reich, P. A., 17, 96, 110, 111, 137,
    149, 294, 296, 303
Reinitz, M. T., 79
Reyle, U., 33
Rho, S. H., 288
Riddoch, M. J., 114, 163
Rips, L. J., 64, 110
Roelofs, A., 7, 8, 9, 46, 47, 48, 49,
    107–38
Romani, C., 147
Rosch, E., 8, 68, 69, 71, 73, 74, 76,
    78, 90, 114

Rosinski, R. R., 66, 72, 89, 111
Rouillon, F., 146
Rubin, D. C., 188n4
Ruddy, M. G., 79
Rumelhart, D. E., 41, 115, 117, 298

Saddy, J. D., 167
Saffran, E., 18, 109, 148, 149, 166, 167, 175, 261, 288, 289, 296
Saillant, B., 162
Sawyer, P. K., 80
Scarborough, D. L., 81
Schank, R. C., 32n5
Schenkein, J., 8
Schlesinger, I. M., 19
Schreuder, R., 6, 7, 8, 9, 23–58, 68, 74, 76, 125, 155
Schriefers, H., 12, 14, 52, 96, 97, 98, 108, 109, 110, 111, 112, 113, 114, 115n3, 130, 136, 159, 203, 204, 288, 289, 290, 291, 293, 294, 299, 300, 306, 307, 308, 312
Schvaneveldt, R. W., 79
Schwartz, M., 109, 144, 148, 149, 166, 167, 175, 288
Segui, J., 69, 71, 77
Seidenberg, M., 288
Selkirk, E., 15, 193, 200, 306
Semenza, C., 161, 265n3, 275
Sereno, J., 10n3
Seuren, P. A. M., 39
Seymour, P. H. K., 8, 64, 67, 82, 112, 137
Shaffer, L. H., 263, 264
Shaffer, W. O., 87
Shallice, T., 148, 150, 151, 152, 154, 155, 156, 160, 164, 261, 262
Shankweiler, D., 167
Shastri, L., 115
Shattuck-Hufnagel, S., 2, 10, 13, 16, 109, 182, 183, 184, 185, 186, 187, 188, 189, 190, 191–93, 195, 197, 198, 213–57, 241, 243, 249, 263, 264, 269, 277, 279, 280, 295, 304
Sherman, J., 76n1
Shields, L., 307
Shillcock, R. S., 2, 261
Shoben, E. J., 64, 110

Shrager, J., 296
Siegel, A., 66, 72
Siegel, S., 228
Silveri, M. C., 173
Simon, J. R., 63
Smith, E. E., 64, 69, 71, 77, 110
Smith, K. L., 279, 280
Smith, M. C., 63, 69, 71, 87, 91, 92, 93, 111, 112, 125, 137
Smith, N., 200, 268
Snodgrass, J. G., 67, 73, 74, 75, 76n1, 78, 94, 99, 112, 115, 137
Snyder, C. R. R., 84, 85, 88, 89
So, K.-F., 63
Sorenson, J. M., 200
Sperber, D., 58
Sperber, R. D., 79, 80, 81, 82, 85
Springer, C. J., 95, 96, 97, 98, 120, 130
Stanovich, K. E., 80
Stechow, A. von, 39
Stemberger, J. P., 11, 12, 18, 109, 110, 111, 117, 128, 137, 149, 183, 184, 185n3, 186, 187, 189, 190, 191, 197n7, 214, 263, 289, 295, 304, 310
Sternberg, S., 79, 202, 307
Stewart, A. L., 80
Stroop, J. R., 86, 112
Studdert-Kennedy, Michael, 6n
Sudalaimuthu, P., 63
Sussman, H. M., 244n2

Tabossi, P., 288
Talmy, L., 49, 50
Tanenhaus, M. K., 288
Taylor, D. A., 88
Theios, J., 63, 67, 70, 77, 78, 83, 112, 137
Thorndike, E. L., 64
Thorndyke, P. W., 46
Tomoeda, C., 148
Townsend, J. T., 118
Treiman, R., 186, 187, 197n7, 263
Trosset, M., 148
Tsao, Y.-C., 63
Tuller, B., 167

Underwood, G., 90

Van der Heijden, A. H. C., 68, 87, 120
van der Hulst, H., 200
Van Grunsven, M., 168
Van Petten, C., 288
Van Wijk, C., 108, 202n8
Vanderwart, M., 76n1
Vermeij, M., 63, 94
Villa, G., 173
Virzi, R. A., 63, 95
Vogel, I., 10n3, 12, 200
Von Eckardt, B., 63
Vorberg, D., 112

Walker, E. C. T., 7, 48, 110
Walker, J., 69
Ward, N., 8–9
Warren, C., 64
Warren, R. E., 87, 88, 89
Warren, R. K., 137
Warren, R. M., 184, 196
Warrington, E., 148, 151, 152–53, 154, 155, 156, 160, 164, 165, 262
Weil, C. M., 79

Weintraub, S., 145, 281
Weisberg, R. W., 18, 289, 296
Wells, R., 183
Welsh, A., 184, 196
Wernicke, 145, 146
Wheeldon, Linda, 17
Whittaker, S., 184, 197, 264, 280
Wilkes-Gibbes, D. L., 5
Williams, E., 37
Wilson, D., 58
Winer, B. J., 133
Wingfield, A., 2, 64, 273
Wright, C. E., 307
Wright, E., 79

Yachzel, B., 76n1
Yaniv, I., 205
Young, A. W., 94, 151, 165
Yule, G., 184

Ziessler, M., 74, 75
Zingeser, L. B., 173, 174
Zurif, E., 167
Zwicky, A. M., 200

# Subject Index

abstract-code hypothesis, 70, 82, 84
activation, 3, 85, 95, 245, 267, 287,
  312
  multiple, 157
  phonological, 291, 293–94, 299–300,
    311, 312
  semantic, 290, 291, 293–94, 299–
    300, 312
  *See also* spreading-activation
    theory
activation metaphor, 23, 57
activation models, 51–55
affixes
  derivational, 29
  grammatical, 282
  inflectional, 29, 246
agrammatism, 166, 167, 168, 169,
  170, 171, 172, 174–75
  *See also* aphasia
Alzheimer's disease, 7, 148
antonymy, 36, 38, 39, 40, 129,
  147
aphasia, 3, 7, 109, 137, 143, 144, 145–
  50, 154, 156, 158, 165, 172, 176,
  261, 288
  agrammatic, 166–67, 169, 172–73,
    174–75, 278
  anomic, 172–73, 174, 175, 281
  Broca's, 145, 146, 147, 168, 173,
    175, 271, 278
  conduction, 262, 271, 273, 278,
    279, 281, 283–84
  *conduite d'approche* in, 269, 271
  jargon, 146, 149, 269, 275, 276
  and neologisms, 274–76, 281
  optic, 166

and phonemic paraphasias, 170–71,
  261–62, 263, 269, 272, 273, 274–
  76, 281, 282
  Wernicke's, 145, 146, 168, 169,
    175, 271, 275, 278
  *See also* paragrammatism
argument structure (AS), 27, 28–29,
  30, 34, 38–39, 43, 44
articulation, 85, 96, 108, 114, 190,
  200, 205, 242, 244
articulators, 25, 26, 43, 53
artificial intelligence, 32, 33

Boston Diagnostic Aphasia
  Examination (BDAE), 145

chunking problem, 34, 38, 39, 40, 43,
  44, 48, 49, 56, 57
cohyponymy, 107, 120, 129, 130, 131,
  132, 134, 135, 136
compositionality, 6–7, 8, 34, 36
comprehension, 41, 167, 168, 172,
  199, 271, 275, 289
conceptual structure (CS), 23, 25, 30,
  31, 32, 36, 43, 44, 48, 58
  and lemmas, 46–49, 53, 110, 157–
    58, 176
  nature of, 55
  pre-linguistic, 26, 44–46, 158
  and semantic form, 30–35, 36, 37–
    41, 38, 43, 44, 45, 46, 48, 49, 50–
    52, 55, 56, 156, 163, 164
conceptualization, 40, 44, 45, 48–49,
  108
conceptualizers, 25, 28, 42, 43, 45,
  48, 49, 50, 58

connectionist models, 18–19, 41, 42
connectivity hypothesis, 47
connotation, 40–41
consonants
    confusable target, 213, 217, 218–20, 226
    exchange of, 16, 183, 215
    and sound errors, 184, 185n3, 186, 189, 194, 205
    syllable-onset, 241
    word-final, 16, 188, 189, 215, 247, 249
    word-internal, 16, 188, 189
    word-medial, 217, 219, 227, 229
    word-onset, 205, 216, 217, 224, 227, 232, 234, 238–41, 243, 244, 245, 246–47, 248, 249, 250

decomposition, 23, 28, 46–52, 56, 108, 109–11, 114n2, 137, 149
    computational, 108
dementia, 143, 148
differential practice hypothesis, 62, 63
distractor-target pairing, 87–89, 93, 97, 99, 122
distractors, 87–91, 94–97, 111, 112, 113, 115, 117, 119, 120, 129
    different-category, 123
    picture, 122–23, 125, 126, 128
    same-category, 123, 125
    and typicality, 123–24, 127
    word, 127, 128
double stimulation, 61, 68, 87
dyslexia, 143, 146, 147, 150, 166, 169, 170, 173, 175

electromyography, 185, 186
encoding
    grammatical, 5–6, 23, 54, 55
    linguistic, 304
    syntactic, 109, 128, 137
    word-form, 108, 109, 112, 114, 117, 128, 137, 190, 198, 203, 205
    *See also* phonological encoding

formulators, 5, 25, 26, 35, 42, 43, 44, 45, 46, 49, 53, 54, 56, 58, 108

grammatical features (GF), 27, 29, 43, 44
grapheme-phoneme correspondence, 63, 66, 96, 170

hypernymy, 6–7, 36, 40, 50–51, 52, 107, 110, 111, 120, 124, 125, 126, 129, 130, 131, 132, 134, 135, 137, 148, 149
hyponymy, 6n2, 36, 40, 107, 110, 120, 125, 129, 130, 131, 132, 134, 135

iconogen system, 66, 67, 82
idioms, 9, 24, 51, 53, 55
information
    conceptualized, 44, 45, 108–9
    contextual, 58
    perceptual, 44
    phonological, 241–42, 263, 264, 274, 288
    pragmatic, 288
    semantic, 181, 182, 288, 289
    syntactic, 181, 182, 192, 288
Int, 33–35, 56, 58
    definition of, 33
    *See also* mapping
interference, 89, 99
    associative, 86
    picture-picture, 93
    picture-word, 3, 7, 52–53, 71, 93, 95, 97, 107, 112, 203, 204, 289–90, 293
    word-word, 67, 72, 93
interfering words (IWs), 203–4
    *See also* interference
internal coding systems, 61, 65, 70, 77
interpretation
    articulatory, 30–31, 34, 112, 115
    conceptual, 30, 35n6, 39–41, 43, 45
    phonological, 172, 176
intonation contour, 182, 196, 197, 199, 200, 201, 203, 240, 306

knowledge
    background, 32, 33
    conceptual, 56
    encyclopedic, 33, 44

general world, 33
individual, 41
linguistic, 26, 32, 50
semantic, 64, 163
situational, 32, 44
*See also* lexical knowledge

language
pathologies of, 143, 144–45, 148
and thought, 44, 45, 144
language processing, 41, 44, 45, 50,
51, 53, 54, 61, 67, 99
disorders in, 143–76
modality-specific failures
of, 160–66
*See also* lexical access
language production
lexical access in, 55–57, 287–312
use of lexical knowledge in, 41–46
lemma retrieval, 48, 96, 107–42, 160,
167, 171, 287, 311
approaches to, 108, 109–10, 144
convergence problem in, 50–52
definition of, 108–9
discreteness of, 289–303, 311
failures of, 154, 156–57, 172, 174
and picture-word
interference, 107
processes of, 108
*See also* encoding; representations:
lemma; spreading activation
theory
lemmas, 4, 5–6, 7, 19, 23, 41, 42, 43,
44, 57, 98, 304
activation and deactivation
of, 52–53, 54, 55, 305
and concepts, 56, 156, 158
definition of, 5
lexical meaning of, 46
and nodes, 118, 120, 122, 123, 129,
130, 136, 137
structure of, 115–17
*See also* lemma retrieval; representations: lemma
lexemes, 3, 12, 40, 41, 42, 43, 53, 57,
67, 109, 111, 115, 117, 127, 137
*See also* phonological lexical representations

lexical access
and advance planning, 303–11
dissection problem in, 7–8
imitation problem in, 8
influences on, 57
in language production, 55–57, 287–
312
processes of, 25, 45
rates of, 2
in speaking, 107–8
temporal organization of, 44, 53, 57
theories of, 6, 109
two-step approach to, 3, 52–53, 55,
97, 98, 108, 144, 287–94
*See also* language production:
lexical access in; time course
lexical concepts, 7
basic-level, 8, 114
combination of primitive, 110
and food, 164
nodes and links in, 107, 111, 115–
17, 129, 137, 193
*See also* lexical access
lexical entries
and argument structure, 23, 29, 39
basic (BLE), 26, 29, 30
as collection of nodes, 41–42, 52
combined with affixes, 29
and grammatical features, 23
memory structure of, 115–17
and phonetic form, 23
and semantic form, 23, 36–41, 56
virtual (VLE), 29
lexical hypothesis, 61, 67, 70–71, 83,
86
lexical items, 23, 24, 25, 26, 28, 29,
30, 39, 57
appropriateness of, 24
communicative effect of, 24
semantic relations between, 36–41
structure of, 30, 53
truth of, 24
lexical knowledge, 24, 25, 32n5, 36,
41–46, 55, 56
and antonymy, 36
aspects of, 26–41
and identity of argument
structure, 36, 39

and identity of derivational
  suffixes, 36
and lexical presuppositions, 36
and phonological
  neighborhood, 36
and synonymy, 36
*See also* language production
lexical meaning, 25–26, 27, 28, 35,
  36, 39, 46, 47, 181, 288
*See also* representations: meaning
lexical selection, 3, 4–9, 34, 52
  disorders of, 143–76
  interaction with phonological
    encoding, 17–20
  major category contrasts in, 172–76
  semantic field effects in, 150–56,
    159
  theories of, 6
lexical system (LS)
  structure of, 26–30, 36, 41, 42
lexicon, 61, 66
  phonological, 264, 281, 282
  semantic, 264, 281
  word-recognition, 2, 95, 96
  *See also* mental lexicon
logogen theory, 3, 6, 64, 66, 67, 82, 96
Luce ratio, 118, 136

mapping, 113, 114, 146, 167, 174
  functions of, 198
  many-to-many, 23, 35, 56
  message-to-lemma, 168, 169
  message-to-sentence, 168
  one-to-one, 46, 52, 192
  *See also* Int; Vbl
memory
  in error processes, 150, 200, 219–20
  long-term, 65, 67, 79
  semantic, 110
  short-term, 45, 262
  working, 65
mental lexicon (ML), 3, 23, 26, 28,
  29, 41, 43, 44, 69
  and comprehension, 41
  and familiarity, 41, 152, 153
  and lemma retrieval, 108, 110, 111,
    112, 118
  models of, 33, 41, 42

as network, 107, 137, 195
  and word forms, 182, 184, 190, 205
  *See also* lemmas; lemma retrieval;
    lexemes; phonological encoding
message structures, 25, 44–45, 153,
  167, 304
  *See also* conceptual structure
messages, 24, 110, 111, 114n2, 129,
  157, 158, 160, 304
  definition of, 144
mime performance, 160, 161, 162,
  163, 164, 165
mind/brain, 26, 32, 33, 41
  modular organization of, 33
morphemes, 10, 67, 109, 128, 167,
  168, 183, 193–95, 215, 246, 265

name retrieval, 64, 85, 95, 166
naming, 68, 147, 150, 156, 308
  auditory, 161–62
  at basic level, 68–69, 70, 71, 73, 74,
    80, 99
  tactile, 162, 163, 164, 166
  visual, 161, 162, 164
  written vs. oral, 160
  *See also* object naming; picture
    naming
naming-categorizing differences, 83,
  112, 113
  *See also* language processing:
    disorders in
naming latencies, 121, 124, 126, 133,
  134
naming time
  vs. reading time, 62–63, 70, 77, 92

object categorizing, 107, 111, 112,
  113, 114, 119, 137
  and selective loss or
    preservation, 151–56
object naming, 44, 107, 111, 112, 113,
  119, 137
  four processing stages of, 113–15

paragrammatism, 166, 168, 169, 170,
  171, 172, 175
PASS. *See* phonological assembly
  subsystem

PE. *See* phonological encoding
phonetic form (PF), 23, 26, 27, 30, 31, 34, 43
phonological addressing, 264, 281–82
phonological assembly subsystem (PASS), 267, 277, 279, 280, 283
phonological encoding (PE), 3, 4, 5, 9–20, 55, 181–206, 213, 244, 246, 247, 249, 268, 295
  backup devices for, 265–67
  control processes in, 265
  defined, 182
  disorders of, 261–84
  interaction with lexical selection, 17–20
  non-words in, 267, 275, 283–84
  slot-and-filler theory in, 9–17, 188, 191–93, 263, 264, 265n2, 267, 279, 295
phonological lexical representations (PLRs), 262–63, 264–65, 267, 268, 269, 271–72, 273, 274, 275, 276, 277, 279, 281, 282
  *See also* lexemes
phonological words, 10–11, 12–16, 52, 97–98
  vs. clitic groups, 10n3
phrasal verbs, 24, 27
picture categorizing, 73, 76, 119–28
  with distractors, 111, 113, 124–25, 127–28, 132, 136
  and picture naming, 61, 68–69, 125
  vs. word categorizing, 70, 71, 77, 78, 83, 92, 94, 99, 127
picture naming, 3, 44, 52, 61–105, 119–28, 156, 160–62, 290, 299
  and disorders of lexical selection, 172, 173, 174, 262
  with distractors, 112, 113, 121–24, 127, 129, 130–33
  important models for, 64–69
  visual processing in, 85, 95
  visual similarity hypothesis in, 73
  vs. picture categorizing, 61, 68–69, 125
pictures

and superordinate labels, 69–78, 79, 88, 90, 91, 92–93, 94, 99, 114, 120, 124
PLR. *See* lexemes; phonological lexical representations
priming, 69, 122, 125, 127, 136, 155, 282, 289, 290–91, 293, 308
  and advance planning, 306–7, 308–11, 312
  mediated, 298–99, 300
  paradigms of, 61, 68
  and picture naming, 79–86, 99
  production, 204–5, 287, 306, 312
  word naming vs. lexical decision in, 308
  *See also* Stroop effect

reading, 61, 62, 65, 68, 69, 76, 77, 79, 85, 90, 267
  aloud, 305
  disorders of, 147, 150, 156, 169, 172, 174
  phonemic errors in, 273–74
  vs. recall, 227–29, 234
  *See also* dyslexia
reading-naming differences, 77–78, 83, 86, 95, 99
representations
  conceptual, 156, 158, 164, 167, 176, 288
  input, 44–46
  interfacing, 109, 176
  lemma, 48, 52, 54, 109, 145, 153, 155, 156, 159–60, 166, 174, 175, 176, 264, 304
  meaning, 162–63, 166, 288
  mental, 31
  message, 165, 304
  motor, 145
  orthographic, 169, 172
  perceptual, 156
  phonetic, 145, 182, 184, 196, 197, 200, 262, 263
  phonological, 169, 170, 172, 176, 182, 184–85, 190, 194, 195, 196, 200, 202–6, 215, 242, 268–76, 288, 293, 304, 311
  speech, 145

structural, 263
syntactic, 167, 304, 311
tactile, 163
word-form, 144, 145, 156, 158, 159,
    160, 162, 184–85, 196–99
*See also* encoding
response buffers, 3, 55, 220, 245, 247,
    279, 287, 289, 304, 311

scan copiers, 182, 191–93, 243, 245,
    247, 248–49
segmental serial ordering, 213–57
lexical stress in, 218–24, 247, 249–
    50
position similarity
constraint in, 215–18, 248, 250
syllable position in, 218–24, 234,
    239–41, 249, 264
word position in, 218–24, 232–39,
    244–49
semantic form (SF), 26, 27, 28, 29
*See also* conceptual structure: and
    semantic form
semantic memory, 41, 44, 61, 66, 100
common-code hypothesis of, 72–
    73, 76, 77, 80, 82, 83, 84, 85, 90
dual code hypothesis of, 64, 65, 66,
    67, 70, 72, 82
sentence construction, 174, 202–3,
    205, 231–32, 238, 240, 303–11, 312
SLIPS procedure, 197
sound errors, 181, 182
analyses of, 183–91
definition of, 183
and haplologies, 187, 261
interacting segments in, 184–91
stress in, 190
and word blends, 187, 267
word onsets in, 188–89, 191, 192,
    195, 196, 204, 205
*See also* speech errors
speaking
and articulation process, 108
and conceptualization
process, 108
and formulation process, 108
speech acts, 4, 70, 114n2, 304
speech errors, 11, 16, 17, 18, 19, 28,
    41, 109, 137, 156–60, 293, 304

analyses of, 2, 9–10, 144, 195–99,
    247, 268–72, 288
distribution of, 230
environmentals in, 19, 267
interaction, 214, 303
and listener judgments, 196
normal vs. aphasic patient, 282–84
rhythmical structure in, 182, 200,
    203, 204
segmental interaction in, 213
sound exchanges in, 128, 133, 183–
    84, 214, 279, 304, 305
stem exchanges in, 128
stress in, 190, 196, 199, 200, 201
word blends in, 113, 128–29, 241
word exchanges in, 113, 128, 129,
    304, 305
word substitutions in, 113, 129,
    146, 147–49, 154, 156, 157, 158,
    159, 160, 168, 171, 172, 295–96
*See also* language processing:
    disorders in; segmental serial
    ordering
speech production, 3, 38, 281
collocation problem in, 8–9
and lexical access, 107–8
phonological aspects of, 213, 249
and slips of the tongue, 113, 128
spontaneous, 01, 202, 206, 213,
    214, 215, 216, 238, 249, 262, 264,
    273, 275, 304, 305
temporal organization of, 53
and tongue-twisters, 231, 185, 197,
    218–21, 224–27, 231–35, 239, 280
spreading-activation theory, 18, 107,
    111–42, 157, 182, 193–95, 198–99,
    215, 244, 289, 291, 294–303
*See also* lemma retrieval
stimuli, 217, 220, 225–41, 248, 250–57
four types of, 222–24, 226
non-word, 232–34, 267
stimulus-onset asynchrony (SOA), 83,
    89, 291, 300
and distractors, 111, 112, 113, 119–
    35 passim
and interference effects, 53, 89, 90,
    98, 123
Stroop effect, 3, 61, 63, 67, 68, 69,
    86–98, 99, 113

asymmetry of, 86, 89, 93, 99
relative-speed hypothesis of, 89, 92, 93
syllables, 10–11, 14–17, 186, 191, 193–94, 201, 204, 205, 213, 214, 215
stressed, 190, 197, 239, 240, 248, 278
and words, 109, 112, 189, 214, 215, 216, 217, 218, 241
synonymy, 23, 36, 37, 129, 147, 157
word-to-phrase, 49, 110, 137
syntactic structure (SS), 31–32, 43, 44, 55, 170, 174, 176, 181
*See also* sentence construction

tachistoscopic experiments, 62, 63, 76n1
target-source tags, 118, 120, 123n5, 125, 127, 137
targets, 144, 145, 146, 149, 153, 154, 157, 158, 172, 173, 270, 271, 275, 287
CVC, 229, 267, 277
and utterances, 217, 244, 308
*See also* distractor-target pairing; priming; Stroop effect
time course, 23, 42, 198, 199, 282, 288, 289, 290, 293, 294, 299–300, 303, 308, 310, 311, 312
and initiation times, 202–3, 204
in multi-word utterances, 287, 291
studies of, 53–55, 112, 113, 119, 137
tip-of-the-tongue (TOT) states, 145, 147, 188, 232, 264
translation processes, 268–82

Vbl, 42, 43–44, 48, 49, 50, 51, 52, 56, 58

definition of, 34–35
*See also* mapping
verbalization, 35, 38, 39, 40, 43, 44, 48–50, 56, 57, 58
*See also* Vbl
verification
category, 82–83
name, 82, 83
vocabulary, 108, 154
closed class, 166–72, 174, 175, 176
open class, 166, 174, 175, 176
*See also* lexicon
vowels, 190, 194, 247
*See also* consonants

weights, 115, 117, 120, 136
Whorfian problem, 19
word categorizing, 61, 69, 70, 71, 107, 111, 112, 113, 119–28, 137
with distractors, 125–27, 128
hierarchies in, 74–75, 148, 149, 154–55, 169, 193
vs. picture categorizing, 77, 83, 92, 94, 99
word frequency, 2, 17, 41, 64, 84, 152, 153, 159, 173, 175–76, 214, 271
relation to reading latency, 64, 99
word-order preferences, 109
word-picture matching, 44, 46
same-different technique in, 71, 72, 74, 77
and three-step hierarchies, 75–76
word stress, 10, 13, 216–24, 239, 244–49
*See also* sound errors: stress in; speech errors: stress in
word structure, 213–57

How do we access words when we speak? Normally we talk at a rate of about two to three words or ten to fifteen speech sounds per second. We select these from a mental lexicon that probably contains tens of thousands of items and also generate an articulatory shape for each word and for the utterance as a whole. The authors of this book provide an in-depth analysis of the cognitive mechanisms that are involved in this amazing skill.

After an introductory chapter by Willem Levelt, the first part of the book deals with lexical selection—the problem of how we choose the appropriate word, given a concept that we intend to express. Authors consider the relation between conceptual and lexical representations, in particular the issue of compositionality, and the extensive experimental research in picture-naming; they also offer a non-compositional network model of lexical selection and a critical review of aphasic disorders of lexical selection. The next part of the book examines the construction of word form. Authors review the vast literature on spoonerisms and new experimental evidence for the specific role of word onset in the phonological build-up of a word. They consider aphasic disorders of phonological encoding from the perspective of normal processing theories. The concluding chapter looks at potential interactions between lexical selection and phonological encoding and adduces new evidence for the existence of a buffering device that mediates between the two.

*Lexical Access in Speech Production* will be important reading for all those who study language, speech, and cognition.

**W. J. M. Levelt** is Director of the Max Planck Institute for Psycholinguistics in Nijmegen and Professor of Psychology at Nijmegen University.

Cover illustration: H. N. Werkman, *De taal der vogelen* (The language of the birds).

ISBN 1-55786-355-5

**BLACKWELL**
Cambridge MA & Oxford UK

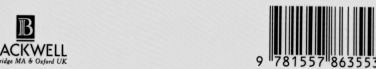